The Peak,
Chimpland.
16th May

Darling Family,

I'm up here waiting for a
gale to subside so that I have a
reasonable chance of hearing anything
worth hearing, or seeing anything to be
seen. It is 4.30, and I had a
very nice time with chimps from
8am - 2.15, so I can't grumble.
Horace and his girls, Sophie and
Sophocles.

I simply don't know where to
begin, telling you about David
Greybeard. He is utterly fantastic.
I think with this moment: I was
staying down to try to take some
pictures of David G. I was expecting
him about 8.30 - 9. I was,
therefore, still reclining in luxury
at 7.30, & Dominic was just
getting my tea — fancy! — early
morning tea! My bed was about
4th from the palm — David's Palm.
I was under my net, gazing
through it at the grey sky. Suddenly
I heard a rustling. David G.

JANE GOODALL

AFRICA
IN MY BLOOD

AN AUTOBIOGRAPHY
IN LETTERS

THE EARLY YEARS

Edited by Dale Peterson

A Mariner Book
HOUGHTON MIFFLIN COMPANY
BOSTON · NEW YORK

First Mariner Books edition 2001

For information about permission to reproduce selections
from this book, write to Permissions, Houghton Mifflin Company,
215 Park Avenue South, New York, New York 10003.

Visit our Web site: www.houghtonmifflinbooks.com.

Library of Congress Cataloging-in-Publication Data
Goodall, Jane, date.
Africa in my blood : an autobiography in letters : the early years /
Goodall ; edited by Dale Peterson
p.   cm.
Includes index.
ISBN 0-395-85404-0
ISBN 0-618-12735-6 (pbk.)
1. Goodall, Jane, 1934 — Correspondence. 2. Primatologists —
Correspondence. 3. Women primatologists — Correspondence.
I. Peterson, Dale. II. Title.
QL31.G58 A3 2000a
590'.92 — dc21 [B] 99-086680

Printed in the United States of America

Book design by Robert Overholtzer

DOC 10 9 8 7 6 5 4

CONTENTS

LIST OF CORRESPONDENTS

Family
Mummy or Mum: mother, Margaret Myfanwe (Vanne) Morris-
    Goodall
Jif or Jiff: sister, Judith Daphne Morris-Goodall (Waters)
Danny: maternal grandmother, Elizabeth Hornmby Legarde Joseph
Olly: maternal aunt, Elizabeth Olwen Joseph
Audrey or Audey: maternal aunt, Mary Audrey Gwyneth Joseph
Uncle Eric or Eric or Rix or Rixy: maternal uncle, William Eric Joseph

Friends
Bernard: Bernard Verdcourt, botanist at the Coryndon Museum and
    Kew Gardens
Desmond: Desmond Morris, author and zoologist
FFF (Fairy Foster Father): Louis S. B. Leakey
Sally, Puffin, Beloved Peach Blossom, Specimen of an Old Friend, Kins:
    Sally Cary
Sue: Susan Cary

Professional Contacts at the National Geographic Society
Andrew: Andrew Brown, senior staff member
Bob: Robert E. Gilka, assistant illustrations editor and director of
    photography
Dr. Carmichael: Leonard Carmichael, chairman of the Committee for
    Research and Exploration and secretary of the Smithsonian
    Institution
Mary Griswold: assistant illustrations editor

Dr. Bell Grosvenor: Melville Bell Grosvenor, president of society, editor of the magazine
Mr. Payne or Dr. Payne: Melvin M. Payne, executive vice president and secretary
Mr. Roberts: Joseph B. Roberts, assistant director of photography
Mr. Vosburgh: Frederick G. Vosburgh, vice president and associate editor

Other Professional Contacts
Paul Brooks: editor at Houghton Mifflin Company, Boston
Dr. Wolff: Nigel O'C. Wolff, director of the Maryland Academy of Sciences

Acquaintances, Associates, and Others
Douglas: Aunt Olwen's friend
Lyn: a visiting friend of the family

Pets
Kip: mongoose
Pickles: cat
Figaro or Figs: cat

AFRICA
IN MY BLOOD

INTRODUCTION

I really do simply adore Kenya. It is so wild, uncultivated, primitive, mad, exciting, unpredictable. It is also slightly degrading in its effect on some rather weak characters, but on the whole I am living in the Africa I have always longed for, always felt stirring in my blood.

— Jane Goodall, first (extant) letter home, April 1957

A ROMANTIC and very young Englishwoman arrived in British colonial Africa in early April 1957 and soon, quite possibly in her first letter home, wrote the astonishingly dramatic, precocious, and prophetic words "I am living in the Africa I have always longed for, always felt stirring in my blood."

Prophetic because she was to spend most of the rest of her life in Africa and because in so many ways — as a citizen, journalist, scientist, activist, and environmentalist — she came to be associated with that continent. Her name was Jane Goodall.

Jane Goodall's fame was initiated by the machinery of the National Geographic Society, which from 1963 on produced a series of glossy articles and television documentaries on her chimpanzee research. That early fame has since been reinforced by her own writing for a popular audience, including award-winning children's books and the 1971 bestseller *In the Shadow of Man,* which has been translated into forty-seven languages and is still in print three decades after publication. With the possible exception of Marie Curie, Jane Goodall must be the most widely celebrated woman scientist of our century.

And yet the very gloss of that celebrity may, paradoxically, have dulled the luster of her actual accomplishment. Hundreds of articles, features, interviews, reviews, and books have told or touched on her life story; but they are limited in scope and too often verge on the sentimental or the iconic. She has been presented as the little girl who thought she could; the sweet Ophelia who dreamed of animals; the feisty feminist in a man's world; the ironic traditionalist in a woman's world; the inspired nurturer; Mother Teresa of the apes; Tarzan's better half; and so on. While each of these images may arise from an appropriate truth, altogether they contribute to a larger untruth, an inappropriate devaluation of what she has actually done.

Based on several criteria — the number of scholarly references in her field directly and indirectly attributable to her research, the number of former students and associates who have reached influential positions in the biological sciences, the volume of data amassed in her forty-year-long study — Jane Goodall ought to be considered a uniquely distinguished pioneer in the science of ethology and the world's preeminent field zoologist. Yet her achievement can be stated more simply and directly: she opened the door to our understanding of the social and emotional lives of chimpanzees.

Wild chimpanzees are dangerous, though before Goodall began her work the dangers were misunderstood and exaggerated. Prior to Goodall's early discoveries, no one knew that chimpanzees ate meat. We had no idea that they or, indeed, any large mammals other than ourselves fashioned and used tools. If we thought that these apes were closely linked to humans in evolutionary history, as Darwin speculated, we nevertheless had no sense how close that link was. More important, we did not recognize what that kinship might mean for our own self-understanding. We did not realize that chimpanzees share with humans a similar repertoire of emotions or that their social systems are startlingly similar to ours. We would not have believed that chimpanzee communities across Africa possess various distinctive cultural traditions. And we could not have imagined that *Pan troglodytes* holds in common with *Homo sapiens* a dark side that includes cannibalism, intercommunity raiding pro-moted by adolescent and adult male gangs, and persistent male bat-tering of females.

Goodall's scholarly tome, *The Chimpanzees of Gombe: Patterns of Behavior* (1986), ranks as the single most authoritative work in primatology, the first encyclopedia for chimpanzee research. Her long-term and ongoing field study of wild apes along the shores of Lake Tanganyika has turned out to be, in the words of biologist Stephen Jay Gould, "one of the Western world's great scientific achievements." Jane Goodall helped create a revolution in the way we study animals, and because the animals she studied are human-kind's closest relatives, she helped alter the way humans think about themselves.

Valerie Jane Morris-Goodall was born to Margaret Myfanwe ("Vanne") Joseph and Mortimer ("Mort") Herbert Morris-Goodall in London on April 3, 1934, between wars; and the great European wars marked her upbringing and character. Her father, who worked as a telephone cable testing engineer in London during the early 1930s, discovered a passion for fast, beautifully engi-neered sports cars. He became a race car driver, a well-liked and highly valued member of Britain's Aston Martin team, competing on the tracks and courses of Europe against various French, Italian, and German automotive teams for excitement and national glory. By the time he finished his racing career in the 1950s, Mort was the only British driver in history to have competed ten times in the gru-eling Le Mans race.

Her father's world of noise, speed, and centrifugal daring — the machine world — seems barely to have touched the young Valerie Jane. "He sometimes took me for a ride in the car, but I don't re-member much about that."* While her father skillfully and coura-geously drove in circles and made a name for himself in that glam-orous milieu, the child was raised by her mother, Vanne, and a loving and steady nanny, Nancy Sowden, both of whom introduced her to a second possible world, that of gardens.

---

* *My Life with the Chimpanzees* (1988), p. 8.

Gardens. Sunlight. Then flowers, birds. Then a pet tortoise and a dog, a dragonfly, earthworms, snails, a pony, a horse, chickens. Most children, possibly all, experience a special identification with small animals and tame nature, a gently atavistic fascination that they usually soon outgrow and forget, or dimly remember in the way one does a dream. But in this instance the public gardens of central London and, after the fall of 1936, a backyard garden in suburban Weybridge, and soon a series of small animals and pets, seem to have impinged fundamentally on the personality of this special child. Valerie Jane combined her father's constitution (focus of intent, surprising endurance, iron stomach, minimal appetite, excellent eyesight) with her mother's sensibility (sociability, effective habits of observation, and literary bent). But who could have imagined how successfully she would gather those gifts in pursuit of her life's goal?

There were a few early indicators of the person she would become. By far the clearest one from her early childhood occurred in the fall of 1939, when she was five years old. Germany had invaded Poland; England had declared war on Germany. The Morris-Goodalls (including now a younger child, Judy), having moved to France earlier in the year to be near the great European automotive racing courses, precipitously returned to England, living temporarily with Mortimer's family. One autumn day, a "golden afternoon" as her mother remembers it, Valerie Jane disappeared. The police were called and began the search. Neighbors and all available family members joined in. Soldiers billeted nearby volunteered to help. After an increasingly frantic search, as dusk moved to dark, the child suddenly reappeared, alone, with fragments of straw in her hair and clothes. "Wherever have you been?" her mother asked. Valerie Jane explained that she had wondered where a hen had an opening big enough for an egg to drop through. To find out, she crawled inside the henhouse, concealed herself in the straw, and lay perfectly still for five hours until the hen raised herself up, wiggled, and provided an answer.

Near the end of that year, Mortimer joined the Royal Engineers. He served his country in Europe and the Far East, and in the process, unhappily, disappeared from his daughter's life. The children's nanny, in ill health, left the family in the late spring of 1940 and eventually married. Vanne, Jane, and Judy then moved to Bourne-mouth, a seaside resort town in Dorset, where they settled into the brick Victorian house owned by Jane's maternal grandmother, Elizabeth Hornmby Legarde Joseph. The house was called the Birches, and from 1940 on, it was the Morris-Goodall family resi-dence: an entirely female household consisting of Valerie Jane, Judy, their grandmother ("Danny"), mother ("Mum"), and two aunts (Olwen or "Olly" and Audrey or "Audey"). Uncle Eric ("Rix"), Jane's mother's brother, a consulting surgeon at a suburban Hamp-shire hospital, often visited.

That Jane Goodall was interested in animals from a very early age is well known and must be obvious. Less so is the fact that from child-hood on she loved language, both the getting and the giving: read-ing and writing. Language use may be the single skill that most im-mediately distinguishes humans from chimpanzees, and it is at least mildly ironic that the one person who has spent her entire adult life understanding a group of often quiet and always wordless animals should be unusually attuned to the expressive possibilities of the hu-man voice.

In any case, she read. She read many of the usual English child-hood classics, but, perhaps starting with *The Story of Dr. Dolittle*, a Christmas gift in 1942, her imagination was profoundly engaged by nature and adventure novels — soon including all the Dr. Dolittle books and the Tarzan series. These books and others thoroughly ex-pressed her own ecstatic feelings about the natural world and, over time, enabled her to develop and articulate "the dream": to study wild animals in Africa. How she might study these animals, how she might actually manage to insert herself into the African wilderness, remained among the vaguer aspects of that dream. She may have guessed that her writing would help. She wrote stories, poems, plays, journals, a nature newsletter to her friends — and letters.

Of course, letter writing today is a dead art. Easier to pick up the phone and visit by electromagnetically transmuted sound. Cheaper to log on and visit by electronically stimulated phosphorescence.

Paper-based correspondence today sometimes seems an almost Victorian habit, bordered by lace and dust, and one can easily imagine that very soon we will see no more collections of consequential letters by famous people, since famous people no longer write consequential letters.

Still, letters have dimension and permanence. They have weight. You can hold them, feel them, save them. You can possess them. You can write them in meditative solitude rather than on noisy demand, and you can read them in the same circumstances. A good letter you can read more than once. A serious letter you will read again and again. A great letter you may save in a box or folder. A love letter you might even press up to your face and smell, hoping to pull away any molecules still lingering from the hands and body of your lover on the other side. And, fortunately for us, when Jane Goodall first went to Africa in 1957, there were no easy or cheap alternatives to written correspondence. Telegraph and telephone were more expensive and less reliable than they are now and, of course, nonexistent out in the forest. Writing letters was a sensible, a natural and normal, thing to do, and Jane Goodall wrote home regularly, every week at first. Many of her letters from Africa, especially the early ones, were very long and sometimes quite rambling. Particularly the letters home to her "Darling Family" — to Mum and Danny, Jif and Olly and Audrey, sometimes Uncle Eric — were frank and open, full of detail and feeling. They were communications from a quite young woman who was, if not homesick, at least strongly and wistfully attached to her family and home in England. Clearly, writing home was far more pleasure than chore. At the same time, Jane Goodall's early letters were and remain simply letters as opposed to self-conscious documents or crafted products. They are candid. The imagined audience is small, intimate, and eternally sympathetic.

When in 1957 the letters from Africa first began appearing at the front door of the Birches — crisp and efficient blue aerogrammes, thick and heavy yellow envelopes, or lighter white ones decorated with exotic stamps and crumpled after a lengthy journey — perhaps none of the family imagined that their Jane would be famous or that these messages would have historical value. It is easy to believe that the family developed a habit of saving Jane's letters from Africa simply because they were delightful, so full of guileless enthusiasm and compelling observation. It would have seemed a crime to discard them. At home they were read aloud again and again. The letters were, as mother, aunt, and grandmother variously declared in their own return correspondence, "devoured," "gobbled up," fallen upon by the family "like a pack of hungry wolves."

"Sometimes now I feel you are utterly lost," Vanne wrote to her daughter in the fall of 1957. "That great gorgeous primitive continent has swallowed you whole — you are engulfed in huge clouds of heat — stolen by a thousand alien voices — utterly remote from this tiny grey island where cold winds take the warmth from the sun." But when the postman drops that mail through the slot, she continued, "an electric thrill rushes round the house."

Jane's letters from Africa accumulated in the Goodall household in England for nearly four decades, preserved in drawers and folders and boxes. Then, one day in March of 1996, Vanne, with amazing trust and generosity, pressed the whole collection into my hands. Many other letters, including a long correspondence between Jane and her second husband, the Honorable Derek Bryceson, M.P., were stored at the home they shared in Dar es Salaam between their marriage in 1975 and his death in 1980. Those were also passed my way, as were additional collections from her voluminous business and research files, both in Africa and England. More turned up one day inside a tin trunk on the floor of a cabin in Gombe Stream National Park. Additionally, as I gradually discovered, further collections of Jane Goodall's correspondence have been preserved in institutional archives, including most obviously those of the National Geographic Society and the Jane Goodall Archives at the University of Minnesota, as well as the Green Library of Stanford University, the Houghton Library of Harvard University, the L. S. B. Leakey Foundation, and the National Museums of Kenya. From the vaults of those institutions some splendid treasures appeared. And even more have come from several of Jane's good and loyal friends: Neva Folk, Professor

Robert Hinde, Paul Kase, Mary Lewis, Dr. Franklin Loew, Dilys MacKinnon, Dr. Desmond Morris, Jean Nitzsche, Sally Cary Pugh, Professor Anne Pusey, Emilie Riss, Joan Travis, and Vivian Wheeler.

All told, I was able to assemble more than 1,800 letters written by Jane Goodall, the bulk of them originals and often torn, fading, and fragile. Typically the letters home were undated, with envelopes and therefore postmarks missing. Postmarks that were available, on aerogrammes, for example, were often smeared and illegible or, sometimes, dated by day and month but not year. I had all the letters typed so that I could examine the contents carefully, frequently if necessary, without damaging the originals. Then, with the substantial help of an assistant, Dr. Valerie Rohy, I sorted them chronologically. Finally, from a total of roughly 1.2 to 1.6 million words I selected the most revealing and representative letters for publication.

An editor's first job is to be kind to the author by keeping out of the way. And with that principle in mind, I have reproduced the selected letters as accurately as possible, being careful to retain habitual spelling idiosyncrasies; useful, significant, or habitual punctuation and capitalization idiosyncrasies; and significant or referred-to typing errors. Since an editor's second job is to be kind to the reader, I have also added commentary at the beginning of each chapter and in occasional notes; regularized the format of the letters; and identified the dates or probable dates when the letters were written or posted. I have cut portions that seemed distracting because they were too long, too slow, or irrelevant. And I have eliminated those occasional passages that might offend someone or violate a living person's sense of privacy. Since Goodall virtually never uses standard ellipses spaced in the standard fashion (. . .) in her writing, I found it convenient to use them as my own indicator for editorial cuts.

Those are the details. The grand concept has always been to preserve the quality and feel of the letters while making them accessible and presenting them together in a way that will create a functional narrative, an epistolary autobiography. Both the personal and the professional correspondence, each in different ways, provide a level of detail, immediacy, and personal drama that all biographies and most autobiographies cannot possibly achieve. Biographies, even very sympathetic ones, are by definition written by people who must remain cool strangers to their subjects' deepest inner lives. And most autobiographies are written well after the facts narrated, with the author standing bravely in the present and squinting weakly into the past, or clawing desperately into the amnesiac maze. Everyone forgets. The best memory retains a shadow of what was. The tenor of the moment, the telling detail, the enveloping mood, feelings and conversations and events, all are always and inevitably fading. Letters therefore remain precious caches of utterance, the closest thing we have to perfect memory, and these particular letters collectively amount to Jane Goodall's only fully realized memoir. They are her autobiography in letters.

1

❧ ❧ ❧

CHILDHOOD
1942–1952

I had been fascinated by live animals from the time when I first learned to crawl.

— *In the Shadow of Man*

J ANE GOODALL'S CHILDHOOD letters take us from early 1942, when she was seven years old, to the end of her school years in the summer of 1952, when she was eighteen. Her family usually called her Valerie Jane during this time, while her friends often referred to her as "V.J." The stretch from 1942 to 1952 is long enough, and critical enough, that we can easily watch a transformation in writing style — including the development of that ironic, mock-literary voice first appearing in letters to her friend Sally in 1951. But in spite of the metamorphosis taking place during those years, as the writer moves from young child to young adult, it is striking how persistently her love of and fascination with animals remains a central theme — replaced to some degree only in the last two letters by the love of and fascination with a man, Trevor.

The earliest letter, written in a pencil-in-fist cursive to "Darling Mummy," addressed from "The Manor House" and dated February 16 with no year, was probably, but not certainly, done on February 16 of 1942. Valerie Jane did not start formal schooling until later in 1940, and it is likely she did not learn to write in cursive until 1941 or 1942. The location and some of the details of this letter might seem to suggest an earlier year. During the fall and winter of 1939–40, when Mortimer first enlisted in the army, Valerie Jane and her mother and sister were regularly staying with Mortimer's mother ("Danny Nutt") and stepfather, who lived at the Manor House, a grand sixteenth-century brick and stone edifice rising out of the shambles of the fourteenth-century Westenhanger Castle in Kent.* Other regular visitors to the Manor House at that time included Mortimer's sister Joan and her fiancé, Michael Spens; but they would not have been "Mr and Misis Spens" until their marriage in 1941. Still, the mention of that "big dog called Jacky who is going to live here untill Uncle Micel come back" reminds us both of the young writer's eager excitement about the animals all around her and of the background drama: the men were going to war.

Beyond the visible carnage of the war during those years (including the 1942 death of Mortimer's younger brother, Rex, in an RAF plane crash) lay the vast if invisible damage of broken lives and families. By the time Valerie Jane's father reentered civilian life, in 1951, the marriage was over. So "Daddy" was nearly always a remote presence, the source of occasional letters and long-distance phone calls and the rare visit on leave. The note in the middle of this chapter, written to "Mummy," possibly in late 1946, describes with only good cheer ("it was jolly good fun") the experience of "seeing Daddy off" on the *Eastern Prince,* bound apparently for Bombay. Mortimer was shipping out to his first posting in the Far East.

Valerie Jane entered the Uplands Girls School in 1945 and began her riding lessons around the same time. On Saturdays she would take a local bus out of Bournemouth to the small village of Longham, where Miss Selina Bush (often called "Bushel") lived in a rambling Queen Anne brick house with field and stables out back. Miss Bush's place was called Longham House, and her assistant, Sheila MacNaughton, was known as "Poosh." Some of the letters beginning with the one of September 1945 refer to the delightful Saturdays at Longham House with Bushel and Poosh.

The bulk of letters from Jane Goodall's childhood have been preserved by her friend Sally Cary Pugh, the daughter of the Honorable

---

* The stepfather was the manager of a nearby racecourse, which included on its property the Manor House; he and his family were allowed to live in the historic mansion rent free.

Byron and Daphne Cary, a couple who had long been good friends of the Morris-Goodalls. Mortimer had gone to school with Byron, and they had been roommates in a London boarding house when, in the early 1930s, Mortimer met Vanne. Sally was born a year after Valerie Jane; Sally's younger sister, Sue, was only two months older than V.J.'s sister, Judy. The girls made a natural foursome, in other words, particularly after the mid-1940s, when Sally and Sue regularly stayed at the Birches in Bournemouth during school holidays. Starting probably during their summer holidays of 1946, Valerie Jane invented for everyone's entertainment a nature club, the Alligator Society, which involved projects, games, rituals, and even — when the girls were apart during school sessions — nature quizzes by mail and an *Alligator Society Magazine,* to which everyone was expected to contribute articles. The girls had an Alligator Camp, in the garden. They walked into town in the Alligator style: single file with V.J. at the head and the other three girls bringing up the tail, strictly according to the order of their ages. They all took on Alligator code names: Valerie Jane, the oldest and therefore leader, was "Red Admiral," in reference to a dramatic-looking butterfly. Sally was "Puffin." Sue became "Ladybird." And Judy, the youngest, was "Trout." Unhappily, there seem to be no surviving copies of the *Alligator Society Magazine,* and we are left with only the few tantalizing references to it in some of these letters.

Holiday sessions of the Alligator Society were enlivened during the later 1940s and early 1950s by all-day visits from Rusty, the black spaniel cross owned by the managers of a hotel around the corner (first mentioned in the letter of March 7, 1951). Rusty was an unusually intelligent dog who found an unusually attentive human partner. He loved to do tricks, including the ordinary (shake hands, play dead, jump the hoop) and the less so (climb a tall stepladder, close the door). Unlike most dogs, Rusty adored being dressed up in clothes and so would sometimes find himself wearing pajamas and being pushed down the street in a pram. But as the girls learned, he had a real personality. If anyone laughed at him while he was dressed up, for example, Rusty "hated that and would walk off at once, trailing clothes behind him." He acted apologetic whenever he did something he had been taught was wrong, but he would sulk bitterly when unfairly accused. "Rusty was the only dog I have ever known who seemed to have a sense of justice," Jane was later to comment.*

The family, deeply religious if cheerfully unorthodox, attended the First Congregational Church in Bournemouth, known, because of its location, as the Richmond Hill church. (Vanne's father, William Joseph, had been a Congregational minister, though never at Richmond Hill.) And Valerie Jane, a passionate and idealistic girl, was increasingly attracted to the grandeur of the church, its gargoyle-lined bell tower, the grand arched bank of stained glass windows, and (as we can gather from the letters of June and August 1952) the new minister, a charismatic Welshman named Trevor Davies. This was an utterly idealized and platonic infatuation of late adolescence. The Reverend Trevor Davies, B.A., M.A., Ph.D., cast his light on the Richmond Hill congregation between 1951 and 1971 and across the end of Valerie Jane's "childhood": the summer of 1952, when she finished school, passed her Higher Examinations, and prepared to enter the world of work and practicality.

*   *   *   *

The Manor House
Westen hanger
Hythe. Feb 16 [probably 1942]

Darling Mummy

the day befor yestoday Mr and Misis Spens broght a big dog called Jacky who is going to live here untill Uncle Micel come back. I dont know how to spell that word. Yestoday Danny Nutt gave me two china dogs and I call them Trouble and Terry. Jublee has got a new dress.† I have got a birds nest and a catepiler in a box of calaig leaves. Now I will drow a pictuer of him.

---

* *My Life with the Chimpanzees* (1988), pp. 22, 23.
† Jubilee was Valerie Jane's toy stuffed chimpanzee, a present from her father for her first birthday.

Today I found a ded rook he died of cold. I hop you can read this letter. I had a bold egg for my tea, new bread and real butter. When I went to tea Gremlin came with me and he stad all night till Gras* came with the tea. Mouse sends you her love and a lik. Kincin is giving you his best bone. Jacky and Trouble send you a lik and the Hen's send you a cluck. Eevry body sends you there love.

with lots and lots of love from
valerie jane

[Possibly November 1945]

Dear Sally

I'm sorry I've not written before but what with school and things I've been rather busy. You must, must, must, must, must, must, must, must, must, must, <u>MUST</u>, come and stay with us this hols. My Ma has written to your Ma to ask if you can, so do write and tell me that you can. I have got quite a lot of caterpillars one is a Lime Hawk Moth looking like this,

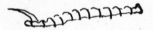

and if you come you will be able to see his skin. Another is a green looper (or stick catepillar) who feeds on mountain ash and he has made a cocoon, another is an ordinary cabbige white, who has made a cocoon, and another is a black hairy tortishell who feeds on nettle. If you come you will be able to see them all. Oh! I have another little yellowy, orang looper who feeds on lime, and a green caterpillar who feeds on cabbage, and has turned brown.

Chase, my Blue Roan Spaniel is sweet. Also he is very mischives and bites anything that comes in his way. He comes when he is called and also I play a cirtain game with him. I run my fastest away from him and soon he gets tired and sits down. Then I lie down flat, and the minute he see's me lying down he runs straight for me at full speed, with which I hurridly rise to my feet, for if I did not, all the hair of my head would be stuffed down Chase's throaght. He is very greedy, and gobbles down his food at a great rate. I have

---

* Grace was a cook at the Manor House.

learned quite a few good poems this term: The Spanish Armardar
by Sir Walter Scott. How They brought the good news by Robert
Browning. John Gilpin by William Cowper. The Leap of Roushan
Beg by Longfellow. It would be nice if you could learn some of them
and then we might be able to have a play with people reciting together.

I must end now!

Lots of Love from
Valerie Jane

not to be read aloud
P.S. In this one code sighns A=R S=E I=K O=V U=W

[Possibly spring 1946]

Dear Sally

I am very sorry I have not written before but with this new school
of mine I am kept rather busy. We have lovely gym there, bars,
horses, ropes and every thing else. Some of the girls are quite nice,
others very nice, and others simply stinking (excuse my word
please). This week I was really top of my form, although, I REALLY
think that — , well anyhow I was. Pauline was top of her form too.
She is in one higher form than me. We are supposed to have a lot of
games, but one day when it was too wet for games and we went for
a walk, some of us were naughty, so for a punishment we have been
going regualy for walks, instead of games. How are you getting on
in your school? By the way, the Prefects and seniors of my school
are jolly decent. What form are you in? The work in my form is
soppy and so far I have only had three things under 8. 6 1/2. 7.
7 1/2. Yesterday we had a <u>horrible</u> thing to do for english prep: —
explain how to do up and adress a letter. What do <u>you</u> think of it.
Last Saturday I had a great thrill, for when we went riding, we had
our first jumping lesson.* Not Judy and Liza, (Liza was in bed) but
Pauline, Jill and me. As there is not a Guide company at this school I
am becoming a Lone Guide. I don't really know how to explain that

---

* At her Saturday riding lessons with Miss Bush at the Longham stables.

to you, but maybe you can find someone who can tell you what it means. Anyhow it means a lot of writting and filling up forms. Do you have a lot of prep. I have three preps a day except Wednesday, and on that day I have two. I expect you are getting bored with this lengthy letter, so now I will end.

Lot of love
V.J.

P.S. I shall have to write again soon, as I have not told you <u>HALF</u> the things I have to say.
P.P.S. give my love to every one in the house.
P.P.P.S. Chase got ill but he is better now.

[Around July 28, 1946]

Dear Sally,

I'm counting the days till you come. Don't forget to bring you bathing-dress with you. We are all very sad, because Chase has been killed. He was in the middle of the road, and a lorry was backing out of a gate (and so could not see him) and he was run over. A man saw him and took him to the vet, but he was dead. It's an awful shame, poor Chase.* How have you done in your exams. Ours were terribly easy, but we wern't helped. Excuse writing, but I'm in rather a hurry. Another of my fishes: —

He's got a nice little dinner. Ha! Ha! We break up this week, me on Monday, 29th and Judy on Wednesday, 31st. On Thursday we're going to the baths, Friday is a pony-club. Thursday you're coming. Friday another pony club. What full days. Don't forget to learn First Class, because you must all pass when you come to stay. If Susie is not sure of no. 2, I will tell here some things. You have to be

---

* Jane deliberately underplayed the importance of Chase's death here; in reality, as she recently recalled, "I cried and cried and cried."

able to recognize 10 birds, 10 dogs, 10 trees and 5 butterflys <u>or</u> moths:

(10 birds) (1) robbin, (2) blackbird (3) thrush (4) blue tit (5) wren (6) house sparrow (7) gull (8) hawk (9) starling (10) wood-pigeon.

(10 dogs) (1) cocker spaniel, (2) terrier (smooth and wire) (3) collie (4) alsation (5) bull-dog (6) bull-terrier, (7) pekenese (8) old english sheep-dog, (9) dalmatian, (10) airdale.

(10 trees) (1) oak (2) birch (3) fir (4) pine (5) sycamore (6) mountain-ash (7) plain (8) lime (9) Ash, (10) Horse-chestnut.

(5 butterflies or moths) (1) Red Admiral (2) Six Spot Burnet Moth (3) Purlple Emperor (4) Painted Lady (5) Privit Hawk Moth. These are only some of the many things. I did not bother to put in ten wild flowers, because here are such a lot that almost everybody knows 7 × 10. I can think of masses to tell you, it would take a book to write it down, and as its Mummy's writing paper, I can't afford to use much. Must stop now.

Lots of love from
V.J. V.J.M.G.

[Postmarked October 18, 1946]

Dear Sally,

This is a very short messy pencil letter. I'm terribly sorry, but I shant have time to get the Aligator Society Magazine together. I come home at 6.0 and do prep till about 7, and on Saterday mornings I do prep and then ride, on Sunday I do prep on and off all day. You see I have 8 preps in the weekends, and about 6 of them are usualy writing ones. I usualy have three preps every night, and I do one of them at school, and bring the others home. So you see, I don't have much time. Don't lets talk about school any more. I've started making Christmas Cards, and I've drawn two. One is a perky horse, pulling an old fasioned handsome cab and a street lamp shining brightly. The other is a tiny picture of Joseph, Mary & Jesus (as a baby) in the middle, and two angels one on either side, kneeling praying. Peter has completely moulted, & is hopping around without a tail, looking very unhappy. I found a little mole out riding, and it bit me hard. Mummy found a hedgehog in the middle of the road.

[Possibly fall of 1946]

Dear Sally

The new Aligator thing will arive soon. I was able to get it ready quickly because I was tossed and got a slight conncussien, so the beastly Doc made me take a short holiday in bed. However I'm getting up this afternoon, thank goodness for that. I am so glad you are going to learn riding. You will be able to ride here when you next come. I have said in A.S. (Aligator Society) that you need not make a badge but if you want to make one each ready for when you come to stay, you can. You must not wear them untill you have passed 1st class. To make them: find a fairly small aligator and trace it out and pin it onto some green material. Cut round the edge of the paper, so that you have a green cloth Aligator. Then get an oblong piece of card board about the size of the Aligator. Cover the cardboard with white cloth and stitch the aligator onto it. Put a safety pin in the back. As all the badges must be the same send me a tracing of the Aligator you use and also a piece of the paper the sieze of the card board. If you have not any green stuff get some green die. Try to use quite <u>thick</u> material. You must make Susie's for her. As I am the leader I will give my Aligator an eye and you must not.

Lots of love
VJ

[On outside of envelope:]
P.S. I meant to send this but [torn] wast of a stamp.
P.P.S. If you wread the inside of this letter you will see about the badge. The aligator of the cover we will use. Make the card-board just smaller than round the aligator.

[Possibly late 1946]

Dear Mummy,

I do hope that you are having a lovely holiday, and wish I was with you. I have just come back from seeing "Hamlet" and it was simply georgeous. We went on the way back from seeing Daddy off. It was jolly good fun. We arrived at Southampton and went to the

wrong docks, & met a policeman with dermithitis or some such disease on his face. We at last arrived on the quay side & there was the
"Eastern Prince". Daddy was up on the 2nd deck looking very
smart in his hat. He said he would come & see us but had to go to
his cabin & we were too late. Olly marched up the gangplank with
his parcels & was stopped by a member of the millitary police. Olly
asked if the parcels could be given to Major Morris-Goodall, on
which piece of information he looked uterly flabbergasted until that
person, very vexed, & having lost his hat, appeared, leaping over
his fellow soldiers, grabbing said parcels, and calling, "comming in
10 mins". He did not reappear until the band began to play and
then Dad appeared on lower deck. The noise was deafening —
from the men, and below Dad's rank & dignity so he disappeared,
& reappeared on the Poop — or some such place. The noise was
deafening as all the men cheered. Then the Millitary Police got
ashore, and were promptly booed & booed by the men. Then the
gangway was hauled up by the crane & the "Eastern Prince" slowly
sailed out of port. Daddy waved until we could no longer see him &
the band played.

The Birches,
10, Durley Chine Rd.
[February, probably 1947]

Dear Sally,

I have written to you so much that there isn't really anything to
tell you. I am doing a lot of things this year to do with nature — and
it is jolly interesting. I have vowed to keep them up for the whole
year, but I don't know if I shall. I will tell you what they are. If you
are not interested, of course you need not read them, but the sad
thing is, that at the moment, I can think of nothing else to say.

Well: —

I am going to keep up my nature log book, in the front, interesting events, such as watching the nest of the Willow wren, and in the
back are my nature walks. I have determined to go for one each

month of the year. If it is an interesting month with nests, I might go for two.

I am going to keep buds of diferent trees in water, and draw them as they open.

I am going to keep seeds and nuts and grow them behind blotting paper — you know, you line a jar with bloting paper (on the inside) then fill the hollow with earth, and press the seeds down between the bloting and the glass. You watch them grow, and draw them at various intervals. In March I am going to get some frog spawn, and if possible some toad spawn. The book says you can find it in the south. I think that is all.

I went for a nature walk the other day, and I found some jolly good things. Almost everything that Enid Blyton had in the diary.* I found a wren, blackbird, song thrush, mistle thrush, blue tit, coal tit, primrose, grounsel, a lovely red beetle, wood lice, a spider, a tiny flie & a funny little insect under an old log. The chestnut buds were geting sticky and the lime's red. I also found 5 Feb. things: — a crocus, a snowdrop & ivy berries. Now I must go and feed the guinea pigs, the time being 7.40 am.

I will end now, and if I think of anything else to say, I will add it as a P.S. or P.P.S. or P.P.P.S etc. Buck up and send your drawing comps. With lots of love to, Daphne, Uncle Byron, Susie, Robert, Rooky, Mandy, Tammy and Tuppy (Oh! is Mandy getting fat yet) and to yourself   from

Red Admiral, Jane, Spindle or V.J.
(I refuse to put Vaalerie)

---

* Enid Blyton (1897–1968) wrote many books for children.

Tel. W'stbourn 63723
May 23rd or — 23.4.47

Dear Sally,

Thanks very much for your letter. Sorry I haven't answered the one before, yet, but I've been busy. Please excuse writing because I've left my pen at school. What did you write to Francis Pitt about? I've now got — oh dear, I shall have to count them all, so hold on. — 67, if my arithmetics right. Oh! Sh! The Robin came right into my room just then, so I must dash down to get some bread in case he comes again. His babies are all over the garden, five of them. The thrush (mistle) has three which she proudly brings into the garden, and to day there were some hedge sparrow babbies. The chafinches have got a nest somewhere behind the hut, but we can't find it. The blackbird is still sitting on her new nest. Yesterday we saw a pair of BULL finches in the garden. I will collect dogs names, and I am going to do it like this: —

KIND OF Dog.	NAME.	KIND OF OWNER.
e.g) Scottie.	Jock	Nice lady. Rather fussy.

Lets say we can't put down a dogs name if we haven't seen its owner, or the person thats with it, but we can count it if we hear it being called. I am at home to day as I have a cold, and I am practising drawing birds from real life. I am determined to get good at drawing them. Yesterday I drew a picture of a forest on fire, and all the creatures running away. It went wrong, but I'll show it you one day if you like. That bird we thought was a lady chaffinch, definatly is a lady chaffinch, as she is always with the male. By the way, the Francis Pitt's, seem to come every other Sunday, don't they. That means there's one this Sunday. I have been to the baths twice. I am glad your going to jump in. Hope Susies quite recovered by now. The baby birds in the garden make such a din you can hardly hear your self think. I am reading all the penguin books, with green covers, that is, all the murders. I must end. Now. Give my love to Daphne, Byron, Susie and your kitten when it comes. R.Ad.

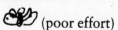 (poor effort)

P.S. Do you like the envelope?

The Birches
10 Durley Chine Rd
Bournemouth.
Tel: Westbourne 63723.
23.11.48

Dear Sally

Thank you very much for your letter. It was a jolly quick reply. I am very interested in your mice and you are jolly lucky to be able to keep them without losing them, especially as they do such adventurous things.

About the Jumping Competition. We had a wizzard time. I showed Bonus, and we got a 4th, but it was feeble as there were only 6 people altogether. If somebody else had showed her she would have got first. (I was not <u>jumping</u> her). Miss Forestier Walker asked Sheila if I could ride Quince* in the Inter Branch Jumping team, for the Portman pony club. She already had one team, but she thought that she would like another. There were only three teams, with four people in each, 2 from the Portman hunt, and 1 from some other Pony Club. We were 2nd. My prize was a nose bag (as it was for all others in the team). Jolly feeble! Then there was the branch team jumping. I was on Urchin, with Hopper on Wellington, Leza on Blitz, and Pauline (notice I put her last) on Daniel. We were not to bad, but you should have seen some of the teams. They were absolutly wizzard. Sheila's team was second, so that meant that Quince had to red rossets. Then came the open jumping, and Hop was in that on Wel, and good old Wel was actually second. Everyone was awfully surprised, as he had refused 3 times, and we were so sure that he had got nothing, that Hopper had actually taken off his saddle, and when they called her no. out, she had to go in bareback.

Then came the bareback jumping in pairs. Me & Hop went in on Dan, and Wel. They were jolly good old men (together their ages add up to 48) and didn't make a single fault, but evidently they were judged entirely on pairs, for the pairs who were 3rd & 4th had rapped many jumps, while we had a clear round.

---

* Sheila MacNaughton's horse.

Then came me on Urch in the under 14.2.

Have you ever had the feeling that on thinking something over, you think how silly you were, and you know that if you had another chance you would do it again. I expect you have! Well, that's how I feel.

Me & Urch. got on fine, and then at the last jump Urch ran slightly crooked, and once you let Urch go crooked at a jump in the Show Ring, you've had it. He is unstopable. He ran right out into the collecting ring before I got him back. Anyhow we had a clear round beyond that, and if they had judged it in the ordinary way, we might have got something but they had 3 faults for a refusal & 1/2 for knoking of with some legs or other, but I've forgotten. Anyhow, I know I could do it right now.

The Birches,
10, Durley Chine Road,
Bournemouth.
<u>7th March 1951</u>

My dear little Puffin,

I am quite positive that it is your turn to write to me, in fact I'm quite certain of the fact, but I will forgive you because I expect you are working for Mock (if you ever do work) or don't you have a Mock. We did, and it was far worse than School Cert, we all thought. I hear that you might do your Maths if you had 2 days in-stead of 2 hours (or was it 2 weeks, months, or even years). Well, cheer up, it was exactly the same with me.

Life is very boring, and, as I tell everyone I meet, but for the thought of next hols, I would stick my head in a gas oven — except that that would be a crime & I might be hung. It would be odd to hang a dead body, wouldn't it. Especially mine! I don't know why it would be especially odd to hang <u>my</u> dead body, at least, odder than anyone elses, only my alive body, is odd, so my dead one would be even odder.

(I hope you have skipped that last bit, only I got in one heck of a muddle. I nearly said H*LL etc)

Well my dear, and how are you? Still the same old 'Lally I suppose! What do you think of these miserable curs who are trying to overule our "blesséd England". Are not they a scurvey crowd of ostentatious thugs? Also, what about "Brittania Rules the waves."?? I have decided to start a civil war, and I shall lead the poor misled, ill-treated, squashed, and long-suffering middle class to a triumphant victory over the pompous upper class (composed of glorified char-women and road-workers). I do hope you will join my noble army. Of course, it will be a well paid job, hours of work 10 am–3.30 pm, Wednesday afternoon off, and of <u>course</u> I shan't expect my army to work more than 4 days a week. Any little squabbles will go before a specially appointed Trade Union of the British Middle Class Defence League. (That by the way is my idea of a Socialistically run Civil War!) I hope you agree with me.

By the way, to cease from penning such utter and complete drivel, do you ever listen to a program called "Any Questions" which is on Friday at 8.0–8.45 pm on the Light Program. If you have tell me and I will tell you my idea for an afternoon's fun next hols, when you (I hope) will be coming to pay this filthy town of mine a visite. If you havn't and you have any odd time over, I should, 'cos it's jolly good fun. It was a hoot last week!

I am going to have a super time next hols (I hope) Hunter Trialing Quince. I say "I hope" because Poosh is quite sure I shall break my neck. Have you been riding since I last saw you, and if so, who did you ride?

Jacob, the turtle in case you'd forgotten, has woken up from his hibernation, and I took walk in the garden on Sunday, as it was so warm and sunny (sorry for the change of ink). Mrs Churcher is moving out to the country in about a fortnight, so there will be no Buds to take for walks anymore, which will be rather sad.* Rusty is still the same as ever, but I think his fighting is getting even worse than it has been before. Hamlette,† that wicked little orange demon, has been awfully wicked. I can't remember if I told you this, but if I did, you must forgive me. Well, we left her in Our Room whilst we

---

* Budleigh was a collie owned by Mrs. Churcher, who ran a candy store.
† A golden hamster.

solomly masticated our supper, and, when we got back we found that the naughty little critter had gnawed clean through the Telephone wire as it went under the door. Was Ma in a bait!!!! It was when Danny was so ill, and we were expecting a call from Uncle Eric etc etc. At least half of the British population decided to give us a tinkle that night, and it was infuriating as we could hear it ringing almost incessantly and were unable to lift a fingur to stop it. As a matter of fact its a wonder the <u>dear</u> little animal didn't electrocute her stupid little yellow body.

At the moment I am frightfully busy typing our form magazine for the second time. I have written hundreds more poems — about 6 to be precise, and one is about the Grand National and is miles long — 144 lines to be exact. That is going in the magazine so I hope everyone enjoys it.

About a fortnight ago I went to a lecture with Audy at the Richmond Hill lecture hall. It was on Reptiles Ancient and Modern and it was absolutely <u>wizzard</u>. I did wish you could have been there, as there were live specimins afterwards. He had a gecko lizzard — the sort that run on the ceiling, an adder, 2 grass snakes, a python skull, and a pickled smooth snake. There was also a "healing serpent" at least so called in Greek Literature — ancient Greek I mean, — but I never caught its proper name. I had it, and a grass snake round my neck, and it was wizzard. Audy & I stayed right to the end talking to him — he was wizzard. I wonder if he has been to your school, as he said he goes to a lot of schools. His name is something like Leucher.

Danny has now gone off to Whipps X for a kind of rest cure, and she is being spoilt most terribly.* All the doctors and nurses pop in all day long and she is never alone for more than 10 minutes. She really is having a wizzard time, and she writes us billions of letters. She has been gone a week, and in that time the family has had two, Judy has had one, I have had one, and Audy has had two, & I think another family one came this morning. All her "boy-friends" as she calls them cluster round her, and would do anything for her, and she has found 2 or 3 which she thinks suitable for Olly. They bring her

---

* Uncle Eric was a surgeon at Whipps Cross Hospital.

flowers, fruit, nuts, books and in fact, she has only to name an object & it will be brought her, even if it means scouring London at mid-night. Hey — ho!

I think it's a swizz that we have to go to school on Easter Monday! Do you have to? I don't expect so. Last Saturday I had to go early to the stables as it was a) Hopper 21st Birthday and she had gone up to London, and — b) Poosh was at Brockenhurst at a dressage affair. The South Dorset Dressage Group were having a sort of schooling by the marvellouse man who teaches Mrs. Beckett, so naturally Poosh and Quince went. Apparently Quince was quite good, but went most terribly badly on the last day, which was rather disapointing.

Anyhow, that left Bushel and I to cope with the school — 7 small, pretty hopeless childeren. Two of them nearly got run away with. My two (on the leading rein) both nearly fell off, one 'cos the saddle slipped round, & the other 'cos the leather came off. On top of that Sally kept trying to run away. There was <u>masses</u> of tack to do, & on top of everything (sorry, I've used that expression twice) Bushel's brother was coming for the night and had to be met by her in the car. On the whole, it was a busy day and I cleaned tack so hard in order that Bushel could finish early and "enjoy" her brother (if I may use such a word) that my arms still ache. Then, after all that, Ruin went and got collic so that Bushel was up half the night. Such is life, but I must not grumble.

And now my dear (sorry to begin with "and") I really must end this nonsensical epistle, and cart my aching limbs up the stairs, unclothe them, and lay them, in all their beauty, between the white sheets. Of course, I hope to lay the rest of myself between the sheets as well, all but my head in fact. I must also submerge all but my brain case beneath the clear water (which will soon become delightfully cloudy owing to the formation of a scum, & will efectively conceal my maidenly figure).

Much love & hope to see you soon.

Give my love etc to all.

Jane (Red Admiral)

[Possibly summer of 1951]

Dear Sally,

Thank you very much for your letter. I hardly dare write to you, and I hardly dare think or talk about you, without feeling the bitterest remorse, as I havent written to you for so long. I am truly most terribly sorry. My remorse is of the very greatest imaginable. Do not however think illy of your freind, for, as the sun sets and rises, and the moon travels around the world, I think of you greatly and truly. I was going to the hospital, to have a truly beloved piece of myself, cut out with a pair of cruel scissors, but I did not, I could have wept for gladness, as a mighty joy swept me from end to end. Please forgive my truly beloved pencil, as although I have a wondrous pen, I have no pure cool ink, with which to make my marks, which are christened writing.

I'm sorry I wrote all that nonsense. <u>Translation</u> I'm honestly and truly terribly sorry I havent written befor, but I was going to have my tonsils out and I didn't because of infitile peralisis.* Excuse pencil, but I don't know where the ink is as I am staying with Auntie Joan, by my self. I am longing to see you all again. How are you all. I got a 4th prize at a gymkana, in a fancy dress race, a little while ago. There are two dogs here, Juno, a black cocker, and Domino a golden dashound. There is also a cat, Smoke, and a shetland pony, Jimpy. There are as well, 6 ponies which Auntie Joan is exercising for a man. Please excuse writing, but it is horiball pencil. I came from London to here by myself. It is very hot here, out in the garden, as I am in the sun, and I am just going to go in, as I have sat here long enough, and Auntie Joan is calling me, so I will finish this lettre in bed tonight and post it tommorrow sometime. There wasn't time yesterday at bed time so I am writing in the morning this — oh! I've forgotten what I was going to say. Never mind. Last night some queer things went past my window last night. I went to look to see what they were, and I found they were one thing. It was very big, and I thought it might be a bat, but it made a whirring noise, and I

---

* A tonsillectomy was postponed for fear that the operation might make her more vulnerable to polio infection.

thought it must be a moth. It came very near the window, but it flew so fast, and fluttered so, that I could not see its shape. I rode the little pony last night, and he bucked a lot, making Auntie Joan screech with laughter. David, her yongest son, is sprawled beside me on the bed, talking away, as he looks at a horse book of mine, and making me forget what I was going to say. I must end now, as this letter must be posted. I hope Daphne is better,

Love to all including Rook.

VJ

The Birches,
10, Durley Chine Road,
<u>Bournemouth</u>.
[Around December 1951]

Dearest Sally,

I am afraid that I have been rather a long time in replying to your last letter, and your reply will have to follow rather speedily if you don't want a nice cold swim. Or do you? I am sorry if I have underated your capacity for enjoying a cold bath. However, enough of this nonsensical monologue — or is it a dialogue? I don't know.

I have just emerged triumphant from my first attempt at sonnet writing. By that I don't mean that I have writen a wonderful sonnet, I mearely mean to impart unto my dear friend — none other than thine own dear self (you see I have been reading a Jeffrey Farnol)* — that I have actually written a sonnet (don't get alarmed, I am not going to send it for your perusal). We have been doing the sonnet in English, and the wretched woman made us write them for prep.

It is a real hoot! Canford School for boys has asked us to a dance,

---

* Jeffrey Farnol (1878–1952) wrote several popular works of fiction, including the best-selling *The Broad Highway* (1911).

and all the seniors and Pre's are going (I don't know if I told you that I was made a Pre?). Anyhow, I have got to spend the night at school. It really is going to be a hoot! Canford School is well renowned for having awful boys — George Elis comes from there, and if he is an example of a Canford boy, they must be pretty ghastly. I am dreading it, but I had to go (I hope I am not boring you).

As I am writing this letter at school, I have not got your letter here, and so I cannot answer any questions you may have asked as I cannot remember them — I hope they were not vital. We are making wizard plans for next holidays, but I don't yet know whether they will work, or whether I am meant to tell you, so please do not get worked up, or dismal or anything which might be your reaction if it did work or really was happening. (I don't think that that makes sense, but you will have to try & see if it does). Well, Ma is endeavouring to take me to see Winter's Tale up in London next hols, as I am doing it for Higher, and she is trying to get them on the 7th, 8th or 9th of Jan, 1952 (not 1 or 3 but 2). We shall then stay the night (probably at Whipps X), and then our plan was for you to come up, and we could either go to the Museum again — as it is all open now I believe, or else we could spend hours wandering round the Zoo. I don't quite know what happens to Sue — she might go on the through train to Bournemouth if she was allowed to go by herself, or come with you, or something. It depends on everything — I don't know. Ma & I havn't even got as far as talking about that. The trouble is that it seems expensive for Jif & I to trail up to London — in fact I'm sure Judy won't be able too, and it seems unfair for her to be left out — I dunno. Anyhow, I don't even know yet just exactly if you can come — so don't imagine this is all arranged. It is NOT. Later I am now very unsure — in fact positively unsure of this arrangement, because we had seats for Sat (next Sat) which Ma was trying to change when I began this letter. Now we know they cannot be changed, so I don't know what will happen. So let me start a fresh subject.

It is now Sunday evening, and I can tell you all about Saturday. Everything went off wizardly except that it was carried out in a howling gale. Oh bother! I have just read through this letter, and observed that you must be quite at sea as I have not mentioned what was happening on Saturday. I am so sorry. Well, I will now proceed to explain! On Sat, the School at Longham got up a Christmas Bazar, and they had a Father Christmas. They asked Bushel to lend Polly & the Wagon. Well, the Wagon was beautifully draped in green velvet curtains with a chair draped in the middle, and beautiful furs down the back and notices about the bazar down the side. Polly's mane & tail were bedecked with gay red and yellow ribbon. We had two choir boys behind the chair in red and black to blow bugles, and Poosh and I were out riders. Bushel was dressed up as a coachman, and you could honestly hardly recognize her — lots of people didn't. She had a top hat, side whiskers, & a big black coachman's coat. Father Christmas sat beside her, and sang occasionally. His hood came halfway down his face. Poosh rode side-saddle in a habit with an <u>18 inch</u> waiste, and a top hat with a veil, and a frilly lace thing as a sort of crevat affair, on Quince. I rode Summer Time, and was her squire. I had Admiral Bush's tail coat, a blue spotted crevat, side whiskers — my own hair stuck down the side of my face — trousers stitched down the side to look like those riding trousers which the very posh show riders still wear, with my riding boots underneath, and I carried my hunting whip. We had great difficulty in a) getting Poosh into her 18″ waiste, and b) getting my hair up under the top hat, so that it was presentable when I took it off to Father Christmas. Mrs McDonald — a person who lives at Longham House now — was jolly useful, and rushed madly around at the last minute. You can't image what a mad rush there was at the last min. There was such a gale that the notices began to blow off, so Mrs McDonald stitched them on, and we were late as we got back late from taking the school out. We had to trot all the time and Poosh got so sore. I was pretty sore as I had to sit all the time as otherwise I sat on my tails. It was super fun. I stayed that night with Poosh which was also jolly dee.

I can't think specially of any more news — certainly not enough to fill another of these large sheets, & so I had better stop. I suppose I told you about the rats killing all the [guinea] pig babies — I can't remember. Don't forget to write me today or tomorrow at the latest — by today I mean Monday when I fondly hope you will get this letter. We have got an extra 6 days of hols because of the fuel shortage.

Tons of love

V.J. Jane: Red Admiral.

The Birches,
10, Durley Chine Rd,
Bournemouth.
[Around June 24, 1952]

Dear Sally,

I am very offended with you. Do you realize that you have upset your old friend beyond words. I would have you know that the Rev. J. Trevor Davies is not yet 50. I would also have you know that Richmond Hill broadcast the other evening and everyone who heard it said it was the best service they'd heard for ages. I would also have you know that I do not ALLOW people to say nasty things about him. Now do you understand. I was going to write a very short note, saying that I should never see you again unless you applogized. Now I have finished Higher, I am so happy that I feel forgiving, and also that it would be a waste of a stamp — BUT! Unless you write and tender your very sincere appologies for so hurting me, I shall not write to you again!!

Now that I have got that off my chest, I will proceed to relate some news to you — not that there is any. My dear, I am being so teased that I don't know where to look for shame! On Saturday I went out to the stables and was not going to ride, and then Poosh said there was some one to ride with, and there wouldn't be next week, so would I rather then. I said yes if it was a nice person. You may guess who it was. Clive! come for a weekend from Aldershot (he is in the army now). Well of course, I'd absolutely had it then. I said I would go if Poosh sent me, so she sent me. As a matter of fact we had a jolly nice ride — I am absolutely sick of riding with either myself or a lot of stupid kids. We both got run away with all the time on Summer & Sol. The worste is yet to come! On Sunday I was peacefully shelling broad beans when Olly appeared to say I was wanted on the phone. You can guesse the next. This time I did not have you as an excuse and I had to go. We went to the Rufus Stone in the new forest, and had tea in a little place where the ponies came and put their heads in at the windows. It was a hoot!

There is worse still! (and this is the most dreadful part of the whole story). Someone from school in my form — saw me!!!!! It really is terrible. She suddenly said before prayers when everyone was there, "Who was that young man you were out with on Sunday?" Of course I went puce, and everyone was in fits. Somehow or other she knew his name (she is going to tell me how soon) and now everyone calls me Clive. But worse was to come! Whilst I was still hiding my face, Wendy (a day girl I come to school with & who I had told about George) said "Is that the one I know about?" And like a fool I said no. My dear, you can just imagine what it was like, can't you.

Oh, I am so happy. Higher is over. 3 weeks with no work, and then I've left — ! Oh! It's so super you can't imagine. I am looking foreward very much to the end of the term as I have arranged a midnight feast for all the Pre's and Senior's in our house. We are having it on the last but one night of term, and we are going down the fire escape and down to the bottom tennis court through the woods. There are about 12 of us and it should be smashing fun. The difficultest (sorry for the coined word) part is getting me smuggled in, but we have worked it out, and I am going into a little 2 room with 2 pre's in it, and no one ever seems to go in there. I shall either sleep on Liza B's bed, under it, or just on the floor. It really will be super, although we are sure to be caught.

Our exams have been foul, I promis you. We had one English exam, "Passages for Comprehension and Interpretation" in which was a poem all about Public Lavatories (at least, very nearly, but there were a few other things in it as well.) I simply popped. I will show it to you when (or rather if) you come to stay. (You can't come unless you take back the words you wrote). That reminds me, there was a picture of him in the Echo the other day. Oh! I do love him.

He knows me now, and next Sunday I'm going to see him, all by my-self, to ask him if I can become a Member of Richmond Hill. You can't imagine how I'm longing for it.

~~(but one night of term, and somehow I have got to be smuggled up to the bedroom. I am)~~

[N.B. I started the letter again after a pause & thought I had ended on page 3. Hence the false start.]

Now I will begin again, although why I have started a new page I can't imagine as I have nothing to say. We (3 of us) finished Higher on Monday morning, and Pongo said we could go down to "Bournemouth" after much persuasion. We decided we wanted to go to Shell bay, and as Hillary had no bike she had to come to our house, & we bagged the 2 bikes (one is unsafe & we are not allowed to use it!) and met Jill and really had a smashing time. We got a pic-nic lunch from home & Jill had some oranges & apples, so we got on fine. Then Hilly and I nearly got lost coming home, which was also rather funny!

My dear, you really should see poor Mrs Jimmy. She is so fat that I'm sure she'll burst if she gets any fatter, and she won't produce. Each morning I go down expecting to find at least 8 pigs instead of 2 — but no go. She can hardly get through the door as it is.

Mummy is away at the moment, staying with Deb (I can't remem-ber whether you knew or have met her, but anyhow, her daughter is Jo — you may have heard of her). Did you hear "Morris Mortimer Goodall" being shrieked over the wireless during Le Mans.* It made me hoot with laughter. Apparently everyone in the motor racing world calls him Morris or something.

I shall really have to buck up now, and fill the remainder of the page with rappid rubbish as it is nearly time to set off for school. It is wiz now as we have no work to do at all so I read all day. I have read my first two novels for about 3 months since higher ended — "The Talisman Ring" and "The Great Roxhythe" both by G. Heyer, and am in the middle of "Royal Escape" also by her. Have you read any of them.

---

* Mortimer raced in that year's LeMans.

You must come and stay in the hols — sometime before August 18th as I am going to Germany then (I'm not looking foreward to it one bit I can assure you). You must forgive writing but the pen is a) full of sand, b) crossed, and c) running out (or not running as the case may be). Must stop, and will post this just as soon as I can find some stamps.

Much love
Jane

P.S. Mind you write & send your deepest appologies.

The Birches,
10, Durley Chine Road,
<u>Bournemouth</u>.
[Early August 1952]

Dear Sally,

Thanks tons for your last epistle (or is it episel — still wrong but you knew what I mean) which I very nearly fell over backwards to receive. I certainly never expected one for weeks and weeks! I'm so glad you are having a nice time, but the G.G's sound quite balmy. Bad luck about your back and shirt — have you managed to mend your jhods yet?

Now! About the great day! It was SMASHING!! Everything worked and went off wizardly! It was wonderful! Glorious! Splendid! Delightful.

Michael didn't come in the end as he went to the Circus — they had the tickets muddled up — at least that was the excuse. Kitty (the little dog) came and she was sweet. Rusty sulked and lay down by the door all the time. Even during cake time at tea he never moved a muscle.

I sat in a little arm chair beside HIM. Danny and Mrs. sat on the couch, and Ma sat behind the tea table on her little setee affair. I wore my white dress — <u>AND</u> <u>he</u>!! said how nice it looked — him <u>not</u> her! We talked about everything under the sun — and oh! he was so wizard. I put a feather and a piece of cotton for him to sit on — I still have them, also his cigarette but, his matchstick and his tea-leaves. I went to bed on the couch that night with his cushion for my pillow. When he first came my chair was quite far back, and while I was handing food round he got up and pulled it closer up!

I have never seen such a lively little man. He couldn't keep still for a second, and he couldn't bear a conversation to be carried on without him. He <u>hated</u> his wife to tell a story, and always managed to get his word — or rather word<u>S</u> in. He had a beautiful long nose and he adores dogs. Of course when they got out of the front door Kitty disappeared and do you know! if I hadn't noticed they would have gone off without her! They must have enjoyed themselves. They'd even started the car. Then Trevor & I looked for her, & Audy found her by the pigs. "Oh hurry Trevor" says Mrs. Davies & he came pounding after me doing exaggerated running — you know — knees up & hands up & head back. It was a hoot. The naughty dog made a hole in the wire netting. We did nothing but laugh all afternoon, and do you know! They stayed from 3.45 till 6.30.

Another wizard thing! They may be coming down to our beach hut and I am going with them to show them where it is. We have planned that I shall take the dingy and Trevor & I are going to drift out to sea — just us two. Won't it be smashing! Judy & Susie have sealed my future — & Michael's. They kept making me laugh in church by saying "There's your husband". Apparently he's going to do Journalism too.

My dear. Something else! I've got Higher & although I only scraped through in Bilge* I got 70% in English which is a distinction only they don't give them now. Unfortunately! Hilary failed hers — Bilge only so that was all she did. Poor thing!

My dear. Do you remember Isabel Abbay? Well, she came here to go to Quo Vadis with me — I never rang her that time I promised, so when she rang again I <u>had</u> to do something. Well, she arrived & we had had trestles made for the ping pong table & were playing. The first back-putting-up thing she said was she wouldn't deign to

---

* Biology.

play with us because we wern't good enough, then that the table wasn't proper, & then that Queen's College (where I hope to go for my Secretarial) was inferior to her place. Ma squashed her wizardly though, & made her go quite pink. My dear! Quo Vadis was simply wonderful — the best film I've seen for years. Trevor told us he'd seen it when he came so of course I <u>HAD</u> to go — though I was going anyhow. We all wept buckets and it was jolly well worth the 5/9 d. Trevor & Alice (his wife) said they have made it do for 2 films so the next one they want to see they won't be able to. Poor man!

I did an awfully silly thing before he came — apart from polishing all the brass till it was so bright it hurt you to look at; polishing all the drawing room furniture; cleaning the drawing room window; scrubbing the entire conservatory floor & washing all the white woodwork, cleaning the window by the door; and repainting all the windows & doors that look into the yard — the one's that were peeling & had things scratched all over them!!! Now, where was I? Oh! yes. The other silly thing. I made a vow that if he didn't take sugar in his tea, I never would. I felt sure he would, & blow me, the man didn't. I have now given sugar up and I <u>HATE</u> it!!!!!!!!!!

We all 3 went to the B'mouth Aquarist's Exhibition yesterday & spent all morning looking at fish. There were some jolly good ones, and some most beautiful aquariums. Also some iguanas and other water loving reptiles.

Every evening now I go to the General Post Office, so everyone loves me because they have till 1/4-9 to write their letters instead of 8.0 which is our last post at Westhill P.O. <u>Reason</u>? Because my trip takes me past the Manse.* It's wizard as there's usually a light, the only blow being I can't see in.

I also gave Rusty a bath on Saturday and he still looks beautiful. I think Kitty must have given him fleas again though, after all my careful de-fleaing.

Jill's Budgerygar (can't spell) is here for a time while they are in France & the poor thing is in awful condition — all its neck is raw & featherless before & its feathers are frayed & its always scratching. Poor Kim.

---

* The Victorian rectory of Richmond Hill church.

Mr. Parry is coming tomorrow & so is Jo so we have to tidy up the house once again. It's shocking.

You should see me my marrow [squash] now. It's simply <u>gigantic</u>! I've seldom seen such an enormous affair. We are going to eat it on Sunday & Mr. Parry will be able to have some.

Do write again soon & tell me some more about your place,

Tons of love,

Jane

2

TRANSITIONS
1952–1957

And then, quite suddenly, my school days were over. What would I do next? I only wanted to watch and write about animals. How could I get started? How could I make a living doing that?

— *My Life with the Chimpanzees*

S O JANE GOODALL has described the quandary of her life following the end of school in the summer of 1952. If she had previously indulged in childhood fantasies about being close to nature, going to Africa, becoming a Dr. Dolittle or a Tarzan, living in the "jungle" at peace with wild beasts, becoming a naturalist or a journalist writing about natural history, now was the time to put away childish things, to move from the dream into reality. And reality in postwar Britain, living in a middle-class family with much love but little money, may have seemed constraining.

Jane had done well enough on her examinations to apply for admission to a university. But the family could hardly afford university tuition, and Vanne urged her daughter to develop practical skills. From September to mid-December of 1952, Jane lived with a family in Germany, intent on learning German but not very successful at it. She returned in time for Christmas at the Birches and then, on May 4, 1953, she began to polish her typing, shorthand, and bookkeeping skills at Queen's Secretarial College in South Kensington. During this period she rented a room in the London home of Mrs. Hillier, the mother of her mother's friend Deb Seabrook, who had married a prosperous apple farmer and lived at a farm known as the Chantry in Kent. Many of Jane's weekends were spent gloriously in the country, riding horses with Jo, the Seabrooks' daughter. The first letter in this chapter, written three weeks after Jane began the London secretarial course, refers to "super times at the Chantry" with Jo.

By Easter 1954, Jane had finished her secretarial training and was back at the Birches, cleaning out her old bedroom, sorting, rearranging, tidying up. She reported, in the second letter of this sequence (April 26, 1954), being delighted to visit once again the Longham stables, finding Miss Bush's assistant, Poosh, to be "suddenly . . . grown up." Her infatuation with the Reverend Trevor Davies continued, though now she described her feelings in tones that seem increasingly ironic and self-deprecatory. As for her earlier ambition to write about animals, to be a journalist of nature and natural history, that too appeared less immediately certain: "I havn't given up the journalism idea by the way, but I have decided that to write anything worth anyone reading I must have lived a few more years and acquired a little experience of life, as they say."

She hoped to find a secretarial job in Oxford, but while waiting for something to transpire, Jane began, probably in May of 1954, assisting her aunt Olly with clerical work. Olwen was a skilled physiotherapist who ran a clinic for children and adults in need of physical therapy. The "dullness of the actual work," Jane wrote to Sally in the letter of June 26, "finds recompense in my interest at being up at the clinic & seeing all the cases."

By early August she had begun typing letters and documents for the Oxford University Registry. It was an uninteresting job, but among its few perks was the opportunity to work in Clarendon House, a superb neoclassical edifice with a grand double entrance, great Doric columns, a dramatic frieze at the central portico, and some serious temple statuary on the roof. Constructed in the early eighteenth century, during the mid-twentieth it housed the registry's various administrators, clerks, and typists. Jane and two coworkers explored the pleasurably "dark & cob-webby" attic (July 27 letter). Her ultimate boss was "the Reg"; her immediate supervisor was Miss Shearer (or "M.S."), who was kind enough to allow

Jane to bring her pet hamster, Hamlette, to work (noted in November 1954). But by February of 1955 Jane would confess in a letter home that "I have been miserable these last few weeks because of the boredom of this foul job."

Imperfectly counterbalancing the boredom of her job was the excitement of being in Oxford and the pleasure of living in a boarding house (at 225 Woodstock Road) with an agreeable landlady, Miss Kersey. Her fellow boarders included Anne (who departed for Italy and New Zealand in the summer of 1954), Rosie Coates-White, and Mr. Davies (disappeared in a huff in November), as well as three others who became during the year her good friends: Stuart Ramsden, John Butler, and Eileen. In the letter of November 1954, Jane relates most delightfully the experience of "jumping with fog-fever" in Oxford. The letter written in early May 1955 describes a timeless spring day (and Oxford's official May Day) spent punting and picnicking with her friends.

Jane left Oxford early in June 1955, and in late July or early August, she returned to London, where she had found a job choosing music to accompany documentary films produced by Stanley Schofield of Schofield Productions, at 6, 7, 8 Old Bond Street. The job had its pleasures, and London certainly did. With what seems a typically high level of energy, Jane squeezed the most she could out of her time in the city, taking classes in philosophy, going to concerts ("I seem to spend my life in the Festival Hall"), and dealing with eager young men — including David and then Brian (first mentioned in the letter of August 7, 1955). Brian had become "B." by May 1956 and was by August or September replaced briefly by a "chap I have met called Douglas." Other young suitors mentioned in the letters include Horst and Hans from Germany and Keith, who was temporarily replaced, on the ship to Kenya, by "not a bad chap" also named Keith.

The position at Schofield Productions lasted until May of 1956, when she received a letter from Africa. It was an invitation from Marie Claude ("Clo") Mange, one of Jane's best friends from her Uplands School days, inviting her old chum "V.J." to come visit her in Kenya, where her father had recently acquired a large farm. Jane instantly accepted Clo's invitation, gave notice at the film studio, and returned to the Birches, where she could live rent- and board-free and walk a short distance each day to her job as a waitress in a large hotel, the Hawthorns. She worked herself "absolutely to the bone," as she declared in a letter to Sally written in August or September 1956. But she was able to save almost everything she earned; every weekend she brought home her wages and tips and hid them under a carpet, saving her pounds, shillings, and pence until the day when she had accumulated enough to buy a ticket to Africa. The last letter in this sequence, written on stationery provided by the S.S. *Kenya Castle*, is her first letter home at the start of a three-week voyage to Kenya Colony, East Africa.

The theme of this chapter is Jane Goodall saying good-bye, in a gradual and unconscious way, to the people and pets and places of her childhood; it is fascinating and satisfying indeed to observe how the central fantasy of that childhood turns out to be the guiding reality of her adult life. The motion of this chapter is a slow drift from place to place and job to job, things begun with wild eagerness and ending in mild disappointment — leading to a final sweep of movement: the invitation from Clo, the waitressing job, the boat trip to Africa: the focus of attention, the direction of a dream, the start of a life's great adventure.

*   *   *   *

c/o Mrs Hilliard,
8, Beaufort House,
Beaufort Street,
Chelsea.
[Postmarked May 27, 1953]

Dear Sally,

I'm dreadfully sorry I havn't written before — at least I don't think I answered your last letter before did I? How are you old thing!

I'm very nearly dead. This shorthand is terribly hard work, and also rather monotonous as it only requires learning, learning, learning. The typing is not too bad, but that again, is a little bit automatic.

I have simply super times at the Chantry at the weekends —

when I don't (or rather can't) go home to Trevor & the Birches as Jo has two ponies and we ride nearly all the time. You can't imagine how super it is to be able to do just what you want on a horse, instead of always having to behave yourself. The weekend before last when I went down we had one quite mad ride when we both nearly fell off from laughing. We had just come back from a dog show, and wanted to take the dogs out. We got onto the horses just as we were, & as I had to take my stockings off, I took my shoes off too. Jo followed suite of course, & so we were sockless, shoeless, johdless, hatless, & saddleless. We went through the orchards (which incidentally were glorious with apple blossom) and Joker kept bucking. That made me laugh, & so I nearly fell off, and then I saw Jo quite helpless with laughter. On enquiring the reason, I discovered that when my skirt blew up (as it frequently did) she could see my suspenders wildly flopping up and down under my knickers. That set me off, and honestly, I've never laughed as much in my life. And as you know it's most queer laughing when cantering. In the end we both had to collapse on the ground, quite helpless & weak. It took about two days to recover from.

On Saturday I went to a horse show, and although it wasn't particularly hot, it was sunny & windy, & for the first time in its life, my face really caught the sun. It is still as red as a beetroot (remember the 'darling' beetroot!) and I only hope that it's not going to peel.

I expect Daphne* told you that she came to Oedipus with me. Oh! It was absolutely <u>smashing</u> and never have I seen a better play. I think your Ma enjoyed it too. I went twice, and I've also been to the Twelfth Night which was also jolly good.

I have heaps more I could say, but also lots of work awaiting me, which must be done. Drop me a line sometime soon old pal, and until then I'll wish you

'Adieu'
love
<u>Jane</u>

---

* Sally's mother.

The Birches,
10, Durley Chine Road,
Bournemouth.
[Postmarked April 26, 1954]

My darling and much beloved peach blossom,*

(So Miss Mary Audey Gwyneth Joseph has told me to salute you.) I'm so terribly sorry that I havn't answered your letter before, but I've been having the most ghastly time imaginable with my room. You know my large white article of furniture with the drawers and the glass cupboard on top? You know the rubbish and piles and mounds of old papers that had conglomerated within? Well, we decided to get rid of it as I was to have a new piece of furniture — brown and much nicer. I was also to have a different dressing table, and move the wardrobe to the other side of the room. Well, you should just have seen me executing said re-arrangements and removals. Gosh, it was a sight you would never have forgotten. For one thing, while the spirit so moved me I decided to untidy everything all at once, so that even if the spirit left me, necessity would force me to continue the good work. So, imagine your little friend one glorious sunny afternoon sitting in a room where every inch of floor is littered with piles of newspaper cuttings, old magazines, file paper, notebooks, old school books, and bits and pieces of every sort and description. Closely piled along the walls are rows and rows of books, while the empty bookcases stare out with hollow empty shelves. Piled onto the bed are dresses, jumpers, vests, knickers, blouses, laddered stockings, socks with undarned holes leering blankly up at the ceiling — etc. etc. etc.! Just imagine it, and spare the poor sweating toiling creature on the floor, begrimed and becobwebbed, a moment of pity in your tender heart.

And I have only just finished it, rehung the pictures, filled my crests with flowers, arranged the ornaments, and got all to my liking. And now, apparently, everything has got to come out for the blasted room to be painted. The thought is driving me slowly but surely insane!

---

* Sally Cary.

But enough of such dismal thoughts, for the sun is shining, and my heart is full of the joys of spring — and fond thoughts of my Beloved. Oh Sally my sweet, I have had such a wonderful Easter, that the memory must surely sweeten my thoughts for all the rest of my life. I think this time of year is the very best of all, and I would rather have an Easter than hundreds of Christmases, because everything is so green and new and beautiful with the promise of new life and sunshine. I' troth, I find myself waxing poetic in praise of the season.

This year I was specially asked for to help with the decorating of the Church, and I was given the most fiddly and laborious job of tying jam jars along the altar rail, hiding them with fronds of foliage, and then filing (sorry 'll') them with water, primroses and wood-anemones. It did look super when it was finished though, and I think it was worth the trouble. I had an old fat dear from the choir to assist me, so while she sat stolidly on her bottom, I had to wriggle backwards and forwards under the rail and between the vases of tulips and daffodils tying knots which invariably slipped and had to be tied again, a process involving more wriggling and crawling. And matters were complicated by Rusty (who was there of course) because every time I squirmed under the rail, he had to lumber through after me, and he had very little respect for the floral decoration, I am sorry to say. However, it was accomplished in the end with no accidents whatsoever.

I must say the Church looked super when we had finished. The window sills were thick with flowers of all kinds, the altar rail blossomed out in green, yellow and white, and on the table in the center was the most heavenly bowl of arum lilies — one of my softest spots is for arum lilies, and, oh joy, after the services were over on Sunday, and I had stayed behind to help clear the church, I was allowed to take two of the beautiful gracious, slender, exotic creatures home with me, together with a basket full of primroses, and a glorious bunch of daffodils and tulips. Truly I felt like an Easter queen.

And you just should have seen the congregation on Easter Sunday morning. We got there an hour before the service began, and even so it was at least half full, and we only just got our front seat. Mummy, of course, was late, and though we just managed to squash her into our pew, it was such an uncomfortably tight fit that I sat on the stairs for the sermon, and was much more comfortable. By about 10.45 every available inch of the church was packed, with rows and rows of chairs down all the gangways and in every nook and cranny possible. And there were about 80 people sitting upstairs in the lecture hall, where Prickles* had laid on a loud speaker the day before, and which we had also decorated. It was quite wonderful, and we had 75 members of the Welsh National Opera Company crammed into that round place in between the choir because they were singing the anthem. They have been singing at the Pav.† all this week. Later.

I was interrupted from this wonderful epistle for the funniest reason. You have heard from Susie, I am sure, of Mummy's Colonel?‡ Well, he is really a sweet old boy. As I was writing this letter the day before yesterday, Mummy was in London, and the Colonel rang up to ask if I would go round and talk to him because he was so lonely. It was about 8.0 but I had to go, and it was a great pity because it spoilt my nice little plan which was to take this letter to the post and then wait for Olly who was at choir practise — and you know why I wanted to do that, don't you? However, I had a very nice little evening, and he gave me the most super volume of Shakespeare. It looks like an ordinary book, only when you open it, inside are four little tiny volumes with tiny print, real India paper, and the most super pictures imaginable.

On Saturday I went out to the stables for the first time in years, and then went with Poosh to the Portman Hunt Point-to-Point afterwards. Poosh has changed considerably — for the better. Quite suddenly she seems to have grown up, and is no longer so silly and giggly and jealous as she used to be. You remember what she said at first when I told her that Pelletier§ was still writing to me — "What

---

* A nickname for Aunt Olwen's boyfriend, Mr. Hollis.
† The Bournemouth Pavilion.
‡ Susie was Sally Cary's younger sister. The Colonel was a close friend of Vanne's.
§ An admirer.

a conscientious young man he must be" — and how horrified I was that she could make such a foul remark? Well, when I told her that he had rung up for my birthday, she was very amused and not beastly about it at all. I told her to test her out in a way.

Did you ever hear that poor old Rack had to be put down? He got some internal stoppage and after being ill for weeks they had to give up hope as he couldn't eat anything at all. Poor Poosh is still very upset about it, especially as her family say she can't have another big dog because it's too expensive to feed. She is riding Quince's foal, Quick, now, and already doing dressage with her. It seems very early to start, but Chasm did the same, and it suited her very well.

Did Susie tell you that I am really off to Oxford to try and get a job? or was I that far when Daphne came here. Anyway, I am going to stay with these people at the beginning of May definitely, and it should be rather fun, as they live outside Oxford in the country, and have lots of ponies and there is a farm next door to them which is almost a part of the family.

And there is another super thing about this Oxford business. Trevor is great friends with one of the Principals of one of the colleges — a certain Dr. Marsh who was at college with T. He is going to write him a letter of introduction — or should I say, he is going to write one for me. Which means I can go down to the Manse to fetch it and tell him particulars. I havn't given up the journalism idea by the way, but I have decided that to write anything worth anyone reading I must have lived a few more years and acquired a little experience of life, as they say.

I enclose this very private poem for your interest and perusal. You can read it to anyone of your family that you consider suitable. I made it up the day before I wrote this letter first, and two of the juiciest lines were composed, of all places, outside the Manse on my way back from taking the mail to the post! Olly and Mummy of course, adore it, and even Danny rather reveled in it!

I am typing this end part of the letter out in the garden. It is very hot when the sun is shining, but every time a cloud comes along it goes suddenly freezing, and the shock makes me type a mistake generally — that's a nice excuse for the shocking typing, but I think the real reason is that I havn't done any for such a long time that I've forgotten how to use the wretched machine. . . .

And now, my dear, I must cease. I hope you will have a nice term, and that you will write again soon and let me hear of your doings and progress etc., etc. I also hope that you have had a smashing holiday as I have, and that we shall meet again soon.

Tons of love, old spud.

Your ever faithful,

Jane

The Birches.

26th June, 1954

My foul & revolting specimen of an old friend,

How I loathe you Madam! You owe me a letter — I hope you have no objection to be reminded of that highly disagreeable fact. Anyway, if I was anyone but Trevor's little lamb, & if I wasn't feeling heartbroken at his departure, I should most decidedly treat you to an infuriated piece of my mind, and a very severe blowing up! None the less, considering that I <u>AM</u> T's little lamb, & all that he would desire me to be, I will forgive you from the heart of my spleen, & turn the other cheek — i.e. write another letter in readiness of not being answered.

How goes the old career, best beloved? All the little children getting on well with their A.B.C.'s eh?

I don't know whether you have heard any recent news from your "little one" but I will assume for the moment that you are in ignorance of your Red Admiral's flutterings, & proceed to elucidate you forthwith.

For one thing I am working for Olly up at the Clinic — I dare say you do know that. I proffer my services for a mere kick-in-the-pants — 2/6 per hour; but even that is better than nothing, & is given for a good cause. Poor little Olly lost her assistant physio & was left single handed. She was so over-worked & over-worried, that she very nearly had a nervous breakdown — she actually gave herself shingles! The clinic was shut for about 4 days while she recovered.

Anyway, I nobly stepped into the breach & am doing all her clerical work — which incidentally is a heck of a lot, & rather boring. But the dullness of the actual work finds recompense in my interest at being up at the clinic & seeing all the cases. Actually one gets a peculiar complex from being amongst crippled children all the time. It makes one realize how damnably lucky one is to have one's body the same as any other ordinary person's. Some of the cases are so pathetic that my heart aches for them, & yet one and all are happy and bright, & they never complain. I have come to the conclusion that it must be a special gift from God to compensate for the loss of activity, or horrible deformity. One poor little girl is paralysed from the waist down & will never be able to walk. She had polio at 8 yrs old, & as she was such an athletic little thing it got her very badly. But I have never yet seen her with a disagreeable face or a cross voice. It certainly teaches one a lesson!

But I think the worst, the very worst thing of all is this dreadful creeping paralysis. It strikes a child at the age of about 7. Until then they are quite normal — they wake suddenly one day & cannot use an arm or leg. There is absolutely <u>no</u> cure, and it just gets worse & worse until they cannot move at all. Luckily they generally die at about 14 of some other complaint as they have no resistance at all — but just think of it!

One boy came up to the Surgeon's clinic on Wednesday with this dreadful complaint. He was 16, and <u>enormously</u> fat. He could just move his hands & head — nothing else. He was incontinent, & how his poor wretched mother managed to look after him I hate to think. Oh dear, life does seem unfair when looked at from some angles!

There is one man who goes once a week (Olly treats 4 adults, who have been to Alton) and he is quite smashing. His determination to get about has enabled him to walk (with calipres & a stick) although the actual power in his muscles is almost nothing. But for sheer determination he would still be lying in bed, or hobbling about on crutches. He is so nice, & terribly handsom. At the moment he is as pleased as punch as his wife has just had their second baby, & he adores children.

I told you about Pelletier ringing me up on my birthday? Well, now he has the nerve to write & ask me to exchange with him. He wants to come here this autumn, & then I am to go over to his house next spring! I ask you! But he sounds very determined to <u>come</u> to England somehow, & my heart is trembling. I shall positively <u>DIE</u> if I ever see him again!

Have you been to "Beneath the 12-mile Reef"? I went last night, & in spite of catching a flea from someone, & a mosquito biting my legs non stop, I enjoyed it so much that I stayed round twice. The first time I was so perturbed as to what was going to happen, that I could not enjoy the marvelous under-water photography. Gosh, how dangerous, exciting, & beautiful it must be to go down under the water. How I should love & dread it at the same time. As they said "You don't know how scared you can be till you go down for the first time into deep water".

I am becoming very musical my dear. By which I don't mean that I am becoming adept at any instrument (though I should absolutely adore to play the harp) but I have taken to going to concerts, & love them very much. Now that my darling is miles away over the ocean waves, music must be my consolation.* In case it interests you, he left last Wednesday from Southhampton, and the passage takes about a week, so he will still be tossing as you read these words. I do hope the sea is not too rough, as Alice anyway, is a bad sailor.

I really wrote to say that if you had any spare time one weekend, it would be super if you could pop down & see me. Of course, money is the greatest problem I know, but it would be lovely if you could manage a visit.

I had a simply lovely time at Oxford, as the people I stayed with are nice & horsey. Next door to them is a farm, & the man breeds horses & has lots of smashing hunters & a few point-to-pointers. His daughter, though only 15, was very nice, & we went for some heavenly rides. I didn't manage to get a job at the time, but I got a letter from the University Registrar yesterday offering me one in her

---

* Trevor Davies and his wife had gone to the United States, probably on a ministerial exchange.

office. It starts in August, & I am taking it as then I shall be on the spot to seize anything decent which is going. Anyway, it will be experience, & I don't feel capable really of applying for a really good job without a little experience — especially as it is such a long time since I left College.

Well peach blossom, I think I've wasted quite enough ink, time, energy, brains & paper in penning this illiterate scrawl. I hope it doesn't seriously impare your respite for weeks to come. But please drop me a line sometime.

Much love,
Jane

Tuesday. 6.35 p.m.
[Probably July 27, 1954]

My darling Family!

How charming & adorable you all are! Thanks simply masses for the Diary, beans, & your letter Mummy. The diary is super, being the larger size, and jolly well worth the extra money which I will give you, Danny, when I come back. I assure you that Butler & Ramsden* won't be jealous of the bean smell — they do themselves proud! By the way, I hope Jif is also charming & adorable — i.e., that she has de-flead Rusty by now!!! Because if he is not done by Friday — Just wait for it, oh sister mine!!!

I have just been composing a very lengthy letter to Sally as today has been slack in the extreme. Sheila, Pamela & I had such fun this afternoon. Sheila was showing us the way up to the roof of the Clarendon Buildings — & gosh, it's simply gorgeous up there, & one feels on top of the world. Then we started to explore the roof — the 'atticy' part, not outside. It was all dark & cob-webby, and there were great long spaces with crumbling boards beneath. Sheila & I were very venturesome, & got all mixed up in a place where some queer soft stuff lay on the ground between two planks. We couldn't think what it was, & took a handful out to the light with us — but

---

* Stuart Ramsden and John Butler also rented rooms in the boarding house.

were no wiser. It was white & looked rather like flour that has become clogged up with weevils — or whatever those bugs are that used to be in Danny's store of war-time flour & appeared baked in her bread on numerous occasions! It felt like dust.

I'm not sure that I shall be able to start on Monday morning — though I hope so. Can't tell till M.S. gets back from her holiday.

Can't stop to write any more now or I shall miss the post — not that you will get it tomorrow anyway, though I don't know why the post here is so bad.

Anyway tons of love, & thanks tons for the parcel. I love getting parcels & letters you know.

> See you soon —
> Jane

> UNIVERSITY REGISTRY
> OXFORD
> 18 August, 1954

Dearest All,

Today is just about the slackest one I have met so far, and already, at 11:30 I have run out of all work. Miss Shearer has been sending me over to the Indian Institute to find out where various people were for future reference — that's how little there is to do. Do look out for a little Johna (Jonah?) to put in her whale Mummy. He can be bigger than I thought — in fact I think my little professor would do, but I don't want to part with him. Will you send him to me if you find him — I'm sure he would feel very much at home in these academic surroundings.

Thanks for your letter Mummy, and will you thank Olly for her super P.C. when she comes back. I'm glad they are having a nice time, but do tell me what she said when she discovered she had to sleep miles away through a wilderness of gorse and bracken. Also I want to know the result of Jif's Scholl Cert. — if you can make out the meaning of 'Scholl'.

When I next come home I have got an <u>Adventure</u> to relate. Now I have tantalised you havn't I? But it is much too long to write decently in a letter that wasn't a miniature novelette, and even though we are slack, I still havn't got time for a work of that sort. At any moment I feel sure I shall receive a great pile of letters to be re-done from the Reg. And Miss Shearer too no doubt because I did all hers on his note paper by a mistake. Not that she will mind really, but she's not in a very wonderful mood this morning.

Last night when it was time to go, it was absolutely pouring with rain — a real deluge. A lot of people, me included, had brightly set out in the morning — a lovely sunny one — in cotton dresses and cardigans. Anyway, Miss Shearer said she would lend me the old mac which she uses to clean the car in. Of course, by the time I had found the car, struggled vainly with a most awkward lock, and retrieved the mac, I was drenched to the skin. It was frightfully funny. But some people had to bike back with no mac at all, so I was better off than they. The really silly part about it was that by the time I had got the mac, returned the key, and tidyed up all my belongings, the rain had practically ceased.

One of the girls here who was on holiday when I started came back on Monday, and I think she is one of the nicest here. I had lunch with her yesterday, and we went round Christ church afterwards. N.B. I am now having lunch once more — an early lunch which means I leave at 12.30 & have to be back by 2.0 in case the Reg. wants to dictate after he gets back. I had to stop typing because, as I said, the Reg rang for me. He gave me a beaming smile when I went in, & actually said "You're getting on rather well you know. I like the stuff you are serving me with". So there. What a clever daughter, grandaughter, niece, niece & sister you have respectively.

There is pandemonium at 225 at the moment. Anne is leaving today — going off for a fortnight's holiday in Italy before leaving for New Zealand, lucky child. All her baggage is strewn around, & she has been bequeathing all the things she can't take to Rosie (Coates White) & me. She has also given me her wireless to house & use for the fortnight. Then, Miss Kersey is busy doing up the kitchen, so all the pots & pans are in long rows up either side of the stove, & the kitten keeps playfully rolling things down so that they are lost amongst Anne's trunks. It's rather a hoot.

I suppose Byron will have gone now — though I shouldn't be at all surprised if not. Give him my love in the later case. Also give love to Colonel, & I'm very sorry I didn't see him. Please thank Madam from me for being so decent if you hear her again (on the phone) & say I am writing to the Loms (doesn't that sound funny) to thank them for having me that evening.

Do take good care of my poor darling little Black Fellow,* won't you? And Judy is to go on taking him out when she gets back. Swartz should have given her great zeal by then. Give my very best love to Deb — & the others, & say I am dying for her to come up to Oxford to see her old school. But it would really have to be a Sunday, & anyway PTO. Since they are off to Scotland she will probably have forgotten when she gets back. None the less! And also (for your ears alone Meine Mutter) what about the B? How is wee Hughie! I shall send Olly the name of that specialist she is to ask Wilson about if you have really lost my long & beautiful letter — which is disgusting in the extreme. I must now go & buy some sugar.

Danny, my frying pan works very well, but the bacon I got is so smashingly lean it makes less fat — so I have to use Magic!!

Tons of love
Your distant <u>Jane</u>

[Probably November 1954]

Darling Mummy,

Didn't we have a smashing weekend? Thanks tons for doing my hair. It's jolly nice now, and I hope it will be so on Saturday.

I have got my lift! From Mr. Butler, (only it's John now!) I went to help him drain his car of water the other night because we thought it was going to freeze. It was Monday night — did you have a foggy journey Mummy? Because here it was the thickest fog I've ever been in, from 6.00 onwards. I had a gorgeous time in it — I just couldn't face the thought of German, so I went into the Library and looked up Unicorns — I can't get the material I want from any of the books

---

* Her dog, Rusty.

in the Ref. Library, so I don't know what I'll do. Anyway, after doing that the fog had not got into my blood and I feebly got a bus.
That however set me jumping with fog-fever, as it crept along at
about 2 m.p.h. and kept mounting the curb with alarming lurches.
The cars in front were making equally heavy weather of it. When I
got back I seized a hunk of bread and a biscuit and had a chat with
Miss Kersey who said that she adored wandering about in the fog
too. Then I sallied forth, and in a few moments was caught up by
Ramsden (only I have to call him Stuart now to make it fair). He
was walking into Oxford to do some work at the lab. So I went part
of the way with him, and then did some smashing wandering on my
own. It was really chronic for the poor wretched motorists, and a
wall and a pillar box were knocked flat — only I didn't see them unfortunately. At last I meandered home, having made myself useful
to the extent of guiding three cars to a turning on the other side of
the road, and helped a man whose car battery had given out to point
out the curb to people. Just there the road was very very wide you
see, and so having left the curb, their only guide, by the time they
had crossed over to the opposite curb they couldn't see it at all. And
when one stood on one side, though shouts and calls came looming
through the fog from the other side, one just could not see a thing.

Anyway, I got back, & John was in a perfect state as he had no
anti-freeze in the car and he felt he ought to go & drain it. I said I'd
help him — I thought the car was in the drive but to my horror I
found it was in a garage miles away. Actually I did not mind much
as the fog was still smashing. We walked about 1/2 a mile — there
and back — all the way up to the roundabout, (only you won't
know how far that is). And when we got there we found there was a
fire in the kitchen the other side of the wall, & the temp. was <u>very</u>
warm in the garage. So he didn't drain it after all.

However, I then went up & had coffee with them, & he offered to
take me on Saturday. So it was well worth my foggy tramp! I rang
Mrs. Lom who said she could have got me a lift so it would have
been OK anyhow — but it's nice to be independent.

Will you send a little bag, or I suppose I <u>could</u> take your black
one? And don't you think I need something on my wrist — or I shall
feel awful naked.

Miss Shearer says I <u>can</u> have a hamster. Won't it be fun. The shoes are fine now, & I like them as much as ever.

Mr. Davies is going. Miss Kersey wrote him a noble little note, & he, in a very childish way, left it lying there all day & wrote her a note saying he thought he would look for somewhere else as it was 'too regimentated' here — he must have guessed what would be in her note. Last night he left all his things lying round in the kitchen. We had not room at all, and Butler got cross & banged the whole lot in <u>Adcroft's</u>* cupboard. I heard bangs and crashes, & went to investigate. I met a spoon flying downstairs — she threw them <u>all</u> out of the kitchen door — in this case I don't blame her!!!

[Probably February 1955]

Darling Mummy and Danny,

I've decided only to write to you two because you're the only ones who ever write to me, so I will miss the others out — oh, Olly does occasionally of course, but only once in a blue moon! Anyway, that's neither here nor there. Thanks tons for your lovely long letter Dan.

Now the thing I want to write about is this vile job. Do you not think it is time I got something else? I have given the matter serious consideration, and have decided I should honestly like another medical job, and wondered if dear Mr. Wilson could pull any strings to get me into the Wingfield Morris, or even Uncle Eric. . . . I have been miserable these last few weeks because of the boredom of this foul job, but now the thought of future jobs perks me up no end. And if I stay here until July, say, and then had a nice holiday at home, wouldn't it be fun?

The next thing I want to talk about is the party at 225. The numbers are increasing alarmingly — thank heavens one is only 21 once, or one would live in a permanent state of bankruptcy. Anyway, can you suggest where I should turn for a cake? I shall probably find somewhere to do one in Oxford, but perhaps you have some advice on the subject. Everyone is adament that I must have

---

* Another boarder at 225 Woodstock Road.

one, with 21 candles. 14 or 15 if Sue comes, will be the number — crikey. Also I am told that I shall have to make a speech as I shall be formally toasted at dinner — now, dear Mummy, come to my rescue and tell me what I should say? Please. I rely on you entirely. Also, I am to be an elegant hostess while the others do all the work — once the guests arrive that is — and they all insist on my getting my red dress for the occasion. What do you think of that plan? It would be rather nice, and a wonderful excuse to get out of all the dashing up and down to the kitchen — which is fun actually, but still.

It is going to be on 26 January — sorry, March, and I really think it should be rather fun, don't you. Have you any bright suggestions as to what we should do at it? Apart from Stuart's repertoire on the piano, and an act which Sandy is to be persuaded to put on, together with an odd game or two such as charades, we cannot think of anything. And Eileen and Stuart have been tucked away with the most lousy colds so that we have not had a really communal conversation and discussion as yet. And that brings me to the fact that such things are happening at 225. It is mainly between Eileen and Stu, and it is all such a muddle that I can't explain it all in a letter, but they want to stop seeing each other for a long time, and Eileen's in a flat spin because her John doesn't come back from Canada until May, and she's getting fonder and fonder of Stuart, and doesn't know what to do. Oh dear oh dear. We were discussing it for hours last night. The sooner they <u>both</u> get out the better it will be. I only hope that in all the confusion of hearts I get a party at all. The only immune heart, so far as I can see, is mine!

Now, I shall really have to stop — for the moment anyway, and get on with a little work. It is M.S's half day, and the Reg is in London, so I am having a peaceful time, but unfortunately I have one or two odds and ends to tidy up to-day. However, I dare say I shall be able to continue this letter at a later time, so farewell till then.

It is now later, and this is no time to write any more as it is 5.55, and, therefore, time to go — and I hate staying here a moment longer than I need. I am expecting a letter from you tomorrow about various matters, so I daresay this will cross with yours. I hope so —

I mean, I hope a letter comes. Have you got my toothbrushes? I can't afford <u>another</u> one. Honestly. D'you know, I havn't done any work all afternoon, and everyone has come in here to chat. The Vienna Boys' choir last night was marvellous, though they did not seem quite as perfect as the ones I heard in Germany.

Tons of love,
Jane

[Early May 1955]
Darling anyone who thinks herself entitled to a letter!

Thank you for your letters Mummy and Danny — or have I written since then? I really don't know. The hamster box should be on its way by now, but if they take as long in delivering it as they did my trunk, I don't suppose you'll get it until about Friday or Saturday. Anyway, I hope she survives until then.*

I had a simply gorgeous time on May morning. We got up at 3.45 and took a smashing breakfast with us. We got to the punt at 4.30, where we met Eileen's friend, Moira, who, poor thing, had had to rise at 3.00 to get there. It took us the hour and a half to get down to Magdalen Bridge — as we got the punt from Tim's at Bardwell Road. It wasn't at all cold, and John and Stu. punted very well. We got a very good place — oddly enough very near the people I met at the Beagle Ball. They looked funny in the cold and sober light of 5.45. We could see the top of the tower, but not the choir boys. It really was beautiful sitting there in the punt and listening to the pagan hymn floating out across the water. All the babble that had been going on stopped suddenly as the clock chimed the hour — all except one stupid fool who chose that moment to leap into the water and swim — in bathing trunks. It was really mean of him — he could easily have waited until the singing was over, but some people must draw all the attention to themselves if they can. As a matter of fact, he didn't, and everyone completely ignored him, so soon he stopped his splashing. We were fairly near the front of the queue for getting

---

* Hamlette was being delivered back home to the Birches.

out, and so dashed away upstream to find a good place for break-fast. We didn't go very far as we were mighty peckish by this time, and stopped at the edge of an enormous meadow round which the river curved on three sides. It was a popular place — but then so was most of the bank as there were a large number of people all looking for breakfast sites. We tied the punt to a tree, and having got the primus going, I supervised the cooking of the breakfast with Moira, and the others built a fire.

The primus really worked supremely, which was just as well as I had to cook: — sausages, bacon, tomatoes and fried bread. At one time John was to have brought three cousins with him, but at the last moment they decided not to come, and so we had all their rations as well. It was scrummy — and cooked to a T. It was most plutocratic having a fire as well, and kept us nice and warm. John and Stu. made toast over the fire — which for camp toast was really very good, though it took rather a long time.

The undergrads. next to us were really quite clueless. They took hours getting their fire going, and then it was so feeble that the sausages they were cooking on sticks were all half raw. And I thought their kettle would never boil, so offered them our primus. But though it started off all right, it soon conked out, and they brought it back. The kettle was still only warm. So I examined the primus, and found it had run out of petrol. So we filled it up for them, and once more they borrowed it — with success. It was a whistling kettle, and when the whistle went off, what cheers there were. They made the tea by pouring the leaves down the spout! At which we went into fits of mirth. Someone fell in just by us. It was very funny, but we didn't laugh for long as we thought how cold it must be. Several other canoes went by containing people with sodden trousers. Near us a large party of people had a gramophone and were doing country dancing, and the other side of the meadow a large crowd first sang, and then a long and energetic game of rounders. It was great fun sitting and watching everything, and thinking that nowhere else in the world could one see anything quite like it. Good old Oxford. I hate the idea of going now, and yet I daresay it is all for the good. Still, I wish I could have seen the summer out.

After we had been sitting there for about 1 1/2 hours we decided to make a move — Eileen was dying to show off her punting. So we set off. She managed very well until we got to a tricky bend, when she first lost the pole behind a sticking out branch of a tree, and then, put off her stride, went round and round in circles, bumping into everything that came along. We nearly died of laughing.

Then they persuaded me to try. We sort of drifted idly from midstream to the bank, and from the bank to mid-stream, and then the pole got caught in a tree. Like a clot, I leant out to try and free it, and the punt rapidly departed outwards. If I hadn't jumped I should have gone flat onto my face. So I jumped!!

Oh it was funny. Really funny. They just sat in the punt and roared and roared with laughter. And I stood in the water — up to my chest — and roared and roared with laughter. And we were so weak with laughing that I had no strength to crawl out of the water, and they had no strength to paddle back and fetch me. Gosh it was funny. And the odd part about it was that it wasn't cold. Not at all cold. Queer. At last they managed to stop laughing for long enough to fish me out, and we set off again. And still it wasn't cold. Curiouser and curiouser.

But that was by no means the end of the comedies of the morning. Really it would have made a dashed good film. I insisted on being allowed to punt again, and was doing fine until we got to a tricky bend. Here the river received a little tributary, in the middle of the entrance to which sailed a large male swan — his wife was on the nest on the bank. Well, you know how dangerous swans can be. I swear it was entirely the fault of the punt, but anyway it began to head for the swan. Straight at the wretched bird. Stu. who was sitting out on the front bit bravely grasped his paddle more firmly and said he'd try and keep it off. All very well, but I knew better. It began to hiss, the punt pole was being unwieldy, and John was foolishly saying that it wasn't at all dangerous. He really thought it, but the rest of us knew better — at least, Stu and I did. Luckily I managed to control the pole hastily, and rapidly backed us away with all possible speed. Danger averted. Then, as the corner was very tricky, and my steering was negligible, the boys said they'd paddle us round — John's paddle being the frying pan. Well, they paddled straight for a low overhanging branch. I was by then in Stu's place in the front, and there was absolutely no room for me to go under — so I did what seemed to me the sensible thing to do — I jumped onto the branch, and the punt actually slid underneath. The others were all sitting actually inside, so it was fine for them. How we laughed again. And some other people in punts nearly split themselves as well.

Then the final joke occurred after they had come back to fetch me off the tree. I was once again punting. It was a straight bit of river, and I was doing fine — really getting the hang of the thing. Stu and John had their backs to me, Eileen was facing me. Suddenly the pole stuck in the mud, and Eileen looked up to see me tugging frantically and nearly overboard. "Drop it! drop it!" says she in a stern voice. John, who was idly paddling with the frying pan dropped it — just like that, and it sank straight to the bottom. I shouted grimly 'I'm not going to' and hung on until the wretched thing came out. That was almost the funniest of all. After that Eileen had another go, and then Moira was going to try but it began to pour with rain so Stu thought we'd better get back quickly and took over himself.

By the time we got back to the car I must admit that I was beginning to be a trifle chilly, but we soon got back. I showed myself to Miss Kersey who was rather worried about me as my cold had only just gone. She took away my skirt and has since ironed and washed it — the other way round of course — as it was all over green stains from the tree. Also the hem was down, and she has hemmed it all for me. She did it last night when I sat and talked to her. Isn't she decent. She also brought me a cup of hot coffee to the bathroom. Eileen had run a bath while I took my sodden garments off, and I sat in front of her fire till it was ready. Spoilt girl, arn't it?

After my bath we all had coffee, and then John's cousins came round, and Stu and Eileen began the lunch — roast beef and Yorkshire Pudding — but nothing like your Yorkshire pud. Danny. I have vaguely asked Stu and Eileen to come for a weekend in the summer — either during my holiday, or perhaps afterwards — they could drive up to London, collect me, and we could all arrive together perhaps. But if that comes off, we simply must have Yorkshire pudding!

I have got to meet wretched old Bob this evening, but seeing I am going to get a lot of going on the river out of him, I don't mind.

Since finishing the last paragraph I have had a terrific row with Miss Shearer over writing letters* — which is quite ridiculous as I have nothing — absolutely nothing — else to do. So I told her this, and we have hardly spoken since. Now there has been a muddle over M.A. taking the Reg. and V.C. to the Radcliffe in her car for a meeting. The Reg thought she had not turned up and actually she had been waiting all the time. So, as you can imagine, MS is now in an even worse mood. Hey-ho. I rather enjoy these rows now that I am definitely leaving.

It is raining at the moment, and cold into the bargain. I had really better stop now I think. I nearly rang you up on Sunday night, but thought it would be rather a waste of money. Give my love to the Colonel. How is Piggy?†

> Masses of love,
> Janey

> 6, 7, 8 Old Bond Street.
> W.1.
> [Postmarked August 7, 1955]

Best beloved family — Hail!

How is my darling black man? and has Hamlette been cleaned — is she being fed? Did Kenneth bring some decent corn for her?

I am really having rather a nice time you know. Dinner & theater with Pop on Thursday — <u>marvellous</u> play. Daddy has seen it twice now & it's most original. Only 4 of the cast speak English. The rest are Japanese. It is terribly amusing & there's a lot in it as well.

On Friday, as I told you, Daddy & I had dinner with a Solex‡ chap & his girl friend. We also took a very, very nice . . . Australian man with us. We saw Eric & Judy during the evening — they really <u>are</u> an extremely nice couple.§

---

* That is, writing personal letters during working hours.
† Rusty.
‡ Solex, a manufacturer of carburetors, was Mortimer's employer then.
§ Eric and Judy were friends of Mortimer's.

Yesterday morning Daddy took me to his Bank Manager and I now have my first cheque book! It is a very nice feeling. He also says that he may pay in a small amount monthly — which wouldn't half help to make ends meet. I hope he does.

I met David at 2.0. He had arranged nothing definite so we wandered round & decided to see 'The Private Life of Major Benson'. It was a most enjoyable film with a gorgeous little boy in it. Gosh he was sweet. Then we had something to eat & went to see Terence Rattigan's play 'Separate Tables' at St. James's. It was excellent. I'm afraid poor David's as smitten as the rest. I've had an invitation from Dora's Brian as well. And Mummy, I've fixed up with Mrs. Hindley* for Tuesday & Wed. next week — or rather, this week.

Tons of love all,
Jane

P.S. Our iron has bust so I'm just off to Pop's flat, + dresses, to use his. Doesn't that seem funny!

Poor David spent all last weekend looking through files of Sheres & Tatlers hoping to find a photo of me when I was presented!!†

Daddy is by now firmly convinced that Judy could do nothing better than learn the Clar-o?-i?-net. Most impressed with the Distinction — I do my best.

P.P.S. Please give my love to Byron & say I'm hoping to see him next week-end. Can you please book a trim with Jean for the Saturday. My hair's nearly to my waist!!

[Postmarked September 16, 1955]

Darling family,

It is a long time since I have owed every single one of you a letter at the same time — in fact I'm pretty sure it is the first time on record. Thank you ALL very much for your letters, etc. (The etc. being a very nice postcard from Audrey — thanks tons old cockolorum — a bundle of postcards from Horst from Olly, and the book

---

* The mother of Jane's godmother.

† Jane was presented as a debutante to Queen Elizabeth at Buckingham Palace; her uncle by marriage, Michael Spens (son of Sir Patrick Spens, lord chief justice of India), arranged the debut.

from Jif. Raymond thought it was wonderful and he chuckled all the way home in the train last night. Also thank you for getting me that bread knife which works wonderfully and I am now able to eat respectable looking sandwiches for my lunch. And the 5/- which you left and which you shouldn't have done because you couldn't possibly have eaten that amount of money value in 2 days even if you'd eaten anything at all which I doubt.)

I'm very sorry that I havn't written before to let you all know that I'm still in the land of the living, but what with one thing and another life has been pretty hectic. I hope that all the invalids have recovered, or are recovering. And talking of such things, I am just developing a lovely cold.

I went to the proms on Tuesday and Wednesday — and was going to go on Monday as well but I had to work late showing some people nice films of cows! Really, I have seen so many films of shorthorns lately that I almost began to dream about them.* On Tuesday it was the planets, Delius' piano concerto, Dvorak's 4th and the Wasps (to put everything in the wrong order). The pianist was Moiseivitsch (I expect that I spelt that wrong!). Well, I didn't realize what a popular concert it was going to be, and arrived at the usual time only to find that the gallery entrance had a notice up saying "Full House" and the arena door had a long queue outside. Just as I had joined the end of this queue a little man came out and said he was sorry, but all the seats were sold. A few people still hung around, me among them. A girl went up to him and I could hear her saying she'd come for miles and couldn't he possibly squeeze one more in, but he only shook his head and told her to try the box office. So a few more people drifted off. I don't know what made me stay, but just after she'd gone this little man opened the door a crack and beckoned to me. He then whispered that if I could slip him 2/6 without anyone in the queue seeing he would get me in somehow, although it was strictly illegal.

As luck would have it I had only a 10/- note on me, but even this did not put him off as might have been expected. He couldn't change it as the top door man was hovering around and my chap

---

* As part of her job at Schofield Productions.

would have got the sack. But he gave me a ticket and told me to go and change the note, and when I returned I was to say I'd had to go and make a telephone call. So off I went and changed the note with a programme seller (after having tried a taxi driver in vain, though he must surely have had some change really) and marched back. There were about 4 officials who clustered round me as I opened the door, and they all told me it was strictly illegal and they shouldn't allow me in at all. It was rather difficult to smuggle the money to my little man without any of the others seeing. Gosh, the concert was worth it though. I don't think there has been one prom which I enjoyed better. I got a very good place, and was able to see Moiseivitsch beautifully. I stood up for all the things except the Dvorak, and within a radius of 5 yards around me no less than <u>three</u> people fainted. So how many there must have been in the whole hall I hate to think. None of them were taken out. Their friends were so enthralled with the music that they just shoved them on the floor, bunged their heads between their knees for a bit, and then left them to recover as best they could. The Brahms 2 which I heard on Wednesday was simply superb — maybe you heard it on the wireless. Mrs. Hindley did and she said it didn't come over very well. But in the Albert Hall it was really terrific — and I really and truly think that apart from my darling Mendhelsohn (that looks a bit odd!) violin concerto I enjoyed it more than any other symphony. It was most probably because I was in a specially receptive mood that evening. Although I thoroughly disliked the woman singing the Mozart aria earlier on. She was vile. The orchestra didn't like her at all either. The sub-leader who was incidentally rather handsom absolutely refused to clap when she had finished — and as half her notes were distinctly wuzzy I was quite in agreement with him.

The Japanese dancing last night was very great fun, and really beautiful. Somehow it was more static than I had expected, but so lovely that I could have watched it all night. The Spider dance was terrific, and the man looked really horrible. Dear Mr. Wilsden lent us some opera glasses so we were able to see very well. We went for some coffee in the first interval because we both had sore throats and it really was funny. We went along winding stone passages, in and out and round about, and by the time we got there the interval was nearly over. So after gulping down the coffee we simply dashed back. We tore for miles along passages that seemed even longer and more winding than they had before, and at last got to a door which we thought led to the gallery slips. We flung it open — only to find ourselves back in the buffet! There was the same woman finishing off her coffee, and the same man smoking his cigarette. It really was most terribly funny, and when we finally got back we laughed and laughed.

There really isn't very much news. I met Daddy for lunch yesterday — he came along to the Overseas Club with me to try and get some addresses — we got a lot, but they were mostly too expensive. Then we went to the Sports Car Club, and there I met Daddy's boss — a really charming man, who insisted that as he'd never met me before he be allowed to give us lunch. So we had an excellent meal — and I was about 2 hours late back!

I've just had a postcard from Brian H. He is having a lovely time in South France — lying around in the sun all day and getting fat he said.

And now really there is nothing more to say, and since I want you to get this letter before the week-end I must go and find an envelope and get John to post it. Also it is very nearly the end of my lunch hour — and I don't want to have a lot of extra time today after yesterday.

Thank you all again, and I'm longing for next week-end — I must collect some warm cloths when I come home. At the moment I am shivering in cotton dresses while everyone else prances round in thick winter wool. Most unfair, but there is nothing I can do about it. We havn't heard about Ray's scripts yet. He was simply thrilled with the Sammy stuff, and is firmly convinced that that is the best script. It is really a mixture of Sammy's and mine, because I wrote out all the dope for him, and he has used a lot of it practically word for word.

Incidentally, Mummy, I never found that 3d piece. I and an old porter searched around for ages, and in the end had to give it up. Perhaps someone picked it up while I was waving to you.

Now do give my love to all the other people I have not mentioned — is Uncle Eric still there? And Rusty, Hamlette, etc. Also to Trevor please if you see him. I keep dreaming about him which makes life very much pleasanter.

Tons and tons of love,
Jane

6, Courtfield Gardens,
London, S.W.5.
27th March, 1956.

My dear Sue,

This is very naughty of me as I have a great deal of work to do, but I was so upset when I had a letter from Eileen saying that you had rung Miss Kersey after all. I still don't quite understand how it all went wrong — except to start with I didn't get there on Friday evening after all and so was unable to prepare 225 for your call.* But when I rang them on Saturday they said no one had rung, and so I presumed that either you were away, or else had been unable to make it. I really do apologize for all the muddle — when I come to think of it perhaps it was rather a stupid arrangement, but it was all I could think of at the time. It was a great shame that I couldn't see you — I havn't for simply ages.

The next I'm going to Oxford is the last week-end in April, so you must write and let me know in good time whether I might be able to see you then. As you may have noticed, I have now changed my digs, and my present room is a hundred percent nicer than the old one. I don't know if you heard about the vile dark little place I was forced to live in for so many months, but when the spring weather started coming I decided I simply could not endure waking up and wondering whether it was the middle of the night any more. Luckily Olly happened to glance through her physiotherapy journal quite by chance one day — usually it gets thrust away and never opened.

---

* On a visit to Oxford, Jane intended to meet Susan Cary, who was to call and leave a message at Jane's old boarding house at 225 Woodstock Road.

And she saw that a physio was advertising a room for £2 2s. at the above address. I went along and saw her, and there I am. Of course, I can't really afford the extra 7s a week — but my goodness, it really is worth more than that when I wake up in the morning and see lovely sky. Added to that the room looks out over the garden in the middle of the square, and there are trees, and even an odd blackbird sometimes sings — not to mention sparrows and pigeons of course! It is only very small, and right up at the top of the house. It is a huge place, and so far, having been there only two weeks, I have hardly seen any of the inhabitants, but so far as I can gather they are mostly medical students or physios. Up on my landing there are four medical students! Mummy came up to London last week-end to inspect my new abode, and she roared with laughter — fancy landing up next to four young men — she thought it was quite typical. One of them has the most beautiful skull — it cost him £8 12s 6d. Apparently it would have been even more had it had its own teeth. But the poor fellow must have lost his, and had someone else's stuck in with glue. This particular chap is also madly keen on motor racing, so we have quite a bit to talk about.

I have just been watching a film called "The British Midwife". It is most interesting — it shows you everything about the birth of a baby — well, not quite everything because it doesn't start early enough!! Margaret, the girl who works here with me, can't bear watching it, but I quite like it because I think it might come in useful — you never know when you might be the only person to hand in an emergency, and to know what is supposed to happen, what is normal, would be very useful. Does midwifery come into your training at any time? I suppose it must do.

I had better tell you the sad news — unless you have heard it already from Jif. Poor old Rusty got run over two weeks ago. It was apparently instantaneous death. I was so upset when I got Mummy's letter, that I didn't think I would ever be able to go home again — well, you know how I loved him. It was a pretty grim weekend really. There would be long pauses when we all knew what we were all thinking, but nobody said a word about him. When a dog barked, or anything occurred which might remind me of Rusty

everyone tried to think of something, anything, to say. Really it
made it much worse. Danny burst into floods of tears when I set off
back to London, but luckily not before. It is so sad, but I suppose it
is just one of those things which has to happen sometime — it was
better I suppose than if he had got old and blind — but that was
such a long way off.

Dear Alvar Lidell* took me all round the B.B.C. the other day,
and it really was most interesting. He had been round here doing a
commentary for us, and afterwards, as it was about lunch time, he
just took me off to lunch. I felt very grand being whisked away by
him, leaving everyone else just standing — they all worship him
here you see, and Stanley's secretary was mad with jealousy when I
got back. He is such a very nice man. We had lunch at the canteen,
and then he took me on a conducted tour of all the studios. The
drama ones were most fascinating. They have all sorts of doors with
locks of different kinds, latches, chains, squeaking hinges — everything. And windows of different sorts, and stairs — leading to nowhere — which are concrete down one side and wood the other —
to produce the different effects you see. He showed me the room
where the commentator was sitting (I forget his name) when the
bomb exploded in the B.B.C. during the war. It is quite a famous
story. He was reading the 9 o'clock news, and suddenly he heard a
terrific bang followed by a tremendous scuffling and commotion.
Clouds and clouds of muck came pouring down the ventilation
holes and covered his script with a thick layer of black muck. But he
saw that the red light was still glowing — i.e. that he might, with
any luck, still be on the air, and so he calmly brushed the dirt off his
paper, and continued to read as though absolutely nothing had happened. Alvar said that all the other commentators were green with
envy — and quite sure that had they been in his place when a bomb
had exploded they would never have had the presence of mind to
just carry on so coolly. It was pretty good, wasn't it.

Honestly, I am getting as bad as Judy as far as music is concerned

---

* Lidell, well known as one of the great BBC "voices" during the war, was a friend of
the family. He helped Jane get the job with Schofield Productions.

— though not so mad — at the moment she is trying to make a flute out of a bamboo chair leg!! Rosemary is to take her flute round, and they are going to measure up the various distances between the different holes! But I seem to spend my life in the Festival Hall — well, as much of my life as I can afford. I really do love music now, and of course, London is the ideal place to be so far as that is concerned. I have been booking tickets for months ahead, and now have about 8 — I shall probably forget when they are for. But the thing is, if you book early enough, you get very good seats very chaply — that word is supposed to be 'cheaply' — whereas if you leave it until nearer the time you are faced with paying about three times the amount for a seat which may not even be so good — some people may like being right up in the front, but I don't. It gives me great pleasure to set off by myself to the Festival Hall. I am quite in love with the place I think.

The other thing which is great fun at the moment is my philosophy class. I go to lectures once a week, and perhaps the most interesting part is the people one meets there — people of all descriptions who have all gone along for various different reasons, and have all got caught up in the swing of the course. I must admit that it is not the type of philosophy I was expecting — there is no studying the great philosophies of Plato, Spinoza, Hegel, etc. If we study any recognized philosophy at all, it is the ancient wisdom of the east — she is always quoting passages from the Upanishads and Buddha. But in the main it is a philosophy distilled from all the ancient philosophy which might help the school to grasp what it is trying to teach — the New Testament is also often quoted. I'm not at all sure that I shall go with them very far along the path they are trying to lead us. It has tremendous possibilities, but you have to really march forward with no looking back, and I'm not so sure that it is a good thing. To go so far, with one's eyes wide open — yes. But after that, I think enough is as good as a feast. But we really do have fun after the lectures. About 10 of us or more go round to one of the little coffee houses, and get down to a good old discussion about all sorts of different things, and it is most entertaining. There is one very nice man — we nicknamed him Mr. Immaculate before getting to know him, because of the way in which he dresses. He assumes a very earnest manner, and wears a beard, but there is the most delicious twinkle in his eye. He asked me round to a little party at his house the other day, but unfortunately I couldn't go.

It is now a little later on in the afternoon — which, incidentally, seems to be never ending. I simply had to go and view some prints that came in as all sorts of people had been screaming out for them all day. As a matter of fact it is quite strange having so little to do. For the past three weeks we have been working so hard that we all nearly collapsed from exhaustion at the end. I had to come in for two solid week-ends, Saturday and Sunday, and we were here almost every day for that time until 9 or 10 o'clock at night. But I don't suppose this sounds particularly impressive to you. I know how hard nurses have to work. Most people, when I tell them the odd hours we have to work, say "Well never mind, just think of all the extra overtime you are getting". To which statement the answer is easy — we don't get a penny. Then they say we are silly to do the work for nothing, but in a job like this one can't just lay down tools — there is a certain pride in the work, and we don't like to see a film go out that isn't as good as we can get it in the time.

I have decided to get another little water turtle like Jacob and install the vivarium in my new room. Later on, when I have got to know the landlady a bit better — and the woman who cleans — I may try to keep a hamster, but I couldn't have one in the room because they do make such an infernal noise with their chewing at night. Did you hear that poor little Ham died as well? And I'm sure that Pickles won't last much longer. Actually, my great desire is to have a budge,* but unless Stanley is amenable to my keeping it here during the day — or during most days — it will be out of the question — because I should never see the poor little thing otherwise.

One other thing I must tell you before I close. Uncle Eric has got a Bentley! Did you know that it was his overwhelming desire to possess one of these cars? The thought has haunted him for years, but I don't think any of us ever thought he would satisfy it. But a Harley Street specialist upon whose wife he operated had to give his up,

---

* A budgerigar.

and as he wanted it to go to a good owner, and was not particularly bothered about the price received, he let Uncle Eric have it for £400I. That, incidentally is supposed to be four hundred, and not four thousand and one! It is a 3 1/2 litre 1937 model in simply superb condition. It has really been looked after marvellously, and shines and glistens like new. Every time Eric approaches it a terrific beam spreads all over his face — he has only been the proud possessor for about 3 weeks. Apparently he rang up Daddy and asked him to drive it out to the hospital as he wasn't insured — and a very puzzled Daddy rang me to know if I knew a thing about it — he just turned up at the Birches in it the weekend before last, and kept it as a surprise. I have not yet been in it, but he collected Mummy and took her home on Sunday, the start of his holiday.

I really must stop now, because although I have attended to all the pressing work, there are one or two matters that I must clear up while I have the chance. It is very peaceful up here. Margaret is having two days of her holiday, and poor old Ted has gone to the dentist. So I am in sole charge of the upper cutting room.

Do write if you ever have a moment and let me know how you are getting on — and whether there might be anything doing at the last weekend in April.

With lots of love,
Jane

[Probably May 1956]

Darling Mummy,

I have <u>had</u> to give in my notice under force of circumstances. I have also had a letter from Clo & it really is O.K. to go out there next year — though not <u>quite</u> so early as I had hoped. However, things are nicely arranged in my mind & I <u>had</u> to leave here. Stanley has behaved very badly over the whole thing — by which I don't mean he is on bad terms with me at all — but I will explain all at the week-end. Is it really O.K. for B. to bring me down? I shall give you the £1 I should otherwise have spent on the coach — otherwise I shall not come. Don't do anything extra for B. I have decided, even more firmly than when I spoke to you on the phone, that he is no husband for me. He knows how I feel too, so he is just coming down as a kind of repayment of hospitality which I feel is due. Heaven alone knows what we shall do. I hope the Healey will be mended by then & perhaps I can have a driving lesson. I could take him onto the Swanage downs — make him climb!! Any suggestions welcomed.

If you want to know any reasons for my never marrying him I can let you have a string — e.g's television, too settled, too fond of creature comforts, doesn't like books etc., doesn't stand up straight, too fat, not handsom — I could go on for ever, but it boils down to the fact that I just don't love him one bit, so that's that — AND he knows it.

Will it be O.K. if Margaret* & I come on the 15th — or 16th June or something? We are as excited as kids over the idea of sleeping in the hut — but don't <u>DARE</u> to tidy it till we come — that is half the fun. I'm so looking forward to living at home again, especially in the summer. Can you get jobs for us or not? Because soon they will all be booked up. I don't mind how hard I work. But if you <u>can't</u> you see, we <u>MUST</u> get something arranged. They are advertising for living in waitresses all over the place at the moment, but soon we shall have no chance at all. I am very sorry to thrust this on you — I can pop along for interviews this week-end if you hear of anywhere — I will give you a commission!! Must do some work. All news later.

Tons of love,
Jane

10, Durley Chine Road,
Bournemouth.
[August or September, 1956]

My dear Sally,

Thanks for the post card, & I'm glad you had such a lovely time on your holiday. I am working myself absolutely to the bone. It really is dreadful during the peak of the season. We only get one day off a fortnight, two afternoon teas & one late night per week. I hon-

---

* Margaret Arthur worked as a receptionist at Schofield Productions.

estly can't remember whether I last wrote to you before or after I got my job at the Hawthorns — I feel it was after. However, I am still there, with a huge station of my own now, and apart from the ghastly rush of some meals — more especially lunch when we are all up the wall — it is quite entertaining. I have met some really delightful people — one television producer who is a darling — unfortunately engaged. His engagement to this girl — who joined him during his second week — is a really romantic and wonderful story which I must tell you when you come & see us — I presume you <u>are</u> coming in the fairly near future? There was also a very nice man from Halifax who unfortunately fell for me & insisted on coming down for another week. I had a nice time with him but it is a bit exhausting being proposed to every few minutes. At the moment I have two delightful families — one husband writes children's books, the other one act plays. No 1 has a son of 17 or so who will be incredibly handsom when about 25. No 2 has a daughter of about the same age — very pretty. No 1 has a girl of about 8: No 2 has a son of about 10. Both wives are charming — No 2's has long chats with me about Kenya. Last week I had a party of 7 to look after — 4 children. That really was exhausting & I had them for a fortnight. But they were very charming. Pop was a doctor. They gave me £3.

Brian came to stay with Dora a few week ends ago & it was rather awkward as we both knew it was all over between us. However, we had a dinner party & invited another chap I have met called Douglas, & it all passed off fairly well. B took me out to tea both days, & of all places he suggested Wimborne — I told you Hans was staying there for 2 weeks, didn't I? My heart was leaping around all over the place — I thought I should literally pass out or something equally daft if I should see him. Brian kept asking what was the matter. However, all was well.

Since writing the last word I have fallen sound asleep. I was lying in the garden in the first hot sun we've had for about a fortnight. Add this to the fact that I've been to bed at about 1.30 for the last week & you will realize the reason for my slumbering. I should still be asleep but Audrey arrived with a nice little tea on a tray.

Last week end dear Horst arrived for a night from Oxford — he leaves for Germany on Tuesday & will not be returning — anyway for 8 years. He left here very sadly. All the family seem to think he is quite devastating — even Danny thinks so when she isn't frantically asserting that he's a German. But he simply doesn't appeal to me in the slightest.

One very sad thing has happened. The gales blew down the silver birch — the one between this garden & the bottom. Uncle Eric actually saw it snap off. It went right across the lawn and was like a living tent of green. Poor tree. I almost cried over it. . . .

Do come soon — absolutely any time will do. I won't write any more just at present because I must write to Brian & return the cheque for £40 which arrived this morning towards my passage!!!

Lots of love to you and all your family,
<u>Jane</u>

10, Durley Chine Road,
Bournemouth.
[October or November 1956]

My dear Sally,

Thanks for the letter — do come here at half-term. I am now not sailing until after Christmas because the family were so woebegone at the idea of my going just before. I finished at the Hawthorns on Friday and am having a well-earned holiday — so far I havn't even <u>looked</u> for a new job. My goodness, I don't think I've ever had such a physically strenuous summer as this. It really was hard work round there from the start to the finish, and during August & September it was most sheer unadulterated slave labour. But I have now safely got my outward & return fare with a certain amount over & above — most of which latter I have almost decided to spend on a winter coat. I have it in the room on appro. at the moment.

I certainly seem to have chosen the best time of the year for my holiday. The last few days have been really delicious and I have been having a good 'go' at the garden. You never saw such a mess as it is at the moment — though it is a little better since I started on it.

In spite of the hard work I have managed to get a good deal of fun out of my strange job, and a very great amount of amusement.

The trouble is that I just can't remember when I last wrote to you. Did I mention Douglas? The boy I met at the Marine beach party? Well, whether I did or not, I have been seeing him quite often during the last two months and he is great fun — the first man of my own age I have ever liked and not got bored with. During my last week at the Hawthorns I had 8 people on a conference — at least the 4 men were — the wives were with them merely. They said one morning — "Would you like us to try and get 2 tickets for you for the reception & dance at the Pavillion tonight?" I thought it might be rather fun so I roped old Douglas in & got him into a dinner jacket so that I could wear evening dress which was optional. And it really was fun. We were late but the people had kept two places at their table and when the refreshments came round they said ha, now it was their turn to wait on me. They were very charming. . . .

Little Poosh came over to supper the other day. She has just got back from Malaya where she was staying with her brother & his wife — & my goodness it has improved her enormously. She has quite matured now, and is a normal person to speak to. She enjoyed herself tremendously & would love to go back — but she is now caught up in the old Longham regeme (however you spell it) all over again. She wants me to go out & ride her horses sometime & now that my slaving has stopped I hope to do just that.

Gosh, I am so tired just at the moment that I can hardly focus the paper. Well no, not tired — sleepy. I used to be tired after a day at the Hawthorns. After a day of sweeping, chopping and bonfires I am that other much nicer thing — sleepy. This is further induced by my sitting right in front of a glorious fire on the floor — oh dear, it's me on the floor, not the fire of course. I've got on a funny little thing that was sent from America — it's shorts (very short!) and blouse all in one, doing up down the front. Green. The rest of the family are in winter clothes and it is rather amusing.

Later. (Next day). This morning I dashed out with great zeal to creosote the hut. Pot of creosote in one hand & brush in the other I leapt, sylph-like, onto the table. But oh, most unsylphlike was my descent when the table overbalanced. And I was covered in the horrid black stuff. Dripping and slightly hysterical I went & dripped in the yard. Mummy & Danny with exclamations of horror dashed out, stripped me, & frantically rubbed me down with bits of cloth. Just then Audrey arrived and was at first horrified to find a completely naked niece, & then furious because I fled to a bath and didn't have it on to show Olly when she came back for lunch! I laughed for some time — but my clothes, I fear, have had it.

We have now embarked on clearing the entire air raid into the out house so that it can be decorated.* As the out house floor has collapsed this is likely to become highly entertaining. I can just see Mummy staggering out with armfulls of bottling jars & hammers & disappearing through the floor. Also I am moving back to my room which was let all through the summer & everything taken out — including all bookcases etc. Think of it. I rather fear I shall not even be able to get into bed tonight. Also the scullery floor has to be painted. For all this we have despatched Danny off to Swanage for a few days. At the present rate I fear she will be back too soon.

Olly & her Douglas have been on Shell Bay in the rain all afternoon. They leap around in the sand dunes and play red Indians amongst the grasses!!

Must stop as Judy is just being driven out to the post. Luckily my hair is wet — as I washed it. Much love, & please let me know when you can come.

Love,
Jane

[March 14, 1957]

Darling Family,

It is now 4 p.m. on Thursday and I still find it difficult to believe that I am on my way to Africa. That is the thing — AFRICA. It is easy to imagine I am going for a long sea voyage, but not that names

---

* During the war, the family's standard steel air-raid shelter had been kept in a small, closetlike room. That room was ever after known as "the air raid."

like Mombasa, Nairobi, South Kinangop, Nakuru, etc., are going to become reality.

We are just going into the Bay of Biscay — and out of 365 passengers over 200 are sea sick. And that is not counting the stewards etc, a good many of whom are invisible today. The rest of my cabin are languishing in misery on their bunks, fortified slightly by Eric's pills. They had all forgotten to buy any. I havn't even thought of taking one.

But, after all, they are very nice, except for the old girl in the fur coat. The girl from Uplands is Helen Paterson — she was a form or two below me. Pam is a very pretty girl — & rather mad like me. We both went on deck last night after dinner & discussed our respective love lives while the other 3 went to bed. The remaining girl, & I'm not sure what her name is yet, is the nicest of the lot I think. She has the bunk below mine & each time my dressing gown or sheet starts falling between my bunk & the wall she pulls it down. However, I can retaliate by tickling her face with my belt, or even better, turning her air blower on & directing it into her face. So I really have the upper hand! Poor Pam succumbed in the middle of breakfast. It suddenly got very much more 'swelly' and the dining room emptied rapidly. The other two just got through lunch.

I had to move my table. It was simply <u>ghastly</u> last night at dinner. There was the old fur coat misery, and the other two were both foreign. One, I believe, is travelling as a sort of companion or governess to two children. No one spoke more than 4 words the whole dinner. The funny part was that the fur coat woman had made a mistake. She should have been at another table. But the man who was there at lunch time, having been temporarily put at a single table, asked at once if he could stay there. So the Head Waiter came over to W & said she could stay. All girls together he said. What great fun. I spoke to this man afterwards — he thought it was I who had made the mistake as I had not been there at lunch time. Had he known it was Fur Coat, he said, he might have elected to return to the table! However, I am now sitting with Helen & the nice girl. They are a larger table with a very charming older couple, a dear old foreign lady, and a ghastly young man with a mustache. We all took our hats off to him, however, for coming down to lunch at all. He was simply pea green. And he sat looking at his dish of fruit salad for fully 10 minutes before making a rather rapid exit. It is now so rolling about that I keep sliding off the chair which doesn't make writing any too easy.

When I really started looking round in the cabin I suddenly noticed that there were two large vases of flowers for me. One from Poosh & one from Keith. The other 3 young ones also had a rose each so it is absolute heaven in there now. I put Keith's into two — the smaller ones looked much better in a glass — & they are now on the shelf over my bed. I only hope they havn't slid off onto my bunk in this swell. Then today there was a native saying that a parcel had arrived — well, it arrived yesterday but they weren't sorted out till this morning. Some sun glasses from Keith. And I was just going to buy some, too. They are smashing ones — light as a feather, rimless, & tested in Paris by the Institute d'Optique. They really are beauties.

There is only one handsom young man so far, and I think he is married. So Pie* quite safe so far!! I have been out on deck all afternoon. I have found a favourite spot as far forward as one can get. There one gets more movement than anywhere else. Sitting there watching the waves is simply heavenly. One is right in the teeth of the wind and no one else goes there at all because it is so cold. Just under the ship the sea is dark inky blue, then it rises up a clear transparent blue green, and then it breaks in white and sky blue foam. But best of all, some of this foam is forced back under the wave from which it broke, and this spreads out under the surface like the palest blue milk, all soft and hazy at the edge. Here I had a long chat with a very handsom young waiter who told me that soon I would be able to watch the porpoises gamboling around scraping their sides against the ship. And at night all the water glows with brilliant phosphorescence and phosphorescent fish swim below the surface.

Unfortunately we stop at Las Palmas during the night so we shan't see a thing. A shame. All my letters are taken by a homeward

---

* A nickname for Keith.

bound castle vessel and posted in England. So it will be some time before you get this letter I suppose.

I feel quite absolutely helpless about thanking you all for everything. You did far, far, far too much, and spent 100% too much money. All I can say is — just wait till I come home. Thank you Jif very much for your birthday presents. The ear rings are simply sweet, and the nail things just what I need.

I must finish off this letter now as we are nearing Las Palmas and everything has to be packed by 6 o'clock. We are going ashore despite the midnight arrival. I am going with this fellow from Uganda — I don't think I've mentioned him yet. He's not a bad chap does Engineering, 26, good fun. But what is quite horrible is his name — Keith. I just couldn't believe it at first. Still, I suppose one can get used to anything.

It is a whole lot calmer now, & we have begun playing deck games — tomorrow I think there will be water in the pool.

We had a dance last night which was quite fun. There are two foul Germans aboard — I have told Dora about them at length so she can tell you. I have also told her that you will tell her any other news from this letter.

I discovered that <u>THE</u> sea sick pills, which really revived Pam from the dead, are the ones Charles gave me. Marzine.

I am down in the cabin just now, as up on deck or in the lounge it is impossible to get any peace. The High Commissioner of Malapin is going to give me & a boy friend a wacking great night out if I'm not married this time next year — in Malapin.

I will write a longer letter from Cape Town, but there is really no more news just now. So far, & I don't think there are any other sufferers confined to their cabins at present, this Ugandan is the only presentable young spark aboard. He's certainly full of life. The chap Helen has fixed for is tall & good looking & has knocked round the world — but he can't speak the King's English. The two chaps we saw the first day, Ginger Top & friend, are quite good fun of their type. Ginger Top made advances, but was gently laid aside, the second day. Mossy Face, the sickly young man on the table, is going out to a leper colony for 3 years.

You will be nice to poor Keith, won't you? And find the books of mine on the list to lend him. I'm sure he will like the Durrell books. I am sending him the penicillin — disguised as pen & pencil! I hope it gets through.

Honestly, the food is wonderful, & what with that, sleep, & fresh sea air, I was taken for 19 last night. So you can cease worrying. Our waiter, Mick (and a real darling — big & handsom) says it is the best ship for fruit he has ever been on. We live on it.

I miss you all a lot if I let my mind dwell on it too much, but in these circumstances it is best not to.

Thank you again, 10,000 thousand times for <u>everything.</u>

Tons & tons of love,
Jane

<u>P.S.</u> After spending hours wrapping up that <u>blasted</u> penicillin for Keith, and wondering what on earth to say it was for customs, one can't post it. The only way is to try to do it from beyond the dock area in Las Palmas — unlikely to work at 3 in the morning even if we <u>do</u> go ashore — or else from Cape Town. If you could get some more it would save a lot of bother — it seems a little silly to spend pounds doing it from the Cape. But I should be very pleased if you could tell Keith I have sealed his letter up, telling him I was sending it disguised as pen & pencil.

I have just saved the cabin from a flood as the gale turned into a squall & it is absolutely pelting.

Romantic music is being played over the speakers, rain is falling into a rough grey sea from a leaden grey sky and people are now talking or frantically writing last minute letters. I must end, so again good bye, God Bless, many thanks, and I'll post to you again from the Cape. By then there will be porpoises & tropical sunsets to describe I hope.

Tons & tons & tons of love,
Jane.

<u>Sunday.</u> P.S. The girls are going to put on the zip!! It is now blowing up a gale again, & the sea far from calm. I went to the service this morning.

3

❧ ❧ ❧

KENYA COLONY
1957–1958

I think that during those weeks at Olduvai Dr. Leakey realized
that my interest in animals was not merely a passing one.
— *My Friends the Wild Chimpanzees*

THE *KENYA CASTLE* docked in the port of Mombasa at dawn
on April 2, 1957. The young Englishwoman cleared customs
by noon and soon was rolling upcountry on the train to Nairobi station, arriving on April 3 — her twenty-third birthday — to
be met by Clo Mange, Clo's father Roland ("Papa"), and a friend,
Tony. They drove north out of Nairobi, climbing higher and higher
on a rough dirt road into the Kinangop (also known as the White
Highlands), turning onto the South Kinangop Road and stopping at
last, not far from the tiny trading center of Naivasha, at Greystones,
the Mange family farm.

So began Miss Jane Goodall's African life. From her arrival in
April 1957 to her departure on December 1, 1958, her stay lasted
some twenty months, primarily though not entirely within the bor-
ders of Kenya Colony. Those months were exciting but chaotic. She
lived in more than a half dozen places: the Mange family farm, a
hostel on Kirk Road in Nairobi, the flat of an acquaintance (Gillian
Garret) in the Kinangop, the Leakey camp at Olduvai Gorge in
Tanganyika, a room in the women's halls of Nairobi Technical Institute in Nairobi, the Leakey home in the Langata area outside of
Nairobi, the house of a friend (Jean Hyde) in Langata, and finally,
starting in April 1958, her own apartment in staff housing (the Mu-

seum Flats) behind the Coryndon Museum in Nairobi. The latter residence she shared with her friend Sally Cary, who came out for an extended visit in late April of 1958, and then also with her mother, who arrived in September of that year.

Jane was socially active as well. She flirted regularly, was courted frequently, pestered often, proposed to at least once, and fell in love (or into a serious relationship) once. She also met her life's mentor, Dr. Louis S. B. Leakey, and, without fully noticing it herself, moved from one social circle to a second. Her first two or three months were spent within the privileged orbit of the White Highlands set. The currency of this group was horses — the breeding, racing, and riding of them — and Jane quickly shone as a superb horsewoman. Soon after meeting Louis Leakey, though, her attention shifted. She found some excellent and loyal friends among the museum staff — including entomologist Robert Carcasson, mammal expert Derek Fleetwood, ornithologist John Williams, technician Norman Mitton, and accountant Gerry Hillings — and by September of 1957 was becoming involved in an extended if stormy affair with Brian Herne, the son of a camp manager at Ngorongoro Crater in Tanganyika. Brian and Jane shared a love of adventure, animals, and wilderness, and with Brian and his family and friends she regularly explored the wilds of the Serengeti — as well as of Nairobi, where they danced, went to parties, frequented nightclubs, and in general behaved like young people of high spirits and great energy. The most serious problem with that relationship may have been Brian's love of hunting and his plan to become a "white hunter."

Her first meeting with the legendary anthropologist Louis Leakey happened simply. After Jane had been in Kenya for less than two months, Clo mentioned Leakey to her. "If you are interested in animals," so the words were later recalled, "you must meet Louis Leakey."* According to the second letter in this chapter, written on

---

* *My Life with the Chimpanzees* (1988), p. 35. Whether it was Clo or her father who said this, how the introduction actually happened, and other details are not perfectly clear. The letter of May 30 probably recalls the story as accurately as we can hope for.

May 30, Jane telephoned Dr. Leakey at his curator's office at the Coryndon Museum, told him "how interested in animals I was," and was invited to visit him at the Coryndon at ten o'clock on Friday, May 24. The meeting was momentous, arguably the single most important event of Jane's Kenya Colony experience.

Louis Seymour Bazett Leakey was born at Kabete Mission Station, Kenya, on August 7, 1903; he died on October 1, 1972. The son of one of Kenya's pioneering missionaries, he was raised in unusual circumstances. His playmates were members of the Kikuyu tribe, and Louis grew up fluent in their language, adept at their games and hunting skills, and entirely knowledgeable about Kikuyu culture. In early adolescence he underwent the secret Kikuyu circumcision rites, marking his manhood as an African and his entrance into the tribe. He was, as he put it in one early autobiography, a "white African."* Louis combined that unique experience with immense personal energy and considerable intellectual brilliance, graduating from Cambridge University in 1926 with top honors in anthropology and archaeology. He soon became convinced that, contrary to the prevailing wisdom of the time, *Homo sapiens* had first appeared in Africa, and he set as his life's work the uncovering of human origins on that continent. In that task he and his second wife, Mary, were supremely successful, digging up at various sites in East Africa tens of thousands of ancient stone tools and thousands of fossilized bones and skull fragments from hundreds of human precursors.

When Jane walked into the Coryndon in May 1957, Louis had already established his reputation as a great, if eccentric, anthropologist. He and Mary had already begun their pioneering excavations at Olduvai Gorge. And he had already begun speculating that long-term studies of humankind's closest living relatives, the great apes, would prove extremely useful for our understanding of how ancestral humans lived. Of the four great ape species still living, three — chimpanzees, gorillas, and bonobos — could be found in African forests. As early as 1945, in fact, Louis had been aware of the chim-

---

* He used the phrase as the title of a memoir published in 1937.

panzees living in a protected patch of forest on the eastern edge of Lake Tanganyika. According to Leakey biographer Virginia Morell, he may have tried to send a young man out there to study the chimpanzees around 1946.* A decade later Louis once again attempted to launch an ape research project, this time with mountain gorillas. He sent his secretary at that time, Rosalie Osborn, out to Mount Muhavura, Uganda, for four months to locate and observe the apes. Four months, unfortunately, was simply not enough time to produce significant results, and in January 1957 Osborn returned to England.†

By the spring of that year Louis was still actively pursuing the ape-studies idea, and thus the appearance on Friday morning, May 24, of an eager young Englishwoman with steady gaze and hazel eyes was fortuitous — for her and for him. As Louis soon recognized, Jane Goodall was superbly suited to and ready for the task, sharing with him a powerful fascination with animals and nature, an interest in paleoanthropology, and exceptional energy, endurance, and fortitude. Her lack of formal training was a plus, in his view, since she could begin her studies without any foolish academic preconceptions. That she was a woman was also positive, Louis believed, since a woman would be less threatening to a male-dominated ape community.‡

The latter theory was reasonable, but Louis also had a less rational fondness for women, particularly young and pretty ones, and his reputation for informal relationships with his young protégées had been well earned by then, as had Mary's burning jealousy. Jane started to hear the gossip only after she began work as a secretary at the museum in September, but it appears that her secretarial prede-

---

* See Virginia Morell, *Ancestral Passions: The Leakey Family and the Quest for Humankind's Beginnings* (New York: Simon & Schuster, 1995), p. 239.
† Osborn did succeed in tracking gorillas and making preliminary observations; her work was extended by a subsequent volunteer, Jill Donisthorpe (Morell, *Ancestral Passions*, p. 246).
‡ Male dominance is certainly a characteristic of chimpanzee and gorilla society. Among bonobos, males and females are codominant. That is to say, dominance is more a matter of social class (who your family and friends are) than of sex and politics (who your friends and allies are).

cessor, Rosalie Osborn, had nearly become, in the words of Richard Leakey, "the third Mrs. Leakey."* Thus Jane's description of Louis's special concerns about how Mary might react to his new candidate for secretary, as we read in the letter of July 3 or 4, 1957, takes on added significance. And Mary's heavy drinking and disturbingly erratic behavior during the safari to Olduvai (as recorded in the long letter written in late July) become more comprehensible. Quarrels in the Leakey household had become increasingly noisy and violent after 1955, when Mary began to realize that Louis's affair with Rosalie was "quite serious."†

Leakey recognized Jane Goodall as an extraordinarily promising candidate to undertake a study of apes. At the same time, his motivations in dangling that tantalizing opportunity to "study a strange tribe of chimpanzees" (mentioned in the letter fragment from early September 1957) must have been more complex than she first reckoned. When Louis began to assert his romantic interest directly (noted in the October 1957 letter), Jane's candid reaction was of alarm and disgust. She resisted directly, emphatically, and regularly until he finally gave up. The process took longer and was more complex than will appear in these pages, but over time Louis's relationship with Jane shifted satisfactorily from suitor to mentor.

A generally understated background to this group of letters includes Kenyan colonial politics, particularly the Mau Mau rebellion, the Emergency, and the independence movement. More than forty different tribal groups lived within the region called Kenya during this period, of whom the most powerful, rapidly growing, and politically attuned were the Kikuyu. By the late 1940s the tribe included some 1 million people — compared to around 32,000 white settlers — and they had particular reason for resentment, since from the earliest days of its colonial administration the British had reserved Kikuyu land in the highlands north of Nairobi for white settlers only. In the 1940s a radical group among the tribe created the Mau Mau, a movement that at first focused its energies

---

* As quoted in Morell, *Ancestral Passions*, p. 244.
† Ibid., p. 245.

on a secret, compelling loyalty oath. That oath eventually included a sworn agreement to kill Europeans, and soon it was being administered forcibly to any resisting Kikuyu. After several assassinations of prominent Kikuyu moderates, as well as a series of chilling attacks on whites living in isolated farmhouses near the forests of Mount Kenya and the Aberdares, in October 1952 the British colonial government declared the Emergency. That declaration justified invoking supraconstitutional powers and rounding up many alleged leaders of the Mau Mau, the best known of whom was Jomo Kenyatta.*

At the start of the Emergency, some 15,000 Mau Mau militants fled Nairobi and the Kikuyu tribal lands and formed a guerrilla army in the Aberdares, continuing from their hidden camps a reign of terror. The great majority of the victims were Africans who opposed the movement. Comparatively few European civilians were killed — perhaps fewer than three dozen altogether — but those murders were unusually brutal and certainly horrifying to the colony's whites. Among the white victims were Louis Leakey's cousin Gray Leakey and his wife, Mary. A gang of Mau Mau guerrillas broke into their farmhouse, strangled Mary as her elderly husband watched, then dragged him into the forest and buried him alive.

As both a prominent white and a distinguished Kikuyu moderate, Louis Leakey was a prime target for the Mau Mau. His sympathies for Kikuyu land claims were well known, but he could never have been sympathetic to the brutal and often bizarre methods of the Mau Mau. He publicized his vehement opposition to that movement in both deed and word — including the books *Mau Mau and the Kikuyu* (1952) and *Defeating Mau Mau* (1954) — and in return he received death threats during the Emergency. By the time Jane arrived in Kenya Colony, though, the Mau Mau rebellion had been crushed. The final significant leader among the forest guerrilla army, Dedan Kimathi, was captured in October 1956 and hanged on February 18, 1957. So the "emergency" was actually over by the

---

* Sources include Morell, *Ancestral Passions*, pp. 163–74, and Nicolas Best, *Happy Valley: The Story of the English in Kenya* (London: Martin Secker & Warburg, 1979), pp. 172–203.

spring of 1957, though officially the Emergency did not end until January 1960.

The penultimate letter in this sequence treats another subject: Jane's menagerie. This collection began within the first or second week after her arrival with the purchase of Levi, the bush baby, at a pet shop in Nairobi. Levi accompanied Jane to work at her first job, at the Nairobi engineering firm of W. & C. French, and then, starting in September, her second job, at the Coryndon Museum, where he usually slept curled up inside a large gourd in Louis's office. Later in the year Louis helped Jane set up a fish tank in her room at Nairobi Technical Institute; around the same time Brian Herne brought her an orphaned bat-eared fox, Chimba, from the Serengeti. Chimba, mentioned briefly in the letter of February 1958, was stoned to death by some ignorant passers-by in March. Then came Kombo, a vervet monkey; Kip, a mongoose; Tana, a cocker spaniel puppy; Nanki Poo, a Siamese cat; and eventually Boozy, a large bush baby; Dinkie, a hedgehog; Lettuce, another monkey; Mrs. Kip, another mongoose; and various other visiting critters, including snakes, spiders, a rat, and another dog or two — all living at one time or another in Jane's apartment at the Museum Flats. "But can you imagine," she asks in the letter of June 1958, "how paradisical (if that is the correct word?) it is for me having all these animals round?"

Years later Jane Goodall concluded that people should not take exotic animals as pets. "It is almost never a good thing," she noted in her autobiography for young readers, "to keep wild animals as pets. They are adapted to live in the wild. They can't cope with human ways as our dogs and cats can."* In point of fact, the Museum Flats menagerie seems to have been both delightfully amusing and mildly distressing. It was a personal zoo, a hothouse wilderness of sorts created by someone who intuitively, passionately, and obsessively intended to live "among the wild animals" but had not yet figured out quite how to do so.

Jane's mother came to visit in September 1958, bunking in with

---

* *My Life with the Chimpanzees,* pp. 43, 44.

Sally, Jane, and the menagerie at the Museum Flats. By the end of the year Jane, preparing to return home, had released some of her animals and found new homes for others. Only Kip and Boozy were sent on to England. In early December, possibly the 1st, Jane and Vanne sailed on the S.S. *Kenya* out of Mombasa north through the Suez Canal, arriving back at the Birches in time for Christmas. Sally stayed in Nairobi a few weeks longer. And Louis S. B. Leakey, now Jane's fatherly friend and mentor, worked diligently to find a sponsor who would enable her to live truly among wild animals.

* * * *

[Around April 15, 1957]
Most Darling Family, and, in particular, Mummy, Danny, Olly, Audrey, Jif and Pickles,

Hail, one and all! Also, with a capitol HAIL, most beloved Rixy, greetings. (Sorry, I'm feeling rather mad!) Quite honestly. I really do simply adore Kenya. It is so wild, uncultivated, primitive, mad, exciting, unpredictable. It is also slightly degrading in its effect on some rather weak characters, but on the whole I am living in the Africa I have always longed for, always felt stirring in my blood.

Thank you for your letter Mummy which arrived yesterday. I was so terribly sorry about the exam again being a flop.* It's such a shame. However, they always say third time lucky so we'll all cross our fingers for the next shot.

Since last writing I have been having a very gay time — also the rains have started which does rather mean the <u>end</u> of a gay time. Now, I must apologize for the pencil, but Clo & I are baby minding for a charming couple — he is Danish & she Swiss. They have 4 small boys, the eldest about 5 — & there is another due in June. It is a lovely house, a beautiful garden, heavenly orchard — but no ink! So I hope you can read the pencil. We have to stay here the night as it is quite in the cards that they will get stuck on the way back from Nairobi — we did last night. It is rather a hoot — Tony is busily falling in love with me! Clo is quite fed up with him — in fact he

---

* Judy was auditioning for admission to the Guildhall School of Music.

never was in love with her — so she is thrilled. She couldn't go into Nairobi with him yesterday so I went — he said I was easily the nicest girl he'd met in Kenya & that the evening was by far & away the best he'd had during his year out here. He is going home on 9th May for 3 months & suggested, Mummy, that he should meet you in London to tell you how I was & how I was getting on. Also Clo is very keen to borrow "My First Two Thousand Years" and the two books of Prof. C. S. Lewis — 'Out of the Silent Planet' & "Voyage to Venus" — not the other one. So Tony can bring them out when he comes.

On Friday Ivor* had booked 4 seats for "The King & I." Clo, I, himself & his son, Hugo. Ivor, as I may have told you, has pots of lolly and a Merc. We set off, Ivor, Clo & I, at 9.30. . . . It was full moon & Clo told Ivor & Hugo how I went moon mad & worshipped arum lilies at midnight. So I said it was quite true & that if I didn't have the lily to worship I pretended my partner was one! So it was all very gay & jolly & Hugo was asking for tips on looking Arum-like. Then, quite suddenly, the engine stopped. Ivor & Hugo disappeared under the bonnet & were joined by an Indian. Ivor was busily issuing instructions to them both to suck different tubes & poor Hugo kept getting mouthfuls. In the end Hugo was sent on into Nairobi to fetch a breakdown lorry. We coasted downhill for a few miles before reaching the escarpment & then came to a woebegone halt. A Land Rover stopped & out got one of the chaps who works for W. & C. French.† He practically took the car to pieces & got old Ivor sucking petrol! He is very very handsom & Clo & I sat in the car admiring his bottom & feeling sorry for him because he was getting filthy & oily & we knew he was on the way to Nairobi to meet his girl friend. He was very much your type of masculine beauty Mummy — like the boy from the Eagle Hotel you fell for. He pulled the whole engine out & when he put it back it was 30% worse! So we then — Clo & I — stopped a lorry for a tow rope — Hugo had been gone about 5 hours by then. We got a rope &

---

* Ivor Yorke-Davis was a Mange family friend and neighbor.
† Jane started work at the engineering firm W. & C. French about three weeks after this event.

started off — me & the bottom man in his Land Rover & Clo & Ivor in the Merc. After a few miles we met Hugo — & had a ghastly trip — through pouring rain, thick fog, & <u>clouds</u> of huge flying ants into Nairobi. Our windscreen was half the time inches thick in red mud turned up by the lorry. . . .

We had to get up [the next morning] at 11.30 as some people came to see one of the horses which Clo wants to sell. We have been schooling her madly in the intervals between our gallivanting & the heaven's downpouring. The silly clots arrived in a real torrential cloudburst & could only see the horse in the stable. But they liked her & are coming again to ride her — which gives us longer to school & is therefore good. We are embarking on a 2nd youngster next week. It is absolute bliss riding here. Shoes are unheard of as one never meets a tarmac road — there <u>is</u> only one in Kenya!

When these people had gone we were invaded by 5 people from the Belgian Congo — all down for a meeting of the Pyrethrum Board — of which Clo's father is a member. This pyrethrum is a white plant for insecticide — grown by everyone on the Kinangop. The plan is that we should all go to the Belgian Congo in September — smashing if it comes off. And then after riding all afternoon, in the evening we went round to some charming people for dinner. They had a new record player — and a Hi-Fi speaker. Reproduction was just about 100% & we had a marvellous evening — Grieg Piano Concerto, Beethoven, Sibelius & some lovely popular stuff. They also had a projector & screen where we saw some marvellous colour slides of Big Game. . . .

It is evening at the moment & Clo & I are collapsed in exhausted heaps in front of the fire having worn ourselves out by playing with the children — I gave them all piggy backs, bucking, and started swinging them round by the hands & various other energetic tricks. They are now silent in their beds & we are just going off to ours. Ivor came this afternoon & asked Clo when she would like him to divorce his wife! So Clo said, Never & he said that if he died it would be her fault! What a thing to say.

When Tony & I were driving back last night it was ghastly —

thick fog & blinding sheets of rain. We had to stop several times & never thought we'd make it. We managed to get nearly up to the house & then got well & truly stuck. Tony had said we'd be back at 11 & it was only 12 — but Mrs. M was in a real state — said she felt responsible for me & all that. Tony, of course, had to stay the night & in the morning the old man was simply livid — in one of his real rages. Poor old Tony. I doubt if he will turn up again for some time now!

This really will make you think I'm daft. When we were in Nairobi — Clo & I & Tony — Clo & I went into the pet shop — & I saw some bush babies. Oh, they are such darlings. I simply had to keep the one she showed me — £4!!! But he was so sweet. Only about 2 months, hardly weaned. Everyone said he was too young & that the altitude of the South K would kill him. But he has a wonderful appetite & is doing fine. I have called him Levi, & will send a photo soon. He already takes flying leaps onto me from any strange place, & clings with his tiny hands. They have teeny-weeny nails.* He really plays with me, hiding behind cushions & leaping out at one's hand. He loves sleeping under my jersey. Clo & I have made him a sweet little cage.

Oh yes, I have seen some giraffe!! Very near the edge of the road — one was in the road & walked away in a most condescending & stately fashion. They are even taller and more impressive than I had imagined.

I must tell you one other thing. I have found a most romantic lover. Every night he wakes me up, very gently, at about 2.30. He then creeps into my bed and makes love to me until I want to go to sleep again. I'll tell you more about him later — but I feel Dora would appreciate this. Clo is very jealous about him because formerly he was her beau.

Later. We are now in Nairobi. Papa† is in a foul mood & has gone off with the car leaving us to cart mounds of shopping in the sweltering heat. I have an interview with the French branch manager af-

---

* Levi was *Galago senegalensis,* a lesser galago or lesser bush baby, a nocturnal prosimian (primate) widely distributed in Africa.
† Clo's father.

ter lunch,* but I think I am plumping for a very well paid job — up country at Kitale as by doing this I can save up more money in 3 or 4 months than I could in 6 months living in this very costly city of Nairobi.

I must stop now. Clo is discussing rabbit illnesses in a Veterinary store & I am finishing this at a table in the corner. I will write again soon & let you know about jobs, etc. And, to relieve your minds as to the propriety of my conduct in Kenya — my midnight lover is Patch — the dog. He has firmly adopted me — & I like him best.

Tons of love to <u>everyone,</u>
Jane.

P.S. You really shouldn't send me anything for my birthday, but if you do send me something, I do need, rather much, a dark coloured pullover — you know, a thing with long sleeves & v neck — well, any sort of neck, but a cheap sort of thing to muck around in & that won't get so dirty as my white one does. But I would much rather you didn't send anything at all. Honestly I would.

P.O. Box 30132
[May 30, 1957]

Most darling Family,

I was most upset when I kept getting letters from you saying you hadn't heard from me for months and months, because not one single week since I left home has passed without my writing home — not one week. However, now you have got them, or most of them I think, so all is well. You should have had three typed from here, this being the fourth. I can hardly believe I have been here one month already. Thank you all for your letters. I had a real feast of mail when I got here this morning — two from Clo enclosing one from you, Ma, and one from Brian. And then one from Keith, another from you, mummy, with Jif's inside. And on Monday I got your letters,

---

* W. & C. French was an English firm with a Nairobi branch. She had arranged to work for the firm before leaving England but had to have an interview with the branch manager.

Danny and Olly. So I feel very satisfied and spoilt. Keith is a conundrum — and I assure you I'm not pining for him, only you needn't tell him so!

Since I last wrote an awful lot has happened. For one thing I have had a great deal of work, now happily disposed of into various files and envelopes. Friday — when, as I believe I told you we have a bank holiday out here, only I had to work on Sat. morning and so couldn't go away — was my nicest day in Kenya. Here in Nairobi is one of the best Natural History Museums there is, with all the most up to date and modern methods of showing and arrangements, etc. The Curator, who is responsible for all this, is a man called Dr. Leakey. He is the expert on the Kikuyu tribe, being himself a first grade initiated elder of the tribe amongst whom he was brought up. Despite the fact that in the emergency they buried his brother* alive as a blood sacrifice, he still thinks they are the best tribe in Kenya. He is also considered to be the authority on most types of African animal — he is about 60 incidentally. Anyway, Clo told me about him, as they had taken an Aard Wolf to the museum to be stuffed — for the museum, not them! She promised to introduce me, having met him on one or two occasions, but of course, she didn't. So I rang up and asked to speak to him, told him how interested in animals I was, and left the rest to him. He immediately suggested I should go there on the Friday morning, at 10 o'clock — which I did. And for the whole morning he took me round the museum, pointing out why one species of antelope had its head set on at a particular angle, or one type of pig had horny developments in one place and another sort in another. He showed me all the snakes, about which I was naturally very interested. He has a snake park in his garden, and I am going there to see them. He told me about experiments they are carrying out on the lung fish, and how these remarkable creatures have been proved able to remain in their dried mud holes without a drop of water or a bite to eat for — you just couldn't guess — 3 whole years!!!!! They were still alive, but very weak, and Dr. Leakey decided it wasn't fair to try and make them survive longer. At first

---

* Gray Leakey was his father's brother's son.

he dried them up for one year — most people thought they could only last out the dry season at that time. They were full of energy and very lively when water was added. So, after a few good meals they dried them out again, and left them for two years at the end of which they were still lively, and a little more hungry. So then they were left for a further three years, and even survived this. Isn't it incredible. He told me so many fascinating things, that it would take me pages and pages to tell you, so I won't. We then had some coffee. Now comes the amazing thing — and it is just as amazing whether it comes off or not. You must realize that he had never seen me before, and knew absolutely nothing about me at all. Over coffee we were talking about Levi, etc., when he suddenly said "Can you ride?" So I said that I loved it, etc. etc. Then he looked at me intently and said "Are you good with dogs?" So I answered in the same vein. Then he said "Would you be interested in living at my house while my wife and I are away, exercising the horses and seeing that all the animals are all right?" It absolutely took my breath away. He has 5 horses. 3 dogs. Several bushbabies. A very rare animal from Tasmania. Tree hyrax. A 12 foot tame python. And snakes in the garden. I told him his house sounded my idea of paradise, and he said of course he couldn't definitely say whether or not this was possible, and he had to discuss it with his wife. He is taking me out into the National Game Park tomorrow evening. And I am being armed with collecting bottles etc to collect spiders for the museum as the entemologist is not frightfully keen on them. So there for you !!!!!!!!!!!!! I havn't yet got over the shock. I was there yesterday evening talking to the entymologist who showed me all his most fascinating specimens. . . .

Tons & tons of love,
Your little Jane.

P.O. Box 30132.
[July 3 or 4, 1957]

Darlingest Family,

I really have slipped up badly and missed out a whole week without writing. I am so very sorry. Thanks tons for all your letters — or rather, I have only had one from you Mummy, since I last wrote. There was a reason for my not writing. I wanted to make certain of my future plans before letting you know them as possibilities or no possibilities. In fact I have been living under great tension for a few days. But I suppose you may as well know all the details, now that it is all over.

I hadn't heard from Dr. Leakey for about a week last Friday. On the Friday I wrote to Bob* & told him I would go & stay up at the Falls during the last two weeks in July. He wanted me to go for a 10 day trip round Lake Victoria in August — which I wrote & said no to.

On Saturday I was supposed to be going for the day to Kisumu — 200 miles away — with Jim Grant — the chap with the put on Oxford accent who gave me a lift to Nakuru — remember. At 3.30 on Friday he rang to say the trip was off as he had to go to Nanenki on the Sunday, but we would meet at the New Stanley for a chat at 10.00 on Saturday. While I was talking to him & feeling most annoyed because it was by then too late to arrange to go to T. Falls (Bob having asked me to the Hunt Ball up there & me having said no because of going to Kisumu!) the telephonist (Win!)† came in with a scrap of paper — "There's another call for you on the other line". So I said goodbye to Jim, & it was Dr. Leakey. He had just that day got back from safari. He would come & collect me from French's to bring me some more chapters of his book & have a chat. I had absolutely given up any idea of safari-ing with him & was frantically thinking how best I could inveigle myself into some other expedition. I planned to ask him that evening. Well, he turned up at 4.30 in his safari waggon — a vast van with a ladder up to the flat roof where one can put a table & eat or something. He gave me 3 more chapters & then asked me if I still wanted to go with them to Olduvai if I could? Well, he said, he would talk about it to Mary that evening. If she said no at once then it was all off. If she thought

---

* Bob, who was briefly a boyfriend, lived outside Nairobi in the Thomson's Falls area. At one point he proposed marriage — and he was kind enough to take care of Levi while Jane went on safari to Olduvai.
† A telephone receptionist at W. & C. French.

it vaguely possible I must go over there on Sunday. There was a hunt for which he would try & get me a mount.

Well, you can imagine how I felt. He was going to meet me on Saturday morning to tell me which way the wind was blowing — at 8.0 in the morning on his way to the museum. I felt in such a state of ghastly suspense, & yet all the time I felt sure it would fall through & almost hated him for raising my hopes again. Making a project given up once into a possibility. After tea I was sitting in my room trying to read to take my mind off my fate — which was possibly being decided as I sat there, powerless to waft the decision in either direction. Suddenly there was a knock at the door — Tony. I was in rather a vast rage with him for not having been to see you, but found he was very nearly engaged & so I forgave him.* Apparently the film was taken on the wrong exposure, so you couldn't have seen that anyway. I said I'd go out to dinner with him because he seems like an old friend & I thought there was such a lot to talk over that I might be able to stop thinking about things for a while.

We had a very pleasant evening. He really is mad, is Tony. He is madly in love with this Italian girl who is very nearly his fiancée. But when I told him I should have been going to Kisumu with Jim he told me it was just as well I wasn't because he wouldn't have liked it at all! We had a good dinner and then sat in the car & talked until about 11 o'clock. After which I went to bed & was most grateful that I should know my fate — or at any rate a part of my fate — <u>early</u> in the morning. I got up & had breakfast & went down to the bottom of the drive. I found a fascinating little scene amongst the grass stalks. A lady beetle was climbing up a grass stalk, purposefully followed by a prospective & hopeful husband. He caught her up & she turned round to say "hello". And then wanted to bustle on about her own concerns. He had other & more amorous ideas. But she was a woman of determination & character. She was busy, it being a Saturday morning, & very firmly told him that there was a time & place for <u>everything.</u> I was chuckling to myself when I looked up to see the huge safari van approaching. I put on a brave face & went to meet it. "Well, the answer is yes!" he said. "Yes to

---

* Tony, Clo's friend, had said he would visit Jane's family while he was in England.

what?" I nearly flung my arms round his neck. "Yes you can come out on Sunday, & if my wife likes you, you can come with us". He couldn't stop then, but said he was going out into the Masai reserve in the afternoon. . . .

[On Sunday morning] I had just finished grapefruit & a large helping of cornflakes when Paul* said "That wouldn't be Dr. Leakey peeping round the door would it?" And it was. Oh, he is such a darling, my Dr. Leakey. I fled out, grabbed my bag, & told him I'd just got back. He asked if I'd rather go to sleep & not go over there!!! There was a professor of anthropology just back from Oldoway Gorge, in the Land Rover & we had to go round to the museum to try & get some skulls out of their cases for him to study. But the keys were lost! How typical. And so the poor fellow — Dr. Tobias (isn't it lovely) had to be content with peering through the glass — and he had corduroy trousers & a beard!†

Dr. Leakey & I then set off for his house — 12 miles out. On the way he told me he couldn't call me Jane yet because his wife would think it dreadfully familiar. I wasn't to tell her he'd taken me in the Park. There had been a row about his last secretary because Mary (his wife) thought the secretary had been making eyes at him. I began to be petrified of meeting Mary. "She takes violent dislikes or likes to people for no reason at all" he said. And you know me & wives!

We stopped at the dukha (village shop) to buy pop for the pony club members — the Leakeys run the Pony Club. And then on to the house. I couldn't hunt because the other horse was lame, but we were going to follow in the Land Rover & I was going to ride Mary's horse home.

We got to their house & collected 2 children — aged about 7 & 8 — little boys — who were following with us. One was known as "Peanut"!‡ I was introduced to what seemed like hundreds of large bouncing Dalmatians — Mary Leakey has the champion of all

---

* A friend and fellow boarder at Kirk Road House, a hostel in Nairobi where meals were eaten communally.

† Philip Tobias was a professor of anatomy at the University of Witwatersrand.

‡ Louis and Mary had three sons, the youngest of whom, Philip, born in 1949, was nicknamed Peanut; the older boys were Richard, born in 1944, and Jonathan or Jonny, born in 1940. Jonny was the snake collector.

Kenya which is quite an achievement — that is, champion of all breeds, not just Dalmatians. Here again is a comic nick-name — "Bottom Pincher"! Actually there are 5, and two belonging to a next door neighbour. I was also introduced to the two hyrax — the twins. Then we dashed off to the meet. And there I met Mary — but only for a moment or two — a small, lean woman, with blackened teeth, a perpetual cigarette, & short wavy hair. A little distant. I had no time to judge, as the hunt moved off, whether she liked me or not. I also met Gillian Trace,* the other girl going to Oldoway. She is absolutely sweet — 19 & she looks — & behaves! — a bit like me. I liked her no end from the moment I saw her, & apparently she said to Dr. L "How did you find such a nice person" — & we'd only seen each other for 10 minutes. A mutual click.

It was wonderful fun following with Dr. L. I know Land Rovers can go where cars can't — Dr. L's goes where Land Rovers can't! No other car was able to get even to the place where hounds found — & this was a drag hunt because Dr. L wouldn't let any of his family hunt an animal. We only came up on the hunt 3 times — but that was an achievement. Speaking Kikuyu as he does we had no end of co-operation from the Africans. The sun shone — & I was so happy. We had to keep getting out & making surveys to see whether the gari† could possibly get through some quagmire or over some vast ditch. We lost the hounds right at the end & so went back to the meet — or vaguely in that direction and met them there. I mounted Mary's wicked little pony who made an exhibition by firmly walking backwards.‡ There is absolutely <u>nothing</u> one can do when a horse does this, but it does make one feel such a fool. It was a blissful ride home. I talked to Jonny, the son of the 1st Mrs. Leakey.§ He is 16 & the one who is dead nuts on snakes. We talked snake. There was a very nice girl — about 14 — who rides beautifully & wants to show jump. Her parents are rolling in lolly & are getting her a

---

* A friend of the Leakey family.
† Vehicle in Swahili.
‡ This was Shandy (see the letter of February 1958). Mary must have known Jane would have trouble with this retrogressive horse.
§ Actually the son of Mary, the second Mrs. Leakey.

horse from England, but she is quite unspoilt. Then another of Leakey's boys — 10 or so, another little fellow, another girl, & a friend of Jonny's over for the day. We rode back through divine country, Jonny occasionally leaping off for frogs for his snakes — he has about 30 — & the younger brother chasing butterflys. I nearly got a large furry bat!

We got back & found the others had started lunch because they were half starved. Dr. L, carving, asked if I was hungry. I said "fairly" & Mary said "That means 'starving' only she's well brought up". A good sign I thought.

After lunch I looked at the fish — 19 tanks in the house. And then the python was brought out — he is now a good 13 feet & was in a bad mood. He bit his master's arm. A Jackson's Tree Snake, harmless, & about 4 ft long was the next favourite — almost identical to look at with the deadly Boomslang, Africa's most poisonous snake. These two — the python & Jackson live in their own houses.

Then I was taken to the snake garden where Jonny, to his father's slight horror, walked barefoot amongst deadly night adders & puff adders. He is not a polite child — indeed, none of them are. They are treated rather as grown ups and a little spoilt.

As we were still snake-ing there had come an urgent phone call. 2 miles away a leopard had taken a man's Irish wolfhound. The boys* had tracked the dragged body & found it about 1/2 mile from the house. Would Dr. Leakey go & set the trap. This was because leopards are wanted in the Tsavo Park where the baboon & wild pig are getting out of hand owing to hunters practically wiping out the leopards. Two have been sent there already. So Dr. L & I leapt into the Land Rover with the two youngest boys who came with butterfly nets. First we had to collect the trap from a nearby farm. It is about 8 ft long & 4′10″ tall & wide. It is strong mesh all round, and doesn't look very heavy.

We got to the house where we were met by the dog's owner, an old boy with heart trouble, and his beefy son-in-law. 6 Africans

---

* "Boy" was commonly used at the time to denote a man, typically but not necessarily African, who worked in some comparatively menial capacity. The term was not then considered racist.

helped us with the trap & we set off into the forest. As we went over rocks, through thorn bushes, across streams, & forced our way through dense forest the trap got fairly heavy. But we were fresh. Also it was <u>very</u> hot. Suddenly the undergrowth became very thick & the boys told us that the dog was just ahead. So we put the trap down & Dr. L went to see the best way of getting the trap through. Great consternation — the dog was gone. And it is most unusual for a leopard to come back to his kill during the day. So the boys were sent on ahead to follow the track again. We followed more slowly behind — without the trap. Suddenly there were excited voices ahead — the boys had seen the leopard up a tree & trying to drag the dog up. It had buzzed off when they came upon the scene.

It must have been still hanging around because the son-in-law's Alsatian was looking into the forest, his hackles rising. It was really ghastly to see the great Wolfhound lying there, all its guts hanging out & two holes in his throat where the leopard must have killed him. The poor old boy was most upset. And he was such a huge dog that it took <u>2</u> Africans to drag him along the ground. So you can imagine the vast strength of the leopard.

At first Dr. L thought we would have to drag the dog back to the trap because the path was pretty impassable the way we had come. But one of the Africans thought he knew a better way. We left the old boy <u>and</u> his son-in-law behind. They thought I should stay there too. But no fear. We got back to the trap. 6 Africans, one an oldish man & one a little boy — & another only about 15 — [and] Dr. L & I. Honestly, I havn't worked so hard for ages, & the going was ghastly. But one thing pleased me no end. Sometimes there would be a large boulder or a very thick thorn bush to one side of the track — not really a track — simply the way we had come. Then the people on that side would push those on the other side further over to avoid the obstacle. On this occasion there was one on each side — & Dr. L pushed harder than me — since I couldn't go through, over or under a very thick spiny thorn I had to let go — & they dropped the cage. Which proved my worth. We had to put it down every 5 minutes as it was.

When we got to where the others were waiting, the young man did look a little ashamed — & helped us for the last 10 yards or so!

We set the trap, saw that it worked, and went back to the house. Dr L said "Thank you" & we two walked together, some way from the others — reward enough.

When we got back he said to Mary, "Well, she can work anyway". And on the way back he said to me "I think you've been approved". I was so, so happy. I can't tell you how happy.

After a large tea — & Dr. L. would keep leaping up & handing me things, Mary took me back — Jonny's friend had to go back to school & so I went at the same time. Before going I was introduced to the Tenrec — oh the funniest darlingest wee animal you ever saw in all your life. He is about as long as your thumb, & half of that length is nose. His head is this shape: —

A tiny weeney little eye & long long whiskers. The rest of him is a bit like a hedge hog — as yet his spines are like thin white hairs except for one or two thicker yellow ones. He runs very very fast & eats worms. He will eventually grow about the size of a hedge hog & is a relation to a shrew.

After dropping off the friend Mary said to me "I hear you might like to come with us to Olduvai". So I said I wanted . . . nothing else in the world so much. "Well" said she "I think it would be an excellent plan — providing Gillian doesn't mind". My happiness I then thought was complete. But she then suggested I should help her school her pony for jumping & go hunting on him the Sunday before we leave. Honestly, no one in the whole of this huge world is so lucky or so happy as me! Gosh I was happy.

I got back & went into Paul's room with him, Jack & Mike* & we heard Finlandia & I lay on the bed & still didn't feel sleepy — only wonderfully, beautifully tired.

On Monday he rang up & said "Louis here" & this gave me ridiculous satisfaction. He met me outside the hostel at lunch time & took me to the Museum — where the lunch club eat on the roof — & there we met Gillian & he told us what things we would need.

---

* Friends at Kirk Road House.

Because, my beloved family, this safari is imminent, it is almost upon me. And I am so unprepared. We start on the 16th July. I am going to the Leakeys' on the Friday evening to help get ready. Gillian has a birthday party on the Sat to which I am going. Hunting on Sun. morning. Oh, the bliss, bliss, bliss. On Monday afternoon I just couldn't keep the excitement at bay any longer. I had said to Dr. L that I couldn't believe I was really going, & he said the only reason that could possibly prevent my going now was that I should change my mind! And somehow that shook away my last fears. . . .

At lunch time yesterday — Tuesday — I met Gillian & we had a hot dog & coffee & talked. We are very alike. We both wanted to ask each other what we were going to do with our hairs — both being in the same state as regards length etc — & decided to turn ourselves very prim by tying it back — dirty greazey hair — we only get a bowl of water each per day, the nearest water being 50 miles away — looking better thus than hanging in strands if we cut it short.

We are on a dig, incidentally. We shall have to do a lot of plaster-of-paris casting. Dr. L. asked us whether we liked milk or plain chocolate — & if we wanted gin or brandy after dinner!! — I mean before. We said orange squash thank you. He wanted to know if there was anything we couldn't eat — & if we'd had our appendix out!! . . .

I am now sitting in the bathroom, which opens into the bedroom. Gillian* is asleep, but late at night is the only time I have for writing letters at the moment. Life is too full. I have a vast tome on archaeology which I am supposed to digest in less than a fortnight & I havn't even started it. And lunch times are out as I have to go into Nairobi to buy things. We actually have one bath per week! in a canvas bath. And I shall be able to write, & so will you, but I shouldn't write me more than 2 at the most because it may take ages to get to me. Letters are fetched & posted when the van goes in for water once a week — laundry is also taken in. . . .

---

* Two Gillians are mentioned in this letter: Gillian Trace, who would be going to Olduvai, and Gillian Garret, an acquaintance with whom Jane was temporarily sharing a flat.

I really think that I must go to bed now. It must be well after 12 o'clock & we have to get up at 6.30 in the morning. Also I can't afford more than 2/6 — & soon this letter will become a parcel! As it is I doubt whether it will go into an envelope.

Oh, one last thing — the nicest compliment I have ever been paid I think. I was telling Dr. L. on Sunday morning that we had watched the sun rise over the Rift Valley. He told me there was only one place in Kenya to watch the sun rise & be simply amazed by the breathtaking beauty. He has <u>never</u> taken any one there because, he says, people must talk when they see something beautiful — talk & ruin it. He described the beauty. And then he said "I don't know yet, but I think I am going to take you there with me one day". Wasn't it sweet.

If I'm not fixed up with Jean Hyde when I get back from Safari — I do hope I've written since I saw her? — I am going to stay with the Leakeys until we can fix the museum flat, or until I can go there — so I rather hope I can do that!!

And now, to bed. I am getting bitten, sitting here with nothing on.

Tons & tons & tons of love to you all. Good luck in your exams etc Jif. Hope you had a good holiday, O.

All my love,
Your Jane

c/o Dr. L.S.B. Leakey
c/o G. Harvey, Esq.,
Warden of Ngorangora Nat. Park,
Tanganyika Territory.
[Third to fourth week of July 1957]

Darling Family —

I simply can't believe that it is <u>I</u> who am writing to you from here. I don't think I've <u>ever</u> had such a marvelous time in my life. Just imagine. Here we are — a charming Dr. L (and he hasn't got a temper at all providing he likes you. He is never, <u>never</u> cross, no matter how bitchey his wife is. He is terrified of a row. But more of that later.) His wife, Mary, who can be sweet. Gillian, whom I like so much, & myself. Then there are 7 Africans[*] & the two dogs. Dalmatians whose correct names are Victoria & Flicker, but who are known as Toots and "Bottom Biter"! (This because he really does come up and nip one in the seat, just when you least expect it.)

We are camped right in the middle of the Serengeti Plains — no one anywhere nearer than 40 miles away, and that is the Ngorangora camp, on top of the crater rim.[†] The Harveys live there, & 2 more charming people it would be hard to find. Apart from them, & a few tribes of Masai, we are about 100 miles from any form of civilization.

I will go back to the beginning now, and let you know the story from the start.

We set out on the Monday morning after I wrote you that letter from Gillian's house. There was, as there always is, a certain amount of last minute shopping so we loaded everything into the Land Rover and went into Nairobi. By the time everything was in there was just a tiny space in the back for 1 person & 2 dogs. 3 sat in front & we took it in turns to go behind — Mrs L only went behind once & LSB drove, so it was mainly Gillian & I. Things were piled up all round — & the back part is twice as long — or 3 times even — as that of an ordinary Land Rover. The only place out of which one could see was the window between the back & the front compartment. We lay on a little nest of bedding rolls — with our feet in the dog baskets. The 2 dogs were really more nuisance than anything else. I didn't mind. I just lay in a muddle, sometimes on top of the dogs, sometimes underneath them, or even in between, like a

---

[*] The Kikuyu crew did not socialize very much with the Leakeys and their guests. Their leader was Heslon Mukiri, Louis's lifelong friend and, ultimately, scientific colleague, according to Mary Leakey in *Disclosing the Past* (New York: Doubleday, 1984), p. 57.

[†] The great Serengeti Plains and Ngorongoro Crater (the caldera of a long-extinct volcano, now a small, semi-isolated kingdom of wildlife) are in a general sense part of a single 15,000-square-mile ecosystem; they are, however, separately defined within legal boundaries protecting about one third that area. When this letter was written, Ngorongoro was within the eastern boundary of the Serengeti Park; today it is administered as the Ngorongoro Conservation Unit. Gordon Harvey, the warden in charge of the eastern Serengeti, lived with his wife, Edith, in a house at the extinct volcano's rim.

sandwich middle. Then we all three looked through the little window & were happy. I got the technique of sticking my head right through so that I looked out between Gillian & Mrs L, & then I could see just what was going on. Gillian didn't like being a dog pillow or eiderdown & so wasn't as well off. It was a lovely journey, the one sad thing being that we saw no big game at all — nor have we up to date. Poor LSB keeps promising me we will meet lions & rhino around every bush & all we see are tommies & dik-dik!* We stopped at a lovely hotel for lunch where the grounds were full of red head agama lizards, each proudly gazing out from his house top — a pile of stones. It was the most peaceful place. On we went, steadily climbing through Masai Reserve Country with Mount Kilimanjaro faintly visible on our right and Mount Meru in front, tall & jagged against the sky. We paused at Arusha to see if the lorry was all right. This had gone on ahead with the boys to collect some equipment. Unfortunately we let it go off ahead of us from Arusha & it went much too fast. We found a lovely place to camp but couldn't stop until we caught up with the lorry. And then, of course, we found nowhere so pleasant & it was nearly dark when we eventually stopped. We put up 2 little travelling tents — not so very small either — while Muli, the cook boy, got his fire going. We were soon sitting out under the stars — freezing cold — eating steak & kidney pudding. Gillian & I slept on mattresses in our little tent & loved it. We were woken by Muli with a pot of hot tea at about 6.30, when it was even colder. We were away as soon as breakfast was over, to start the long climb up to the rim of the Ngorangora Crater. As we climbed it got colder & colder, & we could only see a few yards in any direction because of the dense white mist. As we climbed the mountain side it was quite wonderful looking out into the swirling white clouds. The tops of trees appeared out of the dense whiteness below, strange & mysterious.

When at last we reached the famous Ngorangora Camp we got out to pick up the water trailer, which holds 200 gallons, & wait for the lorry which was following. While LSB fussed around, Mr.

---

* Tommies are Thomson's gazelles; dik-dik are small antelopes.

Harvey, the Warden, took Gillian & I to look over into the crater. We just had a glimpse of the bottom before the mist closed in again.

When the lorry did arrive it was with a broken spring. With great difficulty it was extracted & then as it couldn't be mended on the spot, LSB & Mrs L. went off to Olduvai* to get it mended, leaving Gillian & I to have the most wonderful day. As we said afterwards out of all the miles & miles we had covered, the lorry broke down at the one place where we could have chosen to spend some time. We were literally frozen stiff by this time, so Mr. Harvey took us back & sprung us on his poor wife. They were both utterly charming, & had the most delightful house & garden with a view across the mountain slopes. In the evening they told us they saw buffalo & rhino from the drawing room window. Strange that my first taste of Mango — <u>delicious</u> — should be hundreds and hundreds of miles from where it is grown!

After lunch Mr H took us in his Estates car — van rather — down the new road they are making to the floor of the crater. The present one is right round on the other side & it takes 3 hours to get from the camp to the bottom so there was not time! When the new road is finished it will take 1/2 hour. They have to pick through solid rock, the work being done by prison labour. They have been at it for 2 1/2 years & expect to finish it by the end of next year. We saw 1/2 way down & he showed us distant spots which, he assured us, were hippo, rhino, lions etc. We gazed through his very powerful binoculars, but were no wiser really! Then he took us up into the bamboo forest — along a very narrow track with the tall whispering bamboo trees on either side. Hundreds of dim buffalo tunnels led out to our main track, & he said one must be prepared to meet <u>anything.</u> Half way along we got out & walked the rest of the way — he was going to inspect the stream where the Camp's water supply came from. It was all such tremendous fun, especially going with him. The night before he had been keeping elephant away from some native shamba† & had no sleep. When he curled up for a few minutes

---

* Probably an error. Arusha would have been the likely destination for repairing a damaged vehicle part.
† Garden in Swahili.

on the floor of a store house, he felt something cold & clammy under his chin. He put on the torch & found a toad nestled there! Very Gerald Durrell-ish I thought!

We met the Leakeys as we were on our way back to the Harveys' for tea. They were in a great hurry to move on so that we could camp at a lower, slightly warmer altitude. So we leapt into the Land Rover & bade Gordon Harvey a fond farewell. (Subsequently, we both agreed that had he been a young & unmarried man we should have fought over him like cat & dog!)

After getting the spring back on it was about 5.15 & we were expecting the mist to rise at any minute. So off we went to get as far as possible while it was still light. We found a lovely place — still in the Serengeti National Park, of which Ngorangora is a part. It is a huge park, shared by Masai & animals, & one of the most famous parks in East Africa. Camping in it is not allowed except in special cases. As we drove along, Gillian & I kept thinking that this was what rich Americans paid £100 a week for doing!

Camping was again fun — but even colder. Thank goodness we didn't have to camp up at the top. The wind shrieked over the plains — which rise & fall and are covered in golden sun-baked grass and clumps of scrub & thorn trees. We heard the laughing call of a hyaena & had to put away shoes & anything leather or they may pinch it during the night. LSB had one story of when he was sleeping out in the open with one boy. He took his boots off & put them under his pillow. The boy merely unlaced his & left them on for warmth. In the middle of the night LSB was woken by a shout & in the moonlight saw a hyaena dashing off with a blanket trailing after him. He had smelt the pong-y leather, grabbed it through the blanket, & made off — the boot, being unlaced, slipping easily off its owner's foot! They never got either back!

We heard lions that night too. It was most exciting. And at dawn the next morning the red rising sun showed herds of Tommies, Grants & Eland — all right on top of us & grazing unconcerned.

The last 30 miles were tremendous as we had to make our own tracks. No one ever goes to the place where Olduvai Gorge is situated — very few people have heard of it. Unfortunately we never see many animals around here because there is no water except a very foul rhino wallow about 7 miles up the gorge from us. We did see a wild cat on the way — very rare. And the most beautiful cheeta who walked along beside the car, quite unafraid, before turning rather disgustedly from our noisy machine & bounding leisurely into the nearby thorn thicket. She was my first cheeta. We had a burst tyre at a place where a lioness has her cubs. Gillian & I explored & there were lion tracks everywhere — But unfortunately we did not see her. She was there all right because the dogs were most uneasy.

We arrived at about 11 & it took the rest of that day to organize camp. We camp at the bottom of the gorge — which runs, winding & twisting, for about 50 miles, with numerous side gorges running into the main one. The rainy season is only just over & everything is still very green. There are a lot of trees at the bottom of the gorge, which is about 3/4 mile across & roughly 30–40 feet deep. Sometimes the walls are precipitous — at all times steep. Often they are grass covered, but equally often they are composed of rock or shale.

I never, never dreamt that I would ever be out in the wilds excavating animal bones from thousands of years before. It is sometimes very hard work — we spent two solid days with pick-axes getting one of the sites ready before we could start digging. Then one uses a sheath knife until one finds a bone, after which you use a dental pick — really. You must tell Dibble! Often we are working in such hard rock — as at present — that we have to use a hammer & chisel. But digging out a perfect tooth or perfect bone is ample reward. The great aim here is to find the man who made all the tools — primitive pebble tools & the beginnings of the more evolved hand axe. So far 2 teeth have been found — 2 years ago. The day before yesterday, just as we were coming home, there was great excitement because I found what could — and still may — be a human tooth. LSB is not sure yet. It might be a female baboon. Then Mrs L found a ghastly moth eaten old femur, with no articular ends — which is almost certainly human — But with no ends it tells one nothing. It is most peeving. However, we still have a long way to go on this site, & our hopes are high. I spent one utterly fascinating day collecting minute mouse bones & teeth — LSB gives me a star for record eyes! This should amuse you as I seem to remember odd remarks about my mouse skulls at home! When a bone is <u>very</u> fragile it has to be exposed & then plastered before being taken out of the ground. To do this one first wets pieces of Bronco lav. paper & plasters them over the bone with more water. And then you mix the plaster of paris & coat the bone with strips of either plastered [illegible] or bandage, depending on its size. I can't make up my mind whether it's a good advert. for Bronco, or not!

I <u>do</u> so hope that if we find a definite piece of Man it is LSB who finds it. He is <u>so</u> sweet, so utterly adorable. Both Gillian & I adore him & would do anything for him. With his grey hair tousled & falling over his forehead & his grey eyes twinkling, he looks for all the world like a naughty little boy.

<u>Nothing</u> is too much trouble, & he is so sweet to us. He is a wonderful cook — he once did the cooking & catering for a boarding house with <u>40</u> people! There is <u>nothing</u> he can't do. Our cook, Muli, is also very good & we feed most tremendously. Tonight we had roast chicken (we brought live cockerel with us) & potatoes — think of it. Superbly cooked with stuffing & all, over a camp fire in the middle of wildest Africa! The site we are digging at present is about a mile from camp, so we cook our own mid-morning coffee & tea there, but come back for lunch. We get up at 6.0 — or 6.30. We are generally at work by 8–8.30. We have lunch at any time from 12.30–1.30. And then a very short rest time — mainly because Mary insists. Then we clean, sort & mark specimens during the hottest part of the day, & then back to the site until about 6.0.

After this Gillian & I climb the sides of the Gorge. And we can never get over the heaven of being able to wander around on the famous Serengeti Plains. Admittedly we <u>don't</u> meet lion & rhino around every bush. But we do see Gazelle and dear little dik-dik — klipspringers walking on the extreme tips of their one modified toe of each foot, jackals, mongooses, & an <u>occasional</u> snake. I am disappointed there are not more of these. I found the most adorable chameleon — LSB christened her Melone. We kept her for 2 days on a branch hung from our tent roof. But she was not really happy so we took her back & freed her. One of the things that appeals to me almost most is the fact that everyone here is the same about insects & things as me. If we see a spider or beetle while we are digging it has to be rescued & taken to safety. We all spend hours watching bees & strange flies eating off our [illegible]. And LSB knows about almost every thing. Nothing gets killed. If by some sad mischance an insect is damaged, none of us want to kill it, so LSB comes & takes it sorrowfully away from prying eyes & executes it with due regret. The atmosphere is friendly & joking & oh so pleasant — until dinner time. This should be best — but "Lovey One" or "Mary Mine" drinks brandy beforehand until she is reduced to the staggering stage. She totters up to the table, unable to focus across it, & is quite tiddly every night. She can only think of her darling dogs. She does not get jolly — just blotto. She always serves out the veg — a most hazardous occupation. One is liable to get 1/2 a bean & 6 potatoes — whilst all the cauliflower goes onto the table. Gillian & I think it tremendous fun, but we get so worked up for LSB's sake afterwards. He will do anything to avoid a row & really <u>panders</u> to her. She knows this, & plays up to it no end, while he maddens us by waiting on her hand & foot. Dear darling Louis. And all she can say a good word for is her wretched dogs.

For a solid week "Mary Mine" complained about the soup in the evening. She said Muli made it wrong. So LSB came to make it — & thickened it with milk powder. It poured out of the jug in a thick, solid sick-ey looking mess & Gillian & I thought it was foul. We discussed it afterwards. The next evening we suggested that the milk made it a little thick, so he gaily said perhaps it should have less. The point was that neither of us liked it at all — it went into lumps. That evening Mary was staggering about even more than usual, which made us giggly to start with. Then the soup was poured out — thicker than ever, & we caught each other's eye & had a hard job not to laugh. Then we caught eyes again when we were each squashing out a lump of milk powder — & we exploded. It was dreadful really. I pretended to cough & Gillian pretended she'd burnt herself on the soup. It was a hoot.

They sleep in the lorry which has two pull-down-ible bunks.

Gillian & I have a very large tent with a bathroom at the back. We only have the tiniest drop of water to wash in — & you've no idea how economical one learns to be — in 1/2 inch of water one first washes one's face, then sponges the thick layer of dust off the rest of one, & finally washes out pants or bras. So far we've had one bath in a canvas bath — really <u>great</u> fun. You hang out all round & only have a minute drop. In which you first rinse your hair . . . & then do masses of washing. It's great fun.

We sleep on our two beds outside under the stars. It gets pretty cold at night sometimes, & once, when it was so windy we both slept with our heads under the blankets, the jackals stole the bacon from the cupboard almost next door! Often LSB roams round at night with his torch. Once the lions roared quite close. Another time LSB & I both heard a large animal walking round — a rhino. He saw one the first morning, but when we got there it had gone.

There are <u>thousands</u> of ticks around here — & they all <u>love</u> me. I have such a reputation that when the others get a tick they ask me why I can't keep them to myself! 15 is my record after one of our walks! There are very few mosquitoes. The worst insect worry are <u>thousands</u> of minute flies that bite like stink. They arrive in clouds & get into one's hair & one's ears & nearly drive us quite mad. There is nothing one can do. Luckily we only get them when there is no wind — not very often.

It is very late now. Everyone is asleep — LSB is snoring in the lorry to my left. Gillian is sleeping outside to my right. I am at the entrance of our tent — literally "burning the midnight oil". I must stop now & get some sleep or I shan't feel like leaping out of bed to greet the dawn tomorrow. I have to have this ready by tomorrow evening for when the boys leave to get more water from Ngorangora, but I will <u>try</u> to do some more during rest time tomorrow. So I won't end now, but simply say "Goodnight" & creep into my little warm bed under the stars. Oh yes, there <u>are</u> scorpions here, but so far we have only seen two — one of Mary's & one of mine. Both of which were solemnly executed by the boys as their bites can keep one in bed for a day or two.

I must apologize. I have not yet thanked you Mummy, Danny &

Uncle Eric for your letters. I feel it a very great honour, Uncle E, to have had such a long letter from you all to myself. I will answer it when I get a moment. You wanted to know, Mummy, if I have changed & become a new Jane. Most <u>certainly</u> not! Why on earth should I? I am doing the things I have always dreamed of doing, but it is the same person doing them as dreamed of doing them — if you see what I mean. I do, very often, wonder if I am dreaming — & if not what I have done to deserve such luck. Because not only am I actually where I have always wanted to be, but ever since arriving here <u>everything</u> has gone right. It really is too good to be true.

Since I last wrote another day has gone by — & a really lovely day. Mrs. L was <u>such</u> a 'B' yesterday that Gillian & I were wild. Today she has been sweet. When we got back, <u>very</u> hot, at lunch time, we found our dear Mr. Harvey had arrived — with two girls who had been dumped on him for the day. The poor man was fed up with them — & I'm not surprised. One was very plain & obviously on the shelf. The other wasn't too bad — but honestly, their clothes! They were both in dresses with sandals all open showing nail varnished toes. And they had little heels, & posh handbags. I ask you! For a day on the Serengeti Plains! We took them into our 'bathroom' to wash their hands & gave them good measure. We produced 'Shekel', the little snake, from his box under our pyjamas. Then we tipped out a bowl of <u>black!</u> water in which we'd both washed our feet & our pants. And being canvas, when we put some water for them it was filthy because we didn't rinse the settled dirt sediment. Amongst our brushes, combs, nivea baby powder etc we casually pointed out some of my museum, emphasizing the porcupine & dik-dik dung! I am collecting dungs so as to learn them. There were some lovely skulls grinning there as well — quite probably all maggoty!

When Harvey's son, Hamish, comes out, he is coming here to do some work for a day or two. We think he is coming home for the long vacs from Oxford because he has had a sordid affair with a bar maid or something. As soon as Harvey first saw us he said he would send Hamish out to see us, & the Leakeys think he has a nice little plan that we are the answer to his prayer — we are the two girls, ar-

riving as an answer to his distracted prayer, who will pull his son together & make him realize there are better things in life than the bar
maids! So we have to be very glamorous. He is only 21, so I have
given Gillian a free hand, but Mary thinks he may develop a passion
for me. So they are going to have a sweep stake on the affair. All this
discussion was at supper time. She was quite boozy as usual, but
terribly sweet. She said she compared his "two girls" with "our two
girls" & there was no comparison. Harvey himself would gladly
have swapped! It is one of the highlights of camp life — pulling visitors to pieces when they're gone!

I really must stop now. We shall be up at crack of dawn tomorrow, & the water trailer leaves at 6 with the washing & mail so I
must get it all ready — & it is late now as G & I have been planning
an attack on poor Hamish!

This letter is most incomplete. There just isn't time to say all I
want to say. But I <u>must</u> stop now, so tons & tons of love to you all,
& I will send some photos — if any come out!

Tons & tons of love to you all

Jane.

Olduvai Gorge

[Around August 10, 1957]

Darling Family,

I am only going to write a little just now, but I must start this letter to tell you how marvelous it is to sit here and write in the <u>moon-
light.</u> It is full moon tonight, & sleeping under it is quite glorious —
knowing me & moons you can imagine the effect. Poor Gillian is
quite worried! She says she feels responsible — fatal where I am
concerned.

I am sitting half way up the slope leading up from our camp. All
around the crickets are singing their nightly chorus — and so many
different types of song it is hard to imagine. The wind, which has
been very strong all day, blowing the dust into our faces, is now a
gentle and caressing breeze — blowing my long tresses around in
what I'm sure is a most romantic way! Gillian is in her little bed be-

low me — beside my empty one. An owl is hooting about 1/2 mile down the gorge, and before supper we heard the weird call of the hyaena — which means His Lordship the Lion is around somewhere. I can just hear the murmur of the boys as they sit gossiping around their camp fire. The whole gorge, lit by the cold moonlight, is strange and very still. It looks so different from the hot, dry, sun bathed gorge that we know so well. It is 100 miles long altogether, & this is only a side gorge — but just now there is one little tiny speck in the vast wilderness that is "home". 4 little tents & the lorry — & the cho* (about which I will digress tomorrow, if there's time). At the moment I must stop, and after sitting up here, quite alone with the wind, the moon, the stars, the whole immense vastness of Africa and the Serengeti with the mysterious universe all around and very real, creep into my bed and build up enough energy in the minute atom that is Jane for tomorrow. And you will have to excuse the complexity & length of the preceding sentence. I am actually quite tired & it is very late, & we are getting up at 5.30 tomorrow to try & see rhino. So for now your tiny atom bids you goodnight.

* i.e. Lavatory!

[Early September 1957]

. . . I adore working for Louis! He wrote this letter for me to pop in this morning. You see what he says about me working to be a Research Assistant? Well, he is getting hold of a very wealthy man & is going to try & get enough money to create such a post for me to fill. Isn't it super! And there is the vaguest possible chance that little me may have the chance to go right out into the wilds of the Northern Frontier for two or 3 months to study a strange tribe of chimpanzees who may be a new species, or sub-species. That is too heavenly to even think about. He says (Louis) that it might be hard as I'm a woman & one has to get the help of the D.C.* there. So I said he was to leave that part entirely to me!! . . .

---

* District commissioner.

P.O. Box 658,
Nairobi.
[Mid-September 1957]

Darling Mummy,

I have been going to write for the last few days, but have been waiting for a letter from at least one member of the family. Complete silence. I am writing to you particularly because it is your questions that I want to answer, and one or two things which I want to communicate to you. This is the very first moment to myself I have had since arriving at the Museum — it certainly makes a difference when one has a lot to do of the sort of thing one likes. But now we have caught up on the last two months' letters etc. and there is more time for even nicer things — Mr. Williams, the bird man is showing me about birds, teaching me the main groups, etc. Mr. Carcasson, the entomologist is helping me begin my study of spiders, Norman, the technologist is all set to teach me casting. And, naturally, Louis shows me everything! He is off to Nakuru this afternoon to give evidence at a hand writing case* — and, naturally, is taking his personal secretary with him! It should be great fun as he is going to show me a delightful sounding place called Hell's Gate on the way there, by Lake Naivasha. Then, after the case we are meeting the mayor and other high up members of Nakuru County Council to discuss the plans for making Lake Nakuru into a bird sanctuary.

Last week I had to entertain a charming Portuguese professor who came to see Louis who was out. I had to talk to him for three quarters of an hour, and at the end of it, when we had discussed art, archaeology, architecture, history, and music, he told Louis that he had had a wonderful time, that I was so interesting because I had such a wide outlook and so many interests, and he invited me out to lunch on Monday. Unfortunately he had to leave earlier than he had intended, and so wrote a charming note saying he would be delighted if I could join him for lunch in Rome!! Also he would love me to visit him in Lisbon, stay with him and his wife, and see the

---

* Handwriting analysis was one of Louis's many areas of expertise.

Museum there — the Arts Museum of which he is Curator. He studied in Oxford so we had long talks about it.

On Sunday I went out with Louis and another — and very weedy — V.I.P. seeing some of the prehistoric sites. It was a lovely day — Gamble's Cave in particular is most enchanting. They have excavated it and there are countless levels, one after the other, of all the prehistoric people who lived in the cave by the lake shore. . . .

As it is nearly lunch time and we are off after lunch, and as I want to post this before we leave, I must get down to the essentials. The rest can quite well wait until I write again to tell you all about Nakuru and the Mayor — and I am having dinner with Brian* the evening I get back.

What I am really writing about is this. You will have realized that I couldn't possibly come back before Christmas. It would not be fair to this wonderful opportunity I have to stay in this job only a few months. Dr. Leakey goes on home leave next year, probably about July, and the plan is for me to return with him. While he is there I may have to help him carry on with his fossil horse research at the Natural History Museum. As Judy will be in London too, the obvious answer is for you, Jif and me to have a flat there. But I am still jumping on past what I want to say. I have thought and thought about you coming out here. And I can't make up my mind that it would be the best way of spending the money I shall have saved up. You can still do that if you think you would love it — but would you like the heat? And what would you do while I was working? etc. etc. So I have thought of an alternative, which seems to me to be a better plan. And this is that I should meet you somewhere on the way home and we shall have one — or even two months holiday — and that will depend on whether you can save up any money too. I have worked it out that I shall need £300 for my return fare, your return fare to wherever it is and back, and the holiday. So far my thoughts have turned to Rome and possibly Venice as well, Spain — or, indeed, wherever else you would like. So would you please start

---

* Brian Herne. It appears that Jane had not yet explained to her family who Brian was.

thinking about this seriously and deciding where best you would like to go, which place or places best appeal to you — or whether you would still rather come out here. I still don't really think you would like it. Only I have been getting rather worried — a few months ago I wrote saying it was practically arranged for you to come out — since when you have heard nothing and so, naturally, will have presumed that it was just a passing fancy and one which I had then proceeded to forget just because a fascinating job came along and I was particularly happy. Although perhaps you know, really, that I am not a person like that. I hope so anyhow. So now you will please to think about it.

I am now really getting down to collecting instruments for the Mummerys* with Louis's help — I havn't ever forgotten them. Would they like a photograph of a very, very early paleolithic instrument — practically the first ever made — a type of whistle? I was hoping to get a cast, but the one here is a cast already, so that is not possible.

Lousi (sorry!) Louis has just come up and said that if you come out here you can go to his house boat on Lake Victoria for 3 weeks and I can come with you. Also he can think of lots of places up country where you could stay and I could come for weekends. I still worry about the heat. It's never hotter than a heat wave in London, but I know you and the sun. Anyway, I now leave every decision in your hand. It would be fun if you did come out — it would also be fun to meet en route for England. So please do think about it very seriously. Now I must quickly do some letters before we set out.

Tons & tons of love to all,
[Jane]

[Probably October 1957]

Darling Family,

"The cat's away"....... Not that he keeps his mice in great order when he's here, but it does mean that the work I have accumulated

---

* Family friends in England who collected old and rare musical instruments.

can stay in a pile unobserved. And it can worry about itself when he gets back and, for now, stay in obscurity. Anyway, thanks for all your letters. I had one from you, Olly, which you wrote ages and ages ago, and posted to Olduvai apparently without a stamp. So Hamish sent it on to me from there where it had arrived by sea! Anyway, thanks for it, and for the other one. I do hope that by now you have had another parcel from Hamish — I thought you and Douglas could nibble cakes off them at Sunday tea, or put out a few of the sweets from the little rustling paper bags. They are rather attractive, don't you think? Thanks also for your letters, Mummy and Danny.

My situation here is really getting more and more tricky every day. Old Louis really is infantile in his infatuation and is suggesting the most impossible things. I have absolutely no intention of getting involved with him in the ways he suggests. For example, this weekend he left for a handwriting case in Mombasa on Friday. And suggested I should meet him on the way back to see Savo National Park. But imagine my dismay when, just before leaving, he handed me a railway ticket and said he would meet the train at 12 MIDNIGHT!!! We were to camp at the entrance to the Park so that we could go in as soon as it opened in the morning! In actual FACT it would have been O.K. I know I can trust him. He's much too fond of me for any monkey business. But suppose it got round? Suppose Mary got to hear of it? And, more than all that, it is the principle of the thing that is the most important. Don't you agree? I couldn't tell him all this just before he left as the room was full of the Full Board of Trustees, whose minutes I had just been taking. He rang up yesterday, and Hillings was in the room so I had to make an excuse, saying I had flue — which was true, but it wasn't worse, as I told him, but better. I caught it from Brian last week — oh yes, there is a lot to come about this Brian who you seem to think I have not mentioned in my letters. But let me finish about this first. The Technologist, Norman, is an absolute sweetie — and he too is madly in love with me — really in love actually. He knows all about Louis — the other staff may guess, but he, because he likes me so much, knows. He is the one who made me the house outside for little Levi, and is always doing things for me. He told me, roaring with mirth, that it had gone too far when Louis came and asked <u>him</u> for mealworms (which he breeds for various technical reasons, for use in cleaning etc.) so that he (Louis) could give them to me for Levi. Norman said to me afterwards that if anyone gave me his mealworms for Levi it was going to be him! But the other Sunday morning, after I had been out late on the Saturday and was having a well needed sleep (no more getting to look like I did before leaving England thank you — my lesson was well learnt!), I was, as I say, sleeping peacefully, when I became aware of bang bang bang on the door. Eventually I shoved on my dressing gown and opened the door. A hand appeared round the corner with a red rose — a token of his love. I ask you! At 8.30 on a Sunday morning! He really does behave like a child over this — and I begin to see why Mary has taken to the brandy. The trouble is that one simply can't get annoyed with him. He is such a complete darling and so childish and means so well. But he has a horrid habit of making one feel a pig when really one knows it is for the best. For example, and this is typical, I was talking to Norman once instead of having a Kikuyu lesson with him, as I often do in the lunch hour. He was hurt. So instead of being annoyed or anything he went and hammered a lot of waterproofing over Levi's cage. You see! And then I felt quite mean. However, I have Norman on my side. It was he who took me to the station to fetch back the money.* I do feel also a bit mean about letting him know everything, but dash it all, I'm not going to have all the staff thinking I'm madly in love with Louis — it would be too sordid. . . . Forgive all this, but it is rather an important and fundamental problem I think — you will see vaguely what it is I am getting at when I tell you more about Brian — is your curiosity about Brian being aroused!

Right. I will now unwhet your curiosity and tell you about Brian from the beginning. And right away I must admit something I am ashamed of where Brian is concerned — I have judged a character wrongly from a first impression, and not only his, but those of his friends also. I don't like to do that. Mind you, I did not make a bad

---

* A refund for the ticket to Savo.

mistake — I did not take a nice person for a nasty one. I just took a negative point of view — decided that I did not particularly like a certain crowd of people who have now turned out to be the <u>nicest</u> and most sincere that I have met since arriving here — of young people that is.

So. Brian is the son of the camp manager at Ngorongoro — he was lying in plaster from head to foot when I first met him as he had been in a lorry that had gone over the edge of the escarpment there — we saw it on the way to Olduvai, when the breakdown lorry was trying to pull it up. The poor boy had both femurs jammed up into his abdomen, breaking the pelvis on both sides. He was in plaster for 4 months — should have been longer. As soon as he was out the madcap got straight into his brother's M.G. and drove to Arusha, stayed there for a week, and then came to Nairobi — still hardly able to walk more than 8 steps at a time (Incidentally it was not his fault, the accident. The lorry was being driven by an African. He was trying to change down and couldn't get into the lower gear — and the brakes went. He managed to steer it round about 8 of the sharp corners, but the slope is very steep coming down the mountain, and they were getting faster and faster. Just imagine the feeling. The African was killed). Anyway, Brian turned up at the Museum for Hamish's address — and <u>not</u> to see me. We hadn't clicked at all when we met at the Rest Camp at the Crater. But then he came to see me again, and then he asked me out. This was the occasion when I met some of his friends. An Italian couple, and a family of Afrikaans called Enough — (Eenoff). That evening I just didn't sort of get on with any of them — not even Brian very much. However, Brian persisted, and I went out with him on his own. He is a White Hunter — very young, and has an external layer of the typical hard bitten and tough white hunter about him. But when I got him on his own it was incredibly easy to get through that layer, and I began to realize that the character underneath — and by no means hidden by this external layer — is one of the very nicest I've come across out here. Loyal, honest, faithful, etc., etc. (Incidentally, I'm not saying all this prior to announcing an engagement or anything! It has just struck me that that is what it might all sound like.) Brian was only supposed to be in Nairobi for 10 days. He stayed 3 weeks or more — because of yours truly. And I went out with him quite a lot and found him nicer and nicer. Gordon — dear Gordon* — likes him very much apparently. . . .

I started [this] letter on Saturday morning. And had a funny day. Let me relate it because I had better. Just before lunch Gillian popped in to say "Jambo".† She knew that I should have been meeting Louis at Savo & wanted to know what I had said when he rang the day before. I was just telling her when we heard a familiar Land Rover (the silencer is broken). Louis! And (I regret to admit this) I quite lost my nerve & my head & obeyed blind instinct. I fled. Out through John Williams' room, through Bob Carcasson's room — before their astonished eyes — & down to Norman. My heart was literally pounding & my legs were shaking. I stayed there for 5 minutes recovering from the shock & then went up to face the music. (It all must sound incredibly stupid to you!) Anyway, he wasn't in the office but downstairs looking for me. Gillian had gone — she told me today (Monday) that she had fled so as not to answer any questions! John Williams must have got vast amusement out of the situation — he wasn't born yesterday, he has eyes, & he knows Louis. Then Louis came in. "Why did you lie to me?" & while I was telling him that the telephone is not always private both ends, he said, coldly, "You have let me down — let me down by not speaking the truth". And went. And here again I was childish & ran to dear Norman & cried just a wee bit on his shoulder & then got over it. I was just going to set off home when Louis drove up. "I've come back to apologize. I was rude & beastly & I'm sorry". So I told him he had [no] reason to be, & it was really I who needed forgiving. And we went out the lunch club gallery, raided the kitchen & had lunch together, & then he gave me a lift into Nairobi. He had bought 3 bunches of sweet peas & left them, with a letter (written on the Friday night when I should have met him) outside my door — before coming to the Museum. . . .

---

* Gordon Harvey.
† Hello.

Oh dear, there is such a lot to tell you. Next, about Mrs. Mitchel — I'm not sure of the spelling but the Scottish way. She is one of Hamish's aunts — sorry if I've told you.* She lives next door & has 3 children & is <u>sweet.</u> When Mish heard I wasn't having breakfast he said, "Oh, I'll fix you up with my Aunt". Which I took as a joke. Then I met her — at the Airport seeing Mish off — & she said "You're Jane? Well, you're coming to breakfast". It was most embarrassing but she persisted so now I have breakfast with her each morning. They are a delightful family — in return I am to baby sit for them. (Though 'Baby' is hardly correct as the youngest is 6 (Hilary), then Arnold, about 8, & Fiona who is, I should say, 9 or 10.) <u>Please</u> Mummy, will you write to her to say how kind she is, etc., etc. Please. And Louis is hurt because you havn't written before. Also, Olly, Clo was <u>most</u> upset because you never wrote to thank her for the hanky. <u>Most</u> upset. And so please will you, & if so congratulate her on winning with her mare & foal at the Royal Show. Thanks.

Last Monday — it now seems months ago because this weekend seemed <u>weeks</u> — Louis took me into the Kikuyu Reserve. And I had the most <u>wonderful</u> time. We went into a council of elders in "Chief Charles'" village, & there Louis spoke to them about the new Governmental plans for land consolidation — which are <u>wicked.</u> Then we went into Charles' house — a proper house, but small, & like a European peasant's house. Clean. We met his old mother. Her husband was a dreadful Mau Mau — former chief of the village. He is now a prisoner, & her elder son is a political one in England — he killed one of his brothers in front of her & very nearly her as well. But she is such a sweet old lady. She only spoke Kikuyu — but she says that although she knows her husband was wicked, if only he could come back to her she could die in peace, feeling God was with her. Charles' wife spoke a little English & was sweet, & their two daughters are both in London, one doing Domestic Science & the other training to be a Nurse. We had tea & sandwiches & bananas,

---

* Eve Mitchell lived in a house very near Jane's residence on Protectorate Road in Nairobi and became her good friend.

& then left them for Harry Thuku. Harry was one of Louis' boy-hood friends, extremely intelligent. He began one movement & so inspired his followers that it ran away from him, as these things sometimes do. In order to convince his followers that they could gain nothing by being so wild he allowed himself to be deported to England — otherwise he would still have inspired fanatical follow-ers. But the authorities knew he was not anti-British & have al-lowed him back. He now plays a very prominent role in African af-fairs — behind the scenes.* We were going there to meet several African V.I.P's so that Louis could discuss land consolidation, a very, very real problem just now, & incredibly tricky.

Well, his house, built himself, would have done credit to <u>any</u> mid-dle class European, & was 50% better than most of them into the bargain. He has a lovely garden, & is starting coffee behind the house — he has 2,000 trees already. He was charming, & so were the others. There was a minister (a church one that is), the under minister for African affairs — really nice & most intelligent — a wealthy farmer (who spoke no English) & another one, looking <u>so</u> like William! — who did. And a young chap who was very good looking & most brilliant & witty. They had their talk — for 2 hours — in Kikuyu. But after that tea came in — 3 kinds of cakes, lovely china, & a little table each — and they all spoke in English for my benefit. I can't tell you how honoured I felt. I am now having Ki-kuyu lessons! The wife of the non-English farmer we had met be-forehand. Louis had gone to his house to see him not realizing that he was going to be with Harry. She gave me 12 eggs. Wasn't it sweet?

Now, Harry's wife is at this moment in London to perfect her English so that she can better help her husband to entertain — Eu-ropeans often stay in his house you see. It would be rather nice if

---

* Harry Thuku founded the Young Kikuyu Association. In 1922, he urged his fol-lowers to protest the issuing of compulsory identity cards by the British and so was arrested. When several thousand supporters turned up at the Norfolk Hotel to protest his detention, frightened Kenyan police opened fire and killed at least twenty-five people. Thuku was exiled to the northern frontier, and his Young Kikuyu As-sociation disintegrated — soon replaced by the more militant Kikuyu Central Asso-ciation.

you went to see her, Mummy? Would you like to? If so I will send you her address & get Louis to write to her. She is called Tabitha, & very sweet according to Louis. She is going to be away for 18 months. . . .

Honestly, I <u>MUST</u> stop — though there is really more news. I will write it in another letter.

Lots & lots of love,
Jane

[November 1957]

Darlingest Family,

Thank you all for your letters — you can't imagine how eagerly I await them all. . . . I must apologize for not writing for so long. But all sorts of things have been happening, & your little Jane has scarcely had time to write letters — or even to do any washing or ironing so that she has almost been reduced to going to work in a birthday suit. . . .

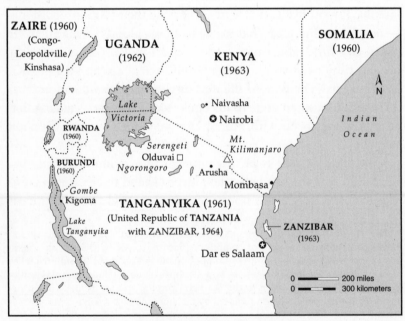

East Africa, 1957–1966

When I last wrote I think I was off to Ngorongoro. . . . Brian was meeting me in Arusha, half way, & I was lucky enough to get a lift — through Louis — with Noel Simon — a big wig, being the Director of the Wild Life Society of Kenya. He was going there for a big meeting on the Serengeti. On the way I saw one animal I'd not seen before, the beautiful Gerenuk. This is one of the antelopes, about the size — height rather — of an Alsatian, but with a very long neck. It loves to eat the leaves of trees, & by standing on its hind legs & reaching up with its long neck, it manages very well.

I was staying in Arusha that night — there are two hotels & I was in the best — a lovely room overlooking the garden. Hotels out here are not one compact building as they are in England — except in places like Nairobi. They sprawl, & usually are only one floor with gardens & courtyards in between. The New Arusha is, actually, fairly compact, but in a lot of the up country hotels a lot of the rooms are separate 'bandas' — round hut affairs with thatched roofs — very attractive.

That evening in Arusha was not particularly fascinating. We met David* & a photographer called André & had some dinner at this famous 'Beehive'. The 'Beehive' is the be-all & end all of Arusha. It is a restaurant, coffee house, bar — & even night club, all rolled into one. But there was no one very nice there that night, & we did not stay out late.

The next morning I was booked out & waiting for Brian by 8 o'clock. I chatted to a very charming American who had just got back from a Safari — photographic. His name is Mr. Pon, and I thought he was quite sweet — about 50, for your information! I havn't yet started falling for handsom rich young Yankees!

Before leaving Arusha we went out to David's farm. He is under manager of a big coffee estate, recently taken over by a large company, & managed by a very charming Italian count, Marco. He & David live there, & are just getting the place into shape, getting the house properly furnished, etc. David is getting good money for a lad of 20. David came back to Arusha with us — a 10 minute drive — & we had a cup of coffee — at the Beehive of course! — before set-

---

* David Herne, Brian's younger brother.

ting off. The drive to Ngorongoro was very hot & very dusty. The country round there is lower than Nairobi & very much more tropical. There are a lot of palm trees, sugar cane etc. around the little streams. In between are great stretches of the real true Africa — yellow grass, patches of scrub, and the still, patient green of the acacia trees. We arrived at about 2.30 & found a cold lunch all spread out & awaiting us. Mrs. Herne — her name is Peggy & so I am to call her — is simply sweet, & David senior is a charming man as well. Peggy has to work very hard up there, in comparison with other wives out here. She has no cook, and the business of looking after the camp never stops. No sooner has she got the garden ship shape than the Elephants & buffalo trample it down & break the fence. She never seems to have time to sit down — which makes their house seem much more like an English one than most of them out here.

After lunch & talking to them a bit, Brian found a spare Land Rover and we went out to look for animals. We drove well off the beaten track & saw eland & water buck. And then we drove up the track through the Bamboo Forest which I have described before — the one Gordon drove Gillian & I along the very first time I ever went to the Crater. It is the sort of place where you can feel, & even <u>hear</u>, animals close by, & know they are there watching you, but seldom <u>see</u> anything. But luck was with us in a very, very big way.

Suddenly, lying across the track ahead of us, we saw a large cat lying — a leopard. It lay there, not moving. So Brian decided to get closer to try & take a photo. We shut the windows, as their dog, Hobo, was with us, & slowly edged the car forward. He let us get fairly close — let us say the distance of the front door to the swing door, & then got up, looked at us, & disappeared into the bamboo. Did I say 'disappeared'. When we drew level with the place, there he was, one or two yards off the track, setting peering at us through one or two bamboo stems. Brian found it almost impossible to believe — he has never before met a leopard one could watch like that. He was a lovely creature — a large & dark-spotted forest leopard, and his green eyes gazed with calm & deliberate interest at Hobo moving about inside the car. After about 3 minutes he rose, and slowly padded away out of sight — we could only watch him for a few steps before he was swallowed up into the bamboos. We went on up to the water hole, stayed there about 5 minutes, & then turned back. And the most incredible thing happened. About 100 yards further down the track from the place where we had seen the leopard — we suddenly saw him in front of us <u>again!</u> We just glimpsed a dark form disappearing. This time, when we reached the spot, he was lying just off the track in one of the buffalo tunnels — so that we could see him even better. We watched him for another 3 or 4 minutes before he went. Do you know, only 65% of the people out here see a leopard at all. And of that 65% only about 2% have ever seen one as clearly as we did that day. It is obvious that I was <u>intended</u> to come out & see animals.

We saw nothing more that day. It was very unfortunate that while I was there Gordon was away — on an anti-poaching operation in the other part of the park. He left me a letter saying how sorry he was.

That evening we all were asked if we could give dinner to a V.I.P. who was arriving for 2 nights. Edith was coming to dinner anyway. And it turned out to be none other than Noel Simon. He hadn't ever been to the Crater, and as the meeting was very much connected with it, had decided to take the opportunity of coming to see it.

This proved lucky for me, as it was arranged that Brian & I should go down with him the next day — & this gave us the benefit of the very best driver & guide. Amtiye is a really nice African & he knows that Crater like the back of his hand. He also knows how to handle the Land Rover when a rhino charges etc — which makes quite a difference.

I woke up early & it was a lovely morning. So I dressed & jumped out of the window to run to the edge of the crater. This was unfortunate. When I got back I found I had created quite a scene. Poor Brian had been rudely awakened from a deep sleep, by his Mother shaking him & saying "Where's Jane? Where's Jane?" To which Brian, somewhat naturally, replied by saying how the hell should he know, he didn't have radar on me, & I was probably in the Crater. Things were calm again when I got back.

Then followed quite the most wonderful wonderful day. We saw

8 rhino. I suggested we should drive up the hill where we had lunch with Gordon that day & from where we had seen so many rhino. Sure enough we saw 3 from there. So we got Amtiye to drive down. This little hill is right at the edge of the floor of the Crater, & behind it the country is not suitable for driving — not even Land Rovers. How he got through at all I don't know, what with holes & tree stumps & fallen logs. I was up on the roof & how I stayed there I don't know. But we saw our Rhino. We were looking for the 3 of them, all together. Brian thought they were on the right, Amtiye on the left. It was me who saw them — directly behind us. One had a good long horn. They were coming straight for us — but until they got very close they didn't even know we were there. Then they suddenly snorted & tossed their heads — but were in no mood to fight. Just as they had gone we saw another, to the right, & I saw, from my elevated perch, that she had a baby. She was making for the open plains at a brisk trot — so we followed her — an incredibly bumpy journey, during which only by miracle was the car saved from over-turning. But we got out at last & soon came up with Mamma & in-fant. She charged us, twice, & baby thought it was all a huge joke, capering round mum & making her more nervous than ever. Gosh, he was a darling.

The herds of zebra & wildebeest were quite fantastic in their numbers — it really gave one an odd feeling to be amongst so many animals all at once. And I then saw another animal new to me — the wild dog. These [are] pretty animals, a little like Alsatians. They hunt in large packs, & their method of hunting is very cruel. They have tremendous staying power & stamina & they just run after a poor animal until it tires & then close in, snapping off chunks of meat & beginning their meal even before the wretched prey is down. We came across a pack of 14 & were able to get pretty close.

We had lunch near the little cabin in the forest — known as Lerai. There is a cold stream & banana groves — & it is quite lovely. After lunch we stayed there for about an hour — at midday it is too hot to see animals. They are nearly all resting in the shade except for the plains herds. Brian was pretty tired. Although he is walking much better now, his hip still gets pretty sore, & it has a shocking jolting in the Land Rover. He went into the cabin & had a little sleep on one of the bunks. Simon read a magazine — & I climbed one of the huge & gnarled old fig trees growing over the stream. And then I got so near to a herd of Tommies that they were practically grazing all round me.

We set out again, by now the clouds were gathering & it looked a little like rain. We waited & watched 7 half-grown lions waking up from their daylight sleep, playing together like kittens. One of them, named by Brian the Spit, with the most beautiful eyes & the start of an absurd little mane, was playing with an empty tin. If one of the others tried to take it away, they got a smack over the ears from the Spit. We think that in a year or two he will be the most sought after young blood on the Serengeti!

We met one other old lion, a little scruffy in his mane, but quite handsom nonetheless. Then we came upon 3 altogether — A lion & two lionesses with a 3rd lioness some way away. One of them — the lion — let us go right up so that we were almost touching him. Simon, with his telephoto lens, got simply half a face in his view finder! After about 10 minutes he got up & peered in at Simon — nearly bumping his nose on the lens! He was a wee bit annoyed, & for half a second Brian thought he was going to bound onto the roof — where he & I were. Well, we wern't sitting on the roof — merely standing on the seat. But it was on the way out that we saw quite the most heavenly & beautiful lion. In fact I realized then that I hadn't really seen a lion before. He was huge, beautifully proportioned, sleek, glossy, & with a thick silky black mane, & elbow tufts about 4 inches long. And he was wild & unused to humans — he wouldn't let us anywhere near him. We were whizzing along the side of the Crater slope — Brian insisted we sit inside the car, because we really thought it was going over at any minute we were at such an angle. We only had to get one of the lower wheels into a hole — & over we'd have gone. But we didn't!

All we didn't see that day were elephants. And, in fact, I began to think the elephants didn't love me because though they were all round, we were never lucky. . . .

After lunch cum tea (at 4.30) [on Sunday] Brian did his first shooting since the accident as Peggy wanted some guinea fowl. He nearly killed himself by walking far too much on his leg — but men will be men. And David (senior) drove the car into a pot hole & tore a ligament in his arm, nearly fainted, & was in agony all the way home. So we were a subdued little party that got back rather late that night. David kept moaning and groaning all night. Suddenly I was woken from my sleep by an animal jumping through the window. There are no lights there of course — only lamps. And I had no torch. So I shouted out "Brian, there's something in my room". They all rushed in — Brian leapt out of bed so fast he nearly broke the other hip! Peggy found a torch as she ran — & standing in the middle of my floor was — "<u>Hobo</u>"!! I shall <u>never</u> live that one down!!

The next day was my last. Brian & I just messed around & enjoyed ourselves. In the afternoon we went out for a long drive, returning at about 4.30 & intending to collect Peggy & take her to see if the leopard was there. As we got to the camp gate David senior stepped out. "I've got a nasty shock for you — Leakey's here". They told me I went quite white. I had told Peggy that she <u>must not</u> let him start off with me late in the afternoon, whatever happened. (Actually, Brian & his father had concocted a lovely plan. L.S.B. was due to arrive on the Tuesday — not Monday as he did. And they were going to spread me out in bed, surrounded by bottles & medicine!) Anyway, we rushed over to Peggy, who said she'd seen him, & he had said "But Jane <u>must</u> have got my note saying I'd changed my plans & was fetching her today". He was very nearly saying he refused to believe that I hadn't! Just at that moment the lorry arrived from Arusha — & the driver handed L.S.B.'s note to Peggy — before his eyes! Lovely! Anyway, she had told him we were out & probably wouldn't be back till 6.30 or so — so we leapt into the Land Rover, Brian & I, and fled! That last drive through the Bamboo — & we heard a rhino but no more — was exceptionally vivid & very beautiful. When we got back LSB was there — very tired as he'd been driving since 4 am.

We planned to start at 6 the next morning. Peggy rushed in to me at about 6.5 to say she'd just heard the Land Rover door slam —

LSB was sleeping in one of the cabins. I was up & dressed & ready in a few seconds. Peggy said goodbye, & tactfully disappeared so that Brian & I could tenderly bid each other farewell!

And then came the beautiful climax to that heavenly holiday. We got outside, & I was just getting into the Land Rover when the chap at the gate rushed up. "You can't go yet, there's an elephant outside the gate." Brian & I rushed out — & that's the closest I've ever been — as near as the tall boy & the Drawing room window! It was feeding. When it heard us (Brian purposely going very close & LSB coming too of course — both trying to get nearer!) it turned round & moved a few steps towards us, ears outstretched. Oh, it was heavenly. There is something about the African elephant that captures the whole magic of Africa — something majestic, awe inspiring, giant & rugged. Something that one knows could be incredibly savage & terrifying. So departure, instead of being the normal anticlimax, was just the opposite. . . .

We got back, in a positive deluge, at about 9.30 on the Tuesday evening. On the Tuesday afternoon Brian had driven his father to Arusha — as he couldn't drive because of his hurt arm. He'd promised to ring me on Wednesday — which he did at 2.30. Imagine my horror when I heard "David (junior) has been beaten up by the Masai. He's in hospital & it's touch & go". It was ghastly. It had just happened & Brian knew no details. . . . [so] in desperation we rang the hospital. Thank God we got a sensible person who told us Dave had a very bad cut on his head from a knife wound, a suspected broken arm, & was under morphia & suffering from shock — but was off the danger list. He'd lost gallons of blood — had a [transfusion] lasting 6 1/2 hours. Poor, poor Peggy. She does have unfair things to cope with.

I rang all over the place next morning to try & get hold of Brian. No good. Then I heard a very welcome voice on the phone — André the little photographer, had just arrived from Arusha, laden with messages from Brian. . . . David had been driving the Masai cattle off the maize — & been deliberately set on by 10 Morani — ie, warriors. Thank goodness only one of them had a knife — or scemi — or young David would not be alive now. How he crawled away from them — he couldn't stand — no one is quite sure. Anyway, the police who went after them were driven off the first time — but they are all caught now.

Brian had set off back over the 100 miles to Ngorongoro, taking his Father back & fetching Peggy. She, poor thing, had just had a ghastly fall on the concrete floor, landing on her coccyx. The day before she had hardly been able to move from her bed. When Brian & David senior arrived she had heard nothing about Dave's beating up. Poor thing. . . .

Does my work fascinate me or is it the hearts thrown at my feet — oh, the work — the atmosphere & nice & interesting people at the Museum, staff & otherwise, the fact that I can have animals, talk animals, study animals. And also that I can get time off when I want or need it.

As for the questions of leave or permanency when I come home next year. That I don't know a bit as it depends on a plan which is afoot — & which you will know of first as soon as I know if it is going to work. Anyway, you, Mamma, whether you like it or not, are coming out here, about the middle of next year, & we are going home together. If my present plans work out, anyway.

I have been out with Peter this weekend. You would all approve of him vastly. Clever, won essay prizes, Chesterham, 6ft 5ins, dark, fairly good looking, likes music & literature, good manners, good job, money, nice to his mother, excellent dancer, dresses well — etc. ideal you would say I expect — 28 years old.

However, just now, Brian is No.1. And now I had better stop as it is late, & I got to bed at 3 last night after dancing at the Mogambourth & eating a chinese meal — I tried chopsticks! And we stalked some giraffe this afternoon in the Rift Valley.

Tons & tons of love,
Your little Jane

[February 1958]

Darling Family,

Thank you for all your letters. I do so apologize for making you weep & for wasting your rouge & valderma, Olly! I'm not feeling miserable just now at all. I am sitting in my bed having chatted to Mrs. Ellis — who <u>adores</u> me & is always giving me cake, bath salts, & meat for Chimba. I had a bath in her flat & then thoroughly cleaned my room, cleaned the bathroom, tidied & changed Chimba's earth box. He is lying contentedly on the bed beside me, & it looks as though he has been reading "The Oxford Book of Mystical Verse". (Actually I have!!) I am waiting for Brian who may not turn up for hours as he is trying to get his car going with Paul. He got back from his safari, & the poor chap got stuck for 3 days with no water and food. He had <u>some</u> of each, but no decent food (he couldn't leave the car because of Masai) and had to drink rusty water from the petrol tank. He also got knocked over by a wounded buffalo — luckily it was so weak it only tore his trousers — but it was a close shave.

I have been given a HORSE!! Let me hasten to explain this stupendous phenomenon. You know I have been riding Shandy & trying to school him in jumping. Well, Mary suggested I should go over with them on Sunday to the Pony Club meeting — a ride of about 10 miles — 15. It was a nice ride — a whole contingent of us. The chief instructors are Major & Mrs. Piper, whom I had never met before. Their P.C. doo's* are quite different from ours — <u>much</u> more fun. Gay & carefree & everyone happy. The kids have much bigger horses (you can't get them small) & they ride better, on the whole. More confidence. Anyway, they had a treasure hunt in the morning, & then, after feeding the horses, the kids had picnic lunches & all the grown ups went into the lovely old house for a <u>vast</u> spread — cold meats etc. There were at <u>least</u> 12 dogs of all kinds. (not to eat!!)

Then came jumping. Eventually I got on my devil & he knew <u>at once</u> that it was jumping. The day before I had jumped him & we got on <u>excellently.</u> But there had been no other horses. This time he decided to go backwards. People were laughing & leaping out of the way — & suddenly he wizzed, through a row of scattering old ladies, towards two tables laden with mugs of beer, tea, cakes, etc. The panic was comic. Everyone grabbed something from the table

---

* Pony Club events.

& by the time we hit them not much damage was done. Richard threw a bucket of water at our tail but Shandy didn't much seem to mind. So Major Piper came to the rescue with a hunting crop. That did the trick. We jumped fairly well — by which I mean relative to <u>Shandy</u> & not normal equestrian standards! i.e. we went over <u>all</u> the jumps but one or two were rather the worse for wear afterwards & I had a blister!

Eventually we rode home, & I talked to Mrs. Piper. She asked if I had a horse & if I wanted one. I said that when I <u>did</u> get one I wanted a really nice one I could school myself, & as I was going home this year it seemed silly.

Well, Mary Leakey rang today. The Pipers have a 15.2 thoroughbred. They were going to sell it, but would love me to have it & ride it until I go to England! Isn't it wonderful! It will have to be stabled at the Leakeys' at the moment, but later on I must find somewhere nearer Nairobi because petrol will be too expensive going all out there.

I have to leave my present place, which is a shame. I am going out to Jean Hyde for March, & then moving, with possibly Jean to share, into one of the Museum Flats — quite ideal. Did you know Sally <u>may</u> be coming out?!! If she does, you, Mummy, she & I will share this flat together. Your passage is booked for 1st September, Hurking Clan. I forgot the time it leaves London Airport. (I thought I'd better let you know!)

Tomorrow Mary & I want to save a pony that is to be shot as unmanagable. Muggins has volunteered to ride it & find out what all the nonsense is about! I have got the afternoon off, & we are going over to Limuru. If it is quite tractable we have an owner all ready for it. If not, Mary & I are going to school & sell it & share the profit! So your little Jane is getting into the horsey world again. The Royal Show is in September, so if this horse of mine is any good I shall enter it (don't know its sex yet!) & you, Ma, will feel it's like the good old days. The Pipers want me to be assistant instructress — which also rings a bell!!

I'm getting a car this month. I have to because of going out to live with Jean.

You ask for a snap of the Museum. Oddly enough I walked all round about 6 times the other lunch time & couldn't find a suitable place to get even one. I did take a shot, but it's so big & sort of straggly it won't fit in. But I'm blowed if I send <u>any</u> more photos until you send <u>me</u> some. So there!

Incidentally, Mummy, what did you write to Papa* about his being a boy friend of mine? I am highly intrigued to hear from you. He has been telling me all this about what you wrote to him, him to you & you back again, & I should be interested to hear your version of how it all started.

Now, one little remonstration to <u>you,</u> Ma. You can't have understood me properly over one thing re. Brian. You say that (a) I don't go out with other men because B wouldn't like it, (b) why don't I try peeling layers off what I call 'stuffy' young men. Well, (a) I am <u>sure</u> I said that at present I have no <u>desire</u> to go out with anyone else, except occasionally, & therefore I am <u>NOT</u> unnecessarily giving up my freedom of personality. I did go out with Ian the other day, & I had a horrible time trying to stop him kissing me — though I enjoyed driving the M.G. (b) there's no question of me peeling off layers (here's B. I think). It is, without exception, so far, <u>they</u> who try & do the peeling. I'm <u>sure</u> I've told you that all the young men out here have only one idea — to go to bed with one. (It's not B.). . . .

Oh, dear . . . I've done it again. Pip† on the telephone. He's got it too. What the devil am I to do with all these middle aged married men. They hang in multitudinous garlands from every limb and neck I've got, and most of them are so charming. Hey ho. What did you do some 24 years ago Mummy. I bet you never guessed when I lay so small and waxey in your arms!

Tons & tons of love,
Jane

---

* Louis Leakey.
† Major Piper, chief instructor of the Pony Club.

[June 1958]

Most darling of families — Hail!

I hope you are all as hale and flourishing as I am. My family is growing still, but becoming more and more adorable. The puppy simply could not be more sweet and charming. I have christened her Tana (after a big river full of crocs where Brian is always saying he would take me if he had a Land Rover). She is inseparable friends with Kip now, and they sleep curled up in a box by my bed. Kombo, unfortunately, is still in my bed, but is moving out tonight as Sally is, at this moment (it being Saturday morning) buying him a hot-water bottle. We still havn't got our big cage, but plans for it are forging ahead, wire netting may be materializing from 3 different sources (or it may not!), plans are made for getting the wood on Monday, and Derek is going to help us build it, having just built a very nice one of his own — for his large bush baby, Boozy, who has now, somehow or other, become incorporated into our family. She simply adores Kombo, and the two sit, in each other's arms, and Boozy licks his face while he shuts his eyes in bliss. Poor little Levi is very out of it. Boozy was sleeping with us, in the animal room with Levi, but he was scared by her — for no reason, because she is very willing to love him as well. But as he refused and spurned her love, being all on edge after Kombo caught him when they were playing the other day, it seemed mean to leave him in anguish all night. So Boozy now visits us from about 6.30 to 10. All afternoon Kombo is tied up outside the flats, to the window, on a long string, and Kip and Tana play around with him. This is a highly satisfactory arrangement. It means we can thoroughly air the animal room, and clean it up, and also they get sunshine and fresh air. In this way we can keep the animal room under control — otherwise it's quite impossible. Then, at about 6 o'clock when it starts getting a bit chilly, they all go in. At first we used to have them all loose in the drawing room from about 7.0 onwards. But this got chaotic. I found it impossible to eat more than 2 mouthfuls of my own supper. There would be Kombo and Kip helping themselves from my plate, a bush baby stretching out and seizing handfuls from my fork as they sat on my shoulder, and two pleading eyes from such a charming little puppy face on the floor, that a few titbits had to be spared in that direction as well. So now they are fed in their own room while we have supper, except for Levi who can never eat when Kombo is around, so he has his little plateful in the sitting room, and the puppy, who has hers in the kitchen. In this way everything is well under control, and there is hardly any mess. They come out after supper, but Kombo, after breaking two vases and a picture, and getting very unmanageable in that he refused to be caught when it was time for him to go back, is now tied to the table from where he can do no serious damage. . . .

Sally and I are now really getting our flat organized a bit better. We had a thoroughly good go at cleaning up and polishing yesterday afternoon. Gerry sent me home at 4.0 as there was nothing whatsoever to do, and I polished all the furniture with O'Ceder polish, and Sally said the smell on the duster reminded her of the Birches. We still need a fridge, a toaster and some lamps. Brian and I got a lovely desk lamp the other day, from a queer old Indian who we are sure is a Receiver. This lamp — one of the ones with a wiggly bendy stem — we got for Shs 25. Brand New. The shop next door happened to be an electricity shop, and, as it so happened, there was exactly the same lamp there. So we marched in, leaving our identical one in the car, to ensure the cost. Shs 45!!! So we didn't do too badly I think.

Little Tana stays with me in the museum all morning. In the afternoons, except for twice a week, Sally is in the flat and can look after them all. She is terribly good. When she wants to do widdle she whines, so I carry her down. All the rest of the morning she sleeps in her box. She has just woken up now, as it is 12.30 and nearly lunch time. She isn't being a nuisance though — just gazing up at me with her brown eyes, resting her chin on the edge of the box. So sweetly melting in fact, that I have now picked her up and she is on my lap biting the typewriter rubber. For a purely bred dog I think she is going to be incredibly intelligent and sensible. You remember I told you I might have one of Clo's dogs, and that it fell through? Well, that little dog is the most highly strung creature imaginable. This little girl is really sensible and takes everything in her stride. She hasn't been homesick once. Sally has instructions to buy her a rubber bone this morning, and Kip a ping pong ball which he can crack against the wall. Kombo really should have artificial flowers to play with I think! Flowers have an irresistible fascination for him.

Incidentally, I must apologize for my ghastly typing today. I don't know what's happened, but I keep putting all my letters back to front. It should be worse than ever now because Tana is biting me with her sharp little teeth. Actually, I can't possibly get on, and as it's nearly lunch time I shall stop this now, and continue anon. . . .

But can you imagine how paradisical (if that is the correct word?) it is for me having all these animals round? Of course, they do make a hell of a lot of work, one can't get away from that. But once we have the cage it will be a lot less, and they are worth every minute of it. Kip insisted on coming into my bed last night, and flatly refused to sleep with Tana. This made Kombo jealous, but he just had to be jealous, because I was too tired to tackle Kip for long. And he was comical and wouldn't get up this morning. In the end I just stripped the bed and exposed him to the hard light of morning. Once up he had a lick and a stretch and felt fine and on top of the world. He wanted a real game with Tana — but poor Tana, who always wakes at about 6.0 was by then ready for another sleep! And so it goes on.

Sally really is a hoot. I was thinking about a Siamese the other day, and Brian said he thought that was a very good idea. So I asked Sally what she thought, and she thought it would be very nice. So then I began wondering how to go about getting one. "Oh, you don't need to worry" says Sal, "Now you've decided that you want one it will just turn up!" So she won't be very surprised when she hears that one is coming next week. . . . I hope Clo does come and share the flat because she will really be good fun. I now propose to end.

Tons & tons of love,
Jane

The Birches — etc.
[December 30, 1958]

My dear Sally,

Your letters come pouring in with all your news, and I am so dilatory. I do hope you had a merry Christmas — we, of course, had a simply wonderful one. We arrived safely back in England, to a smiling London — sunny & with a lovely nip in the air — crikey — of course I've written since getting back, surely? Anyway, we were welcomed with a red carpet & Union Jacks, & it was <u>SUCH</u> fun. On Christmas Eve Peter* rang up to say please could he come on Boxing Day with my Christmas present!! Eric also arrived on that day — & oh Sally, how lovely the house was. Jif's friend Rosemary arrived at 2.30 on Boxing Day, with her flute. Peter had his. There was music all day long. In between Peter & I sat in front of the fire, on the floor reading poetry and Shakespeare. Peter fitted so wonderfully into the family that we all — including him — felt he'd been here for ages & that we'd known him all our lives. Our room was the most <u>fantastic</u> sight — literally covered in books, music, & instruments. Peter discovered the violin and played that as well — & we got Jif castanets & a tambourine at Barcelona. Also an Arab pipe from Aden, & there is her Kenya drum! Eric has just had a tape recorder so we recorded Judy playing, solos, duets, singing and reciting. Funniest was when Rix had it on & we didn't know. It's the most wonderful toy. . . .

Gordon rang twice this afternoon, from London, but I was out, buying a coat — on the Never, Never! He told Danny he probably wouldn't ring again so I have to catch the 10.20 tomorrow & meet him at the Regent Palace at 1.30! Oh, I didn't tell you, but Peter brought me the most lovely skirt for Christmas. Wasn't it brilliant. Otherwise I'd have had <u>nothing</u> to wear. As it is I have that & a coat, & can borrow a jumper from someone, I hope. I have been living in my Barcelona trousers & boots & a jumper from the ship since I arrived home. Actually it is lovely warm & spring like

---

* She'd met Peter, a junior officer of the ship, on the voyage home.

weather mostly. Christmas Eve was the worst day — really raw & freezing.

I had Leakey's letter about the animals arriving, & a cable, & so am off to meet them. Gordon, Peter, Kip is my programme for the New Year festivities. I admit that I am looking forward to meeting the last of those gentlemen most!! Dear, dear, Kip. I am taking with me a hot water bottle & blankets and Peter is driving us all home in his car — he only went yesterday — & will be back the day after to-morrow!

Poor Olly is in bed with a stinking cold & I have a foul feeling that I'm brewing one up myself. I have a stinking throat today & am living on Gee's.

You & Nairobi & everything now seems so far away. I have slid so easily back into the family that it is as though I had never left. Nothing has changed. Danny & Audrey are the same as ever. Jif hasn't altered more than a scrap, the house, the shops, Bourne-mouth — all is the same. It is lovely. And it is lovely to be in an artis-tic atmosphere again. I realize now, more than ever before, that I can never live wholly without it. It feels so heavenly to be able to just sit in front of the fire & talk for hours — of cabbages & kings — poetry, literature, art, music, philosophy, religion. It's wonder-ful, marvellous, terrific. I wish Leakey would realize what it really means to me. And I feel so lucky that I've met someone like Peter with whom I can share all of these things. He is frantically artis-tic — crazily artistic. I am going to stay with them over this Ball weekend, & am really looking forward to it. Dear old Peter.

He is the very first, of all my boyfriends . . . whom the family have delighted to receive to their bosoms. I am longing for you to meet him.

I wrote to Hans on the ship — he wants to see me on the 6th Jan — which is, of course, quite impossible. I can't spend all my time rushing up & down to London. But it really hurts me more than anything to have to write and say 'No'. Still, there will be so much time when I get to London.

Sally, I will stop now, because I must wash my hair. Thank you for all that you've done — oh, if I asked you for Browning, forget it. I have a Browning here. But an exercise book & odd things on paper you come across, please could you bring.

V. <u>Imp.</u> <u>Please</u> could you send all the animal stamps you can find from that cupboard. I find I've forgotten them. This is urgent as I have just been given 100 animal ones & the person wants to see my collection! I don't want the album but if there are any animal ones in it could you take them out. Please. Any news of Clo?

Tons & tons of love to you,
& — oh dear,
only to Kombo & Thimble!
Jane

4

WAITING

1959–1960

> It was a whole year from the time when I left Africa to the time
> when I actually arrived among the chimpanzees. Sometimes . . . I
> felt sure I would never get there. Surely, I told myself, it's all too
> good to be true.
>
> — *My Life with the Chimpanzees*

B Y THE TIME Jane Goodall left Kenya Colony at the end of
1958, Louis Leakey had already seriously embarked on his
plan to send her out to study the group of chimpanzees living undisturbed in a comparatively small patch of forest known as
the Gombe Stream Chimpanzee Reserve along Lake Tanganyika in
Tanganyika Territory.

Tanganyika had once been part of the colony of German East Africa, but at the end of World War I the League of Nations designated
it a "mandate" territory, to be administered by the British with
the ultimate goal of self-government.* Thus Louis was corresponding with Geoffrey Browning, the British district commissioner in
Tanganyika's Kigoma region. Browning's response to Louis's request was somewhat ambivalent. Yes, it would be acceptable for a
young woman to go to the Gombe Stream Chimpanzee Reserve to
study the chimpanzees. No, it would not be acceptable for her to go
alone. For one thing, the wild apes were potentially dangerous. To
satisfy the authorities, Jane would have to have an assistant, a com-

---

* For an expanded historical discussion, see Brian Lapping, *End of Empire* (New
York: St. Martin's, 1985).

panion, a second official member of the expedition. According to Vanne's recollection, Louis mentioned this complication to her in Jane's absence; Vanne surprised herself by spontaneously volunteering to be the second member. The new proposed arrangement — two women going into the forest instead of one — was accepted.

So when mother and daughter returned home to Bournemouth in December 1958, Louis had already received official permission for the expedition. Now he needed to raise the money. And Jane, while she waited for Louis to work his magic, would begin her training as a zoologist.

After Christmas (and after Kip the mongoose and Boozy — or Boozey — the bush baby were settled in at the Birches, getting along as well as could be expected with Figaro the cat), Jane moved to London and began working at the film library of Granada Television (Zoo Television and Film Unit), headquartered at the London Zoo in Regent's Park. In subsequent months she informally studied primate behavior with Osmond Hill at the London Zoo and primate anatomy with John Napier at the Royal Free Hospital. Both men were friends and colleagues of Louis's.* While working at the film library, Jane also spent time getting acquainted with the animals inside the zoo. The first letter in this sequence was written soon after she began work at Granada Television as the assistant to Ramona Morris, the distinguished wife of the zoo's distinguished curator of mammals, Desmond Morris. Actually, the letter was written *during* work, within earshot of some of the zoo animals, on Granada stationery.

Jane found it convenient to live at her father's flat at Number 19, The Lodge, Kensington Park Gardens. Her sister, Judy, who was then studying piano at the Guildhall School of Music in London, also stayed at the flat. For transportation Jane bought a "cheap car" — soon named Fifi. And for entertainment the two sisters and some of their friends frequented an atmospheric coffee shop on Old Brompton Road called the Troubadour, a small dark place with

---

* Virginia Morell, *Ancestral Passions: The Leakey Family and the Quest for Humankind's Beginnings* (New York: Simon & Schuster, 1995), p. 242.

exposed beams overhead and antiques on the walls: a hangout where poets came to read, musicians to play, and earnest young people to hear poetry and music, sip exotic beverages, and notice each other. There Jane met a charming, classically handsome actor named Robert Young. The pair became involved, fell in love, and decided to follow their hearts and convention by getting married. The second letter of this sequence, probably written in January 1960, describes the moment when Robert asked Jane's father for permission to marry his daughter.

The announcement of an engagement between Mr. R. B. Young and Miss V. J. Morris-Goodall appeared in the social section of the *Daily Telegram and Morning Post* on May 13, 1960 — very bad timing, since almost simultaneously Louis Leakey informed Jane that her wait was over. He had gotten final permits from the Tanganyika Game Department, at last found a reliable sponsor for the research, and even received the grant money and purchased essential supplies, including a canvas tent, a small aluminum boat, and two plane tickets. Jane's plans for marriage to the glamorous Robert Young were thus abruptly postponed and then, gradually over the next several months, ended.

To most people, and to almost anyone connected with ordinary sources of scientific funding, Louis's proposal must have seemed bizarre: to send a very young woman, slight and delicate-featured, enthusiastic, but possibly too much so, completely untrained, no college degree — a secretary! — out to the "jungle" to live among the wild apes. The idea was improbable to the point of absurdity. Only Louis S. B. Leakey could have pulled it off. The sponsor he located, Leighton Wilkie of Des Plaines, Illinois, shared with Louis an excitement about paleoanthropology (the Wilkie fortune had been made in tools, and Leighton was interested in primitive tools) and an iconoclast's lack of concern over Jane's lack of credentials. The Wilkie Brothers Foundation came up with a $3,000 grant, enough funds to sustain the world's most unlikely scientific expedition for about six months.

On May 31, 1960, Jane and Vanne boarded a plane back to Nairobi. Upon their arrival, though, Louis appeared with bad news:

another delay, another wait. Disputes among fishermen camping along the shore of the chimpanzee reserve were making things unsafe for the present. To keep the two women occupied, and as a serious first experiment in field research, Louis packed mother and daughter onto a train to Lake Victoria, where they were met by Hassan Salimu, captain of Louis's forty-two-foot cabin cruiser, the *Miocene Lady*. Hassan took the two women out to Lolui Island in Lake Victoria, where every day Jane would watch the vervet monkeys living there and register her observations in a notebook. "The short study," Jane was later to recall, "taught me a good deal about such things as note-taking in the field, the sort of clothes to wear, the movements a wild monkey will tolerate in a human observer and those it will not."* On June 30 the women received a go-ahead radio message from Louis. They paused to bid farewell to the monkeys at Lolui — including a favorite one Jane had named Lotus and her baby, Grock — then returned to Nairobi with a book filled with Jane Goodall's first field notes.

Back at the Coryndon, Louis examined her preliminary report, an event briefly mentioned in the third letter of this chapter. Then they packed up the Land Rover and, from July 5 to July 8, were driven by Bernard Verdcourt (botanist at the Coryndon) around eight hundred miles south into Tanganyika Territory to the lakeshore town of Kigoma.

*   *   *   *

[Probably January 1959]

Darling Mummy,

Thank you so much for the letter. Both Jif and I were awake nearly all of last night, wondering and wondering about Kip.† We decided that he hadn't come back because we thought you would have rung if he had. In the morning I remarked to Jif that there would have been time to write and post a letter, so that if there was no good news in the post we should really have believed the worst.

---

* *In the Shadow of Man* (1971), p. 8.
† Kip had a habit of disappearing.

However, all was well, and good news came. I hear that only two photographs are expected to come out!

We had a very comfortable and speedy trip back — we got to Victoria at 9.5, and so were back at the flat at 9.30 and Pa was still up. I asked him about a cheap car, and he was useless. He said, in one breath, that I would never get one under £150. In the next that only last week his mechanic had been <u>given</u> one for nothing, and had sold it for £25. Hey ho! So please will you write and ask Sammy — SOON.

Please don't think that because I am typing this that I have no work to do. I have been HARD at it all day, and it is now 5.30. Ramona was out this morning, and I did some letters for the Zoologist, one Mr. Nicholas Guppy. There has been a vast row about this as Ramona doesn't think I ought to do any of his work, but as none of the indexing equipment has come yet, and so we can't start (the projectionist is away with flu') I am doing stuff for him to start with. He has just come in and told me my letters were beautifully typed. He's a queer fish, and I don't feel he's a super Zoologist. Rather the Fleetwood type, he appears, but I may be quite, quite wrong of course. Anyway, I did his letters, and typed them back. Well, I then looked at my watch — 2.45! When I went down with them, at 3.15 or so, the girl downstairs, Annabelle (and there is a Pauline too) was most concerned, and says she is coming to fetch me for lunch tomorrow. But after being used to starting work at 8.0 it just about made a normal morning — 10–3.0!

Since then I have done a lot of cards, and at the present moment should be typing a script for Ramona, but she is having a row with Nicholas Guppy about his proposed card to be filled in and filed, concerning each animal on each reel of film. I am entirely on her side — it is a ridiculous list, and if one had to put in all that detail, as she says, we should only get through about 1 reel per day — if that. She and I were discussing it when he came in. Which reminds me, he gave me a list to type for him, so I had better do it in case he appears from next door to demand it!

Well, I did it, but it ran off the end of the page, and anyway it ought to be on thick paper and I've only got flimsy up here, and I can't be bothered to go downstairs and fetch up the proper stuff. So he can jolly well wait until tomorrow for his old list!

All day long I have sat here, hearing strange sounds. The familiar roar, last heard across Serengeti Plains, of the hungry lion. The barking grunts of the deer, curious screeches and cries from the birds. Soon the hyaena will probably start laughing, and then I shall be really homesick!

I got here early this morning, not knowing how long it would take — which is about 3/4 hour — and wandered around looking at moose and elk, peacocks and various eagles and members of the crow family. There was the Fisheagle, looking so bedraggled compared to his lucky cousin that I saw, proud and free, on dear old Lolue.* And the Bataleur Eagle, seen so very often soaring over the African landscape. Strangely enough, the very first animal I saw was the Wolverine — the animal that so puzzled Sally and I on that stamp. And now it's time to go.

Tons of love to all,
Jane

P.S. <u>Please</u> get Boo some more meal worms. They won't be in until Wed — they'd run out on Saturday when I went in. 2/6 per oz — I'll pay you back. It's about the only thing she really loves — protein. Did you take back the flash gun?

[Probably January 1960]

Darling Mummy,

Many thanks for your letter — I'm glad you liked the record. I havn't met any of Bob's family yet, but we're off down there this evening. Bob† rang his Ma last night and she wasn't even expecting us. She said Bob didn't say definitely, and, thinking back on it, I think she was right. However, all is arranged now. She hasn't told Papa yet — so Bob said she was not to worry — he would tell him himself. It really is rather comic!

---

* Probably refers to a brief visit to Lolui Island in Lake Victoria in 1957 or 1958.
† Robert Young.

I have had Fifi "Aquatec'd" and she appears to be fine now.* No more trouble. Not that we have had such a lot of rain as last weekend, but still. I have written to Leakey to ask about money for the course, but not told him about getting engaged yet. I want to get everything settled first in case he goes queer — and there's not any chance of him getting to hear of it, because who would get to hear of it in Kenya? I told Sally not to tell anyone out there just yet. . . .

I had a letter from Napier when I got back on Sunday and he wants Boozey for a Television programme on primate hands. This is on 16th Feb — a Sunday. So we have a dance on the 14th — I think — and then have to collect Boozey on the Sunday — and may fit in Eileen and Stuart, who havn't answered my letter yet. Then I have to be at some strange studio by 2.30 although the programme is not until 6.30 — and then I have to go to Napier's house to meet his family and take Boozey to see how they get on with her since she will be staying there for a year. I think I'd better ditch Robert for the afternoon!

I went over to the Bird House yesterday to collect some food for Bishop, and, being bored, decided to wander round. Don, the head keeper, said I might as well feed the giant hornbill, Horatio, with some mealworms. Do you remember me telling you that I fed him before, on grapes — and how he puts them in your mouth if he likes you? Well, I didn't somehow imagine he would feel the same way about meal worms, but to my horror one was suddenly pushed lovingly into my mouth! It wasn't squashed at all, so in point of fact it really didn't matter! My nice gardener — not the cactus one, but [the] one who brings me roses in the summer, has brought me two lovely primulas. I am worried about them at the weekend because they need water every day or else they droop. Never mind, I'll just have to put them somewhere where it's cold.

Honestly, on Monday evening Daddy was in. I met Bob for a quick drink when he finished work, and then we went round to tell Chrispian and Annie we were engaged. We found poor Chris on his

---

* She had her car, Fifi, waterproofed.

own, a grass widower, Annie being away for the week. So I rang Jif, who was nobly coping with supper, and asked her to do the sausages and extra piece of liver. Anyway, we dashed back, and while Jif and I cooked, Chris sat in the kitchen and talked to us, and Bob actually went and said to Daddy "Can I have the hand of your daughter in marriage". We had told him to, but didn't think he would! So Daddy said "Which Daughter?"!! After this, Bob was very amused. He said he could see Daddy really didn't care two hoots about him, or what he was, but frantically thought of all the things which a father should say in like circumstances. When he told Bob his profession was rather precarious, Bob said he thought motor racing must be pretty precarious too, and when Pa said it had only been his hobby, Bob said that the fact that he might kill himself, made it even worse! Anyway, when we went in they were in deep and happy conversation. And then Daddy found out that Chris was going in for photography, and out came all his photographs — he was in his element, with Chris — who has wanted to take motor racing pictures for a long time — and Bob who is interested — both at his feet, while he produced pictures and anecdotes. Jif and I were very amused. Chris is a very charming person indeed — he was in the services in the Sudan, and has as much love for Africa as I have. He is terribly jealous of me, and is longing to go back himself. He immediately thought about being a photographer on my trip — not to begin with, but after it has established itself. But I had to point out that the money would be negligible, and, having a wife, he can't afford the trip for pleasure. Bob is going around his Studios reading "A Field Study of the Chimpanzee"* so as to get clued up — he says he wishes he never had as the more he reads the more worried about me he gets.

I think that is about all the news I can muster up this week — it seems to have flown by so very quickly. Thank you, and all the rest of the family, for a super weekend — and of course, not having done my new dress I now need it for the weekend. But not to

---

* A 1931 monograph by Henry W. Nissen, the only published study of wild chimpanzees at the time.

worry. The dark silk one or my skirt and white blouse will do very nicely. . . .

Anyway, must stop.

More love again,
Jane

P. S. Bob said last night that one of the nicest things about marrying me would be to gain a second family — with reference to the family he would be gaining.

[July 3, 1960]

Darling Family, Kip & Figaro,

I am frightfully sorry I havn't been writing long letters to you, but as Mummy may have explained I really have not been exactly lazy during the last few weeks. Oh, Lolui was a glorious beautiful place, and the monkeys so utterly charming that I hated to have to leave. Did Mum tell you about Lotus having her baby, Grock, and bringing him out to show all the others? How all the other children gathered round to peer at it, & one of them held its tail? And about them having a bathing party on the beach?

We are now back in Nairobi, and I have been working just as hard writing a preliminary report for Leakey, and, in between, rushing round shopping, paying social calls, and trying to develop some photos to send you! So far have had bad luck — the chemicals were faulty, it's Sunday, & I can't get anymore till tomorrow.

Judy, the spare keys to the flat — mine. Bob has. His address now is [blank space] Earl's Court Road. So if you don't see him you'd better drop him a line. He says he saw you in the Troupadour!

The scandals, scenes & situations at the Museum are the same as ever — I think they always will be. Dear old Museum. Little Ann* is thrilled to see me back & has just been ironing a dress for me! She begged to be allowed to!

Thank you for all your letters. I shall try to write more often at Kigoma. At this moment I am waiting for Leakey to finish reading

---

* Probably Ann Mitton.

my report. Great sighs are coming across the room — very foreboding! However, I don't think I did too badly in 3 weeks — & Mummy got some very good insects. All in all I think our little expedition was very satisfactory.

This evening the Mittons, maybe Mum, & the Carcassons are going to the elephant film — Roots of Heaven I think it's called.*

The journey to the chimp place, which commences on Tuesday, is going to take 4–5 days. We camp at nights, & it is going to be great fun. . . . Now my report is read, & I have been told it's fine. I have to go back & finish the job later!

Tons of love to you,
Jane

[July 5, 1960]

Darling Danny,

Many, many happy returns.† We are terribly worried about no present, but Mum will have told you we thought it was stupid to send a silly little nothing. But we shall be thinking of you — & drinking your health — in coffee no doubt! At this very moment Bernard is packing up the Land Rover. It looks quite impossible that all the stuff will fit in & leave room for us and the poor boy who has to do all the work when we camp at night. We both wish that either Bob or Norman was taking us instead of Bernard, but I dare say all will be well. Did Mummy tell you that I now have the ex-Governor of Kenya, Sir Evelyn Baring's revolver!!‡ Isn't it a hoot.

Leakey has just arrived so I must stop. I do hope you have a <u>very</u> very happy Birthday — wish we were with you.

With lots & lots of love,
Your little
Jane

---

* Norman and Marion Mitton and their two children, Ann and Christopher, lived on the museum grounds. Robert Carcasson, the museum entomologist, lived in one of the Museum Flats with his wife and son.
† Danny's birthday was July 13.
‡ The revolver was presumably lent her by Louis; Evelyn Baring was governor of Kenya from 1952 to 1959.

5

FIRST DISCOVERIES
1960–1961

> I wanted to learn things that no one else knew, uncover
> secrets through patient observation.
> — *My Life with the Chimpanzees*

LAKE TANGANYIKA constituted a watery border between
Tanganyika Territory and the Belgian Congo. Upon their arrival in Kigoma on July 8, 1960, Jane Goodall and her mother
discovered a town struggling to handle the flood of refugees from
the Belgian Congo following its June 30 liberation from a repressive
colonial regime. On July 14 the two women boarded the *Kibisi,* a
launch maintained by the Tanganyika Game Department, and were
motored north about twelve miles to the Gombe Stream Chimpanzee Reserve. Their own little aluminum boat bobbed along behind.

Tanganyika Game Ranger David Anstey accompanied them, as
did Dominic Charles Bandola, whom they had hired in Kigoma to
be their cook. Dominic turned out to be a first-rate cook and a
pleasant companion; he was eventually joined by his wife, Chiko,
and their little girl, Ado.

Gombe Stream Chimpanzee Reserve was a rectangular stretch of
land on the eastern side of Lake Tanganyika stretching roughly ten
miles north to south. An erratic rock-and-pebble shoreline defines
the western boundary of Gombe; the edge of a 2,500-foot-high rift
escarpment marks the long eastern boundary. The reserve, in other
words, is an extremely rugged rectangle, with some fifteen or six-
teen streams tumbling precipitously from the high eastern edge into

deep valleys and channels down to the lakeshore. The actual Gombe Stream is one of the southernmost of the streams.

The chimpanzee reserve was never very large, altogether perhaps only twenty square miles; today, as Gombe Stream National Park, it stands in severe ecological isolation, a forest island edged on one side by the lake and on the other three by stripped-down land resulting from overcultivation. In 1960, when the reserve was still part of a larger, semicontinuous wilderness habitat, chimpanzee populations existed to the south, east, and north of the boundaries; nevertheless, the reserve may have protected approximately as many individual chimpanzees then as it does today, around 160. The forest additionally protected (and still does) several other primate types: olive baboons; red colobus monkeys; blue, red-tailed, and vervet monkeys; and the needle-clawed bush baby. Some of the largest and most vulnerable mammals found at Gombe when Jane Goodall arrived in 1960 are now gone, including hippos and buffalo; other rare species — including the leopard and the serval cat — still survive. Bushbucks, bush pigs, civets, genets, and elephant shrews remain abundant, as do squirrels, mongooses, and various rodents. Crocodiles no longer swim along the lakeshore, but Nile monitor lizards are still found at Gombe, as are pythons and several seriously poisonous snakes: night adder, puff adder, spitting cobra, Storm's water cobra, black mamba, vine snake, and bush viper.[*]

The German colonial government first designated that rich piece of forest a reserve, limiting human intrusion, to protect chimpanzees. The English, upon taking over the administration of Tanganyika Territory at the end of World War I, were content to maintain the status quo.

Close to the center of this piece of forest, between Kasakela and Kakombe streams, the Tanganyika Game Department maintained a small camp — a convenient place for government officials to stop overnight during regular trips up and down the lake — as well as a modest, semipermanent station for the Tanganyika Game Scouts, who patrolled the reserve.

---

[*] *The Chimpanzees of Gombe: Patterns of Behavior* (1986), pp. 45–50.

Along with two or three game scouts, Kasakela camp included a few other Africans whose function seems to have been rather informal, to help maintain the camp or simply to keep the game scouts company. Among this group was Iddi Matata, an older man who served as unofficial "village headman." So when the *Kibisi* anchored offshore at Kasakela, the newcomers were welcomed by a small crowd headed by the dignified Iddi Matata. The crowd may have included Matata's two wives and six children, probably the game scouts stationed at Kasakela, certainly some local fishermen who were temporarily camping along the shore, and also possibly a few curious individuals from the fishing village just north of the reserve, Mwamgongo.

As David Anstey made clear, the game scouts could, if they wished, work for Miss Goodall as trackers. From the Game Department staff, Jane hired Adolf Siwezi; from the village of Mwamgongo she hired Rashidi Kikwale and his friend Mikidadi (described in the first letter home as "the chief's son").

Jane Goodall succeeded in *finding* chimpanzees very quickly. As we read in the first letter home, she saw one on July 14, her first day there. Of course, seeing the occasional wild ape — at a distance, disappearing in panic — was not enough. By the end of August (after she and her mother had endured the worst of an extended bout of malarial fever), Jane was able to write home with the excellent news that "I've discovered more — since my fever, in about 5 days, than in all the dreary weeks before." She kept up a grueling pace, rising before dawn, seldom returning to camp until after dark, eating starvation rations, trying to follow uncooperative creatures over jagged terrain through hostile undergrowth for what most people would regard as a distinctly unrewarding goal: to catch one or two fleeting glimpses of a hairy blob behind leaves. Her first three field assistants didn't last long. They were soon replaced by professional trackers brought to Gombe by a Tanganyikan farmer and hunter named Derrick Dunn, who seems to have been in love with Jane. Dunn's employees — Wilbert and Soko and then Short — arrived at various times in September and are mentioned in the letters probably written on September 19 and September 25.

Vanne returned to England in November. Jane left Gombe for a vacation in Kenya from December 1 to mid-January. By then her only field assistant was another game scout, Saulo David — but, as Jane notes in the letter postmarked February 6, "I now climb the mountains on my own, & Saulo comes up later on." Starting in mid-January, the staff also included Hassan Salimu, former skipper of Louis Leakey's *Miocene Lady,* who served as camp manager.

Once Vanne left in November, the Gombe human community was all African except for Jane. She worked on learning Swahili and came more and more to rely on the Africans, who over time became her close companions and colleagues. One gets the impression from several of these letters — for example, the one written on April 3 — that the camp was a very lively place. The arrival of Hilda, the hen, and Hildebrand, the cock, produced additional amusement in camp, along with a steady supply of eggs and, by early April, about fourteen baby chicks . . . then thirteen, then twelve, as the great Nile monitor lizards came out of hiding long enough to claim their share. Occasionally visitors from the outside arrived by boat. They included David Anstey, as well as, once or twice, friends and acquaintances from Kigoma, including (see the letter of February 6, 1961, for example) Robert and Alison Greenshields and Colin and José (pronounced "Josie") Lamb.

In early October 1960, Jane and Vanne were visited by the distinguished field zoologist George Schaller and his wife, Kay, who together had just completed a pioneering study of mountain gorillas in Rwanda. The letter written on October 31 and November 1, 1960, mentions that visit and credits Schaller with the following prophetic challenge: "George said he thought that if I could see chimps eating meat, or using a tool, a whole year's work would be justified."

Goodall made at least four momentous discoveries during her first year at Gombe. The two best known and perhaps most remarkable occurred within a week of each other and followed Schaller's challenge by about three weeks. On October 30 she saw chimpanzees eating meat, as described in the letter of October 31–November 1. Her first observations of chimpanzees using tools — fashioning and manipulating long twigs and inserting them into termite mounds to fish out termites — happened, according to the journal she kept, on November 4. Unhappily, though several subsequent letters refer to termite-fishing, I have not found any that describe her first observation.

The third momentous discovery, which took place after Jane's return from Christmas vacation in Nairobi, is described in dramatic detail and at some length in the wonderful if rambling letter postmarked February 6, 1961: "the chimpanzee rain dance."

The fourth great "discovery" of this first year is perhaps more event or accomplishment than discovery. But we see it referred to again and again and (in the letters written after September 1960) with increasing confidence: her brilliant success in overcoming the normal, natural wariness of these wild animals and eventually habituating them to her presence. No one ever had done this to such a degree.* Field zoology before Goodall arrived at Gombe typically consisted of specimen collection: shooting wild animals and measuring their remains. As for observations of living animals, the few researchers who tried it typically observed for relatively short periods at safe, comfortable distances, and inevitably with a narrower focus. By moving among the wild chimpanzees and immersing herself as fully as possible in their world, this young, scientifically naive woman had chosen to sail right off the edge of the map, to enter the terra incognita of scientific research. The results were astonishing. By her twenty-seventh birthday (letter of April 3, 1961), a few of the apes were actually wandering into camp.

Jane's extraordinary success at habituating the chimpanzees of Gombe was not, of course, the result of dumb luck. She labored at it, following the secretive creatures day after day after day, maintaining with great sensitivity the comfortable distance they defined by their actions, wearing dull-colored clothes, moving slowly, behaving in nonthreatening ways, and so on. But Jane also had help (as we can see from the letters of May 7 and May 16) from one individual chimpanzee she called David Greybeard. David was easily recognizable because of his distinctive gray beard, his calm disposition, and, soon, his curiosity about the strange and slender ape with

---

* George Schaller, who had begun to habituate wild mountain gorillas in the Virungas during his two-year stay there, was probably her most successful predecessor.

yellow hair. He became a quiet friend, and his calm, curious demeanor helped break through the fears of the other members of his community.

The final letter of this sequence, written exactly one year after the "Morris-Goodall Chimpanzee expedition" stepped onto the pebble beach at Gombe, amounts to a first annual report from the field. Jane summarizes her year's progress in getting to know the terrain and the chimpanzees of Gombe with a deep sense of real achievement: "The challenge has been met. The hills & forests are my home. And what is more, I think my mind works like a chimp's, subconsciously."

*   *   *   *

[July 16, 1960]

Darling Family, one and all, Douglas & Kip & Figs,

I'm really sorry to be such a bad letter writer, but there's so much to be done. Ma says, anyway, that she tells you all the news in detail so it would be silly to relate it twice, & I have to write it all to Bob,* you see.

Anyway, after all the delays etc. which you will know about by now, we have at last arrived. We got here, Danny, on your birthday† & mentally had tea with you — just after I had seen my first chimpanzee! I could hardly believe I could be lucky enough to see one on my very first day. We were quite far away, but at least close enough to know it was a chimp & not a baboon. There are lots of Baboon here — one Troop comes very close to the tent each morning to watch us. I went out yesterday afternoon to do a little exploring on my own and saw a beautiful bushbuck — a smallish animal, a lovely reddish gold colour. He flew away almost from under my feet, barking like a dog.

The country here is quite beautiful, but very rugged. The little stream behind the tent rushes down the steep rocky valley, gurgling and splashing down steppes of waterfalls. The water is pure and sweet — doesn't even have to be boiled. 16 such streams flow down

---

* Robert Young.

† They actually arrived a day after Danny's July 13 birthday; Jane exaggerated the coincidence of dates for her grandmother's amusement.

the valleys between the mountain ridges, & along their banks are the forest galleries, the home of the chimps. In between the mountain slopes are fairly bare — really it is ideal country for my job, though at the moment the task seems of a huge magnitude. Anyway, it's lucky I have more than 3 weeks!

At the moment I have 3 boys making a table with a shelter over it for Mummy to type in. They are really very clever at this sort of thing. The fishermen have just presented us with a large fish, an offer of friendship.

We hope to be able to send & collect mail about once a fortnight — the chief's son, named Mikidadi! will go in, either on one of the little motor boats which operates a passenger service along the shore — carrying about 10 Africans per trip, or else with my own boat, as he is supposed to be a fundi* with boats. David & I got the engine working yesterday & went right along the coast to the end of the Reserve. We saw 8 chimp nests in 2 trees quite close to the water, & he showed me the valley where he advises me to look first. I have 3 Game Scouts to choose from to take with me, & also a local fellow who was employed by a previous Game Warden as a guide when he marked out the reserve in 1947. He knows where the chimps are likely to be, & I shall pay him 2/- a day if the Scouts have other duties. I do hope it's all going to work.

David is just off back to Kigoma — taking Mikidadi who will bring back the few things we've forgotten.

Tons & tons of love,
Jane

Chimp Reserve.
[August 30, 1960]

Darling Family,

How are you all? and thank you for all your letters. I wanted to write you a long one this time, but what with fevers and journals and chimps life has been a bit hectic.

However, all is well now. I had a bit of fever again yesterday so am recuperating today. The D.C. & his wife, together with a White

---

* Expert.

Father, are all arriving at any minute now for lunch, after which they will be bearing these letters away.

Did Mum tell you how many chimps I have been finding, up behind our own mountain. I've discovered more — since my fever, in about 5 days, than in all the dreary weeks before. I've seen them walking along paths, I've seen them resting under trees, I've seen them playing. I've seen them 12 yards away, walking along, unconcerned. And, down in one of the cool river valleys I saw just a little baby, peering at me, & then he was joined by the most hideous female with jet black face & beetling brow ridge. She was <u>huge.</u> She swept him up & climbed down the tree. Then another came & peered at me, gazing down from a high fork. Quite pretty with a nice pale face, & ordinary size. Then the most <u>enormous</u> chimp I have ever seen came & peered at me. It was a she — old, with a half bald head & huge great arms. Her face, too, was black, & she was big as a gorilla. She came even closer & waved a tree at me, standing up & flinging her weight from side to side. And they never uttered a sound, & it was quiet except for the odd rustlings in the leaves and the distant rumbling of the thunder, all heard as a background to the gurgling of the little stream.

Oh — here they are. I will write a very long letter next time.

All my love to you all, Douglas,
& Sal if you're there, & Kip & Fig,
Jane

Chimp Reserve.
[Probably September 19, 1960]

Darling Family, Danny, Olly, Audrey, Eric — not you Jif unless you send that address — see further on in letter — I really <u>WANT</u> the book.

It's awful not having written for so long, but I just have not had time to write letters — I hope Mum has told you. Ever since my boys came I have been out every day from 6 am–7.30 pm. And then there's the punishing Journal to be written. That is <u>really</u> quite terrible. After climbing mountains all day, getting back & having a huge supper, one does <u>not</u> feel like writing several pages about chimps. But my chimps are so lovely now. I know where to find them, I know some of them by sight. I know the hideous Sophie with her son, Sophocles. I know the bearded grizzled old Claud, and an almost bald old lady whom, I think, must be Annie. They are getting used to us. When I was up on my own the other day I heard them in the trees down below & yards away — 15 perhaps. They retired, but only just out of sight. I could hear them moving about in the leaves. 10 minutes later 17 adults, 3 females carrying their babies, filed past — only 20 yards away. They all knew I was there, but didn't care a bit. They all sat down to look at me for a while, & then carried on up the slope, unhurriedly. It really is comical when 2 or 3 suddenly see you and stop, & peer, & then sit down, arms over their knees, chins on arms, and stare with intent interest. And then they often go round, under cover, & appear in a nearby tree, peeping through the leaves. The other day I saw 4 chimps being baited by a pack of baboons. It was like a play being enacted, in a little open clearing down below. The baboons got closer & closer until the chimps could stand it no longer. The 2 females climbed trees, the 2 males chased after the nearest tormentors. Then all was as before. One baboon came very close to the tree in which a female was — she leant down, waving her free arm up & down, & screaming at the top of her voice! The baboon moved sedately a couple of feet away. In the end the chimps walked off, & the baboons followed them to the edge of the clearing! But when the chimps — about 6 — were all feeding in a tree, & the baboons arrived, the chimps looked in alarm & swung out of the tree. It's terribly fascinating — I don't <u>think</u> anyone knew anything about the relationship between the two before, though I may be wrong.

Please JUDY — my ADDRESS book, or anyway Charles' address — I do think you're mean. You can always look up Burroughs Welcome in the London Directory. And now he's written to me & will never believe I wrote well over a month ago. Please make her, someone.

It's getting quite cold up on the mountains at dawn, now. An icy wind sweeps over the peaks, & one longs for the clouds to be swept away from the sun. Then, at 12 when the sun is hottest, the wind stops altogether & one nearly dies of heat! I am rapidly becoming like a piece of tough brown leather. Even when I slip down a few yards of shale, I find the skin on hands, elbows, legs, etc. is not broken! It's rather a hoot! Today is my day for doing paper work — the 1st for 2 weeks when I have not been out. It feels very strange to be staying in camp all day. But there is <u>such</u> a lot to do. I havn't written any letters for <u>weeks.</u>

I hope the news about your knee is good, Olly, poor you. I was pleased to hear from Sally that Kip is not too <u>fat!</u> And thank you, Dan, for looking after him so beautifully. We've only just had your letter about the washing machine & things — it had no stamp! We <u>adore</u> getting your letters. We hear all the news of everyone. Thank you. Love to all, Douglas & Kip & Fig.

Love,
Jane

<u>Chimp Reserve</u>
[September 25, 1960]

Darling Family,

We are supposed to be going to Kigoma this morning — in one of the little African boats because my engine is not working. But the man who was supposed to stop the 5 am one did not, & now we are loaded with the possibility of having to wait for hours & hours. Luckily — well, only in this respect is it 'luckily' — really it is awful, but my chimps have all but vanished. I have come to the end of my month's work on home ground, & am now all set for a great search party. Yet <u>another</u> of Derek's boys arrived for me yesterday! Ma & I are getting giggly — we expect all his labour will be here soon! The farm will then cease to run & he can come here himself! It is very grey & cloudy here this morning — typical of your English summer I should think. We have just heard that Sue & Ron went to Bournemouth for 3 days of their honey-moon — what a hoot — & spent all their time with you.*

Yesterday afternoon I went along the stream to collect the fruits

---

* Sue Cary (of the Alligator Society) had married Ronald Featherstone in August.

the chimps had been eating. I had Wilbert — one of the original 2 of D's staff, who is 6 ft 5 in — & the next one, Short — about 5 ft nothing! It was a hoot. I had them both nipping up trees after chimp food, & trees for our plant collection. We had an <u>enormous</u> polythene bag which, draped over Short's shoulder, reached the ground. Of course, they all had to be pressed that night — ready for our 5 am start! — so I laid them out in families & noted their description in hurricane lamp light while Ma bunged them into presses. Day before yesterday saw a Ma chimp lift her baby from the branch where it had been hanging while she ate, & hold it to her breast, human fashion, for its feed. It was the sweetest thing. And then, half an hour later, I saw it lying, face downwards, on her lap while she groomed its back. I love my chimps now — at first I was only homesick for little vervet monkeys. There are a lot of kinds of monkey here — & I've seen one very queer one that I've never seen before — or heard of. Wouldn't it be fun to have a Cercopithecus goodalli!*

Mummy is now rushing round in great agitation because we don't know how to preserve the large fruits which the chimps eat — for identification purposes. It's a job I don't like — collecting food plants. Another part of my job is messing around in dung, under their nests, to see what they've been eating! What a life, eh! Sometimes it suddenly comes over me how strange it all is, really. Here I am, an ordinary person, with my staff of 3, a camp, unlimited funds, and doing what I have always wanted to do. Not stuck away in some horrid office, out of the sunlight, but out in the open, sleeping under the stars, climbing the mountains, watching all the animals. Is it possible? Can it <u>really</u> be me? Or is it some strange hallucination? The only sad part is that it's so far away from all of you. If only you were all in Kigoma, or even Nairobi. Or if my chimps & their reserve were in the New Forest. But, of course, one can't have everything. You must look out for the Watney's advert — Bob's the chap drinking beer!!† He appears to have a bit of work now — about time too! Poor old Bob. It's now 9 am — seems <u>hours</u> since I

---

* Possibly she had seen one of the occasional hybrid blue/red-tailed monkeys.
† Robert Young, her former fiancé, had found temporary employment.

got up, ready for the non-existent boat. It is hours. Sometimes I love getting up at 5.30. Sometimes it's awful!

Love to all,
Jane

Chimpland.
[October 31 and November 1, 1960]

Darling Family,

I feel so guilty for not having written a long letter for such centuries. I console myself with the fact that Mum gives you all the news anyway. How are you all. How's the Bentley, Rix? You'll have to forgive my writing, but my hand is frozen stiff, & I'm sitting in a hurricane on a rock on a cliff top. When such a wind blows the chimps always stay on the ground, generally in the river valleys, so there is no hope of seeing them just yet. And I happened to have these rather scruffy bits of paper in my pocket.

I dare say Mum has told you about the visit of George & Kay Schaller? The American who has just done such a superb study of the gorilla. It really was nice to talk to someone who really understood what I was doing, and why, & who didn't think I was completely crazy. He did not envy me my mountains or my heat. He, poor man, had the most freezy wet climate. When in their little cabin they wore layers of sweaters & shivered, & he ate porridge for breakfast. It rained regularly every day — usually 4 times — often more. He said he sometimes used to sit on a branch & watch the gorillas below. The branches were all covered in long moss — it looked lovely & soft, but when you sat on it it went "squelch" & was cold, soggy and nasty. He used to get very embarrassed at presenting the boy, time after time, with pants that were a queer greeny brown colour!!

It was a pity all my chimps departed on his arrival, not returning till the day after he went! But he had only come to look at their habitat, the possibilities of the Reserve and, mainly, to spy on me! He admitted as much to me before he went! Which proves, I think, that he was not too horrified by my work.

Now I must recount two chimpy things. One I just mention because it is rather exciting. George said he thought that if I could see chimps eating meat, or using a tool, a whole year's work would be justified. Well, yesterday we were lucky enough to see a male chimp with a piece of pink meat. I think it was a baby animal of some sort. In the tree with him were a female with a tiny baby clinging round her, and a 6 year old child — and a small collection of baboons. It was the funniest thing. At first it was all rather noisy — the baboons & chimps were chasing each other. But it quieted down, leaving Pa with his meat, and all the others sitting round gazing at him. His wife beseechingly put out her hand, but he tucked the meat firmly under his arm. She made no other move — just sat, gazing longingly, & occasionally putting out her hand & touching his. No response. But he did let the child have a taste. The comical thing was that he sat with the meat in one hand & a bunch of leaves in the other, taking a bite at each, alternating. For all the world like a bloke with a pork pie in one hand & a stick of celery in the other! Then another male chimp, with his wife & tiny baby, climbed up the tree. And every time the lucky chap moved, they all followed him in a row, the baboons behind. It was both comical, fascinating, and scientifically valuable.

Oh dear, how cold it is. Soon it's going to rain I think. Then I shall retire under my polythene sheet (which George gave me).

Now my next item, which is far more exciting in a personal way. I was sitting, waiting for some chimps to arrive & climb into their fruit trees on the other side of a little stream. It was cold, & I had the aforementioned polythene sheet folded round my shoulders. I suddenly heard footsteps in the leaves behind me. Thought it sounded like a chimp, & did not want them to see me just there. So I lay down, half hidden by a tree. Kept very still. The footsteps approached. Then I heard very small, surprised, puzzled exclamations. "Huh" "Hoo hoo". High little sounds. The footsteps stopped. A few more comments. The leaves rustled nearer still. I closed my eyes — if they thought I was asleep, & did not know they were there, they probably would not bother unduly. "Huh" "Huh" — it sounded as though 4 or 5 chimps were conferring over this peculiar object, done up in polythene.

There was a silence. Then one voice behind me grew a little louder. Short sharp hoots, with an occasional little wimpery noise. I did not move. The sounds, I judged, were about 10 feet away. Then I heard branches shaking. For the first time I opened an eye. A few feet from the tree I was under was another little sapling. Up this a male chimp was climbing. He sat there & hooted at me. Screamed a few times. Then he climbed into <u>my</u> tree & sat on a branch not far above my head. For about 5 mins. he shrieked at me. He hit a leafy branch over me, & then hit the tree trunk with his hand, making a drumming noise. Then he seized the branch with both hands & shook it vigorously. I was showered with (rain!) twigs & buds & leaves. Then, back to the little tree, & out of sight. A second male climbed this tree & sat silently looking at me. And a female with her baby appeared, down the slope in front of me. Meanwhile my friend was behind me, hooting excitedly. He had worked up a lot of courage by now. The hoots were closer & closer. I heard breathing. Still I did not move. He retreated & paused for a moment. Then, with a last defiant hoot I felt his hand brush across my hair!! You see, if only you wait long enough, the chimps will establish "contact" with you!

Well, at this point I thought the old boy had got excited enough, so I slowly raised myself on one elbow & turned to look at him. He shut up at once, and retreated. The other male climbed rapidly down & joined him. The female disappeared discreetly. Extraordinary what an effect movement can have. A last defiant series of hoots & they all drifted away. Very excited. I heard him calling out to the other chimps, saying what a brave chap he was, drumming several times on the trees.

Wasn't that fun! And I can dine out on it for years. You wait till I tell Cliff Mitchalmore on Tonight, with full sound effects — I'm quite good at them by now.

We had another visitor here last week — David Anstey, the Game Ranger who greeted us on arrival & helped us to get set up. He was very nice, though he did come up on the mountain with me, which was annoying, & rather mucked up a morning. Still, by 12 am he'd had enough, so the afternoon was all right. He is removing the bane of my life, Adolf the Game Scout. How happy I shall be. And sending a well educated English speaking scout who has been trained by the Govt. Biologist. So he should be O.K.

Now that these rains have come the chimps seem to be going down to the lake shore, which is wonderful. Perhaps in the long rains I shall be able to take my tent to the beach & do all my observing from within!

It is a day since I started this — see change of pen! It is now about 10.30 pm, so that I must end or I shall be asleep before I'm in bed. I walked miles & miles today — & if I'd stayed at the camp there were chimps here all day!

Douglas, I wanted to write to you at Whipps, but by the time a chance & post arrived we guessed you'd be out again. I do hope the opp. went off O.K.

Danny, as for you & Douglas & the tree — well, we were quite stunned. What a work, & for you, Olly, too.

I meant to write more. About the exquisite wonder of the flowers which have sprung up like magic since the rain. You cannot imagine how strange it is. For months I have trudged through the heat on a parched dry soil, rocky & barren. Now, a magic wand is waved. Beautiful lilies, striped with pale purple, sway beneath the trees on the lake shore. Little bells, like hair bells, bloom delicately in the woods. White orchids push, leafless, from the damp moss. Beautiful scents wherever you go. And a really <u>fantastic</u> plant is a flower, rather like a yellow nasturtium, in the middle of a cone shaped, thick single leaf: cross section (too late to draw!!!)

Shall write a longer letter soon. When Ma goes, the official scribe of this expedition, having more time, I will make an effort.

Tons & tons of love,
Jane

Chimpland.
[Postmarked February 6, 1961]*

Darling family (except my ex-Sister whom I forthwith excommunicate, disown, & cut from my will [i.e. she will not be left my superfluous gym shoes and my boxes of love letters!]),

I do <u>hope</u> you have had some letters from me by now. I was rather a long time writing after Christmas — but <u>so</u> were you. I almost sent you a cable to see if you were all right, until at long last, a letter came. To which I immediately replied, only the reply was lengthened out between Nairobi & Kigoma.

Anyway, thanks for yours, Mummy (2), and Olly and Dan. I'm dreadfully sorry about the high blood pressure — I must tell Norman — that is his complaint. He has to have 'de-compression' pills! Poor old you. And I'm sorry to hear you're under the weather Dan. Hope you'll be O.K. by the time you get this. The dress, Olly, I didn't have the chance to wear this time — being mostly at the Coast where it was too hot for anything more than shorts. Also, camping, we didn't wear dresses at all. But it will be smashing for when I return to Nairobi in June — for my photography course — if I have it.

News from here is mostly a trifle damp! Oh dear, Danny, I often think of your horror when I plod around in wet cloths or sit on the wet ground. Luckily, being Africa, it's not the sort of damp to give you rheumatism.

I now climb the mountains on my own, & Saulo comes up later on. I leave little notes in polythene bags saying where I shall be, so that he has a sort of paper chase each day — rather fun for him!! But just now, with the chimps so erratic, I see no point in two of us getting wet all day, when one can get just as effectively damp, all on one's own! So my mountain climbing cloths are now practical, if slightly unconventional. I tie my trousers round my waist, & my polythene sheet round my waist too, & there I am. The top half doesn't get too wet. Occasionally, if I am forced to walk about in the rain, I bare that to the elements as well! It's the same old polythene

---

* Written in stages between January 29 and February 4.

sheet — my new one is surrendered to Hassan who has a hole in the roof of his tent!

Well, José and the Kibisi arrived last Saturday with all my things, as planned + + +! Collin, the Greenshields, Dominic's wife, Hildebrand & Hilda, and 3 "Tobacco gentlemen" as they were introduced to me. Do you remember Mum, from Belbase days, a young man in the tobacco trade — Mike I think — Shawe or something? Well, he was one, & 2 others. Well, Robert went off for a baraza* with old Iddi Matata, & Colin & the 3 tobacco gents all whipped the tent up in no time, with Hassan & Rashidi helping. None of the others helped! They all returned to the huts — I think because Robert went there to talk business & they didn't want to miss anything. But Rashidi turned up real trumps and worked like a Trojan. We had tea, & then they departed, leaving me with a <u>superbly</u> erected tent, and absolute <u>chaos</u> around the place. Saulo appeared from the baraza, & he & Rashidi & Hassan & Dominic & the Askanzi father all helped me to pile everything into the tent. Hildebrand & his new wife had made themselves quite at home, & José had brought a large box for a hen house. She said he's had a <u>rotten</u> time with her — her cock had chased him all day long & he'd had to sleep, an outcast, on the woodpile. He is now in his element, & has learnt to crow very nicely.

That night the heavens descended. Of course, we hadn't got round to making a ditch, so the 'verandah' was like a toddlers' paddling pool! I struggled with the guy ropes with my failing torch, & was soaked to the skin when I got back. It was lovely to lie hearing the rain on my new roof. The next day I got back a bit earlier than usual, & made everything ship-shape. You would love it now Mum, really you would. I have a great box of surplus — coo — here are my chimps. Bye.

Well, after that interruption to the tune of 23 hours, here I am again. I had been sitting overlooking the Pocket — I am again, when I suddenly heard loud chimp screams. Baboons joined in. I didn't have a very successful time — I picked out two chimps — a

---

* A meeting.

long way away, & saw them make their nests, & Ma & baby climb into one & the other into the other. And this morning I got nearer & saw one getting up, but the other had already got up when it was light enough to see. And they silently vanished baby & all. So I've been working on Red Colobus all morning. Now, back to my vigil again.

Where was I — oh yes — a box of extra stores in the bathroom — which is now large! From this Dominic keeps a smaller box filled with day to day requirements. Hassan had made the most lovely hen house, door & legs & all. This lives at one side of the verandah & acts as a sideboard. On it, in a shining row, are 7 large tins from Bimje,* for sugar, flour, etc. The other side, low down, is Norman. He has cups & plates etc on him.† And in the middle — where there is still a lot of room, is my new little low camp table. This can be moved easily. I usually have supper outside unless it's actually raining (often is!). Also, after supper, it's just the right height for me to write at sitting on my bed (albeit balanced on two pillows & a folded blanket!). It is always kept quite clear except for whatever it is being used for.

Derrick gave me 3 tin ammo boxes. One is outside, by Norman, & has biscuits, spaghetti, cigarettes, etc. in it. One is at the top of my bed — all my books fit in it, backs upwards, so that it's like looking into a bookcase, only it's been lain on its back. The 3rd has oddments required daily, or fairly often, such as NIVEQUIN!!!‡ extra torch, batteries, etc. The blue trunk has all my papers in it. The black one contains only things likely to be wanted once in a blue moon, or not at all. On this is the clock, baby powder, Pier, and George. George is a beautiful white ivory elephant presented to me as a souvenir of days hunting of the real George. (I take it you did get my long letter all about the trip home? — about 18 pages?)§ Hassan has dug huge & beautiful trenches all over the place, direct-

---

* A shopkeeper in Kigoma.
† A storage cabinet named Norman, possibly made by Norman Mitton.
‡ Malaria medicine.
§ On her way to Nairobi during the Christmas holidays, Jane visited with Derrick Dunn in Arusha; together they went on a safari that included elephant "hunting" (without guns).

ing the flow of water, so I'm in no danger of being washed away. And with a piece of corrugated iron from Robert, Hassan has erected a fine banda* for the kitchen. And I am looked after as though I were a Queen. Terribly spoilt. . . .

Now I must tell you about the chimps. I saw 7 resting [in] a big tree for over an hour. The lady made a <u>nest</u>! Two old gents groomed each other. It was very nice indeed. Then, the same evening, I saw 2 chimps making nests in the Pocket. Next morning I was up close before light, & I saw a mama & her baby waking up. There were 3 others that I didn't see, only heard. They got up as soon as it was light & screamed & crashed around. Baby leaned along Ma's leg to see what they were doing, & then flopped back to bed. She was lying on her back. Babe went off for a walk, came back, & crawled on her chest, putting his face down to hers & lay on her tummy. At last Mum got up. She just sat in her bed. Looked round. Yawned. And sat. Babe kept going off having little walks. Then she sat at the side of her bed. Babe came & sat with his arms round her. Then she groomed him. Then he went past her & lay in the bed, & she held her hand over him & he played with it. It really was all too sweet for words. She never saw me till she was actually down on the ground, & even then I saw babe, sitting up on her back, & just appearing above the grass, <u>very</u> close before she saw me. It was a really good day — thank <u>goodness</u> for it, or I'd really be miserable by now.

Yesterday, right at the top of Sleeping Buffalo, in one of the open spaces, I saw <u>at least</u> 25!! There were too many to count accurately, anyway!! But they all disappeared again — didn't come down at all. So I'm left with the 2 & the baby, who move silently.

Hello again! Can't remember what page I got to so these are A, B, C etc. Now, I'm going to tell you something — it's raining! Honestly! I'm in the same place as before, but two days have elapsed — already both have taken on a dream-like quality & I find it hard to believe in their actuality. However, let me tell you about them — what a pity you arn't here now, Mum — for once you would have had a <u>really</u> excited Jane — more than the meat, more than the termites.

---

* Thatched hut.

The day started well. I heard chimps by Linda, went over, & saw them down by what I call the Bottom Bump — you know Mum, where the stream goes out into the lake, & the slope is all thick with trees. It's stopped raining. Well, I managed to get reasonably close — on the opposite side of the valley. One could easily see sex, face colour, etc. I watched them playing in the trees — mostly young ones, all morning. Then they vanished. I moved a little way down the slope, & heard the angry hoots & squeaks of the males. They'd seen me. I sat down, and soon saw them — 5 large males and one adult female. They were all feeding away in some trees opposite. This they did for 30 mins. Then they climbed down, & I first saw them climbing up through odd spaces in the trees & grass. They arrived at another tree and climbed up. There they rested peacefully. Suddenly the rest of the party appeared — seemingly out of thin air! All the children and at least one more male & a young lady of skittish temperament. The romping began all over again — the poor grown ups just had to lump it. The games went on for an hour. I could see better this time — wrestling, chasing — all silently, as it had been all morning.

Then it began to rain. I expected them all to get down to shelter under the trees. Not a bit of it. They stayed where they were. Then one old male climbed down. He has a pale face — I knew him of old. He sat on the grass under a tree & just looked around, hunched. A very young male (who rather hero-worships Paleface) ran over and sat very close. Slowly they all climbed down from the tree. Half of them came to join Paleface, the other half went and grouped themselves about 50 yards away. It was most organized. A mum with a child on her back headed Paleface's group — 5 all told. They began moving sedately, in line, up the hill. The other group also started off — just a little behind Paleface, & headed by 'Bare Bum' — you remember him, Mum?

(Interrupted there. Now next morning — and it's <u>raining!</u>)

Well, they were almost at the top of the slope. When they started off they left the tree, & there was about 100 yards or more of grass above, with single trees scattered around.

Suddenly Bare Bum left his troop and galloped, full speed, at the other line, swinging his body from side to side, arms flailing in a scything motion. There was an outburst of panting calls. He moved on up a hill & as he reached the top, stood up and swiped at a bush with his hand. Well, I thought that was that. But no. They all began to climb trees. Pale Face then turned & began to charge diagonally down the hill. As he went he snatched at the branch of a tree, tore it off, waved it above him, & charged on, dragging it with him. Then he dropped it & climbed a tree. But another large male was on the move, charging down, breaking off his branch. Then two hurtled down, one after the other, leapt into a tree, seized branches, & leapt to the ground — 30 ft. at least, taking their branches with them, charging on, reaching a tree, seizing it, swinging round & leaping up into the branches. I think only the males took part in this "Rain Festival". The others staying in their 'seats', watching.

I don't think I have ever watched any performance which gave me such a thrill. Mostly the actors were silent, but every so often their wild calls rang out above the thunder. Primitive hairy men, huge and black on the skyline, flinging themselves across the ground in their primaeval display of strength and power. And as each demonstrated his own majestic superiority, the women and children watched in silence, and the rain poured down while the lightning flashed brilliantly across the grey sky.

For thirty minutes this wild display continued — and as I watched I could not help feeling the display was for my benefit — it was to me they were proving their strength and might — me, the poor miserable weak human who dared to intrude upon their lives. The place of the Festival was a natural out of door theatre — a curve in the hillside, with trees all round. They looked so black and gigantic, slightly above me, against the brilliant green of the grass.

When it was over they all sat in trees — 3 in one, 2 in another — but Pale Face sat alone, centrally, reclining at ease in the branches. Eventually they began climbing down, one by one, and walking quietly to the brow of the hill. On the skyline they looked even larger. One or two climbed a tree for a moment, waiting for the others to catch up. But at last they had all gone — all save Pale Face. He was last, & before finally crossing the ridge he stood up, one hand on a tree, and looked back at me for a long minute. The actor taking his final curtain.

Can you begin to imagine how I felt? The only human ever to have witnessed such a display, in all its primitive, fantastic wonder? I fear I was not able to report it as exactly as science might wish. I had no thought for exact numbers, or seconds — nor could I write as I watched — a) for fear of missing one second, and b) because it was far too wet.

I was interrupted yesterday by a troop of Red Colobus, which I watched until Saulo arrived. This morning I gaily crested the peak — & there, not 15 yards away, was my sedate old gentleman friend, the bull buffalo. He was lying there so peacefully, chewing his cud & having 40 winks! He never even saw me. Ye gods — it is pouring! I'm endeavouring to keep the paper dry by holding a polythene bag over it — without overmuch success. If it had done this an hour ago I shouldn't have climbed till it was over. Hassan & I got the new pressure lamp going last night, & today he is erecting a frame for the large towel. So I shall be moth catching in a big way. He's quite a carpenter is Hassan. And Dominic is zealous with his dudu* catching. I've got the little net living up on the mountains now, so am able to do a bit myself in between the chimps — & the rains!

Well, I still havn't related the second day. When I climbed up there were chimps calling all over the place — one big group up Sleeping Buffalo, & more behind me, very close. These arrived from Linda at about 9.30, & I suspected they were my 'actors' of yesterday. Anyway, I set off to investigate. I decided to go into the forest, rather than climb up to look down. I could hear them close to me, but they seemed to be on the move. However, I kept on, even though I had a suspicion they knew I was there. Suddenly I found I was very close. And it began to rain. For a while I stayed still, under my sheet. Silence from the chimps. So I thought, to blazes with the rain, & moved off in the direction I thought they had gone. Well, the thing was, they hadn't gone. And suddenly loud angry hoots sounded, almost overhead. So I sat me down. I was in a bad place — a small clearing with thick undergrowth all round. For a few minutes I heard nothing. Then I saw branches moving — perhaps 15 yds away. I could only see by lying down. So I lay down. There was

* Insect.

a large female, eating away, about 20 ft. up. As I looked she turned round, gave me a contemptuous stare, & went on feeding. All at once my eye was caught by a bush moving, about 6 yards away. There was Bare Bum, on the ground, regarding me. He turned & moved into the thick undergrowth where I could only tell he was there from an occasional stirring leaf. There were sounds of other chimps moving in the trees, but I just could <u>not</u> see. Did not like to move again. Then came a low 'hoo' from Bare Bum. A reply came from the bushes to my right — even closer. But I could <u>not</u> see a chimp. These little "hoo's" went on for some time. Then the rain, which had paused, started up again. Suddenly there was a loud "hoo" & a deafening chorus of hoots & screams of defiance — almost all round me! Certainly on 3 sides. Well, I thought they'd better have something to keep their minds off how much they didn't like me, so I diligently dug for insects, making little grunting noises. This kept them quiet!

After this it was wonderful. A small child came down, looked at me, climbed a tree, & sat regarding me. (Maybe Spray). Another large black female came & stared at me through the bushes. For 3 hours the whole troop was round me, feeding. I could hear the smacking of their lips and the little pleasure grunts.

Where the ink starts* is another day — 2 days since I last started. Since when I have been working on Red Colobus — good work. Very close. Mating etc. And tonight the chimps came back.

Now Hassan has just informed me he's going to Kigoma tomorrow to send his wife some money, so I'm <u>frantically</u> finishing this off, together with other urgent ones — poor Norman will have been trotting vainly to the P.O. for weeks! At present I'm sitting by the big towel, erected in a large frame, under the pressure lamp, leaping up every now and then to catch dudus! Hassan has also made a frame for the mosy† net, so I sleep unmolested.

I met more buff. the day I stopped writing! Also, it <u>really</u> rained.

---

* She changed from ballpoint to blue fountain pen in the middle of the previous sentence.
† Mosquito.

And last night it never stopped. I wasn't able to get up the mountain until 11 — & I stayed in bed until 7!!!

We,ll, tons & tons of love, and I'll drop a line again as soon as poss.

Jane

Chimpland.
3rd April [1961]

Hello all,

Thought I must pen a few lines on my Birthday. It is a funny one and no mistake — a nice one too. It started off with a mountain climb in the moonlight and 8 dear little chimps in their nests. One poor young lady, while it was scarcely light, was woken from a deep sleep by an amorous suitor. With a scream horrifying to hear she leapt out of bed — no time to make up or anything. Dear me! From the sound of things she was not permitted a peaceful breakfast either! They all went away after that. I sat up a tree over by Linda, and then came back to look at the nests. Had done half of them, & was busily poking about in dung, when I heard chimps. The trail led me back to camp! Where I saw 3 just up behind for a while.

Since then it has been raining hard. I found Dominic cursing the fire because it was spoiling my cake. No mere 'safari' cake this — it has everything on it — every egg D could lay hands on, tins of butter — my word. I have been left to put the icing sugar & candles on when it's cool. Jellies are made. And yesterday D, on his own bat, made a loaf of "sweet bread". Iddi and bibi,* and the Scouts —

Well!! <u>What</u> a birthday present (only one I might add). I had just penned the last word when I heard a noise, (I am <u>in</u> the tent, on bed, as it's cold) & saw a chimp hanging on the end of the frond of the palm tree outside. <u>Not</u> the bathroom one (anon) but the one where (I keep writing one letter of one word followed by first letter of <u>next</u> word!) we had that table Mum! He climbed up. I lay on my tummy & looked up at him. A second walked across to the frond. I suppose

---

* Wife.

it's 5 yards away. Then I think the one up there may have seen me. Anyway, he looked down & hooted at the one below who went across the grass & into the bushes opposite. Here he climbed a bush. Then both of them gave loud angry calls — at me? The old man up the tree went on stuffing nuts into his mouth. Made a funny little cross hoot to himself. The other climbed higher and ate some fruit. After 20 mins the old boy climbed down his frond, reached for the trunk, got to the ground, and went into the bushes. They're both gone now. It's still raining as hard as ever. This is the way to watch chimps! The bathroom episode was these same two. Chimps appear here every other day now. As it usually rains about 1 pm & there were no chimps up top I decided to try my luck here. And these two were already up the tall palm — nearer the lake. They saw me come & climbed down. I went into the bathroom & peered out — there was the old boy sitting in the rain scratching his chin. Suddenly he got up. Passed me by about 3 yards, no more. And re-climbed the palm! He was up there for an hour, but the trouble was I couldn't see him properly. The following day I spent another 2 hours on the bathroom floor, with no luck, so I abandoned the idea. WHAT a pity you're not here now Mum.

Ma. Must tell you a funny thing. You know the parcel of dawa* you sent? Well, it arrived via Adolf 2 days ago. (Just wondering if I've told you about the bathroom?) It's thundering now. I'm eating peppermints — got them as a treat — havn't had any choc this time — choc eats though! Anyway I thought to myself, seeing your writing, 'Good old Ma — at least she has got a present here in time'. I carefully didn't look at the declaration of course! So I opened it at lunch time — well, if 3 pm is lunch time, but I had opened a tin of bully beef, with D's new loaf — and how I laughed. — 'Can you send word back in time for me to send a present to reach you on THE day?' Well, old bean, I guess I can't! So sorry!!

It's thundering now. I'm very glad I am down here, apart from the chimps. I can't begin to tell you how wet everything is. I opened my camera — in case I got a chance to do the chimp — & it won't shut

---

* Medicine.

again. Everything is covered in mildew. What a life. All Bob's*
dudus are rotting away gaily.

I was tackling at least 2 hours of Journal last night when Iddi &
a troop came along with their lantern — giving the pigs a good
scare for once. Oh dear — an ill baby, an ill bibi — and two "kich-
was"† — I don't think! Long chats of course. He sent me some
meat today — don't know why. Mutton, D says.

Don't think I'll write any more now because this won't go until
Hassan does on Thursday. So I'll add. Who would be cross if I said
T.T.F.N.‡ Since I don't think I've ever said it, I wonder what put it
into my head. I hope by then (Thursday) there'll be a letter answering some of my questions. Can't remember what they were, but I'm
sure there were some. I've just iced the cake & stuck candles in it.
Dominic came to make me some coffee & disapproving 'cos I
hadn't done it! Hildebrand is crowing in my ear, & Hilda has wandered off with her 14 babies. I'm sure the monitor is eating them
all, but I can't leave her shut up anymore. (It <u>DID</u> eat one!)

Adieu.

Hi! Thought I'd better finish off today. It's 7 pm. Still very light
these days. It's just stopped raining though luckily it's only been
spitting since 5 pm. I'm sitting up by my deserted kitchen accompanied by Hildebrand. I couldn't face a meal tonight! The jelly wasn't
set, so, with great glee the kids are coming round tomorrow. My
party was a great success I think. Iddi and family sauntered up while
Dominic and I idly thought we had another hour. So they all sat &
watched me cut up the "sweet" bread. Dominic & Hassan arranged
the tea etc, & the oldest son was despatched to tell Saulo to bring
more cups & chairs. It was quite a gathering. Iddi with <u>two</u> bibis. 4
small watoto.§ 2 big ones. Saulo. And we 3. They consumed the loaf
and innumerable cups of tea, & I related the soko episode** — they
all said he came for my birthday. I had a weird fruit I found in chimp

---

* Robert Carcasson, the entomologist at the Coryndon Museum.
† Headaches.
‡ "Ta-ta for now," an expression her mother hated, used ironically by Jane.
§ Children.
** The chimpanzee episode described earlier in the letter.

dung which was handed round. No one knew it, but Iddi said his big son might. I think he's a bit dim! Anyway, he came back & I handed it to him & asked if he knew what 'tribe' it was. I <u>JUST</u> managed to stop him putting it into his mouth!! How everyone laughed. I had hit his hand hard, & we had quite a job to find the precious specimen! Hassan made a speech saying he wished me and my sister many happy birthdays. Then, the great ceremony of lighting the candles — which fizzled ominously in the rain — & D explained the custom of wishing for me — so they all — well, I <u>wouldn't</u> go that far — sat and wished. Then we thought the monitor was caught — but the trap had been sprung from the outside. Then we found Hilda only had 13 babies, not 14. Very sad. I solemnly dosed the small ill child — which seems a <u>bit</u> better. And presented Iddi with a bottle of orange juice.

The sunset is lovely. Hildebrand has just stalked off to join his wife & family in the henhouse. It is getting dark, and is peaceful and lovely. It's been an odd birthday, compared to all my others, but I must say I've enjoyed it. A wind is springing up and I shall probably go in in a minute. The Congo Hills are so clear nowadays you can see the valleys & the forests. It's fantastic. And as for Ruanda — you feel you could walk there in a couple of hours — right at the North of the lake I mean.*

The ointments, etc, which, in the joke of it, I forgot to say thank you for! — actually came just at the right time because I got bitten by a mosie last night — she was in bed with me! Oh yes — 2 more things. (1) did I tell you that D and Hassan respectively guessed I was 14 and 16!!!!

Iddi wants a picture of him & me to put in a large frame — an enlarged picture — to hang in his house! Isn't it sweet. Now, goodnight.

P.S. I havn't a <u>clue</u> I realize, of Sue's name!† Never heard it!! Can you address this envelope — making at least the <u>NAME</u> look like my writing!

---

* The territory of Ruanda-Urundi, which is now the nation of Burundi with Rwanda to the north.
† Sue Cary's married name.

Chimpland
4th April 61

Dear Bernard,

Sorry to plague you unmercifully, but I have to write when I <u>think</u> of these things. This one is, I imagine, <u>quite</u> out of the question, but it was just a notion I had — that it would be interesting to know the food value in the things the chimps eat — their main foods that is. Now, for instance, they seem to eat only a certain yellow blossom for whole days at a time. Is there any way of finding out such a thing? (I'm thinking of my thesis!)

I had the most lovely birthday present yesterday. It started off nicely when I climbed the mountain in the moonlight & saw all my chimps wake up in the morning. Then I came down early because of rain. And 2 chimps climbed the tree outside my tent & ate there for 30 mins! I just lay on the floor & watched them. They knew I was there too — just yelled at me! as though I had no right to be in my own tent!

And such a sweet little birthday party I had. Dominic had made "sweet" bread, a superb cake, & jelly, & I had the old boy who lives here, his two wives, 4 little boys, 2 big ones, & the game scout — a new & very nice one. Such a ceremony over lighting the candles on the cake, & they all had to wish for me when I cut it!

I now have 14 little chicks just out for Easter. At least I <u>did,</u> though now the vile monster has eaten two, despite Hassan & Dominic running after them like nannies all day, & specially made hen coops, etc. The old devil much prefers my chicks to the smelly piece of meat in his specially constructed trap!

Dear me, how it does rain. And rain. And how the grass grows. I've been treed by 2 buffaloes! And the day before yesterday was really thrilled to see my leopard — albeit a <u>little</u> too close for comfort. But he is so very beautiful.

I am frozen stiff at the moment, but luckily a nice hot curry is on its way. Let me know how things are with you. Incidentally, if you feel the need to sort yourself out, the mountains are the place to do it. I'm sorted out completely.

Love
Jane.

[May 7, 1961]

Have to write a few words, simply because it can't be true. It can't. David Greybeard is up the palm. I am sitting outside the tent. D. is washing up after my breakfast — which I ate sitting outside the tent. I have walked all round the tree taking pictures — sadness — only one film & that, I think, spoilt by damp. Even from directly underneath. We have talked. Can it be true? My filming difficulties, re. termites — are as good as over. I can just walk up to the ant hill & film David G. This is unique. I can get my own fabulous pictures. Only the sad thing is it's not salt he's after — it's palm nuts & they are nearly finished. Still, as I proved the other day, he doesn't mind me up in the mountains either. I keep looking up & not believing it's a chimp — not a real one. How I wish you were here Mum. He'd soon take food from your hands, come when you called! He's sitting contemplating now, scratching his chin. I have just been under the tree talking in a loud voice to him. He didn't even look! Rayed out below are: 1 tin baked beans, open. 1 plate salt. 1 plate sugar. 1 glass lime juice!!! I am drinking coffee! Isn't it too ridiculous for words? Better than George's "Junior"* who sat 25 yards away. This is not 25 feet. I'm longing for him to come down.

Sadness — it began to pour & he climbed down & vanished. Never mind — from 8–10 he was there.

Tons of love,
Jane

The Peak,
Chimpland.
16th May [1961]

Darling Family,

I'm up here waiting for a gale to subside so that I have a reasonable chance of hearing anything worth hearing, or seeing anything to be seen. It is 4.30, and I had a very nice time with chimps from 8 am–2.15, so I can't grumble. Horace and his girls, Sophie and Sophocles.

---

* A gorilla so named by George Schaller.

I simply don't know where to begin, telling you about David Greybeard. He is utterly fantastic. I think with this moment: I was staying down to try & take some pictures of David G. I was expecting him about 8.30–9. I was, therefore, still reclining in luxury at 7.30, & Dominic was just getting my tea — fancy! — early morning tea! My bed was about 4 ft from the palm — David's Palm. I was under my net, gazing through it at the grey sky. Suddenly I heard a rustling. David G. He glanced up casually at my bed, climbed 5 ft. up the trunk, reached out for his usual frond (which he then swarms up) & only then noticed me under the net. He gazed harder, then, almost visibly shrugging his shoulders, he ascended and sat above me, chewing nuts. Did not look at me again.

Another moment. Waking up at 6.15 and waiting for it to get light, peering up at the outline of the tree where David is sleeping. Still too dark to make anything out when I hear a sound like someone pouring a kettleful of water down from a tree top through leaves — which is almost what it amounted to, anyway! Then Olly's famous card cow-pats. Then silence. As it got lighter I was able to see David G. on his tummy, head sideways, eyes closed. Suddenly his eyes opened wide. He blinked. Gazed round. Glanced at me. I scratched. David G. scratched. Stretched. Closed his eyes once more. Then turned over out of sight. 10 mins passed. Dominic peered out of his tent, grinned, and walked along the path, avoiding my bed which lay across it, & went off to cook me a sausage! David G sat up & scratched. Then lay on his tummy, propped on his elbows, and gazed at me between <u>hiccoughs!</u> Then he slowly got up, stretched, sat nearby, & swung over my bed to his fig tree above Hassan's tent. H's face emerged, & said jambo to me and Bwana David. Retreated. I had my breakfast gazing at David G in the fig, having his breakfast. Then, I sat waiting for him. Up the path he strolled. Gathered up his bananas, & sat on the ground, facing me (on the ground) 12 feet away. Up his Palm. I laid out more bananas. He finished his nuts, climbed down, picked up 3 from the ground, sauntered over to the tent (I was opposite) helped himself to 3 from the table — right at the <u>back</u> of the verandah, walked upright with his haul to the tree where you, Ma, made your clinic sit, & ate them.

Another moment. I was climbing Ogre at 5 pm having waited

182 Africa in My Blood

vainly at the salt lick. Just by the place which I think was your "1st plateau" Mum, I heard rustlings. I stopped. They approached. A black head emerged onto the path some 20 yards in front. Stood looking at me. I stepped aside. He stopped. So I turned round and went back along the path. Looked round. He was following! He did not follow me <u>all</u> the way back along the path, but used his own some of the way. He gave me 5 mins to get things ready for him, then strolled in from the kitchen!

Can you imagine it? We all keep saying how sad it is that Memsahib Mkubwa* isn't here.

He is a lovely specimen too. All his hair, scarcely any baldness of the forehead, long cheek hair, beautiful beard, dark handsom face — <u>very</u> handsom chimp. Rather like old Dick† at the zoo in fact, only I reckon he's bigger.

The time he made his nest we had all been watching him in his fig. He sat there, in the sunset, sucking away at the lump of pips in his lower lip. Dominic went off to start the supper, & Hassan & I lay on our backs & watched him cross over, climb the tree, and make his nest.

At 2 am Rashidi went to Dominic's tent with some dagaa‡ for me, with a lamp. David G. was most annoyed, & told everyone so! Rashidi, who did not know he was there, says he ran off to start with! Then put his lamp out & returned in the dark!

I think the rains are almost over. I thought they were 4 days ago, and then: — well, at 12 midnight I felt a few drops, decided it would pass, & so merely dropped my polythene sheet over the net & frame. This was fine. I dozed off. Was dimly aware of rain pounding on the roof of the tent — lovely sound. It wasn't till I was lying in a good several inches deep that I realized I was <u>not</u> in the tent, but in a sodden bed, lying in a <u>river</u> of water which was charging through the camp. Well, the bed was beyond hope, so I made a dash for the tent, pulled out the two spare blankets, rolled up in them, and spent the rest of the night on the floor. It did not stop. At

---

* "The senior madame," that is, Vanne.
† A chimpanzee at the London Zoo.
‡ Small sardinelike fish.

Valerie Jane Goodall, about two, out for a stroll in a London park.

*Feeding
the birds.*

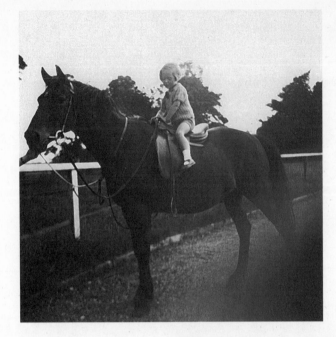

*Trying out
a horse.*

*Valerie Jane holding
Jubilee, her stuffed
chimpanzee, with her
younger sister, Judy,
and their nanny,
Nancy Sowden.*

Mortimer and Vanne Goodall with their daughters.
Mort joined the Royal Engineers in 1939.

Valerie Jane at six or seven.

The Manor House in Kent, where the family stayed just before the war.

The family at Bournemouth. Left to right: Judy,
Aunt Olwen, Danny (Jane's grandmother), Aunt Audrey,
Valerie Jane, Uncle Eric, and Vanne.

The Alligator Society. From the top: Red Admiral (Valerie Jane),
Rusty the dog, Puffin (Sally Cary), Ladybird (Sue Cary),
and Trout (Judy).

Jane riding Daniel.

Jane as a teenager with her beloved dog.
"Rusty was the only dog I have ever known who
seemed to have a sense of justice."

The charismatic Reverend Trevor Davies.

May Day picnic breakfast at Oxford.

Louis Leakey at Olduvai Gorge about 1957.

Dancing with Brian Herne at Ngorongoro Crater, Tanganyika, December 1957.

Jane Goodall, age twenty-three, Kenya Colony.

Jane drove Annabelle the orangutan to the Granada television studio for a program by Desmond Morris.

Flo and little Flint. Flo was "quite won over to the idea of popping in for the odd banana."

Jane's cartoon of life at Gombe Stream Reserve in the early years.

Jane and Hugo van Lawick were married on March 28, 1964.

Flo's Flint reaches out.

David Greybeard was the first of the chimpanzees
to overcome the fear of human contact.

9 am when D. appeared it had <u>just</u> begun to <u>slightly</u> ease off. He and I shrieked with mirth at the sight of my bed — it <u>did</u> look a mess. Earth had rushed over it & through it, with the stream, & the weight of the wet net had pulled the frame inwards. Added to which a large & v. poisonous centipede — about 8″ long & 2″ wide — was curled up under my pillow! D. says their bite is as bad as a snake — not fatal of course.

The rain continued until 4.30! David G arrived in a slight break, at about 3.30, and was still with us when it finally stopped. Yesterday we had a very heavy storm, with thunder. I suppose we shall get these odd deluges till the end of May.

My gale is still blowing. It would be dreadfully hot otherwise, and as I don't really expect to see any more chimps today, I'm not too sorry.

It seems quite amazing that we are over half way through May. And when I go to Nairobi I shall be half way through this year's watching. In some ways this is rather alarming. One thing's for sure — I shall not have seen all I want to see when I have to go. But one good thing — I can check up on all sorts of minor feeding points, etc, on David G. And he will be <u>invaluable</u> for filming the termites!

I don't know whether I shall be able to post this. I am putting it with one to José, & leaving it, in the hopes that a 'Rafiki'* will be going into Kigoma soon. Otherwise it will have to wait till end of May.

All the bibis are very friendly nowadays, including the one who had her baby. The husband, Yosef, is a good pal of Dominic's. Rashidi is now <u>so</u> willing & helpful. Because David employed him again as a porter & I think he knows it's thanks to me that he wasn't turned out of the Reserve. It's very nice for me — he cuts posts, & helps Hassan with things — & supplies me with fresh dagaa when I want it.

He also climbed David's palm with a dead rat! Which David G <u>completely</u> ignored, although nearly bumping his nose on it. He didn't even <u>look</u> at it — as though it was quite an everyday occur-

---

* Friend.

rence to find dead rats hanging on old shoe laces under his nose! You never told me if you got the photo of me and Colin that José took?

I'm sure that at some distant point I shall be asked what I want for Christmas. By when I shall have forgotten what has just occurred to me, so I will tell you <u>now.</u>

(1) Any of [blank space] Anthologies — I have "the Book of Love". There are 3 others — of Pleasure, of England — & Beauty! Beauty is the one I should prefer I think. But I don't know, as I've not seen them. (2) A reproduction, if there are such things, of a picture by [blank space] called [blank space]. I am utterly enchanted by the little girl in this picture.

Oh, I think it's going to deluge. What fun. I shall go if it does. I am now going on a tour to examine various chimp spots — with no expectation of seeing anything I might add! . . .

So tons of love,
Jane

Chimpland.
13th July [1961]

Darling Uncle Eric,

Please do forgive one of these nasty little things,* but I'm so busy nowadays that I can scarcely fit it all in. For one thing now that it has stopped raining I have no opportunities, or few, of writing letters up in the hills — as of yore, beneath my polythene sheet!

But it is really wonderful now the rain has stopped. Do you know, towards the end of the wet season I honestly wondered how I was going to exist through these last months. I didn't even feel like coming back after the week in Nairobi.† But oh, how different it is now. Already I feel the time speeding away, so much to do. Chimps are <u>extremely</u> friendly — I don't mind how far I scramble after them now because I know that there is a very good chance that they will <u>not</u> go away when I eventually reach them. At last I know most of

---

* The flimsy blue aerogramme on which the note was written.
† She took a brief holiday from Gombe in late May and early June.

the ♂ individually — as well as David G. (did you like his pictures?). There are Mike, Horace, Hollis, Huxley, Lord Dracula, the Hon. Mr. X, William, Winston and No. 3! What a collection of names! Women are <u>very</u> difficult & I can't usually get so close. Only to Barbara, Wilhemena, and Mrs. Maggs. Children are hopeless to recognize, except by the ♀ they are with. All the photography ahead alarms me considerably. The camera I have can only be used when one is almost shaking hands with the chimps, though it's the largest tele lens you can reasonably safely use hand held. Now Geographic have sent me all this complicated stuff — you will have seen from my other letter.

I meant to thank you for your letter to start off with. Anyway, I do thank you for it. It's jolly decent of you to find time to write because you're even busier than I am.

Next week — I hope — Derrick Dunn is bringing me a tape recorder. He's on a safari, & going to drop it in as he goes through Kigoma. This is another rather alarming aspect of the business, but one which I must cope with somehow. Though I've a feeling that the equipment isn't going to be good enough for the quality I want.

You heard of the Schallers — chap who did gorilla & came to visit Ma & I? They have a baby in a month & George is most anxious that Kay keeps it with her from the moment it's born — he feels the early mother/child relationship is particularly important — <u>after</u> studying his gorillas!! I only wish I could see a birth. <u>Most</u> unlikely.

Anyway, drop me another line when you have a moment.

Love to Peggy, lots of love to you,
Jane

<u>Chimpland.</u>
14 July [1961]

Darling Family,

If you can work this* out you will be clever. But I must write it on small sizes because of the gale. And small because all I have is this

---

* Her cramped handwriting on small pieces of paper.

thick paper. Oh, maybe biro will help. It's not meant to be blotting paper, but not much good for ink.

Mum, I do hope your colds & throats are <u>quite</u> better now. I wonder if there was a recurrence of our fever. When I told Dr. Grant about it, he said we should have made a blood slide. I told him Ugo said there was no malaria, and he said "B — " well, he said a rude word! And how horrid — about the machine needle going through your finger. Made me shudder all down my back. I hope that, too, is better.

Dan, your letter about Kip in Dennis's drawer — note, O & Jif, drawer, <u>not</u> with an S. What a time you all had to be sure. And there he was all snug & safe & laughing at you.

I am beginning to get in an awful flap about the way time is going. Do you know I have been back a <u>month,</u> already! And today is the anniversary of the first arrival of the Morris-Goodall Chimpanzee expedition! As a matter of fact it does seem a long time ago in many ways. Yet sometimes I can look at the peaks & valleys & see them with my early eyes, & how different they seem now. Then they were alien, strange, confusing — a challenge. And indeed, so were they in the rains. But now — now life is so wonderful. The challenge has been met. The hills & forests are my home. And what is more, I think my mind works like a chimp's, subconsciously. For when I take a track through the forest, selecting one from a maze of little trails — sure enough, if chimps are around, some old chap will be on the same road. It's happened <u>so</u> often. And I can't put it down to my cleverness at all — often it's a very <u>bad</u> track — for me. And often I choose one which I think I took before, & find it's another — & there is a chimp. It's most peculiar.

Although I'm not, at the moment, finding out anything startling, and <u>very</u> little that is new to me, none the less, life is good. Yesterday I made another friend. Another David G. Only this one is up in the hills and is all my own. I think it's the one we used to call Winston. I met him in my 'wood' the other day — he got to 4 or 5 yards from me, saw me, & bolted off. Not far. Anyway, yesterday I saw him plodding around the shoulder of Bald Soko so I decided to take a chance & go to his path in the wood. I only just got there when there was a rustle, & lo, a black face looking at me. Well, for one and a half hours he moved round me, picking up fallen mbula fruits from the ground. Sat in the sun with his back to me for ages — & this only 10 yards away. At times he came even closer to reach for a fruit. I prefer a tame chimp up in the mountains than in camp. I didn't take any photos — not the first time he honoured me with his company — because there are mbula trees ripe throughout this wood, so he definitely chose to be here because of me. I say "here" because I am now in the same spot. I don't think he'll come, because Mike & his woman, & another group, went across in his direction this morning & I dare say he has joined them. Still, I followed them for miles beyond Linda, but they weren't in a mood to hang about, so I left them. Then came the gale, so I thought I might as well wait here as anywhere. It is 4.30 pm.

You will probably all be delighted to hear that I have become ul-tra civilized. Now that Camp II is so very luxurious, I make myself a mug of coffee at some point during the day — when I get back from one of my safaris. Talk about the height of luxury!

I havn't yet mentioned, have I? that Derrick & Likens are coming here in 2 weeks with my tape recorder. I rather doubt it'll be good enough for the job, but I shall get D. to help me install the thing. They come just at the right time.

They come on 27th, & at the end of the month I have to go & look at the tree in Mitumba* — its name is lovely — Msululu. (The one you lost Mum!) So on the 28th we can play tape recorders, and on the 29th I can take D up Mitumba & get some hints on hide building, and on the 30th they can go, & if the tree is ready† I can organize my safari there. So it all fits in beautifully.

Robert & Alison come tomorrow for the night. They will hope to see a chimp on Sun. morning & then, I HOPE, Robert will drive the "Soko Muke"‡ back to Kigoma — if he will. Because Hassan is due back next week & can return with the boat & stores. Works very

---

* A valley at the northern end of the reserve.
† Ripe with fruits to attract chimpanzees.
‡ Jane's small aluminum boat. *Soko Muke* means "chimpanzee lady."

well. And if, for some odd reason, Hassan can't get here, it is not very long before Derrick can bring it.

The weather is <u>perfect</u> at this time — everything is late this year, because it's much cooler than when we arrived, & the grass still green in many places. I hope it doesn't affect the termites.

The dreadful morning gales have, at any rate for the moment, stopped. I say there is a gale now, but it's mild compared to what I have been coping with, & anyway it's not so bad in the middle of the day, because by then the chimps are either here, & you know where they are, or not here, as today, & you know they may come later on when the wind drops in the evening.

2 Lowrie birds are having a terrific flirtation just here. Such a flipping of wings and tail from the ♂, and a funny whirring chuckling call. I presume that I <u>did</u> tell you about my chimps all lying on the ground & grooming, etc? That was the start of my present mood — everything lovely. I don't know if it was obvious in my letters — I hope not too much so — but towards the end of the rains I began to wonder how I could exist through these next 4 months. The last few weeks before I went to Nairobi were the longest I can remember. I was not looking forward to returning. And when I first got back, I still expected to feel the same — so that I did for a few days. But now, as I say, the days are speeding along far, far too quickly. I think it was a combination of rain, grass, heat and general "unfitness" on my part. I don't know why I wasn't fit. I looked OK except for being rather skeletal. But everything was such an effort. Now I don't mind how far I go, how often I get up here before dawn, how often I return in the moonlight. I am just in love with the mountains & the chimps & the monkeys — Oh, & everything. Obviously I am still looking forward to coming HOME — but because it's home, and not, as before, because I near the end of my sojourn here. . . .

Sorry this is a measly letter, but I don't have much time these days. I always seem to be up in the mountains before dawn, & never down till dark fall — kazi!* Anyway, it's rather late now so I

---

* Work.

shall cease. The Greenshields won't be bringing mail as a Scout brought it yesterday, so there won't be anything to answer, so I'll end here.

Tons & tons & tons of love,

Jane

P.S. Ma, when the Ansteys come you might have a chat with Margaret about her Ma in Cambridge. Re. me.

Also, if you're in London, go & see Napier — & how can I find out why Ramona won't write?

Did I send any pictures of David G. in his fig tree — reclining, etc? Or just the 2 tent ones & one in the rain?

6

❧ ❧ ❧

PHOTOGRAPHING GOMBE
1961–1962

> The National Geographic Society . . . wanted to send out a pro-
> fessional photographer, but I was terrified at the thought of a
> stranger arriving on the scene and ruining my hard-won relation-
> ship with the chimps.
>
> — *In the Shadow of Man*

B Y THE END of her first year in the forest, Jane Goodall had
gotten closer to wild chimpanzees, seen more, and learned
more about them and their daily lives than any other human
ever had. Louis Leakey's faith in the energy, endurance, passion,
and intuition of his young protégée was vindicated.

At least for him. For the rest of the world, the vindication was
more complex. The young Miss Goodall's lack of formal scientific
training may have been an advantage in terms of her raw field work.
She approached her task and subjects from a fresh point of view,
without the limits of a theoretical filter. In terms of communicating
her discoveries, however, that lack might actually become a great
disadvantage. Who would ultimately take her work seriously? And
so, to bolster the quality of her research as well as her credibility,
Louis Leakey lobbied the academic authorities at Cambridge University to admit Jane as a doctoral candidate in ethology, the science
of animal behavior, under the distinguished tutelage of Professor
Robert Hinde.* Louis's potent reputation, along with his summary

---

* Professor W. H. Thorpe was originally to have been her advisor at Cambridge.

of Jane's actual accomplishments during the first several months of field research, was persuasive; she became one of only a handful of students in the history of Cambridge enrolled in a doctoral program without having first completed the undergraduate degree.

Jane left Gombe in December of 1961, returned to England, and settled into a bed-sitter at 1 Magrath Avenue in Cambridge. During the subsequent university term she attended lectures, regularly met with her advisor, and produced various papers and reports. Meanwhile, she was invited to talk about her work at scientific conferences in London and New York and to submit papers for publication. She finished her first term at Cambridge in early June of 1962 and by early July was back at Gombe, where she remained until December.

If her first year in the forest (July 1960 to July 1961) had focused upon approaching the apes and making those great first discoveries, her second year (July to December 1961 and July to December 1962) concentrated on communicating the discoveries broadly through her own writing and through photography.

The National Geographic Society of Washington, D.C., had taken over the funding of Jane's research in the spring of 1961, starting with a grant of $1,400 to Louis Leakey earmarked as support for the work of his "chimpanzee research assistant" in the field. The grant was finalized in a meeting that took place on March 13, 1961. By the end of the month, William Graves, an editorial staff member of the Geographic, was visiting Louis in Nairobi and discussing the possibility of an article about Jane and the wild apes, complete with brilliant photographs, for which *National Geographic* magazine, of course, was famous.

Photography was the problem. Beyond the standard technical challenges anyone would need to master — the usual conflicts between light and lens, film and focus, shutter and aperture — a photographer coming to Gombe would have to deal with photonically elusive subjects: dark-haired creatures skittering through dark places, shy beings more likely to absorb than reflect light — shadows inside shadows. As well, a photographer would have to be concerned with the effects of high heat and penetrating moisture on delicate instruments. The heavy, clumsy equipment would have to be lugged up and down, back and forth. There would be the isolation, the confinement of camp, the supply limitations. There was the problem of potentially hostile fauna — poisonous snakes and such — and that of invariably hostile flora — thorns and thickets and mazes. Malaria was a likely problem. And the unavoidable treachery of the terrain, those steep ridges and plummeting chasms. Moreover, the chimpanzees were likely to be physically elusive — why should they stick around? Why would they pause and pose? The Gombe environment gave chimpanzees a vast physical advantage over humans, and if they chose not to be photographed, it would be almost impossible to do so.

Still, in the summer of 1961, Jane and the African staff optimistically built "hides" or "blinds" at a few critical spots in the reserve, hoping to predict where the chimpanzees might go and imagining that they might tolerate a person plus a big glassy eye on top of a pole if the person and glassy eye were half obscured. Chimpanzees inhabit pretty much the same perceptual world as humans. A blind would no more fool them than it would fool a person, but it might make the photographic snoopery seem less intrusive.

Partly because National Geographic was funding Jane through their larger grant to Louis, much of the early discussion about photographing Gombe initially took place in a loop of correspondence between Washington and Nairobi, with Jane remaining to some degree outside.

Louis was at first very optimistic. Jane's progress in habituating the chimps was successful enough, he informed Graves, that possibly a professional photographer could go out to Gombe by July of 1961; but, he insisted emphatically, that person would have to be a woman. As Graves paraphrased Louis's words in a March 29 letter back to Washington: "Miss Goodall spends unbroken weeks in the bush and for her own sake and for appearances it would be very unwise to send a man out there." So, yes, a woman photographer might be acceptable by July but "only if Miss Goodall agrees and things are going well."

Within a few weeks, the Geographic had assigned to the task a staff illustrations editor with photographic experience, Mary Griswold. But almost immediately the idea was reconsidered. "I know Mary is going to do a magnificent job," noted Graves in an internal memorandum, "but it occurs to me that her problems — at least for a short time — will be every bit as great as Miss Goodall's."

By the end of May, Melville Bell Grosvenor, president of the society and editor of the magazine, had written to Louis noting that the Geographic had "reluctantly come to the conclusion that it would be unwise to send someone inexperienced in working with wild animals." That meant Mary Griswold was out. But, Grosvenor thought, perhaps Louis's son Richard might be acceptable to Jane, "since he is no stranger to her." Additionally, Richard had photographic experience and also "knows the animals and would not be unduly alarmed about being alone with them in the jungle." Grosvenor concluded by noting that the Geographic had already air-expressed a wide-angle Rolliflex camera, a supply of high-speed Ektachrome film, and some special cartons to expedite the return shipments of exposed film. Ideally, the society would want enough photographs of the study to produce twelve to fifteen pages of "top quality" pictures.

Louis replied in a letter of June 7 that there was "no possibility" of sending Richard to Gombe. Jane arrived for her brief vacation in Nairobi soon after that first letter — and just after the wide-angle Rolliflex arrived. Thus, in a letter of June 12, Louis noted that Jane had tried the camera and found it "far too heavy and clumsy, and [therefore] will not take it with her into the field. What would you like me to do with it?" As an alternative, Louis had purchased a much lighter instrument with an easily portable telephoto lens. That could serve as the "camera round her neck" — but it would be important for the Geographic to send a second camera with much better telephoto lenses and a tripod to support them.

Jane returned to Gombe with the "camera round her neck," and National Geographic airmailed the additional camera, stronger lenses, and other equipment Louis had requested. In a letter to Gombe written on June 22, Joseph B. Roberts, National Geographic's assistant director of photography, informed Jane that he was shipping out a Nikon reflex 35mm camera with three telephoto lenses of 50mm, 105mm, and 300mm; an electric motor drive powered by eight Type C batteries in a battery case; a relay box; a fifty-foot extension cord for remote control operation; a General Electric light exposure meter; fifteen rolls of Kodachrome II film; a Globe Trotter carrying bag; aluminum tripod; and a set of caption cards and film shipping cartons. "Now," Roberts went on, "for the shortest correspondence course in photography ever written. I presume that you have had considerable camera experience on previous scientific expeditions."

The situation was absurd. Jane wrote her family about the letter, which she found "quite horrifying." And, after about five weeks of apparent anguish over the Geographic shipment, she responded to Roberts (her letter of August 14) with the declaration that "I am not proposing to use your equipment until nearer the end of my work here, as I feel that a determined effort at close-up photography will very definitely upset the animals."

She also sent at that time a "test roll" taken from the neck-hanging camera. That roll, when processed at the National Geographic laboratories in Washington, proved to be more disappointing than anyone had anticipated. "Of 37 exposures on this roll," noted an illustrations editor, Robert E. Gilka, in an internal memo, "16 are so underexposed as to be unreadable, 10 are spoiled because of camera motion, and 6 are not useable for other reasons. We are left with one picture we might possibly use, a shot of Miss Goodall sitting on a hillside scanning the area for chimps."

Meanwhile, Louis and Jane had come up with an alternate plan. Why not send out Jane's sister, Judy? She could take time off from her job — she was by then working at the British Museum. She had "already had some experience of color photography," as Louis noted in a letter of July 17 to Grosvenor. So would the society agree to pay her air fare and expenses, plus perhaps some compensation for her time off from work in London? The reply, sent by Frederick G. Vosburgh, the Geographic's vice president and associate editor, was quick and rather stiff, if not downright stuffy. "The production of satisfactory photographs for the National Geographic requires considerable experience as well as aptitude, and this assignment would tax the skill of even a professional photographer."

Louis persisted, however, and eventually — in spite of Vosburgh's continuing resistance — Judy did go to Gombe to work the big camera. Jane by this time was "obsessed with two things," as she noted in her letter to Aunt Olwen on September 4, 1961: to observe mating behavior and to get some good photographs. And when Judy arrived toward the end of September, for a brief period the weather and the chimpanzees cooperated enough to produce a wealth of solid photo opportunities. But soon the weather stopped cooperating, as did the chimps. Jane's November 9 letter to Louis (whom she was then addressing as "Fairy Foster Father" or "FFF") provides one indication of how discouraging the situation had become.

Jane and Judy both left in December: Jane to Cambridge to begin her first term at university, Judy to London to resume her job at the British Museum. Back in Washington, Illustrations Editor Robert E. Gilka was scanning the latest rolls of film. As he wrote in a January 2, 1962, letter to both Jane and Judy: "I wish that we were in a position to publish an article on your subject because it is an unusual and fascinating subject. However, there is a lack of good pictures of the animals in their natural habitat. This shortcoming is so serious as to preclude attempting to illustrate a story." Incidentally, Gilka went on, where are the camera, lenses, and tripod we lent you?

By this time, however, society president and magazine editor Melville Bell Grosvenor had become convinced that the Jane Goodall story was, as he noted in a letter to photographer David S. Boyer, "fabulous" and the Geographic "must make every effort to get it." He then wrote to Louis in Nairobi and Jane in Cambridge, proposing that the Geographic pay Jane a handsome sum to leave Cambridge for about three weeks during February and fly out to Gombe with Boyer to get those pictures. Both Louis and Jane wrote back and declared the idea impossible: too difficult for her to get out there in so short a time, too hard to find the chimps in February, Jane too busy with her studies, and so on.

Still, the Geographic had begun to support Jane's work seriously, both her studies at Cambridge and her continuing field work at Gombe. Additionally, at a meeting in March of 1962, the society's board of trustees voted to provide a travel grant so that Jane could fly to Washington and present her initial findings (which she did in April) and also to give her the Franklin L. Burr Prize for Contribution to Science (which included a cash award of $1,500). March was a good month, in short, and Louis's wonderful news made it even better. He reported to Jane that he had met an excellent professional wildlife photographer who ought to satisfy everyone involved. Jane mentioned this reassuring bit of information to a friend, zoologist and author Desmond Morris, in a letter of March 12.

About a month after Jane returned to Gombe in the summer of 1962, a handsome Dutch photographer, Baron Hugo van Lawick, showed up at camp. Vanne had been enlisted to come out that summer as chaperone, theoretically to salve any stung conventional sensibilities, but she showed up a few weeks after Hugo did. Back in Washington, Gilka was himself mildly concerned about convention. He described to Jane in a letter of September 14 an earlier photograph that, though it was not successful, still had been a nice concept. "I've told him [Hugo] in my letter of several shots I want him to try," Gilka declared. "One of these pictures is a picture of you washing your hair. It is possible Hugo might be too embarrassed to ask you to do this for him." Jane wrote back on September 26: "You will by now have had stills of me washing my hair — though Hugo is going to take some more in a more forested part. You needn't worry about him being embarrassed. I haven't noticed it yet!"

Hugo proved to be "just the right person for the job," as Jane wrote in early September to Melvin Payne, Geographic's executive vice president and secretary. And by the end of the season the National Geographic had enough superb color photographs to proceed with the chimpanzee article. Jane had virtually finished her first draft by December 19, as she noted in the brief letter to Vosburgh. And in August 1963, Jane Goodall's "My Life Among Wild Chimpanzees" appeared in 3 million copies of the glossy, flatbound magazine with the bright yellow frame around its front cover. The feature began with a romantic silhouette of Jane Goodall sitting in front of a campfire above Lake Tanganyika and proceeded to display three dozen extraordinary visions of Gombe life, including a remote view of a chimpanzee carrying meat (evidence of meat-eating), three closer pictures of chimps fashioning twigs and using them to fish for termites in termite mounds (tool use), a photo of Vanne dispensing medicines in front of the tent, a few more of the African staff and fishermen and other local people illustrating various local activities, some shots of David Greybeard and Goliath, an artist's conception of the "chimpanzee rain dance," a photo of Jane sitting on a hillside and scanning the distance for her quarry, and one of Jane standing knee-deep in a stream and washing her hair.

*　　*　　*　　*

Chimpland.
[July 5, 1961]

Darling Family,

All hail! Wot, no chimps! Actually, there are some, but they are not nice to me these days.

Thank you, Mum and Dan, for your two letters. As I said to Jif, I am about to disown knowledge of an Aunt Olwen. And as for the Aunt Mary Audrey Gwyneth — never heard of her! I've certainly forgotten who she is! Now, Danny, you are <u>not</u> to write me letters with a hurting neck. I suggest you talk them into the tape recorder & Ma can type them!! Or else dictate them to Jif who is supposed to be learning short hand isn't she? You will by now have had various letters from me — since these 2 (yours Mum & Dan) were sent on to me from Nairobi. I think all you wanted to know you will now know.

May I mention a little business first? Mum, did you ever see Napier? Because he's now not answering my latest letter, though I suppose, actually, he's not had it long. But I just wondered if you ever did see him? Also, can you think of a way of finding out if Ramona is O.K.? You remember the long & sweet letter she wrote me? I've penned her two since then, & not a word. I hope she's O.K. I <u>did</u> have a letter from Poosh. DID YOU SEND ON SUSIE'S LETTER??

The only real news I have is quite horrifying. A long letter from National Geographic with details of the equipment they are sending me — camera with 3 lenses & 1 tripod & automatic controls. It makes me feel so utterly helpless & despondent. It's a good thing you wern't here when it arrived, Ma. I was still awake at 3.30, & taking painocils for a raging headache! Have recovered a bit now. The man presumed I was already an experienced photographer after photographing my other scientific studies! It's bad enough having to battle with mountains, heat, tired body <u>and</u> chimps — let alone tripods & lenses & lengths of wire etc., etc. If they only realized the conditions — & this includes dear L.S.B. For instance, yesterday I was inching my way up a mountain side, clinging onto rocks & roots. And I bumped into some chimps. Well, there they sat, yelled at me a bit, ate a bit, scratched a bit, & went on their way. Wonderful view. Super photos — <u>if</u> I could have taken them. But as I hadn't really enough hands & feet to secure me to the mountain's surface, <u>how</u> could I take out my one simple little camera? Let alone if I'd had millions of lenses & tripods stuck all over me!!

You remember when we first got here, Mum, how I went off to Mitumba with my "merry men!" Well, I set off — <u>walking!</u> — with Andreano and Rashidi 2 days ago, to have a look at the tree. Made me quite homesick for Mitumba Valley! But the tree is going to be at <u>least</u> a month late this year. No signs of fruit, or even flowers.

(Must interrupt here to say that I now feel quite homesick for you, Mum. One of my hens is <u>snoring</u> — & it sounds just like you!!! Did you know hens snored? Nor did I. Do please ask Douglas if he has heard this? It's the most <u>incredible</u> sound!)

However, we made a hide — a dear little wee house of palm fronds where I shall sit when and if they come — almost in the tree with them! . . .

It now feels <u>very</u> late — it isn't in <u>fact,</u> but for the last few nights I've just lain awake. Back to me old tricks! I've read recently on the Nivequin pamphlet that a side effect of <u>that</u> is insomnia! But I feel they meant that only when one was taking large dosages, not simply the small preventative amounts.

If the D.C. brings letters from anyone I may add to this, but probably not until Robert & Alison. So tons & tons of love — to all members of my family not yet ex-communicated!

Jane

c/o The District Commissioner
Kigoma
Tanganyika
14 August 1961

Dear Mr. Roberts,

Many thanks indeed for your letter of June and let me quickly offer you my sincerest apologies for the delay in replying. This is partly due to the fact that it stayed in Kigoma for some time before being sent to me here in the Reserve — since then I have been hopelessly trying to make arrangements concerning the equipment — very difficult as Dr. Leakey had been away from the country.

You will have heard from him that I am not proposing to use your equipment until nearer the end of my work here, as I feel that a determined effort at close-up photography will very definitely upset the animals.

Has Dr. Leakey told you that for the present I am using a 35 mm camera with 135 mm telelens? I am sending you, in one of your cartons, a test roll from this camera — which is very disappointing. Since receiving the film from you I have had the worst month of my entire research period! Not only no opportunities for photographic chimps — scarcely a chimp at all. True, one comes to expect these sort of set-backs when engaged on such a study, but it is a disappointment.

The main difficulties here, so far as photography is concerned, are two. Firstly, the nature of the country (as you will see from the couple of habitat shots on the test roll) renders the transportation of equipment extremely difficult. The chimps are seldom in the same place for more than an hour at a time. I must work and travel about, alone if possible. And most of the time I have to be crawling through dense undergrowth or scrambling up and down sheer mountain sides. However, the camera I am using at the moment, to its possible detriment, accompanies me during all my wanderings.

Secondly, and even more trying, is the attitude of the chimps. I cannot say that they are frightened any — far from it. But they do not like to be watched. And to approach them within 50–100 ft., unless it be in bush so thick as to make observation, let alone photography, difficult, is often not possible. However, there are occasions when the troops gather together when a certain tree bears fruit. When all the big males are there, all will be well. Also I have established hides near these trees, in readiness, and shall set up the big telephoto lens there when your equipment arrives.

I have gone into all this, probably unnecessary, detail to put you in the picture a little and to let you know that I feel sure that I shall get the necessary pictures despite a somewhat unfortunate beginning.

As for general background pictures, these will be admirably provided by the dagaa fishing. The tribesmen are allowed to camp along the shores of the lake during the season and spread out the fish on the beaches. I plan to get some fascinating pictures. The canoes setting out at dusk, the lights on the lake, the giant "butterfly" nets which they use to scoop up the fish — all these are very attractive pictorially. And I have several other ideas for "local colour".

Again, my sincere apologies for the delay in answering, in fact this is only the second opportunity of sending out mail since your letter eventually got to me. Any further tips you can give me will be very welcome. I am not in the position of having had previous camera experience I'm afraid. None the less, I am quite certain that when my chimps return again I shall get the sort of pictures you are wanting — as well as the sort I must get for my report — habitat, nests, positions, etc.

Sincerely yours,
Jane Goodall

Chimpland.
10.30 pm.
[September 4, 1961]

Darling Olly,

Just had your <u>letter</u> — wonders will never cease! However, I was writing to you anyway to wish you a very, very happy birthday — I'll be with you next year & can give you a present properly, & everything. But for now, will you just have a whole heap of 'good wishes' from 'chimpland' — where <u>both</u> your nieces (by then) — by <u>now</u> — will be thinking of you & sending "Happy birthday dear Olly" resounding across the mountains like mad!

I only <u>hope</u> I'll be able to get this sent off so that it does get to you in time. It's the 4th Sept at the moment, but Hassan is away — child ill — & unless a Scout goes in, or some other trustworthy bod. — I don't see how I can send it. Still, I shall just <u>hope.</u>

The time is flying past so quickly — that August is over I find almost <u>impossible</u> to believe. It's horrifying really — I am now obsessed with two things — photographs and sex!! Sounds bad, doesn't it! A sort of "chimps' pornography dept!"!!

I'm sitting here, with my pressure lamp. Out on the lake the fishermen's lights are gleaming across the dark, still water. Every so often they bang on their canoes, making the fish jump. A very noisy pig is crunching up dry palm nuts — what a loud sound. The crickets have the orchestration to themselves now — the little tree frogs are silent for some reason. And way up the dark valley a baboon keeps barking — the sentry is uneasy — something is lurking in the black shadows — the unknown terrors of the mountains at night.

Dominic is out in my boat, busily fishing. He keeps me well supplied with delicious fish. Small, but tasty. He had a silver pile of dagaa for my supper tonight — the hens ate it all! My chickens will taste odd soon — they eat so much dagaa I shan't know whether I'm eating fish or fowl!

O — I must stop (not "oh" — "Olly"!). I'm really too sleepy to know quite what I'm writing. I saw my <u>darling</u> David Greybeard again this morning. He was in company. Mike, Hollis, Olly! — the "Terrible Twins" and an unknown lady & gent. It was <u>so</u> nice to meet him again. Don't know where he's been hiding away.

Anyway, I do hope you have a 'super' Birthday. Give my love to Douglas.

Tons & tons to you,
Jane

The Tent.
Chimpland.
[September] 14th. [1961]

Darling Family,

You will probably be wondering if I am still alive — it seems ages since I last wrote, though I don't suppose it is really. The fact is that my chimps have come back, & I really, honestly & truly havn't had a single moment till tonight to pen a line, though I did have the chance of posting one, had I written it! Well, Judy will have arrived in Nairobi today — what a joke. Charles* (D.C.) sent me a note to say he had millions of letters & telegrams from Leakey, all cancelling each other out! She is apparently arriving on 23rd — at least, that is the latest telegram. (I've noticed my writing is turning into a sort of long short hand. It comes of my Journal — it's about 5 or 6 pages every night & these days I'm climbing & returning in torch light — still, I have got some chimps to watch.) But oh, what a tragedy. Two days ago I broke the camera — & today what <u>lovely</u> pictures I could have taken — William 12 ft away, standing up with one hand on a tree, saying, very gently, "hoo" & then sitting there gazing up at the trees looking for figs — Mike, the same distance, chewing a lovely pink wadge of palm nut fibres & fig pips. Mrs Maggs followed by her baby. It was no use for anything else — they were on a safari & did not stop. But superb for photos. And it is the first time in 2 months I've had the opportunity. Makes you weep. I frantically despatched the camera to Nairobi hoping Jif can bring it with her — the shutter's gone. One scout was in Kigoma, the other couldn't go till he got back, so I sent off Dominic's wife. I hope it got on the train O.K — she hasn't come back yet.

The Boma† has been secretary-less for 2 weeks, so I've not had any mail for ages & ages. There is a letter from you, Mum, to answer, & I will do so when I have it by me. I can't post this yet awhile, but decided I'd better start a letter to you all.

Poor Hassan has a very sick child & had to go off to Kisumu. I'm hoping he'll be back next Thursday.

---

* Charles Campbell-Whalley, the district commissioner.
† An old German fort in Kigoma, site of government offices, including the post office.

I saw 2 little children, 2 years old, <u>dancing</u> yesterday. I can't really call it anything else. They were pacing up & down, a distance of 4 yards or so, passing each other, turning, & re-passing, walking bipedally, & stamping down each foot — sort of Conga step, bringing the arm down in time, & nodding their heads. It only lasted a few moments, but was rather fun. All the gents are in fighting fettle just now — everywhere they go they charge around, swiping at trees & yelling & screaming and flinging their arms about. One, followed by a rather bewildered young ♀, came right down from practically the very tip top of Sleeping Buffalo, to the valley. About 1/2 mile I suppose. Yelling nearly all the way.

And oh, so funny. I saw a very neat little group of 3 — gentleman, old lady (in 'interesting' condition) and a pretty and glamorous 'teenager'. They were the same side of a valley as I. They vanished, down to the stream. Then the gentleman, followed by glamour-puss, appeared, walking rapidly up the other side. They did not pause, nor did they go by the usual route, but turned off sharply when they got to the top of the very steep part, & entered a karonga.* Vanished. About 4 mins later the old girl appeared. She was rather like a fat old lady wanting to catch a bus — every few yards she broke into a sort of loping run for a few steps — awful effort — it was <u>very</u> steep. Oh dear, she'd never catch them up. Her pink behind waggled ponderously from side to side. At last she got to the top & paused. Gazed upwards — where they <u>should</u> háve gone. Not a sign. She looked anxiously in the right direction, but obviously could not see them. Hurrying still, she climbed a bit higher to get a better view. Not a sign. Go up again. No good. So it went on, right up a completely bare hill side — 1/4 mile. Finally, she reached the trees at the top. She sat for a moment, still looking round. Not a sign. They <u>must</u> have gone up there after all — better hurry on. So she hurried on. But when the fat old lady spies some extra delicious home made pastries in the shop window — well, bit of a risk — bus might go — <u>must</u> have some of those. And so the old girl could not resist gathering some tasty fallen fruits & stuffing them in her mouth en route! Well, she got right to the top — no

---

* Ravine.

sign — so she climbed a tall tree & sat there for 30 mins. At last, wearily, she plodded off alone. "Oh well, boys will be boys — but talk about cradle snatching!" And she disappeared over the brow of the hill!

We have had the first heavy rain storm — do you remember, Mum, the first last year. It was earlier — just after my first fever, when I saw the two giant ladies in Linda, & you were whisked into the Kibisi by Audrey Knight* & Co? And then the second when I was with Wilbert — I thought we'd been <u>so</u> far — we walked back, early, along the beach, & Wilbert collected shells for you, & thought he'd get a fever from having got wet!

It has got incredibly hot again — though not quite so bad today after the rain. I was sick for 2 days — don't know what the matter was — some old bug or other. It was an effort getting round, but had to be done, and was worth it. Now I am fighting fit again — seem to be fitter than ever. (N.B. Not serious or I'd not have mentioned it!)

I despair of 2 things — (1) — seeing mating (2) Jif or I getting any photos — it's <u>not</u> a question of the capabilities of <u>taking</u> them — it's getting in the right place at the right time. Really one needs about 6 people, all with telephotos, all sitting in all possible places, in hides every day for a couple of months!! As it is, Jif will have to hopefully dash from hide to hide, & they'll never go the right way at the right time. What a life. Since I last wrote I found the home of some more Banded Mongooses, & got some pictures, 16 feet away, of them at their entrance. If <u>only</u> cameras didn't click I could have got many more, but at the 'click' they run for their lives. Surely someone could invent one that <u>doesn't</u> click? Also a ♂ bushbuck, 18 feet away, looking at me. He didn't mind the click. And a very grizzy frankolin† with his greedy, non-stop-pecking wife — 14 feet away. I think they're a new sub-species, or a west African race, & I'm hoping JGW can tell from photos. And now — no camera. (I must say it's <u>bliss</u> going around without having to lug the weight about).

---

* A friend in Kigoma.
† A kind of partridge.

I am now going to put out the light as it's late. Shall continue anon. . . .

Next day

Well, another 24 hours of my life have vanished — 25 actually. I had a delightful morning, with chimps all over the place — & very nearly saw mating — saw mounting anyway, & then, with her lover still clasping her amorously, the lady stood up & held onto a tree. Maybe they did mate, but I couldn't see properly — a most odd way of doing things if so! And then they did a sort of dance round the tree on their two legs, & joined by a 2nd ♂ also upright. It was most entertaining. They all vanished utterly at 10.30, so I did some work on 2 hides this evening. I am doing them myself so as to put them up gradually, a little more every day. . . .

It's now considerably later than it was last night, & I'm going to stop once more. Adieu. I'm going to bed now. My fingers are so sore with writing 11 pages of today's Journal, & it's awful late, & I may be able to post this tomorrow.

Saw about 30 chimps today — & oh where, oh where was my camera. It really is too bad — I was relying on this fig time for the best pictures — & how right I was. Chimps all around me. What a day — chimps near, chimps far, old men, young men, ladies, children, babies, teen-agers — the lot. I don't really like these days — it's wonderful to see them all, but such a muddle.

Like the Boma — they are the limit. Hassan got back today — he asked for my letters — they gave him one which arrived today. What have they done with my last 3 weeks mail. However, the Kibisi passed today & Dominic sent a stern message back to say I wanted my mail — wouldn't they send it via Kibisi when she comes back to collect the tsetse man from up the Lake.

It's too late to be coherent. Hassan's child is in hospital, but getting better. No more news anyway.

Tons & tons of love,
Jane

The Tent
11 pm
[Around September 25, 1961]

Darlings all,

Hail. How are you all? Well, Jif has arrived. It seems a <u>hoot</u> — yet in a way quite normal. She was waiting when I got back on Saturday. I wanted to be here to greet her, but Mike was mating, & I was involved — I don't mean what it sounds as though I do!!! Dominic is thrilled I think, & is working even harder. We eat outside with a fire. He makes puddings. His bibi made us an 'African Cake' today — <u>delicious.</u> Tastes like doughnut. He madly tips baths in & out, washes & irons, etc., etc.

As for Jif's introduction to chimps — more than 25, all spread out over the Pocket! Mating! Walking on hind legs! Dragging branches! And, today, making a nest! Not bad! She hasn't had a chance to take pictures yet as I'm taking the camera, close up to my darlings (mine is due back this week). It is a good thing — she is getting to know the lie of the land, & finding her feet. She is bearing up remarkably — excellent at spotting chimps, & <u>most</u> useful — I wish even <u>more</u> that I could have had an assistant for longer as one can get so much more out of it with 2.

Incidentally, Mum, in one of your letters you were looking over at your youngest, sleeping all pink & white & peaceful. You hoped she would sleep as well here. Well, she may be a little more pink than white!, but as to the peace of her sleep, that is unquestioned. She sleeps most blissfully as I lie wakeful. I have just finished my journal! And am having my customary late night nibble! (Bit of D's new loaf, tiny slither of the cake — well, I'll have the paw paw now, not tomorrow. Cup of coffee? May as well. Oh, there's the cheap choc Jif got in Kigoma — square or 2 would go well with coffee! Etc!)

I think I'd better stop for now. I have a <u>very</u> early start tomorrow. Though it will probably avail me little as it's such a complicated place to get to that I'll probably get lost & arrive at the time I would if I started later!! Goodnight.

Well — I didn't get lost. And Poosh woke up over my head and very nearly wee'd all over me! Just missed! Mike came along, hit a tree at me & climbed it — only 20 yards away. 2 days before he went to <u>sleep</u> on a branch 30 <u>feet</u> away!! And he & Poosh & Humphrey sat & groomed etc, quite unconcerned, for an hour. It really is fabulous. As for mating — you'd have really laughed the other morning. It was early. Few calls from the valley. Then a female jumped up into a big tree, followed by her 5 year old child. With yells & shrieks, full of the joys of life, 5 large males bounded up after her. All masculine strength and virility they swung from branch to branch, calling wildly, huge and black in the cool clear morning. One of them bounded up to the lady. She screamed — but she played the game all right. Well, she coped with No. 1. He sat beside her for a moment, then swung away, out of the tree. 2 of the others had vanished. No 2, allowing no decent interval, bounded up to the lady. Well, she saw nothing wrong with 2 before breakfast. She didn't even scream. Over quickly and he went happily away. No 3 wasted no time. Like a flash he charged across. The lovers passed each other en route — "Have a good time" says No 2. "Good stuff, eh?" says No 3. He evidently finds it so, for he repays her by laying himself at her feet, offering her the privilege of grooming his head. She accepts the invitation, and then they sit sociably side by side, passing the time of day. But what's this? More business by the look of things. "Well, it was nice while it lasted, but you must be on your way, my love". No 3 can take a hint — and No 4 is sitting on a branch at the bottom of the tree. "You sure like taking your time" he remarks, as No 3 swings down past him. Up he goes. He knows what they like — all women are the same. Cave man stuff & all that. Be forceful. Bursting with masculinity he charged to the fray, yelled, shook the branch. "Come on, Woman". She played up all right. Screamed, pretended to run away — but how quickly she succumbed and yielded when he grabbed her.

And, hello — No 5 is queing, down on the bottom branch. "Thanks Big Boy, but don't hang around". No 5 leaps out of the way as No 4 charges down. Then up for his turn. Soon over, & off he goes. Now perhaps a girl can have a bite of breakfast. She settles comfortably. The child comes up & sits beside her. "What's that, my dear? — oh, don't you worry your head about it — your turn will come, all in good time. Just eat your breakfast!"

Hello — what have we here? Another suitor? Well, a most embarrassed and coy young man. He peeps round the trunk. Takes a step towards her. Yes, he will. He takes another step — but oh dear, she's such a woman of the world, so experienced, while he — he dangles, bashful, by one arm. He looks away. He swings his legs. Perhaps he can get some Dutch courage. He hopefully shakes a branch to prove his superior strength, his budding malehood. He takes another step. No good — he just can't. <u>Next</u> time he will. It's too late now, anyway. Giving him a condescending look, my lady swings gracefully past. Young men nowadays — what are things coming to. Her daughter follows. "Let the men do all the chasing, dear" her mother always says. So she too gives the youth a haughty look. But he's rather good looking, all the same — she peeps back. He is looking after her — just a little wistfully — or is she imagining it?

I'm going to stop now. There's no more news, & any there is I dare say Jif has told you. I <u>can't</u> believe there are only 2 more months. Ma — can you find out <u>somehow</u> whether Newnham* will approve of my starting off with M's mother? 'Cos one must be in 'approved lodging'.

Tons of love,
Jane

October
The Tent.
[Probably November 3, 1961]

Darlings All,

How goes everything? All these preparations — really! What with new lino, straightened tiles, new covers, hoards (spent!) under carpets, & rows of permanent waves, I shan't know anything. Maybe I shall walk into O.R., view the covers, & burst into tears because they arn't the same old chairs.

---

* Her college at Cambridge.

Thank you so much for the last 2 letters, Mum & Dan. Danny, you say you are a "bad letter writer". I've <u>never</u> heard such rubbish in my life! You are a fabulous letter writer — & don't worry — I shan't breeze into the arctic house, leaving all doors & windows open in my wake for Kip to depart through in unaccustomed glee — which is what it sounds as though you fear will occur as soon as I set foot over the threshhold.

We are making plans too — at least, we are already saying — in 39 more days we shall be in the Birches. It doesn't seem possible. Where have the 18 odd months gone to I wonder? It is very mysterious.

Dear me, how it does rain here to be sure. I really have ceased worrying over photography & begin to laugh instead. Hordes of frogs, not even gracing Chimpland in the long rains, have arrived to celebrate the "water water everywhere". Only there are plenty of drinkable drops. Yesterday visibility was nil up top, & two very drenched — sorry — 3 — people dripped into camp at 4 pm. And there we remained. The rain was still coming down in buckets at 9 pm, & we cooked eggs, beans & corned beef on the primus. D was prepared but the poor fellow is dreadfully ill with — probably flu I should say.

Had a funny thing with John Napier — he wrote and asked me for a title for my paper in April. Which gave me a heart attack as I think I told you. Anyhow, I asked him what lines the symposium was being run on — to do with human evolution, or what. I suggested, if he was really desperate for a title, he invent one to fit the bill. Well, then Moshi* arrived & I wrote to him again — about 1 week later — to know if he wanted Moshi as a founder member of his new Primate Unit. And I thought I'd really been rather foolish & said, if he thought it O.K., I'd call my paper "Ecology & Behaviour of the Free-ranging Chimpanzee". (Jiff thought Free-<u>living</u> sounded immoral!) This crossed with John's answer to my original letter sug-

---

* When some fishermen brought a baby vervet monkey to Gombe one day, Judy named the monkey Moshi and "adopted" it for the duration of her stay. After Judy left, Moshi was given to people in Kigoma.

gesting we call my paper "Observations on the ecology & behaviour of the Free-living chimpanzee"!!!* Rather a hoot!

I am planning a farewell party — back to the <u>original</u> birthday idea of an evening curry. I have been discussing it with D — we think 2 hours will be enough. There will be 14 adults & goodness knows how many children. Iddi & 2 wives, Saulo, Rashidi, & Severino with their wives, H & D with Mrs. D, & Jiff & I. And then all the strings of infants. Quite a "doo" — Or am I only allowed one "o"?

What — do I hear someone saying "she hasn't mentioned a chimp yet!" A chimp — what, pray, <u>is</u> a chimp. I fear I've forgotten. Quite honestly, the last few weeks have been a waste of time except that we have termite pictures. And I should, of course, tell you about when David G came to the termitery. He sat on top of the hill, gave the hide a passing glance, & set to on the bananas. "Click" went the camera. He glanced across. Ate another banana. "Click". Another look. "Click". Banana. "Click". No attention. Etc. But, having finished the bananas he very slowly & deliberately climbed down & proceeded up the 30 feet of path to the hide. The "door" is a low hole across which grass is pulled. Slight pause outside — then a hand grasped the "door", pulled the grass to one side, & a face looked in. (The hide is <u>just</u> big enough for 2 people & you can't stand upright.) Well, he said "hoo", retreated a couple of steps, paused. Then marched solemnly back & got on with the main business — termite eating. But it got funnier. At one point I held out a banana to him: He didn't like me doing that. Anyhow, I threw it — it misfired & fell about 4 feet away. Well, I didn't think he'd paid much attention. But after 5 mins he began shaking a branch. This got more & more violent. Then he climbed the tree & shook that. Then, wildly hitting everything, he arrived in a small tree over the hide & shook that about till I expected him through the roof at any moment. Then he sat. Then he leapt down, drummed a few times, & returned to the hill. I could not decide what it was all in aid of.

---

* This paper, finally entitled "Feeding Behaviour of Wild Chimpanzees: A Preliminary Report," was given in 1963 at the Symposium of the Zoological Society of London.

Then, after 5 mins, he began to march up the path again. And got the banana. All that was because he was annoyed that the banana was too close to me for his liking!! Well, he vanished. The walls are very thick. I heard much rustling just outside, where there is a lot of long grass. But could not see. Silence. Then fingers appeared — literally 5″ away from my foot. Again, I wondered what on <u>earth</u> was going on. It was a banana skin Jiff had poked out through the grass, & he wanted it!! It was terribly funny. Then he went back to termite eating again!

We made an amusing discovery when C.W.* was here. He told us he had nearly been christened "William" but his Godfather said <u>anything</u> but that — with a surname like his he would be "Willy Whalley" (pr. "Wolly") for sure. We immediately decided to call him just that. And Jiff happened to announce that I'd once been "Weary Willy". We got quite hysterical & he said that if ever we met in public — "Hi Willy Wolly" — "Hello, Weary Willy" people would shrug "They've been in the bush too long"!! Did Jiff tell you the dirty fellow forgot his bath, refused ours, said he'd use the lake, and never did more than wash his hands & face?! D. was horrified. I've never known a "bush" person before who didn't have baths whenever possible.

Did I tell you I saw a Colobus clasping her dead baby? It was so sad & upset me dreadfully. It had been raining, and it was all sodden & limp, & she kept trying to groom its poor little coat. Oh, it was heart rending. I'm only so glad I've never seen a chimp with a dead baby. I just couldn't bear it.

Today, when I was inspecting a termite hill the termites were leaving — you know, on their nuptial flight — oh, sorry — I must not refer to "that certain behaviour" — even in the bees, the birds or the flowers?† Anyhow, I caught a lot and we ate them as "toasties" before supper! I gave them to Mrs D who de-winged them, & they arrived all crisp on a plate. You know those little tiny things you get

---

* Charles Campbell-Whalley.
† Danny had recently written to Jane saying that she hoped she could trust her granddaughter, when surrounded by erudite scientific gentlemen, not to disgrace the family by referring to "that certain behaviour."

at cocktails? Can't think if they're prawns or what. Well, the ants taste just like those — Jiff was rather horrified when she saw the plate, but having closed her eyes & munched a few she liked them, & polished off the plate. Moshi was in his element!

It is 10.30 pm. Still raining. I was a gorgeous brown when Jiff arrived. I am now rather lily-like! Perhaps 'old parchment' would be a better description!

We are starting to sing carols! We hum them as we go up & down Ogre. I laugh to think of Jiff "running up ahead of me"! Though she is a little less grampus like. But then, she doesn't lead an energetic life — her job is sedentary at present. If the cherry trees ripen she will need a bit more energy.

Must stop now. Hassan will go to Kigoma tomorrow — oh, Christmas lists — I sure <u>do</u> need a warm cardigan. Apart from that — I <u>will</u> try to think of some little things & let you know in next letter.

Tons & tons of love to you all,
Jane

Wish it was!
9th ~~October~~ November [1961]

My dear FFF,

You will have heard the news from Judy, who has explained <u>again</u> about the speed of the film — oh, unless you are reading this first, in which case see other letter.

I am <u>Shs 1,000!</u> overdrawn. This is most alarming, & due to the fact that the duka* forgot to send me any bills. How <u>is</u> the money situation? I hope it's better than the photographic one — see Judy's letter.

She has told you all the news, so I won't repeat. Life is depressing — wet, chimpless, and, it seems, impecunious. We are doing our best, but I cannot — repeat <u>cannot</u> — contend with FATE. What else is it that makes it <u>pour</u> when I get close to chimps, or else my camera fails — the new one. Had to send Judy into Kigoma to get it

---

* Store or shop.

repaired — mechanical fault. Cost 20/-. Will send bill for insurance? Fruit not fruiting. Chimps vanishing. Me being ill. Oh, just **** everything.

> A despondent & sad
> FC*

> 1, Magrath Avenue,
> Cambridge.
> 12th March 1962

Dear Desmond,

I'm sorry to plague you, but I'm wondering if you can help me on one point. I'm suddenly faced with having to write a paper on nesting which is supposed to be finished by 19th March — most unlikely, but still!

I was thinking about the various reasons for the construction of a new nest every night — you know, greater protection from predators, or the fact that fresh leaves are softer and warmer than old ones. For various reasons these do not explain the behavior — even though they may have been the <u>original</u> cause of it. So I began to wonder whether, perhaps, it was simply habit, like a dog turning round and round before he lies down (and this is begging the question as to whether or not the actual nest making is learned behaviour or not). So I wondered if you had any idea as to whether a zoo chimp, if its straw nest is left quite undisturbed from one night to the next, will re-make its bed or simply climb into the old one? Schaller's theory that the gorilla probably makes a new nest each night because it fouls the old one obviously does not apply to the chimp which never, under any circumstances, mucks up his nest.

I have just seen Leakey and am feeling happier than I have felt for a very long time because at long last there is the prospect that I shall get a really suitable photographer. This man is, at the moment, climbing about mountain forests in Africa to see how much equipment he can reasonably carry, and is also experimenting with flashlight on various sorts of monkeys and other animals to see just how

---

* "FC," as in Fairy/Foster Child.

much effect it has on them, and how long they take to get used to it. The thought of someone like this, who is really desperate to [film] the chimps and who is, in addition to being a first class photographer, wonderful with animals — well, it's just too good to be true.

I'll hope to see you sometime next week if you have a minute to spare — which is a good day, sometime between Tuesday and Friday (inclusive), and when I might be able to see Jan too.

Give my love to Ramona,

Jane

1, Magrath Avenue

Cambridge

20 May 1962.

Dear Dr. Bell Grosvenor,

I am horrified that so much time should have elapsed since I returned from America — and still I havn't written to thank you for your wonderful hospitality in Washington. To me it only seems like a few days since I left America, but when I look at a calendar....! Anyway, please do accept my very sincere apologies for the lapse of time. I really do appreciate everything which you did to make my stay in Washington so memorable, and I only wish I could have stayed just a few days longer and seen a little more of your lovely city. It is so white and clean and green — I quite fell in love with it.

I still havn't got over the magnitude of your organization. I knew it was large before I came, but never dreamed of anything quite so tremendous and magnificent. I expect your new building has grown quite a bit since I left Washington.

The temperatures over here still continue below 45°. We have rather given up any hope of summer — we had no spring at all, and the spring flowers are still blooming in bits and pieces all over England, whilst the summer flowers which ought to be appearing now, have scarcely struggled out with an occasional bud. In a resigned way everyone blames atomic tests as they crouch over blazing fires or wrap themselves in thick winter clothes to brave the elements outside.

Thank you again, and I only hope that I can obtain sufficient chimpanzee pictures to justify all your kindness. If I fail I think I shall just quietly disappear into the forests of the Reserve because I shall never dare to show my face again!

I hope very much to see you next March, on my way to Stanford in Palo Alto, and give you the latest chimpanzee news.

Yours very sincerely,
Jane

Chimpland.
17 July [1962]

My dear FFF,

Safely here. I've not had much luck yet, but have had two opportunities for taking photos — 4 rolls in the first week isn't bad when compared with one roll in over a month last time! But, of course, whether they will be any good is quite another matter! And it was nice of David Greybeard to come and welcome me — the same old David as ever, and just as amenable, bless him. I couldn't help laughing when I saw him, sitting up there in the great fig tree, chewing peacefully on his fig wadge, of all the toasts we have drunk to him, of all the places where his name has been in the forefront, in England, Washington and New York. Dear old David G!

One bit of bad news concerns the boat. I thought Hassan had tested the engine before we left, but apparently he hadn't been able to get it out — as it was Sunday of course, and when he said it was all right, he meant it was all there. Anyhow, I despatched him to Kigoma yesterday with the first batch of film, as Geographic are most insistent that it should be sent off at once. And I found when I got down that he had been unable to start the engine and took it in a water taxi, and they don't know if they can repair it or must get a new part. Hassan got back today, and is returning the day after tomorrow to see if soaking it in oil has worked. Good old Jack Granham, the only European left from the "old days" is working on it, and there is a Tsetse man who takes a keen interest in my affairs and helps Hassan when he goes in. Also the African Town Foreman is the most charming and helpful of men, and the D.C. likewise.

Anyhow, if a new part has to be got, I am asking that it shall be got — I only hope that it doesn't because I desperately need the boat next week. The big tree at Mitumba valley, 4 miles up the reserve, should be ripe, and I plan to make a temporary camp up there — it's normally a simple matter to get there on foot, but I had the most hair-raising journey owing to the water of the lake having risen so much, and the way along the beach being, in parts, almost impassable. To carry any equipment along would not be possible. However, if I can't have the boat I shall send the kit with the Scout — or Hassan if he's back — in one of the boats, and myself go across the mountains (If I went with the stuff I'd be charged treble!).

I am industriously collecting your sackfuls of dung. Dominic thinks its a real scream, this "kasi ya mavi!"* But he quite understood when I told him that it was to find out about endoparasites and small things they'd eaten. He's good on that sort of thing which is a help, because he's industrious in the drying. Actually one doesn't find dung in a fit state to be of use very often. Usually the dung beetles, flies etc. have been doing their work.

My word, but it's good to be back here. Even when the chimps are scarce, it's still good. But I've already crashed down onto some rocks and jolly nearly broken the camera. Heaven help me if I do. It certainly hampers one's progress and speed — when one is continually wondering whether each leap or scramble will bash some vital piece of equipment against a rock. However, I've got the original camera (which Geographic were most scathing about!) if the worst comes to the worst.

I don't think there's any more news to relate, so I'll end now and go to bed, since it's a bit late. I don't know if you will have seen the letter I wrote to Mummy — but I don't think Ahamed's overhauled the tent at all. They did the poles — bas. Because there is a rip in the bathroom roof, and <u>none</u> of the guy ropes have been changed — well, some of them certainly havn't. And, into the bargain, there were scarcely enough pegs and the mallet had gone. So you can tick off dear Jimmy Ahamed† when you see him, for me.

---

* Working with dung.
† The Nairobi supplier who had promised to overhaul the tent.

Now I'll really close before I think of something else unnecessary. Hope something has happened to my final feeding paper.

With love,
Your FC

Chimpland
17 August [1962]

Darling Family,

Thanks tons for all your letters which arrived with Bwanas Samaki and Ndorobo (Fish and Tsetse).* Bwanas S and N to my horror had come for the day. As chimps were gaily feeding all round I couldn't very well say I had to go away, and, of course, they sent away poor Charlie. Never mind. They brought stacks of mail, including a super Geographic letter of which more anon, and a hooting parcel from Derrick.† The rail service is still at sixes and sevens, and things get landed at Tabora and dumped for a week or so. Such was the fate of this box of vegetables — it was oozing vile liquid when it arrived in Kigoma — it sat in the Boma for a week, and arrived with Bwanas Samaki and Ndorobo! It took a lot of courage to open it — ugh!!!! A really vile sight — I've never seen such rotten vegetables. So sad. I had to tell him because it would be foolish to waste any more. Thanks for the photos Jiff — and for 2 letters which all arrived at the same time. Staggering. You still haven't answered my letter properly as you will see if you re-read it. I also had a weird telegram from Hugo saying "Arriving 15th". As it was the 13th, I imagined he was arriving 2 days later to have a look round. I was overjoyed as it would have meant getting David and Co on cine, the chance to do which may not come again (grammar!). Anyway, I made complicated arrangement for his transportation — Bwana Fish said he'd bring him, and Bwana Tsetse is pass-

---

* Tanganyika became independent within the Commonwealth on December 9, 1961 (and would become the United Republic of Tanzania when unified with Zanzibar in 1964); the transition to independence was smooth enough to be almost unnoticed in the backwaters of the country. One clear result of independence, however, was that many civil service posts passed on to black Africans, including those in Fisheries and Tsetse Control.

† Derrick Dunn was sending extra food from his farm near Arusha.

ing tomorrow and said if he came late he would bring him. Then my heart smote me when I thought that if he arrived today he would wait for the Kibisi tomorrow and it might be the last morning of David. So when he didn't appear with Bwana Fish by 10 this morning, I despatched Hassan. But it is now 11 p.m. so I imagine, after all, he meant 15 September. I really don't know. Why send a telegram? Anyhow, that's rather later than I feel he should come, but I don't suppose it matters — I really don't think we'll get much worthwhile cine whenever he comes, but so what. Now let me tell you about Geographic — I will quote. It's from the camera editor — no picture editor, beg his pardon. Bob Gilka. Who always seemed so horrid when beastly letters used to come from him saying everything was all wrong, but was so nice when I met him, and he realized what was what. Anyhow. "Your first shipment . . . is the best you've done so far. Good going! In the 4 rolls are the first really readable pictures of the animals in the trees. I feel sure that at least one of David G. will wind up as an illustration in your article, and there is a sequence of one chimp out near the end of a limb, reaching for food, which may also make the grade". He says even the shot of Ma and baby, though marginal as the babe is lost rather against dark coat of Ma, can be made usable with careful work if I don't get better! That is more than I dared to hope. "I am most pleased with the way in which you have mastered the photographic equipment we gave you. With this kind of progress I am sure you will end up with excellent coverage of the study". Isn't it super! The jinx must be over — pity you're not here this time Jiff. Between us we could do fabulously. What pleases me most is that the chimps in the dudu tree are O.K. — when I trailed the tripod and big lens along and all 5 came — the only time I had the lens there — the only time more than one fed in that tree at a time. You see — the jinx working the other way.

I had one bad show — took some fabulous pictures of David and Goliath grooming each other — found, at the end, that the film hadn't been winding on. A whole sequence — David in a bare tree, really close as well. Very sad. No matter.

Here, things go from strength to strength. I found David, Goliath and Charlie all huddled behind the huts the other day. They let me get right close, of course. (Oh dear, every boat I hear I have to run out and listen in case it's Hugo). No! I couldn't think what they were doing. Then I found that David and G. each had half a mat under their arms! Charlie had a little piece. They were tearing bits off, chewing them, and spitting it out. They are straw mats — something to do with dagaa and called Mrago. I've never seen anything so funny. Charlie tried to pinch a bit of David's, and when it was pulled away he screamed in temper — David charged off, holding the mat high above his head — unfortunately all behind branches because it would have been a lovely shot — Hugo could have done it with cine — and Charlie following. David sat, still holding the mat up, and Charlie went on making a scream face without a sound. Then he vanished into the grass and reappeared with a piece — may have got it from Goliath. Later on, Goliath having moved out of sight, David took his piece up a little tree. Charlie, having found, torn up, and chewed, a piece of very ancient patched trousers! — joined him. The end of David's mat was very near Charlie, and after 10 mins. Charlie just allowed one straw to stray into his mouth — a little guidance from one hand that just happened to be there. David didn't mind much. The straw is joined together with string, and he found much difficulty in pulling away the bits of straw near the string. He struggled with one bit for ages, and finally, with such a lordly air, he handed Charlie the part he couldn't manage! (Charlie's hand being outstretched.) He dispenses his cast off bits and pieces with regal condescension — today he dished out his finished banana skins to Goliath in exactly the same way! And today No. 3 (who is going to become Huxley, because I've always thought they were the same, and it means I can probably get Sir Julian* the photo he wants!) — with a pal, also came to camp — I just saw them. Would have had a super time if I wasn't so flippin' conscientious. But, of course, I trailed up Lower Kitanda Valley at dawn, and merely succeeded in seeing two chimps in a fig, who didn't like me and went. And when I got back, Huxley was sitting

---

* The biologist Sir Julian Huxley, whom Jane had gotten to know at Cambridge.

right behind Hassan's tent on the ground — about 10 feet away. Just looking. Most odd! His pal with a very droopy lip was up above, more snooty like. Poor Huxley never got a banana.

Now that 2 or even 3 chimps come here it really is rather fab — it means I can get little details of social interaction at first hand close up — oh, another boat. Hang on. No! The little touches of David handing out his spare oddments are quite charming — not to mention pictures, of course. But, unfortunately, my best ones of 2 together are the roll that didn't take! Still, I have got some with two. Even when they're feeding in the new shoot trees along the beach I can get quite a reasonable picture with the big lens — it's usually rather dark when they're there though. And did I tell you I even got some black and whites of David and Charlie early in the morning? And I got some divine baboon pictures this morning — they are black and white too. The weather is fantastic — for the past three days there hasn't been one single glimmer of sun, and low heavy clouds. Most peculiar. The new grass is alarmingly tall in places. I hope this all means I can get some good Red Colobus pictures. If this goes on much longer I shall find I'm getting camera conscious! Gosh — that was the boat.

And it was my boat — but without Hugo. I had decided, as I may have said, he must have meant 15th <u>Sept.</u> But a letter came from Shirley* saying she was giving him a pair of shoes to bring as he was starting up the next day. I believe the road is still very bad. It is so unlucky I could weep.

Actually I am just writing a few words now to tell you that today is the happiest, the proudest, of my whole life to date. Something has occurred — an achievement which I value far higher than any prize, degree, praise — oh, anything you like.

David G — yes — he has TAKEN BANANAS FROM MY HAND. So gently. No snatching. The first time I held one out he stood up & hooted, swayed from one foot to the other, banged the tree, & sat down. So I threw it him. The next one he came & took.

---

* Shirley Coryndon, a friend of Jane's from the days when they both lived at the Museum Flats.

Even when I stand upright he takes them. I even got Dominic to come & get a picture — unfortunately he was a second too late & D. had taken it from my hand.

Just now I got back — 12.30 — & David was eating bamboo grass near the lake. Then he trundled towards my tent. I waited for a moment & then followed. He was sitting in the tent trying to open the banana box! So I sat outside & held out a banana. He came out, took it, ran back in, & sat inside eating it!! I hope, Mum, you don't mind sharing a tent with a chimp! Also at dawn (having gone to sleep about 4.30 am) I was woken by Shaitani (Devil in Swahili). He was sitting happily by my bed eating a banana. He IS a devil! I shooed him off & closed my eyes. 5 mins later I heard a stealthy foot fall. When I shouted at him he spitefully gave the table a wham & knocked the thermos over! Now I must go & look for some of my other pals — but can you blame me for devoting time to David?

Hi! Super letters came from you, Danny and Mummy. Thanks tons. Danny, how you can say your letters are dull and uninteresting I just don't know. Far from it — I was breathless with suspense when reading of Kip's wasp, and horrified when you couldn't find him — though I knew it was O.K. cos I'd read the bit on the outside sending me a spit-y kiss from him. More to the point if I send him such a kiss I should think. Oh no — your letters are very very far from being dull. They are some of the nicest and most interesting and most well written that anyone ever sends to me.

Fancy Uncle E — you going all the way to Bournemouth in Annable! The typewriter always insists on corrupting her name! Good luck in your next test Jiff — I guess you'll have an English driving licence before me anyway!

Ma — I think you'll still be in England when this letter arrives, though as I don't know when I can post it I can't be sure. I shall probably write this to Nairobi as well — but don't bring a netting thing for the veranda. There's no room for it now. What I do suggest you get is a proper net for your bed — WITH PROPER FRAME! This will mean you can sleep under it — tuck it into the mattress and no dudus can creep into your bed or fly down your neck to cause those alarming upheavals and grunts as I'm about to drop off!

That is the answer. The other thing is a) quite expensive and must be properly made, and b) as I say, there's no room, we're so elegant with tables now, and c) it always gets eaten by something remarkably quickly. Maybe, if you go to Ahamed Bros. (De la Mere Avenue) and tell Jimmy Ahamed — the boss — you're my mother, he might fix you up a SINGLE piece of netting to go across the inner part of the tent — I. e. if you want to sit inside the tent and I'm on the veranda I can then draw this net down behind me. Get me? IF he made it the right shape — he knows the tent size — large officers — we can sew it on when you get here. That's if you really want it. But since we eat outside and so are not likely to want netting then, and I don't want it anyway — it would just be silly. But DO bring a net. We don't seem to have any here — the old ones may be in that box in Shirley's room! But get yourself a new one — white. Those green ones are dingy. But if they're there, please bring green one for me.

Had to send Hassan and Dominic off to Mwamgongo today — Hassan couldn't get any bananas for David in Kigoma. Luckily Vic* (he is a dear, but such a hoot — came to visit me in Trilby, lace ups, grey trousers, socks and jacket!!) had sent me two bunches of ripe ones — which, of course, was a great treat for David, and may be why he took them from me. Just think — it's taken about 2 years to get to this stage of almost perfect trust. Isn't it really simply and absolutely fabulous. I do hope we get a really correct picture tomorrow — with a bit more light than this morning. Apparently the rains are heavy in Ruanda Urundi now. And today it was so humid and overcast, with thunder and odd drops of water oozing from the water-logged atmosphere. Most sweaty sort of weather — most unseasonable. All the Africans say the rains are about to begin. You'd better bring more polythene bags from Nairobi, Mum — Man's Shirt Pack. Can't get that size in Kigoma. Not a gleam of sun again, all day.

---

* Vic Jones, a friend in Kigoma.

c/o District Commissioner,
Kigoma.
2nd September 1962.

Dear Mr. Payne,

I am enclosing an interim report for August which, as you will see, is encouraging.

One thing which I should like to mention specially is in connection with the taking of film simply for the scientific record. I have stressed to Hugo van Lawick that it is of extreme importance to film some things even when lighting conditions or distance of the subjects from the camera means that the results will be far from perfect. With this end in view I have suggested that we get some fast black and white film for use in the early morning or late evening so as to get records of nest making, etc. which is not possible with the commercial ektachrome. I do hope that the Committee is in agreement with this.

I must say that the filming is going far far better than I ever imagined possible, and if things go on as they are we should end up with some very exciting material both for a scientific record and the lecture film. Hugo van Lawick is managing wonderfully and I think he is just the right person for the job. He uncomplainingly carries huge weights to the most inaccessible places, and waits all day on the most uncomfortable slopes.

I'm afraid all this is a little incoherent as I am surrounded by Africans all talking and the Game Ranger who came to visit the reserve is packing up all round me. Not ideal conditions for writing reports, but it is the only opportunity I have had for a long time.

Please do give my regards to everyone.

Yours sincerely,
Jane

Chimpland.
26 September 1962.

Dear Bob,

Many thanks for your last two letters with the discards. I'm glad they are not too appalling. Just at present we are going through a very, very bad spell, and I'm able to get practically nothing, but I dare say things will come all right again soon. The trouble is that the fig season has failed, and during this time I hoped to get all the "intimate" pictures of chimp life. However, some other chance may occur. Provided we manage to get good frames of the termite eating, the main outstanding gaps seem to be a mother and baby, good social grooming, and a few shots showing a large number together. An awful lot really, when you stop to think!

There are one or two questions I must ask. The first is about the overexposing when I shoot into the sky. In fact, I should aim at a silhouette shot? I was trying to bring out the details of the chimp — a ditto for the exposure of the chimps on the Ridge. However, in the future I won't if you think not.

Secondly, although Hugo is horrified at the idea of my even asking you, is it ever possible to blow up frames from 16mm film? I ask this because Hugo has been able to film some scenes which I probably won't have the chance to get stills of. I don't expect it is, but I can't see any harm in asking!

For your personal information the chimp in rolls 16 and 17 written on the cards as "Ugly" has been renamed. He was due for another name as he isn't, in fact, Ugly. It was a misnomer. When he scratched his back on the tree trunk he made faces just like Hugo does when he's concentrating hard — so he is Hugo! I thought I'd better inform you or you might get confused with all the Hugos!

You will by now have had stills of me washing my hair — though Hugo is going to take some more in a more forested part. You needn't worry about him being embarrassed. I haven't noticed it yet!

Incidentally, I wonder if you could send some more of the small boxes for packing film. We seem to have both run out — I think perhaps some have got mislaid, though I never remember there being many. Anyway, I've hunted high and low and can't find any. The small boxes are definitely the most useful.

The last lot of film I sent off — well, it is going at the same time as this letter — will be pretty useless. Probably none of it worth looking at — I'm talking of mine of course, not Hugo's. But, as I've said, it's the bad spell. And don't worry — I shan't miss any opportunities of taking shots of Buffalo, etc. They don't appear until a bit later, when the rains are well under way, and I shall do my best. I really wish I had a bigger lens, but I'll manage somehow — they are rather shy around here, and it's very difficult to get close — except the one bull who charges on sight! Maybe I'll get some real close-ups of him, one day, from the tree he has made me climb!

Yours sincerely,
Jane

Chimpland.
30 September 1962.

Dear Bob,

Just a short note — sorry I have no stills to send off lately. This business is the most frustrating I can think of. Just lately I've been getting really in amongst my black hairy friends — 20 feet and closer. They stay there, that close, for an hour or more. And even I find it hard to believe that I have not been able to take pictures. There are so many twigs and things between them and me that it just isn't worth it, and, into the bargain, it is very dark. I've taken a few black and whites, but not even a complete roll. However, the closer they let me get . . . the more hopeful it is, because there is bound to be a time when there is not half the African jungle in the few feet between me and my elusive subjects!

I also want to say that I retract all my remarks about silhouette shots when I shoot into the sky — I now have new batteries for my viewer and so I can see clearly that the chimps as well as the sky and the leaves are overexposed! Please forgive me!

And the last thing — in Hugo's latest shipment which he is sending off at the same time as this there are a lot of stills of various African dagaa fishermen. When he first tried to take them they all demanded 5/- and were not very pleasant. However, I talked to them and told them that after all we gave them medicine for nothing when they were ill — and I then told them that if they let their pictures be taken they would be able to see them — at this their faces lit up — could you possibly send a few Polaroids? It means so very much to them, most of whom have never seen a photograph of anyone, let alone themselves. In particular the bloke with the net, the ones turning the fish, the one playing the pipe — and any others who have close ups. I hope you don't mind my asking — Hugo didn't like to ask you, but I feel sure you won't mind, especially as it helps so much with better feeling all round. If you do mind — just say so! And don't let Hugo know I told you he didn't like to ask you! — please. I wouldn't like to jeopardize my friendly relations with my cameraman in order to promote them with my fishermen!!

Shall try and send you more stills in the near future.

Sincerely,
Jane

c/o District Commissioner,
Kigoma,
Tanganyika.
21 October 1962

Dear Dr. Carmichael,

Thank you so much for your letter in reply to mine. I am sure you will have heard by now that the photographic side of this study has been far more successful than I ever dared to hope. The chimpanzees have become so much tamer since last year, and they have accepted the presence of Hugo van Lawick with his tripods and lenses in the most wonderful way. The method I have always followed — never hiding from the chimpanzees, never following them when they have moved away from me, and never appearing particularly interested in them — has, at long last, paid its dividends.

I understand that Dr. Leakey has already written to you saying that I do want, very, very much, to return next year. There are, of course, many reasons for this — not the least being that even if I spent my whole life here I should still have a tremendous lot to learn about chimpanzees! However, in particular, there are three main reasons for my wanting to follow up this year's field study as soon as possible.

Firstly, the way in which the chimpanzees now tolerate the presence of an observer is so remarkable that it seems wrong not to take as much advantage as possible of such an opportunity for learning more about the social interactions between the various individuals. This was a task which seemed formidable at the commencement of my research, and only now is the pattern really beginning to take shape. It took so many months of patience and frustration before these chimpanzees would, in fact, tolerate my presence, that I cannot bear to think of leaving them just when they really will allow me to remain within a few feet of them on almost every occasion when I am able to get close to them.

Secondly, my observations to date suggest that there may be an increase in carnivorous behaviour amongst the chimpanzee population in the area. I cannot as yet be sure that this is so, but if it is then you will realize that it is vital to return in the near future to find out if there is any further increase in the eating of meat. It would be an important development in the life of the chimpanzee — after all, many people think that it was the desire for flesh and subsequent development of the hunting technique which was so important in the history of the first men, or near-men.

My last point is in connexion with filming. As you know, Hugo van Lawick is with me now, and is doing a wonderful job. But we have had a spell of phenomenally bad luck. During September the chimpanzees usually move about, in large groups, over my main observation area. It is this area which is so ideally suited to filming with long lenses. Other areas are more thickly forested, and not only are opportunities for filming much less, owing to fewer valleys and open slopes which can be overlooked from any one place, but it is impracticable to carry heavy equipment for long distances across the mountains. It is one thing to crawl and slide along by oneself — it is another matter to do the same when loaded down with heavy and valuable equipment.

Two weeks ago the chimpanzees returned in force to my home area. Their return coincided with the start of the rains. Had the weather been fine Hugo could have shot some truly remarkable scenes — as it was he had to sit and watch, helpless in the pouring rain. The main consolation is the degree to which the chimpanzees accept his presence, either in some sort of hide (which seldom deceives a chimpanzee for long) or just sitting out in the open. I am hoping that you will have seen, or be able to see, some of the material which we have managed to get so far on chimpanzee behaviour and that, in view of the facts I have outlined, you will agree with me that it is tremendously important that we have a second chance next year. I cannot believe that such bad luck will occur for two years running.

Please do give my regards to your wife, and to my other friends in Washington.

Yours sincerely,
Jane Goodall

10 December 1962.
Dear Bob,

Very many thanks for your last letter with the black and white prints and the slides. They are simply splendid, and it was most kind of you to go to all the trouble of looking through everything for me.

By now you should have got the last shipment I sent — 12 rolls in all. I sure do hope that some of those come out all right, more than anything the ones in the nests. These really are unique pictures — well, so are the termite ones — so, I suppose, are they all! But I'm particularly hoping the nest ones will be all right. There is another roll of nest ones in this shipment. It's funny how one plods on for 2 years and suddenly all the photographic opportunities come right at the end!

I also hope that one of the ones of me in the field with a chimp will be better than the one you had before. Because, quite honestly, it rather looks as though I'm sitting in a field with an exceptionally tame cow! — or something! Do you agree?

There will be a lot of rubbish in some of these rolls — but I am desperately trying to capture some of the social gestures, and they always seem to make these in the most unphotographical places imaginable. It's most annoying. I hope the "chimpanzee tea party" comes out — I think it's the most delightful scene, but the light was awful — sorry about using ektachrome by the way, but I suddenly ran out of Kodachrome. Thought I had a lot more.

The missing roll I mentioned was black and white — the Polaroids you sent I seem to remember came from a Kodachrome roll — people's heads cut off because I had all my hands full of bananas which made picture taking tricky!

Would you like any of the pictures we shot last year sent over? Or not. Or did you keep any that were the slightest bit of use? I was thinking in terms of packing up camp, or things of that ilk.

I don't think I shall be able to get the buffalo — the grass is now about 10′ everywhere, and the buffalo just seem to have vanished. However, you never know.

Thanks again for the fine pictures.

Regards,
Jane Goodall

P.S. By the time you get this I shall almost be leaving. The safest address in England, at the moment, is the Bournemouth one, The Birches, 10 Durley Chine Rd, Bournemouth. Don't know what horrible digs I shall end up at in Cambridge.

Chimpland.
19 December 1962.

Dear Mr. Vosburgh,

Excuse the frivolous address, but as I shall have left here before I could receive an answer to this letter, my correct postal address seemed unnecessary.

I have nearly finished a first draft of an article for your Magazine. It will, of course, be too long! What I am writing to ask is this: would you prefer me to sit down when I get back to England and reduce it to the approximate length required? Or would you rather first see it as it is so that you can see the sort of material. I feel this might be better — it would be discouraging if all the parts which I decided needed shortening were the very incidents you subsequently might think in need of filling out! (Excuse grammar — It's too late I think).

However, I am very happy to do either. It would be best if you could send an answer to my home address in England as I am not sure yet what my Cambridge address will be. That is "The Birches, 10 Durley Chine Road, Bournemouth". I shall have to go home first, anyway, to sort myself out.

I expect you have heard from time to time how well things are going here. The season has been far more profitable than I hoped it could be. Have you also heard that I am returning next year? The family have given up — they imagine that I shall still be coming back to watch chimps when I'm old and tottering. But it's taken so long to get the chimps really used to me that really it's only just starting to be worth while. Well, perhaps that's putting it too strongly. It has occurred to me that this may alter your plans about when the article should be published. If it is decided to hold it over until the end of next year's research — well, the sooner I know the better!

It's too late to wish you a happy Christmas, but I can wish you a very happy New Year.

With best regards,
Jane

7

CLOSE OBSERVATIONS
1963

I must say . . . that throughout the . . . study of the chimps at the
Gombe Stream, I have often felt like an anthropologist taking
notes on a tribe of people, for chimpanzees can seem so human.
— *My Friends the Wild Chimpanzees*

INTUITIVELY, Jane Goodall chose a bias that happened to be rare
among the scientific biases of the time. She thought of her study
subjects as sensate beings who shared with her (and us) a significant array of similar, perhaps identical, emotions and percep-
tions. Her apes lived in a parallel universe, one might say, separated
from hers (and ours) not by an uncrossable gap in feeling and per-
ceiving but by a partly reversible failure of communication and understanding. Apes don't have language. They can't speak. And our
own habits of thought and language had always kept us from understanding very much about them. Indeed, in spite of all we've
learned between then and now, our language still retains that automatic and unexamined point of view. While humans are imagined
to have character and personality, a quality or a value of being,
a *personhood,* and as such are automatically dignified with the
pronouns "who" and "whom," all nonhuman creatures are by
unreasoned definition nonpersonal objects: "it" and "that." Only
humans have "children"; other creatures have "offspring." Only
humans include "men" and "women"; other animals are usually
"adult male" and "adult female." Only humans, by definition, have
"consciousness" and "minds" and "reason"; all other creatures

possess "brains" and "instincts." And thus only humans have "souls" when alive and become "corpses" when they die, whereas animals have nothing equivalent to soul when alive and usually turn into a "carcass" or "meat" at death. Language is a scratched lens, yet such habits of expression are rooted so deeply in our speaking and thinking and seeing that we ordinarily accept them as unassailable measures of reality rather than as what they actually are: flawed expressions of perception, expectation, and habit.

Jane Goodall's imaginative respect for her study subjects as sensate beings with feelings, minds, and individuality may help account for the rapidity with which she gained their confidence and was able to approach them for closer observation. Soon enough, as we have seen from some of the earlier letters, a few individual chimpanzees — the one she called David Greybeard, most obviously — began approaching *her* for closer observation. Apes are curious, and it is easy to imagine that a few of the chimpanzees who paused, gazed at, and even perhaps vaguely approached that peculiar yellow-haired ape who had recently dropped into their forest were motivated by curiosity. But, of course, very few humans in history have been curious enough about apes to trip along in their wake, day after day — why should the apes show any greater interest in humans? Both Hugo van Lawick and Jane wanted the chimps closer, for better photographs and film, for more intimate and consistent and accurate observations. Jane wanted to penetrate beyond the random and still occasional glimpses she had so far been able to achieve. Her ultimate goal, as she suggests in some of the letters, was to "tame" the apes: to make them comfortable enough that she could move among them regularly, daily, and get to understand them thoroughly. If the human ape-watchers were to achieve this goal, their subjects would have to be motivated by more than mere curiosity.

What might entice them to come closer?

The banana feeding began accidentally and developed haphazardly. Bananas were sometimes left out in camp. David Greybeard one day bravely snatched one and ran. Soon after that, Jane found that if she offered David a banana, he would be bold enough to accept. As she wrote home on August 17, 1962, "David G has — yes — he has TAKEN BANANAS FROM MY HAND. So gently. No snatching."

Jane began to recognize the usefulness of leaving out a regular supply of bananas — "provisioning" her study subjects — so she established the camp as a site of temptation. Chimpanzees tend to follow their food source, which can change drastically over the year. When food is widely and sparsely distributed, the individuals making up any single community become widely and sparsely distributed as well. But with seasonal food concentrations — a large and healthy fig tree that suddenly bears fruit, for instance — the chimpanzees of that community will concentrate nearby. When Jane and Hugo began regularly leaving out substantial numbers of bananas, they were creating the artificial equivalent of a very good fig tree.

The apes responded. Soon, as the following sequence of letters written during 1963 shows, they were coming into camp and, "as they daily get tamer," becoming increasingly easy to approach. First appeared the adult males: David Greybeard and his friend Goliath, then William, followed by six-year-old Evered and old Mr. Mc-Greggor. Of course, once the apes lost some of their fear of camp, they began to find many nonbanana objects also tasty or otherwise interesting. Towels must have contained a provocative mixture of sweat and soap; clothes were probably good to suck on for their piquant trace of sweat; cardboard boxes may have provided an enticing taste of glue. Even haversacks were interesting enough to drag away and check out.

Females as well began approaching the camp, including the one who arrived with Goliath (described in the June letter home); she was a "very pink female" who was happy to escape Goliath's apparent coercion the moment his attention wavered from sex to food. The famous Flo also arrived in camp around this time (first mentioned in the letter of late May or early June), carrying her three-year-old daughter, Fifi, followed by her older son, Figan. By then, Flo had been "quite won over to the idea of popping in for the odd banana." And Flo's presence in camp attracted even more of the wild chimpanzee community, particularly during August when

Flo herself "developed her first pink swelling" and "trailed millions of men along here with her." (During estrus a female chimpanzee's genital region becomes swollen and pink, unambiguously advertising to the community's males her condition of sexual receptivity.)

Provisioning ratcheted up the research a notch. Jane was suddenly getting an explosion in the number and quality of observations. But, of course, provisioning also resulted in an increasing level of danger. For starters, the bananas attracted both chimpanzees and baboons, and soon individuals of the two species were competing in sometimes violent battles, including the classic fight (still featured in film clips about Gombe) described in the letter of April 25. The chimpanzees also displayed vigorously and sometimes squabbled violently among themselves, behavior that is normal for them around any good source of high-quality food. The dominant males get the best and the most the earliest, and they assert themselves in the process. Still, the displays and squabbles in camp were genuine cause for alarm. When, for instance, the chimpanzee Hugo "got a fright" and "rushed about with all his hair out" and threw a two-pound rock some twenty feet, Jane found that act "quite fantastic," as she noted in the letter of late May or early June — and she also recognized the danger that the apes would accidentally or unthinkingly or deliberately hurt one of their human observers. Pound for pound, chimpanzees are several times stronger than humans. A weak chimpanzee could tear the arm off a strong human. So large numbers of apes coming into camp brought an increasing danger of some unforeseen, unpleasant conflict between observers and the observed.

Other people recognized the dangers of banana provisioning, including Melvin Payne, executive vice president of the National Geographic Society (whom Jane felt she had to "hasten to reassure" in the letter of June 17), the Coryndon Museum botanist Bernard Verdcourt (letter of July 5), and Louis Leakey (letter of August 30). To mitigate the danger, Jane and Hugo had a steel cage built as a quick and easy retreat should the chimpanzees appear to be getting out of control. At the same time, the pair were working on various ways to limit the number of bananas each individual chimpanzee would be able to take. By 1964 they had developed a feeding area away from the original camp and also were experimenting with remote-controlled boxes to dole out bananas in a manner that ideally would reduce the squabbles.

But the advantages of provisioning, Jane insisted, far outweighed any disadvantages. As she forcibly asserted in her letter to Louis Leakey of August 30: "to be able to follow the interrelationships from DAY TO DAY, instead of simply seeing the same two animals together once a week or even once a month — well, I can really say, now, that I know chimps." Banana provisioning allowed astonishingly close observations, in short, and the superb quality of the subsequent epistolary reports during 1963 reflects this accomplishment. Several of these letters show the increasingly accomplished Jane Goodall at her most candid; they present altogether a set of powerfully detailed, deeply affectionate portraits of creatures who seem, suddenly, less like the "animals" we usually consider non-humans to be.

The last in this sequence is her first extant letter to Paul Brooks of Houghton Mifflin Company, which was to become in 1971 the American publisher of her best-selling book *In the Shadow of Man*. To Brooks, Jane summarized the year's accomplishments at Gombe Stream: "I now know about 30 chimps really inside and out, characters and all — and there are some splendid characters." She also described, notably, her growing intention to establish a "permanent research center" in order that her study of those chimpanzees and their offspring might continue for "years."

*   *   *   *

[Early January 1963]

Best beloved family — Hail!

It is almost completely dark, and Hassan is having difficulty with my lamp. He has been up there for hours. Then he stalked off majestically, and has just gone up there with another one — I suppose it will be explained to me anon. It's lucky I learnt touch typing, because it's far too dark to see for anything else — even writing would be a strain on the eyes.

As for my chimps. They go from strength to strength — that is, David, William, and Goliath. The others have all vanished, except for Pooch* who occasionally appears, but doesn't follow David to camp — though she will come and look for termites on her own. Goliath now always takes bananas from my hand, not always gently. William ditto — but he now takes them gently. The other day Goliath came on his own. He wouldn't take anything from my hand. I threw them to him, and he dashed about in an agile fashion — rather like a heavy weight boxer dancing. He is, in fact, just like a heavy weight boxer, with the temperament of a thug! Anyway, I threw one very close, and he did all sorts of gymnastic leaps and springs on his way to get it — then carried straight on and took the whole bunch giving the table a great hit as he passed and knocking everything off. Dear old Goliath.

Must interrupt, while I think of it. Firstly I had telegram from Hugo to say termite eating fine.† Then a great package of photographs from Geographic which I had asked for to show the people at Dar — Ministers, etc. They are simply super. Hugo has a wonderful one of David jumping the stream — they sent some slides, and 12 huge black and white photos, and a letter from Bob saying to relax on the photographic side — between us we have achieved a "fine illustration package" for the article. Which is very nice, and especially as all that was written before my last 14 rolls — full of two or even three chimps termiting at once, lovely close-ups of William and Goliath, and, best of all, David and William in their nests.

To return. G, W, and E have all been coming together. The last time they all three made day nests and slept for 2 hours — right near camp too. David has brought Pooch twice, but she will not venture closer than the termite heap. As for darling William. He trailed along one day at 5. He wasn't feeling very well — had a runny tummy poor old boy — and at 5.20, all in the sun, just by camp, all visible, he made his nest. I climbed above and took pictures of him lying asleep, still in the sun. And then, after supper, I

---

* Jane had originally named this chimp Poosh, after her childhood riding instructor.
† Hugo had left Gombe and was reviewing the photographs in his possession; Jane was about to leave for her term at Cambridge.

went up there and spent the night with him, watching him in the moonlight. That day I saw him almost every minute until 6.30 — after that the 3 of them appeared up at the top — from the beach — and as that was time for nest building, I really did see him solidly, all day long, plus a night. That's a record for one chimp. Good old William. When he came yesterday, still with the boys, he was still under the weather. Goliath is foul to him. But I see some simply wonderful social gestures with those three — David even made them to me once — put his hand on my arm, with backs of his fingers, making soft hoo hoo noises, and then held my forearm very gently but firmly with his hand. This is how he placates Goliath — but unless he thought I was scared by a sudden crashing of a baboon I don't know why he did it to me. If he gets cross with me he makes louder hoo hoo sounds, and raises his right forearm. Once he was thoroughly fed up with me, and smacked my arm! Yes, he really did, with a lovely nonchalant attitude!

I have been photographing small deformities. I find William has a broken finger and deformed feet — they are just like orangs' feet. Goliath has a broken toe, and David must have once cut the end of one toe almost off. He also has a nick in one ear. William looks as if he had his ribs broken once too. Poor old skinny William. How I do love them all now. Even more than before. In between times I climb up through the ever lengthening grass, but I never hear anything or see much, so I run back to my most darling ones. After all, I tell myself, all during next dry season I shall be with the screaming hordes. I may as well make the most of my friends while I have them to myself with no one messing them about by filming them. Also, as they daily get tamer, Hugo should be able to film this social behaviour if he returns.

Hi again — because it's anon from when I finished the last page. In fact it's several days later, and I'm several days older, and several facts wiser — etc, etc. I'm also rather sleepy as I've spent two nights with William, with one night in my bed in between. He spent last night in bed — and in a bed he'd made two nights previously — with my towel. When I went up to him at 10, in the moonlight, he was there, sitting up and sucking away. David took the one you left,

Mum. I now only have that miserable red and yellow check rag! When William trailed along yesterday Dominic was replenishing his iron in the kitchen. William accepted the bananas I offered him, and then drooped off down the path to the boys. "Tell Hassan to watch the clothes" yelled D. But as I rounded the corner William was heading for the bushes with a white shirt and my towel in tow. He climbed a tree at the top of that ledge there. And do you know, from 4 until 6.30 he was up that tree sucking my towel! After 15 minutes he accidentally dropped the shirt, but though he nipped down smartly to retrieve it, I was smarter. Every time I met his gaze, after that, he rocked, almost imperceptibly. If I didn't know William I shouldn't have noticed it even! And then he climbed down, bundled the towel up carefully and held it behind him to take the one banana I had with me, and then wandered off on two feet and a hand to climb into his old nest. There he sat, sucking the towel, as the sun went down behind the Congo hills. He sucked it when I disturbed him, climbing up for my night's vigil, and then, first thing in the morning after waking up, stretching and rolling onto his back, he reached lazily for the towel and sucked it — an early morning suck. I was only peeved that the mean old fellow didn't bring it down with him as he left it up there in an unclimbble tree. (Good word, that — a climbble or an unclimbble tree!)

But William's evil doing was not over. The odd thing is that he knows it's evil, when he steals these things. I had a new haversack made in Kigoma. Three times already he has tried to take it. He always says "hoo" in an aggrieved way when I say no and hold onto it! Anyway, this morning after his bananas he looked so melting sitting there that I resolved to get him one from the bunch I had hidden in the tent. A shriek from Dominic who was making my bed warned me — too late. William had taken my haversack from the table and was dragging it off, bumpity bump, into the bushes. In it was my camera. Also the 300 and 150 mm lenses. Also exposure meter and my last 5 KII films. Well, I yelled at him and just charged after him. He dropped it just before getting to the bushes opposite the tent. Now this is the amazing thing. I told you he knows it's wrong — I quickly followed him with a banana, but was afraid that I might have scared him badly. Not at all. He came up at once, though he did pause and say "hoo" in a rather defiant way before taking it. And came out again, bold as ever, to try and push me off the box to see if there were more inside. Which proves most positively that he recognized my right to get my property back. He is a real menace — a real cleptomaniac. He stands in front of the tent gazing in to see what he can take. He will even put a tentative hand onto a jersey if I happen to be holding the other end. But if I say no, he simply looks sad and goes away. He is a real "card" is William. That describes him to a T. An old card!!

Yesterday David wandered into a thick patch of that bamboo grass on the lake shore. I was going after him as I havn't got a picture of that. Suddenly there was a tremendous explosion in the grass and a large red pig shot out, almost knocking me over. A startled silence from the grass, and then a bewildered black face peered out and said "hoo" in a very surprised voice. It was so funny. My three blokes all came singly yesterday. First David. Then Goliath. Then David again. And finally William. David was worried that he had lost Goliath and looked everywhere. William this morning was convinced David was coming, and hung around for ages. David never came. But the wretched Humphries did, with an Italian and hundreds of children of all ages.* Ugh! I was just too late hearing the engine to escape! And as it poured with rain most of the time it seemed foolish to announce my departure. They didn't see any chimps, and they did bring me meat and veg. which they wouldn't let me pay for, and had asked about mail. One up to them.

Hi! I intended to finish this epistle in a leisurely way this evening & send it, via Hassan, tomorrow. But Vic Jones passed — my only real friend in Kigoma — stopped the Kibisi especially to deliver mail — didn't come ashore but was rowed in to deliver it to Hassan in person — and is stopping again this evening to collect anything for the post. <u>Really</u> decent.

I am sitting companionably with William who is having a luncheon date with half a cardboard box! I was not invited. It is rain-

---

* Uninvited and unwelcome visitors arriving from Kigoma.

ing. William has been eating termites — they go on & on. Yesterday was wonderful — D, G and W all sat in my veranda sharing a cardboard box, & then Goliath begged from William later up in a tree over the tent — where they were joined by a 6 year old male — Evered! Having rushed up to the Peak & found nothing I went down the valley & said 'howdy' to Mr. McGreggor, & came back in time for the box party. I shall start a new fashion. Can't you imagine, say, William Goldsmith, Byron and Mr. Wilson all sitting round solemnly chewing cardboard & spitting the bits elegantly into a red wagger pagger!* The begging was best. And the little male coming along. And William, not allowed his share of bananas, suddenly running when he saw termites flying, so as to get some of the big juicy winged ones.

Oh — there may be a panic. I was invited to Peterhouse Ladies Day, or something. Evening dress. And at first I wrote & said no. Then I thought that the first night in Cambridge would be pleasanter at such a 'do' than with Mrs. Tweedie!† So I said yes. Well — I don't even know where my green evening dress is, or the whalebone crinoline — &, wherever they are, they are both dirty! The green dress might be with Mrs. Tweedie — in which case she might be asked to have it cleaned — if it's not at home it's with her — 14 Grantchester Rd. And it will mean buying some shoes. And my hair will just have to be tied back! You see, it's on the 14th!

My plan, anyway, was to spend what is left of 13th in London & go to Cambridge on the 14th. Then return to London on the Friday, go to B'mth with Jiff & Annabelle, & stay at home for several days — whilst ostensibly in Cambridge. . . . I do hope Louis is going to send more money. Time is running out & I don't know where he is. I asked him to.

I must stop as I have to scrawl various epistles to people like Tweedie.

Tons of love,
Jane

---

* Goodall family slang for waste paper basket.
† Jane's landlady in Cambridge.

[Second week of April 1963]

Darling Family, one and all, including, of course, Dido.

Many thanks Olly Danny and Mummy for Easter and/or birthday cards. I couldn't work out when Easter was — I no more knew of it than I did of my birthday! Anyway, your letter was a hoot, Mum — saying you had been thinking of me all day because it was my birthday, letter dated 4th April!* Hugo says that in Holland you do give presents to the person whose birthday it is — but only small ones, and the main presents are given to the parents. So the Victorian ladies would have done well, with 22 children!

The most fantabulous things are happening here. Guess who has been to camp twice, and got bananas we threw — why, none other but my adored Mr. McGreggor. I can hardly believe it. We have filmed more baboon fights, drinking and greeting. Yesterday, when David appeared at 7.30 on a brief lonely visit and hastened away I presumed that the others had decided not to come back and so took myself off up the horrible grassy trail to Mkenke. Ugh — foul, and not a chimp. I had started the day by going up Ogre pre-dawn to watch Evered leave his nest — just up Hassan's beautiful main road, which is now only a few yards off achieving its destination — the Peak. However, Evered, with scarcely a rustle to announce his departure, vanished into the dawn, so I wetly trailed down again. It was, unfortunately, (for Hugo) a grey cold day. I found a most comfortable tree way up the Watu path from which I could see both sides, and hear any possible calls for miles around. There were no calls and it was chilly, as I was buried in clouds. By using a vivid imagination I was able to hunch my back, close my eyes, and slowly the sun came out, warming my back with its happy glow. But, if I chanced to open my eyes — cold grey clouds enveloped me again, and the shy sun hid his face with miraculous speed. (I find it impossible to type these days. I guess I typed too much during the past 3 months.)

Well, I pushed down the track, and getting back along the beach was well nigh impossible. It was high tiede (you will have to sort out

---

* Jane's birthday is actually April 3.

the errors in future or I shall be all night at this!) and the waves were right up to the grass — the track along the beach further inland, of course, quite overgrown with impenetrable grass. So — I had to sort of run around outgrowing trees, racing the waves — all most dramatic and wet-making. I got back to a most excited Hugo. In the palm tree in camp (not the one with the water bags) two days before the little black weaver birds began building. Hugo is doing a bird film for Louis and filmed the making of the nests, the stealing by one bird from its neighbour's nest as soon as the neighbour's back was turned, the shredding of the palm fronds for weaving in strips, etc. We were amazed that in two days the nests were almost complete. Now, I read in Dominic's truly fabulous report that Goliath, once, seized two chickens and ate them in a tree — with leaves.* Also William took one. On another occasion William seized Hassan's hen who was sitting and dashed her out of the way, taking the poor dear's eggs. Well, this, as you can imagine, far from rousing feelings of false sentiment in evil minded Hugo and Jane filled us with high hopes for getting meat eating. Vile indeed are our plots for the slaughter of the innocent! When I saw these nests I said to Hugo, wistfully, "Wouldn't it be wonderful if William, when the palm tree is ripe, happened to notice those nests". Well, Hugo had been filming David and Goliath greeting, baboons attacking William, and throwing bananas to a yelling McGreggor who was lurking in the bushes. Suddenly, with his usual swift perspicacity he saw Goliath suddenly gaze up at the palm, his hairs all rising at the same time. With lightning speed the cameraman rushed to get the fronds in silhouette — Got the murderer climbing the trunk, pulling down a frond, hand over hand, and then, very carefully, with two fingers, feeling inside the nest on the end. He then repeated the process, let the fronds swing back, the nests undisturbed, and climbed down. Wasn't it super! The birds have not deserted, and we now see a contemplative expression come over Goliath's face when he looks at the nests — the same sort of expression as you see on the face of a

---

* While Jane was away at Cambridge, from mid-January to late March, Dominic stayed in camp and kept a running report of chimpanzee-related events.

housewife when she gazes towards the kitchen where her cake is in the oven, and looks at her watch. "When will it be done". In fact yesterday when Goliath returned he sat resting in a tree, one foot dangling, gazing with delighted anticipation at the little nests whose owners are working so industriously to provide the rapacious creature with a tasty h'oerdoevre (the effect of that sentence, I fear, is sadly lost by my inability to spell this common culinary dish!)

Well, I had scarcely got back, and was cursing fate that sent me drearily off up Mkenke when so many exciting things were going on, when I heard a crash in the bushes opposite — a little 5 year old girl with a cardboard box, and a year old infant. Lurking behind was Ma. The children were most unafraid, but mean old Ma — when I got out my binoculars she seized her infant and moved the family to a further back tree. The children went on playing, and then they all rested from 2 to 3.45. Suddenly, just as Ma appeared to look at us, a sudden yell — William, with a bit of cardboard appeared round the tent, followed by the other two — the scream was from McGreggor — still with the boys. He was quite happily walking about behind the kitchen for bananas which Hugo threw there. It was splendid. The other three climbed up a bare tree to feed, and McG remained up above the boys' tents feeding on his own. But he had quite a good taste of bananas. Finally they all trooped off — just 5 minutes too early — for we had run out of ripe bananas, and just as they had gone Hassan and Rashidi got back with them — with bananas I mean! I couldn't find them, though I looked in all likely places for the next hour until dark. Today I am determined to stay in case McG comes back. That is too good to miss. At 7.30 David came on his own, and was in such a bother. He kept looking for the others to come — we didn't give him enough bananas for his liking, I wouldn't let him have my sweater, he didn't like the only remaining box. He has gone off over the stream in a huff.

But something happened the other day that was quite fantastic. I hope one of my stills comes out because otherwise no one will believe me. I followed David and Goliath across the stream — where Hugo got them jumping and drinking — can you believe all this drinking when I only <u>saw</u> it once before! — and then they went into thick stuff. I after. David lay on his back under a low tangle of vines. Goliath flung himself beside him. After a moment I saw they were holding hands. They began to play with each other's fingers — at first gently, then more actively. And after about 4 minutes they began to wrestle. There they were, two old gents (and I believe now that David is much older than I had suspected) playing about like two year olds, roaring with laughter and tickling each other in the ribs. After a couple of minutes David couldn't stand it any longer and with a final guffaw he jumped up and ran round in a half circle. Goliath followed a little way and then sat to eat a reed. Then David sat down by a sapling with open space round it. Quite light. Goliath once more flung himself at D's feet and sprawled, face down. Suddenly he put one hand on D's foot and held it. D at once put a hand on G's hand. And the fun began all over again. I got one picture — oh how I hope it comes out — of David sitting up, leaning slightly back, head thrown back, and simply shrieking with laughter whilst Goliath, almost hidden behind, tickled under his arms. Twice again D broke away and ran in a circle — and twice again the playing started with holding hands and playing with each other's fingers. It was so completely fantastic that I simply couldn't believe it was actually happening. One of the most delightful things I've ever seen. I'm sad I can't find my hordes, but so much is going on here that I may as well make the most of it. Especially with Ma and infants, and other young ones, AND McGreggor. Oh — the day the two played was the first day dear old William arrived. I knew he had come because as David Goliath and I were dozing peacefully in the shade I heard William's high annoyed barking call from camp. D and G at once sat up and rushed to the edge of the stream. But they did not go to join Wm — after 10 minutes they lay down and went to sleep again. The bark was because Hugo moved a towel which William had his eyes on. He is a worse thief than ever — so is Goliath.

Tons of love,
Jane

[Postmarked April 25, 1963]

Darling Family,

This is the second letter I've started — one got sodden & illegible in my haversack & one is lost. It is simply pouring & blowing such a gale that typing is impossible. I've never known such rain. It was so bad yesterday I could no longer see from the Peak & so I thought I'd come down & see the boys. So I put my clothes in a polythene bag, just for fun, & walked nearly back naked. It was simply super! I was cross, though, that it rained. A child was poking into a hole in a dead tree stump with a stick & licking the end I could see beautifully with the telescope. Only it went when the rain started before I'd seen exactly what it was doing. I also found why they chew cardboard — I saw them pulling off dead wood, chewing it, & spitting it out. So cardboard is a type of dead wood for them. Of course, now remains — Why do they chew dead wood!! Still, it was interesting.

I am feeling very cross. Heard crashing outside, went out — & the baboons have destroyed 3 of the weaver nests. With eggs too. To hell with them.

David, Goliath & Hugo came this morning. Hugo waited up a palm the other side of the stream (now a roaring red torrent) & watched Hugo & I sitting with David & Goliath in the kitchen. I am hoping Mr. McG. will come with William. I met him on my path last night. Flo, Figan & Fifi are around too. In fact I was going to follow G & D hoping they'd lead me to the others when this storm began — there seemed little point in trying then. I prefer to wait for McGreggor. What a way to watch chimps — eh! Never mind. It took 18 months of slogging before I could!

I caught the 3rd rat last night. We decided to kill it & were trying to get it into a snake bag for the purpose. Suddenly — bingo — it was out! Like an arrow it rushed back to my tent! What they do is to collect food in my tent, carry it to Hugo's, & there make a nest. Only this one is trying to make a nest in my bird books in the bookcase.

Oh, Ma, before I forget. When you come, can you please bring the New York Conference book with nesting in it. I forgot.

Have just had a colour transparency of the 'Rain Dance'. It really is very very much better. Only the silly artist hasn't done it in the rain. Mr. Poggenpohl* said he wouldn't fault him, as I did say I'd seen it in good weather, but he thought it a pity. So do I.

We had the most <u>glorious</u> baboon fight. The cheeky baboon, Max, just deliberately ran at poor William who at once took himself up a tree. Then the baboon ran at David who chased it, upright, screaming — turned, ran to Goliath & flung his arms round him. After that the 2 attacked the baboon together — but after about 2 mins, it was Max who drove the chimps away. He is the only baboon who is so brave. <u>All</u> in good light. All filmed. And, believe it or not, the film ran out <u>just</u> as the fight was over! We have also filmed begging, beautifully, and nesting on the ground. Social grooming. Could have filmed Hugo in the palm this morning if it hadn't rained. Ugh — it is so cold.

Well — narrowly averted a disaster. I had just fetched water for coffee, & Hugo came over. Suddenly an extra violent gust of wind, frenzied flapping — 3 guy ropes came out & all the rest down one side almost out of the ground. So I held frantically to the main one in front while Hugo ran for aid. He flew back with Hassan, Anyango & Rashidi tearing after through the deluge, & Condo in the rear. Eventually my tent was safe again. Condo arrived yesterday with a large bald patch in the middle of his head in which was a <u>tiny</u> cut. He had cut himself with a panga while cutting a track! It was a microscopic cut! At first we thought he had miraculously shaved his hair off with the panga! So I had to put a strip of plastic on. Now he has shaved his whole head to match & it looks so funny! He still demands epsoms every other day. Oh — I <u>do</u> wish it would stop raining. New grass is shooting up. We'll never be able to burn it down. It is <u>sickening</u>. Incidentally, Mum, for purchase in Nairobi (or England) plastic table cloth for our table. . . . Can't get in Kigoma. Oh yes — do you know what David took? — your waste paper basket. I was so surprised when Dominic produced it intact — told him how pleased you'd be. Now the three old men have chewed it up.

---

* Art editor at *National Geographic*.

It is very touching how Goliath rushes to David's aid — whether or not this is necessary. Certainly, in the baboon fight, his assistance was most necessary. After I was peering at David's cut, & I put out my hand to groom his back. Suddenly "Look out!" said Hugo. I looked — there was G who had been resting about 20 yards away. He had advanced 1/2 way & was standing, eyes round, all his hair out. It was like an apparition in a nightmare! I have never seen him look so huge. I took my hand away & he returned to his seat. I had to test, so again I groomed David — at once G rose & advanced threateningly, & went back again when I stopped. Most spectacular & very touching.

Yes — Ma — I had a letter from Robert saying he was sorry he'd pestered you needlessly. I hope I've heard the last of the vile thing. He only asked me how a strongyle egg can turn into a hookworm or a roundworm! How on earth he thinks I should know! I have referred him to poor John — who did explain at some point — it went in at one ear, encountered a head full of dominance & sexual behaviour, turned round, and went out again!*

Did I thank you, Jiff, for your Christmas card? It was waiting for me when I got back. Also a letter from Peggy, & one from Pa. I now see what he meant when he asked me, on the phone, about the stamps — in his letter he asked me to spend up to £2 to buy him a set! No wonder I didn't know what he meant! Incidentally, I wonder if he ever got the giraffe tie? He never said.

Well, folks, I guess I'll sign off! There is no more vital news. Just prospects of more rain. The kitchen is <u>full</u> of baboons. All sitting sheltering. It looks so funny. Not friends with them now.

Anyway, tons of love to you all till next week. Don't forget 'nesting', Ma.

Jane

P.S. <u>Mum</u> Another item for you to bring — some of those salt pills — don't bother to bring whole tin — some in polythene bag. Also, from Nairobi, bandages.

---

* Robert Hinde was her tutor at Cambridge; John was probably the primate expert John Napier.

Chimpland.
[late May or early June 1963]

Darling Family,

I meant to write such a long letter — in fact I really looked forward to describing all the things which have been happening. But when Hassan returned from Kigoma, after posting my last mingy blue, he brought back various copies of chapters from Stanford — including mine,* Vernon's, one on Sexual Cycles, and one on Communicative Patterns in Primates. So I have been frantically busy each evening since making comments. . . .

What about my chimps. Oh, they are so fabulous and wonderful that it's hardly possible to believe it's true. Just to give a typical sort of day, let me say what happened today. Goliath arrived at a fig which I saw from a new look out post which scans the whole valley from near camp. Then he vanished. I went to see if he was in camp — he wasn't so I went back. Then I had a note to say others had come — well, Goliath actually, on his own. He clambered up the slope — the poor fellow has hurt his foot so much that he keeps losing his friends who travel too quickly for him. For 20 mins he sat waiting, hoping they'd come. Then he plodded on up. And about 1 minute after he had gone David arrived, leading Hugo and Evered. They all ate bananas. The most wonderful character, Hugo. He is a real gourmet — he just guzzles and guzzles, skins or anything will do. When one throws a banana his hair stands out and he runs for it. Rather jumpy, like Goliath. Evered tried to get one — he ran at it — screams. Evered got it, with wild fear grimaces presented, and was given a reassurance gesture. This is typical of Hugo. He hits out at everyone when he is excited, and then, when they scream and get scared, he is at once very sorry and sticks his hand towards them to reassure them. All his subordinates are continually being reassured. But he doesn't like to take time off eating and as he sticks one hand towards the other's lips or thigh he is stuffing skins into his mouth with the other. This morning, for example, a baboon was being irri-

---

* "Chimpanzees of the Gombe Stream Reserve," that she wrote for Irven DeVore's *Primate Behavior* (New York: Holt, Rinehart and Winston, 1965).

tating and threatening the chimps. As it chased Evered past him he hit out towards the scuffle — which was, after all, disturbing his eating. Then, as Evered ran behind him he hit out again, irritably — but was rather upset to find that in his preoccupation with his bananas he had hit out at the wrong animal!

Flo! Oh Flo! She is, as Hugo and I agree, a hoot! She has the most enormous nose. It is almost human, is Flo's nose, projecting forwards into a sort of beak. She has a small face and rather tight upper lip, with a small lower lip which, on occasions, droops down. She is scraggy and all her body seems out of proportion. She is devoted to Hugo* and, occasionally, we think he hands out some bananas to her. Slowly she is becoming tame — she is quite won over to the idea of popping in for the odd banana — ever since she got an entire bunch, in addition to my haversack. She is a funny beast. Yesterday Fifi was begging from David — how she loves David. She follows him round, sits on his knee, plays with his hand — and sometimes he puts his arms round her. Anyway, he gave her a skin, and Flo wanted it. Mother and daughter rolled over on the ground, Fifi holding the skin out of Flo's reach, and Flo determined to get it. It was very charming really — a sort of good natured scramble with no screams or upsets. Hugo again boobed — Fifi went up to beg from David. Hugo himself had just reached out a hand which David had gently but firmly pushed out of the way. When Fifi went up to beg Hugo hit out — not realizing who it was. A small whimper — Hugo looked round — prostrated himself on the ground as he leaned right back to reassure Fifi of his good heart by touching her on the thigh.

Evered and Pooch are wonderfully tame — and so is Flo's eldest, Figan.† Figan, far from being scared when we throw bananas, runs toward them with his hands out, trying to catch them!!

When he first came into the open Hugo was very rude. He got a fright when a banana was thrown, and because of this he rushed about with all his hair out. On one never to be forgotten occasion he

---

* Hugo the chimp.
† Flo in fact had an older son, Faben, but he was not much in evidence during this time.

stood completely upright when I threw one, and with a forward swing of his arm he picked up and threw, all in one movement, a 2 lb rock which happened to be right under his hand. It was quite fantastic — 19 1/2 feet he threw it. We tried to get him to do it again — he once tried to do the same with a dead palm frond, strengthening our conviction that it was not really throwing at us — simply a reaction.

Now Hassan is about to go — early. I got up at about 6 — but here he is. Continuation in 2 days.

Tons of love,
Jane

"Chimpland"
17 June 1963.

Dear Dr. Payne,

Thank you very much for your last two letters. The cheque has arrived safely in the bank, and I will certainly do as you say and keep a close watch on my funds. I am delighted to hear that there is a little money left from last year's work.

I must hasten to reassure you with regard to our safety here. I know you think that I am rather foolhardy in my attitude to the chimpanzees. In actual fact, although I do have implicit trust in David Greybeard, I do not have this trust for the other chimpanzees at all. In fact I mistrust Goliath very much! I have never pretended a friendship with him. He is slightly mad and not very intelligent. I am telling you this so that I can stress that Hugo and I do, in fact, take very great care not to alarm or upset him in any way. So do not go on thinking that I am just being completely foolish and presuming a friendship — which might terminate at any moment.

The enclosed interim report deals with only about half of the things which I am now finding out about these animals. I feel that I am only just beginning to understand them. One of the most important things with which I am becoming familiar is the real relationships which exist between the various chimpanzees in this community. Normally, under the everyday sort of conditions, it is not possible to observe these actual relationships except on the occasions when I am lucky enough to see meat eating or some other such situation. To see the behaviour evoked by throwing a desired food object amongst a large group is not studying natural behaviour. But, taken in conjunction with the many many hours of observation on normal behaviour, it provides a vital insight into the pattern of chimpanzee life. The only danger would be in describing this behaviour as normal — that is a danger I have seen well in advance and into which I shall not be guilty of falling.

You will have to excuse the terrible English in which I am trying to express myself. I can't seem to keep up with all my writing work these days — so much happens each day that it takes hours to type out each evening, and I am still having to cope with bits and pieces arising out of the chapter for the Stanford book.

I must just warn you that I had a letter from a Nan Russel-Cobb of Aldus Books Limited. They are publishing a book on Human Biology and want a picture of chimps in natural habitat. I suggested she contact you — I havn't the faintest idea whether it would be a good thing to have a picture in this book — they say it will be published in the United States and I thought maybe someone at the Geographic might know something about it. Anyway, I have to leave it to you to say yes or no, if, in fact, they do get in touch with you.

With warm regards,
Yours sincerely,
Jane

[June 1963]

Darling Family,

This is going to be rather messy. I have banana-sticky hands, bare feet, a kikapu* of bananas beside me, & I am with Hugo, Goliath & Evered who are sprawled asleep. We are on the 'pig path' side of the stream, just opposite camp. On the other side of the stream are

---

* A woven shopping basket.

Hugo II* and David. They (mine & David) missed each other by 5 mins — driven from camp by baboons. Blast them. . . . Honestly, if you'd seen McKnew† yesterday threatening Evered — going right up & keeping on opening his mouth in a threat yawn in the little fellow's face, & hitting bushes at him. Just taking it out on him because he couldn't cope with Hugo & Goliath together. Evered tried not to look at him but jumped each time McKnew hit a bush. Hugo charmingly reached out a hand & touched his scrotum in reassurance, & then hit at McKnew (who was not attacking him).

I am in such a muddle as to what I have and have not told you. I should have made a list. However, I <u>do</u> know I was just going to relate the tale of Goliath & his wench. He had been away for 2 weeks. The boys came to say Goliath was there but wouldn't come down. There he was, staring at the bananas. Most odd. He then set off towards camp, still up in the trees. From my veranda the mystery was explained. He appeared up the slope with a very pink female. With mouth — (4.0 Hugo starts eating leaves — ! That was for my note book!) with mouth watering he looked from the bananas to his female. She sat, hands on knees, chin on hands, gazing in the other direction, in a fork. After a moment or two G climbed down and took a couple of steps towards us — then, in sudden panic, rushed up another tree (they were in grass so otherwise he couldn't see her). She hadn't moved. He gazed at the bananas, at her. At b's. Climbed down. Ran a few yards — panic — up a tree. Gazed at her, b's. Her. She hadn't moved. Scratched. Suddenly climbed down and rushed nearly all the way down — ran to the right and stood upright — she was still there. He ran down — ran to the right, stood upright to look at her — she hadn't moved. Got to the banana box. Took a banana — ran towards the kitchen, stood up, gazed up. Still there. Hurried back, got to the veranda. Took 3 bananas. Simply charged back towards the kitchen. Stood up — she'd gone. With typical feminine cunning she'd waited until he was the farthest from her he was ever going to get — & then she'd made a dash for it. Goliath simply <u>rushed</u> up the slope. Bounded into the tree where she'd been

---

* Hugo van Lawick.
† A baboon.

— sniffed the fork, peered round. Leapt down. Ran in all different directions, flat out, all his hair out, appearing up various trees, standing upright to look over the grass. Hugo & I were in <u>hysterics.</u> And he never found her! After 10 mins he came down, seized bananas, crossed the stream, & met up with David who was waiting up a tree. They'd been apart for 2 weeks so there was a splendid greeting and a 2 1/2 hour grooming session.

This is another part of the letter or scrawl which is gradually multiplying in various parts over the reserve. I ought to quote you bits from letters from Geographic people. But one and all, even the most unlikely sort of people, say that the article is one of the most fascinating they have read in a long time, and is likely to be received with tremendous enthusiasm, etc., etc. They are saying this in letters to Hugo as well. I must say it is nice, after using their money and equipment for so long to have produced something which they think first rate, both manuscript and pictures. A pleasantly satisfying sort of feeling. And they are mad with enthusiasm for another article next year. . . .

Now, before I relate any more news — Mummy — millions of congratulations on passing your test.* I am now the only member of my family which has <u>not</u> passed a test!! Which is rather a hoot. Anyway, many congrats — Hugo told me to send his as well. I am being madly bitten as I write. It is early morning and I'm waiting here until they arrive as they left late yesterday, going north, and this usually means they arrive between 7.30 and 9. The trouble is, with Evered and Hugh† still not properly tame, I can't follow them. I hope your mouth is quite better Jif — though if I don't have a letter from you soon you may as well have rotted for all I know. I hear vague bits from the rest of the family, that's all.

Oh — you know how Louis pushes his lower lip forward whilst lecturing? This trait is becoming more pronounced in David every day. He has recently become, officially (though not yet with the approval of his — what is the other part of "namesake"?) David

---

* Driver's license test.

† Hugh (no relation to the chimpanzee Hugo) was a powerful young male who had recently appeared at the provisioning area.

Louis Greybeard. We feel, anyway, that he is of sufficient rank to warrant an extra name to all the other chimps. Let me also tell you — I do hope I havn't — about Mr. McGreggor and Hugh. We had had the most splendiferous afternoon in camp, with Flo and the whole lot. As soon as they'd gone we whizzed up to the mango. In one of the figs there were the two aforesaid gents. Funny thing — I'd come down from that tree for Flo, over an hour before — and Hugh had been there then! Anyway, he was still there, and had been joined by McG. Hugo (let him be I, and the chimp II) arrived, and had been filming for some time. Because Hugh is an absolute hoot. He droops his lip even more than William and, what's more, he doesn't close it when he eats, which gives a very strange effect — with each chew it sort of waggles about! Suddenly they both peered down, and their hair came out. We knew someone was coming. By enormous good luck Hugo I just happened to have them both in the screen — so that he could concentrate on whichever one did the best greeting. Suddenly McGreggor's hand went out towards Hugh — almost at the same time Hugh reached his hand toward McG — and they held hands. I've never known anything so simply amazing — no one would believe it, save that, right from the first movement, it is on film. They held hands for nearly two minutes, peering down. And then Hugo II bounded up, having got rid of Flo, and he and McGreggor embraced. All three groomed each other, and it was super. All in sunlight. We at last got some really good film showing McG's baldness.

I mentioned I'd seen chimps eating bushbuck. McGreggor was prominent in that feast — he had the whole skin and leg bones of the buck. He was dishing out large dollops to Huxley, and wadges, from his mouth, to two of the small children. Also Huxley was dishing out helpings to one of the small ones. And one little incident was charming. It concerned Mr. McGreggor and a female unknown. McG. had eaten or given away all the flesh from the skin except for a piece up at the top, so the whole rest of the hide was dangling down. The female reached out and touched it — she withdrew her hand. Then she reached out and tentatively held it, looking up at McG. All I could see of that gent, because of a leafy branch, was his feet on one branch, and the skin dangling down. The female was on a lower branch. Well, she gently pulled the skin — suddenly a large black foot was lowered, grasped the importunate lady by one wrist, and gently, but firmly, pushed her hand away! It was so funny — I just burst out laughing. But honestly, none of these observations would be anything but for my telescope. I cart it madly around with me. I can learn far more by watching from a good distance, when I can see who everyone is, than by creeping up close in the thick forest — which, super though it is, doesn't give me so much information. It used to be nice for the resting on the ground — but we have that daily in camp. And the telescope is 100 times better for Ma's and babies because they don't have to bother to sit behind thick vegetation, and so I can see exactly what is going on. But can you believe it that huge Fifi still suckles. It is amazing. Still rides on poor old haggard Flo's back.* (Hugo keeps calling her Clo!) Have I told you about Flo's nose? It is a real human nose — on a chimp is quite hideous. But what a beak.

I must now break what may be the most sad news in a long while. This concerns William. William has not been [seen] for well over a month — so long, in fact, that I simply dare not check on the exact duration of his absence. So long that we are full of terrible forebodings; so long that I can't believe we shall ever see William again. I just can't bear it. It has got to the stage when I feel all weepy when I think of him, and his darling groans when he doesn't like bananas, and his rocking — oh, and everything. True it would be worse if David disappeared — but we'd much rather that it had been Goliath. Goliath has given us wonderful things — both film-wise, photograph-wise, and observation wise. But he has not got a really nice character — not like darling darling William. There is just a chance, of course, that he has gone on a long trip, visiting an aged aunt perhaps, who lives outside the reserve. But that possibility becomes less likely with each succeeding day. Every evening we say — William just <u>must</u> come tomorrow — and he never does. Tonight is even

---

* Flo was a very tolerant mother. Her difficulties in weaning Fifi, as noted here, were repeated with disastrous results later with her son Flint.

worse than usual. "We shall never see William again". It's made worse by the fact that not a single chimp came to see us today, and I only saw 3 chimps vaguely from my mango — which is the worst day for a month. Trouble is, as we've agreed, we've been thoroughly spoilt — n.b. it is Hugo who is cheering me up these days!

Now — this, in fact, is the end of the letter, and comes after the other two typewritten pages. There is so much more to relate, and, as usual, simply no time to relate it. For instance, tonight Flo, Fifi, Figan, Hugo, Goliath and David and Evered are all sleeping just along the path. It is too good to be true. It started with David coming at 10.30 and going almost at once. Then, about 12.30 Flo and Fifi came. And this is what is so interesting. Last week Figan, Flo's eldest, wanted to go off with David, Hugo, Goliath and [Evered]. His mother was going in another direction. He went after them until he could just see them and also Flo. Then Flo climbed down and set off her way — Figan at once turned and ran after her. So, we presume that Figan, until now, has been tied to Ma's apron strings as it were. 3 days ago a whole group appeared in one of the figs in the valley, late at night. In the morning David, Hugo, Goliath, Evered and Figan arrived for bananas. Not Flo and Fifi. The "men" trouped off together. In the afternoon Flo came, with Pooch and Fifi. No Figan. She waited all afternoon and went off without him. The next day she came — we didn't see Figan — Goliath arrived. Today they all met up. It was so super. Flo and Fifi were here. Goliath arrived. No greeting. Then suddenly Goliath began standing up and being absolutely fabulous, swaying from foot to foot, all his hair out. Charging off to greet Hugo who was [following] a trail down the path. Unfortunately 4 strangers got so far and then turned and went off — before I even saw who they were. Anyhow, there was a lovely greeting of G. and Hugo. And then we saw Fifi stand upright and go up to her brother, put her arms around his neck and her face to his. Then Figan went up to Flo and they kissed briefly. A very filial and dutiful peck, but lips to lips. It was so wonderful. Fifi and Figan played in the open beside Flo, with Evered lying beside them, reclining on one elbow. Hugo ate so much that every time he moved he collapsed, sprawling, on the ground. Figan made wonderful fear grimaces and presented to Goliath. Fifi half rode on Goliath's back. Fifi cracked half a gourd. Fifi swung and played. Fifi jumped on her mother's back and rode across in the open. Fifi suckled. And then they trailed off. We went up to see if we could see them make nests. Missed the making, saw them in their nests. Hugo went down as it was late and too dark for filming — I heard my signal — went down — David had arrived and Flo and the children had come back with him. He was feeling belligerent and wanted the whole boxful of bananas for himself, but we managed to load Flo up, and the other two got plenty. They joined the sleeping, bloated, banana-full Hugo, Goliath and Evered. The other things that have happened are without number. It is so super. There just isn't time to write letters — I'll tell you more in the next. There has been a gap because Hassan didn't go in last week — my very urgent cable re final script of Geographic went with Ian and his family who came.* I am getting 500 reprints of my article, which is very nice. I asked for 50!

> Tons and tons of love,
> Jane

P.S. <u>Ma. When</u> are you coming? <u>How</u>!!?? To Nairobi? Dar? Train or air? v. imp. Can get clothes as presents in Africa. Chiko & Ado not here. Can you bring <u>ancient</u> sweater or cardigan — David took my yellow one.

P.S. <u>Please</u> Ma — do borrow Olly's ciné if she can spare it.

> 2 July 1963
> Chimpland.

My dear FFF,

I gathered from Ma's last letter that you would be away when she was in N[airo]bi. I gather from Bernard you won't be. I hope she gets the notes I have written her at New Stanley where she said she might stay. This is really just to say: I think I told her to send a

---

* Casual visitors who came for the day, probably from Kigoma.

telegramme to McDonald <u>instead of</u> me. But I've now worked it out we can send it on the 9th & so, all being well, get her cable. So ask her to send <u>2</u> — one to McD & one to me.

Chimpland is still fine. I hear from Mary Griswold via Joanne* that you think you'll be able to stay on in Kenya. Will you? I hear most of your news & views via other people!

Still no William. Letters come from all over the world asking if William has turned up. He never will any more.

The bit on the back of the envelope — I just had a letter from Robert. <u>He</u> thinks the extra term a good idea — he is proposing it to the Board which doesn't meet till 1st week in August. He suggests I carry on on the assumption I shall be here till Christmas, but that I must be prepared to return, at short notice, to fulfill degree requirements. I think I'll write a chatty note to Huxley telling him how important the term is. He helped before — I don't mean I'll <u>ask</u> him.

Have I asked you if you can find out for me at what age a chimp's canines are full grown? Or who should I write to?

Incidentally, the most urgent note for Ma was asking her to arrange interflora flowers for Danny's birthday from me.

Filmed the most <u>super</u> greeting today. David Louis G. did 4 steps of the "greetings swagger", (upright, hair out) flung one arm round Olly, in front of the infant Gilka. Was just about to poke his finger into her backside when Gilka, most agitated, dropped from Ma's back & got in the way. So he stroked her little white tuft instead! It was super.

With love,
FC

"Chimpland"
5 July 1963

Dear Bernard,

Many thanks for sending the two extinguishers, and for your letter. Before reading the end of your sentence about water pistols

---

* Joanne Hess of the National Geographic had hand-delivered mail during her recent visit to Gombe.

filled with ammonia Hugo and I said to each other — "Why didn't we think of that. What a wonderful idea!" and you were about to be bamboozled with requests for millions of water pistols. Then I read the second part — that they are unobtainable! Of course they are. I remember Norman trying to get a toy gun into Kenya which he bought in U.K. for Christopher. Of course he couldn't get it in for love nor money. Still — it was a bright idea.

I trust that you will take everything off the blank cheque. If by any chance you cashed it before we wired for one of the expensive ones, then I trust you will let me know with all due speed and I will send you another. Only please let me know how much you have cashed it for so that I can keep my accounts in order — or Ma can for me!

You needn't worry about being careful. We are. We have a cage built!!!! For us! This is only for when Goliath comes with a group of other males early in the morning or when it rains. At these times his temper is terrible. The trouble is that ever since the baboon episode when Hugo threw a stone at him fearing he was going to join David in chasing me, Goliath has borne Hugo a grudge. He is really horrible to him, and has chased him 4 times. You know what he can be like in a rage, and I'm sure you and Helen both can imagine how unpleasant it must be to be on the receiving end of his rage!* Anyway, though if I'd been just on my own I'd never have considered something like a cage, with such a spite raging it seems only fair. Also with Ma coming out, it's best to be safe than sorry! Another tame one we've got who is still just a bit scared, luckily, has a worse temper than Goliath. That is Hugo. He would certainly join in if Goliath started anything, but wouldn't dare on his own.

However, enough of that, because otherwise everything is simply superb. We have two tame mothers, Flo, the most hideous chimp in Chimpland, and Olly (!). Olly has a darling daughter of about 1 year, and an elder son of about 8. Flo, with her huge nose, her sagging bosom, her ear with the piece torn out, and her skinny little legs, has a dear child of 3, Fifi, and a cute and most intelligent son

---

* Bernard and his friend Helen had visited Gombe and were familiar with the personalities involved.

Figan, who is about 7. Flo, although she's such an old bag, is very popular with the men. Particularly David, who sometimes greets her in the most fabulous way — did I tell you how he once kissed one of her nipples and pinched the other! The men also have a naughty habit of poking a finger up their lady friend's vagina when greeting her!

Honestly Bernard, I am learning so much in such a short time that I sometimes wonder how much longer it can go on. I mean — there <u>must</u> be a limit to the amount I can go on learning about chimps — such large amounts of new things, anyway. Of course, one would expect to go on learning in dribs and drabs for years and for ever — not so much. I have already applied for yet another term here — which means I wouldn't get back to England till Christmas. . . .

Why are you returning to England? Is it because of Africanization? Politics? Or what? And where will you try for a job. Kew? I'm sure you will find it dreadful, after being here, won't you.

Anyway, I hope you saw Vanne (I am having to call her this daily to get Hugo used to saying it. What a pair you are, to be sure!) She will be on her way by the time you get this. She's going to find it a very different camp from the one she knew. It is a camp completely taken over by chimps. The kitchen and choo have both been moved out of the way of photography. We keep cutting down various trees — well, bushes, which removed the light for Hugo's photography. The boys all vanish like lightning at the smallest whistle which indicates that chimps have come. Meals, half cooked, are abandoned on the fire. Bread cannot be made. The boys are in their seventh heaven — they never have to come up to make tea or breakfast, because Olly always comes about that time and mustn't be disturbed. Often they only appear after 7 p.m.! What a blissful life.

I must stop. Incidentally, Mummy may have asked you already, but I couldn't read your writing — the large prickly <u>what</u> growing on the foreshore? And what does it look like? And are those the seeds from the dung which I found whilst you were here? Sorry about all those questions, and there's no hurry with answers. Any old time will do — this year, next year, sometime. . . .

Thank you again, very very much, for all you've done. And all the bother. And please give my love to Helen. I hope Ma did manage to get out to have a meal with you — though somehow I rather doubt it.

With love,
Jane

c/o Box 8,
Kigoma.
20 July 1963

Dear Dr. Payne,

I am enclosing an interim report for 15 June to 15 July. I am sorry it is rather delayed. Although the report is not as long as usual it has, in fact, been one of the most fruitful periods of my research. With such a large group of "tame" animals details of interrelationships between different animals are acquiring more and more significance.

I must tell you now about our cage which, I hope, will finally set your mind at rest with regard to our safety in camp. This cage is designed for us — a retreat in case of emergency, and a more substantial one than the inside of Hugo's tent where we are protected only by mosquito netting! I hope that we shall never be forced to use this cage, but it does provide a really sound safety precaution.

There were several reasons which decided us finally to have such a cage made. Firstly: we now have so many "tame" males that they are inclined to excite each other — and chimpanzees, like humans, do things without thinking when highly excited. Secondly: Goliath bears a lasting grudge against Hugo (because Hugo threw a stone to dis-attract Goliath from chasing me on the day of the baboon fight which I mentioned in my last report). On several occasions since Hugo has been chased.

The cage is foolproof. It has two doors, one as an emergency. Projection forwards with a netting dropping down in front of the cameras while Hugo can nip into the cage and close the door. It was made by Hassan in Kigoma — all metal — and is a really first class job.

I next want to ask you what the position is with regard to my using photographs taken by Hugo in any subsequent books — both scientific and popular. This, of course, will not be for another two or three years, but I intend, ultimately, to write a popular book about my chimps. For one thing I think they deserve it, and it might well help their pathetic relations which are forced to live in captivity. Obviously I should need some pictures of myself doing various things, and, in addition, Hugo is taking a lot more stills of chimps now — many of which will be far better than any which I take. I'd be very grateful if you could let me know about this point.

There is one final point which I hate to worry you with. But I have received another letter from Aldus Books Ltd, which I have enclosed. Can you advise me as to how I should answer these people? Should I tell them to write to you, to wait till I return to England so that I can find out more about the book concerned — or what? Maybe this is the last request for the moment, but there might be others.

Joanne Hess was extremely lucky when she visited us for the day. We thought it was lucky at the time, when 21 or so chimps came to camp that morning. Since then we have realized that she was even luckier — for the following three days there were no chimps here at all — neither in camp nor anywhere in the surrounding country. They had all gone off on a long trek.

I have nearly forgotten the most important item of all! When I started thinking about the tame mothers with their children I realized that it was absolutely vital to get an extra term's leave of absence so that I could witness the behaviour of the infants during the termite season. Dr. Leakey immediately agreed (as you may well have heard by now) and so I wrote next to my Supervisor in Cambridge. He also agreed, but said that he could not give the answer of the Research Board until mid-August. However, he suggested that I plan to stay on until Christmas.

You told me I had a certain amount of money in hand from last year. Even without that I feel sure that I can carry on until Christmas with the money here in Kigoma. So that I feel sure that from your point of view there will be no objections to my staying here for a longer period than was originally planned. I myself am more happy about the prospect than I can say — as I dare say you can imagine!

My mother has arrived safely. And now, with all these chimps coming almost daily, we are finding a third person extremely helpful in all sorts of ways.

It is now well after midnight and I must close.

All best wishes,
Sincerely yours,
Jane

"Chimpland"
30 August 1963

My dear FFF,

I havn't yet had your long typewritten letter re the chimps, and am forstalling it. I know that part of your worry so far as WE are concerned is due to the film you saw in Washington. And that's fair enough because I WAS silly then — and I freely admit it. But as for the safety of the chimps — Louis, can you honestly think that I havn't thought and thought about the safety of my chimps. I have already talked about this very thing with the Game Department, before all these chimps came to camp. Bill Moore-Gilbert and I decided that the best thing would be to keep the fishermen from the little bit of beach where my boys are now — then there are no huts for a long way along the beach. Apart from this, only David ever goes up to the Africans — the others all keep well away.

The cage. This has been erected not really so much as a means of escape, but as a means of removing temptation from the chimps — if they get excited we do not have to try and get out of their way, which might excite them more, but simply sit still in the cage. From which — or outside which — Hugo films when he is here.

Tourists. So far as I can see the only way to safeguard these chimps in the future — I don't mean the immediate future during which I guess things will go all right, but the future beyond which no one can see — is to make the reserve pay just a little. I know that Government, at the moment, is keen on game. But local pressure is still strong, and this particular little Reserve is NOT safe. The game dept. once I have gone, might well change their minds and reconsider a suggestion which was once almost taken up — give this place back to the Africans and make Mahale Mountain area, south of Kigoma, a chimp preserve.

So. All is planned. The attraction is provided — the chimps themselves. Their safety is planned. I myself am planning to put back all the money from my lecture film into the Reserve, in the building of a place for — say — 4 people at a time. I plan to pay for the looking after of the chimps — and I feel some sort of arrangement can be made with Geographic whereby I can give lectures with the film for money for the chimps. The hut for the visitors is to be by the lake. A covered way leads to an observation cage, and a Scout lets them know when chimps are here. Mummy, Hugo and I have planned it in detail. Obviously hardly anyone will come, certainly not for ages. But if bananas are bought from the village which causes the trouble, that will slightly appease them. And if I employ one of their leading lights, as we do now, that will also appease.

Most important of all. If only you came you would see for yourself that things are not as Joanne and Richard painted them.* If you could only SEE my chimps for yourself. O.K. — we didn't quite know how to cope when 20 chimps arrived, the first couple of times. It is now so well taped that there is not the slightest danger of anything happening at all. I mean that. Mum will agree — I expect she'll tell you herself.

And if you are worried about chimps raiding huts after I've gone — they would (IF the banana supply stopped) simply look for a few weeks in the places they know and then presume the tree was out of season and move off. They will not look for them anywhere else. Why should they?

Louis — you had faith in me when the whole project was seemingly hopeless and futile (to me). Do not suddenly lose it just when things are better than I ever dared to hope. The results I am getting now are the sort of things I never dreamed of getting.

---

* Joanne Hess and Richard Leakey, who briefly visited Gombe, apparently commented on problems with the banana feeding regimen.

A few examples, which should be exciting enough. Flo, my mother with the 3 year old (approx). Still suckling. Flo developed her first pink swelling since the child has been born. She trailed millions of men along here with her. I was able to see for the first time the real effect of a sexual swelling on the other chimps, the duration of their interest, and the effect it had on the movements of Flo. I was able to see, close up, the effect of mating behavior, on the child, during the whole of the attractive period. (Throughout which she continued to suckle.) I was able to see the different treatments accorded to this old female and a very young female (Jane!) in the same pink condition (she was almost completely ignored when Flo was present). And another very, very interesting thing — the elder child, probably between 6 and 7, finally left his mother, for days running, during this first pink swelling since the birth of his younger sister. His whole behaviour is changing — he is becoming grown up!

As for the details of social behaviour — to be able to follow the interrelationships from DAY TO DAY, instead of simply seeing the same two animals together once a week or even once a month — well, I can really say, now, that I know chimps.

Louis — I beg you will try to come and see things for yourself. Anyway — I plan to come back here the moment I finish at Cambridge, even before the Pigmy Chimps* (if that is possible) because then Flo will have a new baby and I can see the effect on Fifi — the daughter — not to mention the 101 other things. I CAN'T tell you, in a letter, how simply fantastically exciting everything is. . . .

DO try and come. You would fall head over heels in love with all my darlings — never, never think that I will let anything happen to them through what I am doing. I KNOW it is right. I KNOW that I can work the Reserve the way it must. I KNOW that I shall come back here time and time again until the problems that remain are hardly worth mentioning.

It is after midnight. My journal is usually about 10 pages per

---

* Louis and Jane had planned that she would make comparative observations on bonobos (pygmy chimpanzees) in Congo; the plan was never realized.

night. There is seldom time for a good night's sleep. But the results will so justify it, and your faith — don't, please don't, lose it now. It hurts, you know.

With love,
F.C. Jane

P.O. Box 8,
Kigoma,
Tanganyika.
12 October 1963

Dear Dr. Payne,

I have just received a letter from Dr. Grzimek of 12 August — sent on from England by sea. He wrote after seeing the chimpanzee article in the Geographic Magazine. He is very anxious to publish a translation of a shortened version of this article in Das Tier — which he edits together with Professor Lorenz and Professor Hediger.*

Since August I have been busily refusing articles to hundreds of magazines. So far as this is concerned, however, I am not quite sure what I should do. It is certainly the best animal magazine in Europe. But, quite apart from this, I do not want to make an enemy of Dr. Grzimek. I am sure he was not to blame so far as the Kinloch episode† was concerned and I rather feel that, if we refuse to co-operate with him in this article he may feel that we are holding a grudge. I have a great admiration for his work in Africa — and, since I wrote to him explaining that the chimps would be badly disturbed

---

* Bernhard Grzimek, director of the Frankfurt Zoological Garden, was a great popularizer of animal behavior studies and conservation and, perhaps most significantly, one of the most powerful voices calling for the preservation of the Serengeti Plains; he was also a trustee of Tanzanian national parks. Konrad Lorenz, Austrian zoologist, director of the Max Planck Institute for Behavioral Physiology, shared a Nobel Prize in 1973. H. C. Heini Hediger was director of the Zoological Gardens in Zurich.

† A conflict with Tanzanian officialdom (as represented by Major Kinloch) over Jane's reluctance to cooperate with a Grzimek team hoping to film chimps in Gombe.

if he came here he has not attempted to press the matter further.

As I only posted my interim Report two days ago there is really no further news from here — oh, but yes. There is one thing I really must tell you as it is one of the most amazing things that has happened since I started working with the chimps. Yesterday David Greybeard and I set off along the valley together. He was in a lazy and tolerant mood — after he had vanished through a thick tangle of vegetation I found him sitting (seeming to wait) when I finally crawled through after him. We sat and ate leaves side by side. And then I found a palm nut, nice and ripe and red, and felt sure David would appreciate it. So I held it out on my outstretched palm. Now David is a past master at affecting to ignore completely what he considers foolish actions on the part of his would-be human friends. He gave my offering a scornful glance and turned away. I held my hand a little nearer. For a few more moments he continued to ignore me. And then, suddenly, he turned towards me, reached out his hand to the nut, and, to my astonishment and delight, held my hand with his, keeping a firm warm pressure for about 10 seconds. He then withdrew his hand, glanced at the nut, and dropped it to the ground.

I have explained in my reports how chimps sometimes hold each other's hands — normally the subordinate animal holds out its hand when wanting reassurance and the dominant animal, if feeling friendly, reaches out to clasp the hand of the other. David did not want the nut. But there was this strange creature, holding out its hand, making an offering. So he took it, reassured me, and then demonstrated his complete lack of interest in my offering by dropping it to the ground. If it had not happened to me I think I would never have believed it possible.

The rains are very late — already the chimps are inspecting the termite heaps, but as yet the insects are not ready to fly.

I must close. My mother can post this when she goes tomorrow.

Yours sincerely,

Jane

P.S. Dr. Grzimek wanted black and white stills for the article.

c/o P.O. Box 8
Kigoma, Tanganyika
27 November 1963

Mr. Paul Brooks,
Houghton Mifflin Company,
2 Park Street,
Boston 7.
United States of America.
Dear Mr. Brooks,

Please forgive this messy little "blue" (I hate them) but I felt I must write immediately, upon receiving your letter of 19 November, to express my horror on hearing that you never got my reply to your last letter. This is the third letter of mine which has gone astray in 4 months — including one marked "urgent" in huge red letters for Dr. Leakey. I really am sorry about this.

I am writing just a hasty note — your letter came with the mail today and because the mail brought us a terrible problem — the mail always does seem to! — we are sending in an African tomorrow to send off batches of cables. It is already midnight.

Anyway, thank you a second time for your original letter, and for the extremely kind gesture of sending John Williams' book — which is a very fine one, and has been most helpful. In comparison with Grant and Praed it is a handy book indeed! Grant and Praed is often quite useless unless you have the dead bird in your hand and can measure its various feathers!!

As regards a book — I really and honestly can't tell you anything about that just at the moment. I feel quite helpless about it. I had a letter from the Geographic Society (because a number of publishers wrote to them to ask about the possibility of a book) suggesting that I should make no commitments at the present because there was the possibility that the Society might wish to publish a book. This I should not be happy about for various reasons, but if they really insist there is little I can do about it, being, as I am, indebted to them so greatly. However, when I have sorted things out a bit more I will contact you again. I think the type of book Collins wants is something very different from that which the Geographic wants, and there might be no clash at all.* At present, however, I can only wait and see!

In the meantime — splendid news from "Chimpland". Results are so splendid this year, so much in excess of my wildest dreams, that I have got two more terms away from Cambridge next year, and shall be returning to the Gombe Stream in March. I now know about 30 chimps really inside out, characters and all — and there are some splendid characters. The sad thing is that dear William died — we think he must have caught pneumonia as a result of his cold which never properly cleared up — the last time he was seen he was coughing dreadfully.

However, the splendid thing is that I am pretty sure we can raise the necessary funds to set up a permanent research center here — so these individuals can be studied over a sufficient number of years to make the research really worth while. When you think of the amount of money poured into the social behaviour and psychology of captive chimps you realize how very worth while this scheme will be. After all, the psychological state of a captive chimp, in most instances, must be rather similar to that of a man in prison. The older chimps in captivity, that is.

I apologize again for my seeming rudeness, and I will write again when I can let you know anything definite about the possibility of a book. Incidentally, I was interested that you heard from Fairfield Osborn† about the conference in Nairobi. I am still waiting to hear about that Conference — at which this Reserve was discussed. No one, so far, has told me anything! However, I am so glad Osborn is optimistic about the future of the animals — and with you I certainly hope he is right.

Sincerely yours,
Jane Goodall

---

* National Geographic was to publish one "popular" book, *My Friends the Wild Chimpanzees,* in 1967; Collins in England and Houghton Mifflin in the United States published *In the Shadow of Man* in 1971.
† Osborn was with the New York Zoological Society.

8

MARRIAGE AND RETURN
1964

> Hugo and I agreed afterward that we had never been
> to a wedding we enjoyed more.
>
> — *In the Shadow of Man*

JANE GOODALL and Hugo van Lawick left the camp at Gombe
in late 1963, he returning to Nairobi, she to Bournemouth for
Christmas and then to Cambridge to begin her third term. As
during her second university term, she lived in an old farmhouse
at Cross Farm, Comberton, a few miles outside the city of Cambridge. During her four months' absence from Gombe, Hassan and
Dominic managed the daily operations, and Dominic kept a continuing log of chimpanzee observations. Also present in the winter
of 1963–64 was a young Polish-born mycologist, Kris Pirozynski,
who had come to look at the local microfungi.

Jane and Hugo were by then, as she later wrote, "very much in
love," and the separation of early December was enough to convince them both that marriage should be the next step. Boxing Day
(the day after Christmas) at the Birches was therefore enlivened by a
telegram that said: "WILL YOU MARRY ME LOVE STOP HUGO."[*]

So the term at Cambridge was a very busy one, filled with the
usual pressing research reports and papers and meetings with her
advisor, as well as a quick trip to Washington, D.C., in February
to address a huge and enthusiastic audience at the National Geo-

---

[*] As quoted in *In the Shadow of Man* (1971), p. 90.

graphic headquarters — not to mention planning the wedding. Held at Chelsea Old Church on March 28, Easter Saturday, the wedding was done in yellow and white: daffodils and arum lilies, with the bride in white and the bridesmaids in yellow and white. Perhaps all weddings are exercises in anxiety, excitement, and frantic activity; this one may have been more so than most, as the letter of February 3 to "Kins" — that is, Sally Cary — suggests. In addition to all those "cables and express letters . . . whizzing between here and Africa, Africa and Holland, Holland and here" and the "frantic cables from Africa to Washington, Washington to Africa and to England and from England to Washington about files and tapes and more films," Jane suddenly developed some physical symptoms alarming enough to warrant a visit to the Tropical Diseases Hospital in London.

But Africa and the chimpanzees of Gombe were never far from her thoughts. The wedding cake was topped by a clay model of David Greybeard. Enlarged color portraits of several other Gombe chimps, including Goliath, Flo, and Fifi, looked out at the happy crowds at the reception. Louis Leakey, though unable to attend in person, gave a brief congratulatory speech by tape recording. A telegram from the National Geographic Society informed one and all that the bride had just been awarded her second Franklin Burr Award for Contribution to Science (which included an honorarium of $1,500). And the bride and groom, having thus tied the knot, then trimmed their honeymoon down to three days in order to race back to paradise at the edge of Lake Tanganyika, because Flo had just given birth to a young male (soon named Flint). The couple's return was in fact briefly delayed by a grand reception at State House in Nairobi. There, after a couple of power dinners and a brief side visit to the Leakey house at Langata, Baron and Baroness Jane and Hugo van Lawick showed their latest film on the Gombe research to "H.E." — His Excellency Malcolm MacDonald (governor general of Kenya) and several ministers and other dignitaries associated with that newly independent nation. In Nairobi also they met Edna Koning (a young Dutch woman living in Peru who had written asking for work and was hired as a research assistant) before pressing south, through seasonal rains and unreasonable floods, to "Chimpland" at last.

* * * *

Cross Farm,
Comberton,
Cambridge.
27 January 1964.

Dear Dr. Payne,

I am writing mainly to tell you what you may already have heard — namely that Hugo and I have just got engaged! It must seem rather strange that we were together for so long and then got engaged by cable! — but that's typical of Hugo! Anyway, it is all very exciting and we plan to get married at Easter, after my "ordeal" in Washington.

The other matter, linked with wedding arrangements (plus an endeavour to acquire enough clothes to do credit to the Society in February!) is that I shall be very grateful if you could send me a cheque enabling me to draw about £300 of the money for my last article. I have not got the correspondence with me, but I think the sum is lodged with your London Barclay's Bank account.

Work is going ahead well, and I have broken the back of my paper on aggressive and submissive behavior. It is always a bit of a shock — returning from the chimps to Cambridge. Most exhausting but, I feel, very good for me.

Thank you, by the way, for sending me the cuttings about the chimp kidney transplants. It would feel very strange, I think, to wander around with ape kidneys inside one — it is a peculiar thought — and quite extraordinary that the man lived for so long.

I must close and get on with working out a system for my new filing cabinet — a horrible job!

I look forward to seeing you all again in February, although <u>not</u> to giving the lecture!

Yours very sincerely,
Jane

Cross Farm,
Comberton,
Cambridge.
3 February [1964].

My dear Kins,

I can't think of many people on whom I would dare use up this charming shade in writing paper. However, I seem to remember various daintily coloured pages — or was it red ink — or violet or something — from you in the past — so here goes.

Your letter arrived this afternoon and forestalled me by 3 hours — as tonight I planned to write and tell you the latest. This is that Hugo and I get wed on 28th March, Easter Saturday of all days. It is the only possible day free. I most sincerely hope you are not planning to be away for Easter, and that, if you are, you will give a priority to coming to the wedding. It should be great fun!

It was all decided on in a hurry, and you can't imagine the cables and express letters that went whizzing — and still whizz — between here and Africa, Africa and Holland, Holland and here. My goodness. 7 letters all at once from Hugo. 1 express — did I like emeralds!! So back went a cable — "love emeralds love you"!!! Back came a cable — what size was my finger? Back went an answer — No. J. Another cable — can't find J on the card I was given. Then an urgent one — please cable names and address of your parents for announcement of engagement (there are two cables, both saying this, one from Africa, one from England. They crossed!!) Then a cable to Holland — please what are Hugo's full names. Then a cable from Africa to Holland — have I got christening cards. A cable back to Africa — please cable Jane to ring me. Cable to me — please ring my mother tonight. Horrors! Was I panic stricken. I got through at last, and his mother sounded quite sweet — but the poor thing was in such a muddle, all Hugo's letters having contradicted each other. Was I going to see them before the wedding. Was it a white wedding. Did Hugo really need christening cards — they were burnt by the Japs in Indonesia?!! Oh, I can't tell you what a muddle. And in the middle of all this frantic cables from Africa to Washington, Washington to Africa and to England and from England to Washington about files and tapes and more films. My whole life since I last saw you has been snowed under by showers of express or registered letters and cables! Not to mention film and paper!! I am exhausted in the extreme. Have got the most SUPER wedding dress — white of course. Went home on a sudden inspiration — having booked an appointment for the Tropical Diseases hospital because everyone thought I was about to die. I decided there was nothing I wanted to do less, so I went home instead. Now everyone here thinks I've been looked over, so they do not think I look so ill!! I only hope I don't have any evil disease when I do go or I shall find it hard to explain why they have been so long in finding out! Anyway, went into shop called "Brides Corner". A most fantastic shop, tucked away half way up Pool Hill. They stock over 300 wedding dresses — if you like the skirt of one, top of another, and material of a third they have it made up for you. People go there from all over the south of England. And there I found a dress that would have been at least £50 — oh — sorry — 50 <u>guineas</u> of course! — at Harrods. It is really quite superb.

Wedding plans. Chelsea Old Church, on the Embankment, where I was christened. Mum and I went to see the Vicar, and he was simply charming. Reception — ? Don't know yet. We want somewhere where I can just hire the room, and not somewhere that "does" receptions. Or it will be far too expensive. Aunt Margery, who is a cordon bleu cook, is being asked to do the catering. Uncle E. can get booze cost price. I plan on a bubbling wine, with choice of still wine — I think champaign (I always do spell it that way, it amused the family so!) is just a snob value waste of money! Wedding cake made by Arlene's on top of Poole Hill. Honeymoon of 6 days in Holland before I go back to Africa. We go back to Africa rather!

Other news is quite limited. Flo is behaving well, and I am horrified to hear that Apple* broke down. How very wicked of her. Piston slap sounds vaguely obscene!

Sally, do write back quickly and say you will come to the wedding. It would not be complete without you. I think it will be a

---

* Sally's car.

"fun" reception — lots of booze! You can stay at the flat — there will be space for you, and we expect you to. Can you give me any idea as to whether your Ma and Pa will be back? It will indeed be tragic if they cannot come. Do you think Sue would be able to come?

I am sorry this is such a short and rather dull letter. But I don't have much else to write about — latest news from chimpland was very disturbing — from Dominic to say that Kris had been walloped on the head by a chimp but was O.K.! I simply must get on. I have just added a missed out line to 50 reprints of my nesting paper, and put "with compliments Jane Goodall" on the back, and typed out 50 labels on a long sticky perforated label roll — looks like a miniature toilet roll — and done the envelopes up. This has exhausted me, but I still have about 10 more official letters to do. It is 9.30. So forgive me for stopping, but please write immediately — use another sheet of the airmail pad! You won't feel so guilty every time you happen across it then!

With love,

P.S. Yes — I got to Cambridge that Monday.

Cross Farm,
Comberton,
Cambridge.
11 March 1964

My dear FFF,

Knowing how hectic you must be, I simply hate to bother you with this. However, I feel I must. So let me quickly set out the points I was not sure on before I tell you anything else.

Mum and I went through the expense sheet together. In the first part — costs per month — I have filled in all the costs except (1) food for 4 Africans, (2) Medical supplies, and (3) contingencies. I havn't a clue what to put for these.

The next section is all complete. The final section I just havn't a clue about, and I'm hoping that you just have enough of an idea in your head: 2 large tents, one boys', camp equipment, boat, transport of boat, outboard motor. It is all set out on the sheet.

Anything you think is wrong, too much or too little, please alter. I'm sure you can get a secretary — anyway, the committee won't mind if it's all ink corrections I'm sure.

You needn't worry about the banana bit — I said to the committee exactly what I have written on the report, only in more detail. They were all very happy.

There is one other point I have not mentioned. We are still looking for an assistant (other than my secretary whose salary I want to pay myself) to train during the second part of my stay, to carry on when I go. Should I include that somewhere? Or what? Also, should one mention the fact that the N.Y. Zoological Soc. is extremely interested in the research center — Osborn as good as said that he would be willing, almost definitely, to co-operate with the Geographic on the project.

That, I think, is all for that. I didn't put down film stock for me, because I get all that sent, from the magazine, automatically. I gave Hassan a rise in the estimate — 400/- a month, and Dominic 160/-. Then there are two of 120/- each.

They are taking me into the Tropical Diseases to see if I might have Bilherzia — or however you spell it — just the day before Hugo gets back, which is really mean and horrid of them. Anyway, I couldn't have the treatment now, cos of Flo's baby, so I shall have to go off for 2 weeks in July or August or something — probably it would be best to do it when I have to do the silly T.V. recording. Ugh! Anyway, I don't think I've got it.

The wedding plans are going ahead nicely — only Judy has the problem of somehow trying to get the piano out of the room!!! Because more people than we thought are coming.

I met Richard* in the Trop. Diseases Hosp!!!! I expect you must have heard by now that he was bitten by a flea and paralyzed all over. Wasn't it horrible. I was whisked off in the middle of talking to him and when I got out I couldn't find him or what had happened to

---

* Richard Leakey.

him. Must end as must write more letters. I do hope all goes well — though since you are obviously going to be more hectic than I was I just don't see how you can possibly survive.

With love,

F.C.

Jane

[Early April 1964]

Darling Family,

Well — here we are again. Outside the rain is <u>pouring</u> down in buckets. It has been doing so on & off ever since we arrived — which has been a great bore as we have had to do <u>so</u> much shopping.

First, let me thank you all again for the super wedding and all that you did for it. Hugo has only just learned that the cake was a present & he sends many thanks. It really <u>was</u> a super wedding, wasn't it? And, I do hope you have all recovered & that we didn't leave <u>too</u> much mess behind.

Some news. We got our heavily overweight hand luggage safely to Nairobi. B.O.A.C. were fantastic — I have never had such excellent service since the time Jif & I went 1st Class. Food superb. Smiles & help from all Hostesses. <u>Fans</u> brought round at Khartoum! Iced eau de cologne towels in the morning to freshen up. Nuts, crisps & cocktail biscuits at 7. It was all quite amazing. And a really <u>good</u> breakfast — on the plane & not at a sordid airport.

We arrived & were met by <u>two</u> shining State House cars — one for us, one for our equipment. We were conducted, on arrival, immediately to H.E. — leaving our luggage in the hall. We ordered coffee & biscuits & they brought tea & no biscuits — which peeved him no end! We then had a quiet lunch on our balcony, the two of us — in the same sumptuous suite. And then began at once on our shopping. Dinner with Mrs. & daughter as H.E. was tied up with Prime Ministers. I saw Jonny's* new wife when we went out to Langata.

---

* Jonny Leakey.

Last night there was a dinner in honour of a retiring Air commodore — another MacDonald. There were 20 guests. I wore the new black dress (with loose hair) & everyone was most impressed. I had the distinction of sitting on the left hand of Malcolm — the Air Commodore's wife on the other side. We talked chimp nearly all through dinner — the wife joining in & being nice & interested. The ladies then retired & sipped coffee & liqueurs round the fire; the gents, to Hugo's enormous amusement, followed H.E. into the garden & wee'd in a row! He said he'd heard they did that in Kenya but never known it happen at an official party before.

Tonight is the film show. There are about 60 people coming, including Clo. Poor Clo, whom I spoke to on the phone, is in court all day tomorrow — the same old Erskine business. So we couldn't meet her for lunch. She sounded rather subdued. She is living in her "sordid" flat now — not with Petal any more.*

No word from Miss Peru,† which is worrying.

I have gone & got some VILE shingles. Isn't it sordid. They arrived in the middle of the night. I found one or 2 virugon but have left most with Lyn. The shingles are spreading, & sordid. Ugh.

We have bought the most super tent — super fast engine, super tiny weeny tape recorder, super portable filing cabinets, found the only typewriter like ours in Nairobi & got it for Miss Peru, & various other super things. Including the most smashing 8 mm camera. So you will receive super films. Wack O.

It is now next morning. Cable from Miss Peru, from London Airport last night, to say she was arriving at 8.30. We got the cable at 8.15!! She really must feel she's fallen in clover! What with Washington when she watched our giddy progress, the wedding, & news of Palaces in Holland — & now State House where she has been warmly invited. Later again — she is now sipping coffee with us. We are about to go off & do our last shopping.

---

* Clo, Jane's school friend who had invited her to visit Kenya in 1957, married Francis Erskine, son of the distinguished Kenyan Sir Derek Erskine; the marriage was a troubled one, as this comment suggests. Petal was Sir Derek's daughter and thus Clo's sister-in-law. By coincidence, Petal eventually married Robert Young, the actor who had been engaged to marry Jane in 1960.
† Edna Koning, who had been living in Peru.

The film show was a great success. The ministers were all impressed. Kenyatta was ill & couldn't come, but all the others were thrilled. I think it has done an enormous amount of good. We are having lunch with the most interested Ministers today. Courie was there — ugh! he is revolting. But it really was a good thing.

Must end now as it is getting late. Must put some more gauze over vile shingle.

Tons & tons of love to you all,
& again many many thanks.
Your little 'pudding',*
Jane

P.S. Please send Mrs. Mackenny — the address of Leakey's office — One reprint. Please send us, by sea mail, the tinned food cooking book from drawer in Vicki's room.

Box 8,
Kigoma,
Tanganyika.
21 April 1964.

Dear Dr. Payne,

You will have to forgive me for not writing before, but things got pretty hectic, as you can imagine. It was the most wonderful surprise to receive news of the Franklin Burr Prize on our wedding day — that cable caused quite a stir when it was read out amongst the other greetings telegrams! And I should have written earlier. I do indeed feel honoured to have been awarded this prize for a second time.

The wedding went off wonderfully, and the chimpanzee pictures which you so kindly let us have absolutely made the reception. We even had models of chimps on our wedding cake! We then had a delightful but brief honeymoon in Holland — not a very conventional one as the main purpose was for me to get to know Hugo's family better. I certainly have got some delightful in-laws.

---

* By marrying Hugo, Jane became a baroness. In celebration, Olly had persuaded Danny to make a special dish known as "Baroness Pudding."

We had a terrible time getting back to the chimps, over flooded rivers and broken down trains. But we made it. And my new secretary also has got here — by the last passenger train which is likely to run for some time — the lake has risen so much that the rails in Kigoma are 20″ under water. And they expect the level to go on rising!

Flo's baby — a little boy whom we have provisionally named Flint — is simply the most adorable little object you ever saw. Although I was heartbroken she didn't wait till we got back, reports from the "caretaker" suggest that, in fact, we didn't miss anything. For the first 5 weeks of its life he never saw it move at all — it just clung onto Flo. Then, two days before Hugo and I got here, it began to look around with intelligent focused eyes, and move its arms around, etc. So I think we were lucky and timed our arrival fairly well. He should take his first crawl in a couple of weeks!

The rest of the chimps are all fine and we have already observed one or two new behaviour patterns. Hugo filmed a delightful sequence of David playing idly with little Fifi.

I hope to start work on another article in the not too distant future. There are still a few pressing things to attend to first, and a little more training of my secretary so that I can hand over to her most of the typing out of my taped notes for the day. Should the article be about the same length as the last?

Please give our regards to everyone — and once more, my apologies for not writing before.

Yours sincerely,
Jane

9

BANANAS AND BABIES
1964

Without doubt the most exciting thing that year was being able to record on paper and on film the week-by-week development of a wild chimpanzee infant — Flint.

— *In the Shadow of Man*

UPON THEIR RETURN, Jane and Hugo were informed by Dominic and Kris that the situation with the chimps was veering out of control. Several new chimps had begun wandering into camp from the forest — too many in their opinion. The apes were stealing anything resembling food, as well as clothes and other loose items, and had started chewing on canvas, such as tent flaps, and wood, such as chair legs. Additionally, and most alarmingly, some of the apes had entered the temporary huts on the beach that the dagaa fishermen used; the fishermen were not likely to be so tolerant. There was a legitimate concern that someone, either human or chimp, would get hurt.

Hugo had in February ordered the construction of steel banana boxes that would dispense limited amounts of bananas by remote control (with underground cables that could be pulled by handles at one end and would attach to latch releases at the other). But those supposedly ape-proof steel boxes had not yet arrived, so in the meantime, the couple planned to relocate the banana feeding operation away from the beach. "We discussed the problem far into one night," Jane later recalled, "and eventually decided that as soon as possible we would move the feeding area farther up in the valley."* The successful move is thoroughly described in two letters from late April. A banana storehouse was constructed of corrugated iron, and a sleeping hut for some of the African staff was built. And then Jane and Hugo moved the chimpanzees to the new area by the delightfully simple expedient (as noted in the first letter) of waving an empty banana box at David Greybeard. "Good old David, immediately hoodwinked, gave screams of delight and anticipation."

The new provisioning area had the added benefit of providing a nice sense of romantic seclusion for the newlyweds, since their own tent had been moved up to the feeding area as well. But as we read in the letter of June 1, that seclusion was slightly compromised when the much-anticipated new tent finally arrived. The new tent became their work area at the feeding site during the day, and at night the back portion served as bedroom for Edna Koning, the research assistant. Still, one gets a sense from the fond lingering over domestic details — the new coffee percolator, the "dear little veranda" outside the new tent, and so on — how pleasant their life was that summer. And in spite of the continuing problems associated with banana provisioning — all the competition and squabbles over that rich source of food — we can note the extraordinary, continuing flow of new information about the behavior of chimpanzees. Jane enumerates some details of this new information in the long letters of July 9 and September 24 to Melvin Payne.

At some point during the summer, before the arrival of the steel boxes from Nairobi, Hassan built some "temporary" banana boxes of cement with steel lids and latches (mentioned in the July 9 letter). The steel boxes finally arrived in September (letter of September 24), but even they were not actually very chimp-proof. Within a few weeks an enterprising chimp named J.B. had figured out how to break the control cables.

Edna Koning had arrived at Gombe during the floods of April, within a few days of Hugo and Jane. She seems to have spent most of her early weeks transcribing Jane's behavioral notes from audio-

---

* *In the Shadow of Man* (1971), p. 93.

tape. Gradually, though, she took on other tasks, and in the fall was preparing to study the baboons. In December a second assistant, Sonia Ivey, arrived (briefly accompanied by her friend John Sankey); she was hired to work more specifically as a secretary and typist. Arrangements with the African staff continued pretty much as before; Dominic Bandola and Hassan Salimu, assisted by a cook named Anyango, were in charge of the camp's day-to-day operations. Dominic, though, became seriously ill in August and spent a few days in the hospital in Kigoma, while around the same time Hassan developed back pains of unknown cause and so returned to Nairobi. Other African staff during this period included Rashidi Kikwale (there from the first days), as well as Ramadhani Fadhili, Hamisi Matama, and Sadiki Rukumata.

Visitors to Gombe that year included Joanne Hess, from the National Geographic Society, who came in mid-June to oversee some final details of a film about the chimpanzee research; Malcolm Mac-Donald, the governor general of Kenya, who arrived in September; Vanne, who came for a brief stay late in the year; and two European researchers, Hans Hass, a biologist and diving pioneer, and Irenäus Eibl-Eibesfeldt, an ethologist at the Max Planck Institute, who probably arrived on August 11. Jane, as we can see from the letters home preceding and following that visit, was apparently flattered and delighted at the positive interest and support of these two important men "from the same establishment as Konrad Lorenz."

Jane and Hugo had been imagining a permanent research institution at Gombe at least since the summer of the previous year. In March of 1964 she had mentioned the idea to a National Geographic committee, hoping for support. She had even (as we see in the August 10 letter) located "THE ideal site for the future research building." The distinguished Drs. Hass and Eibl-Eibesfeldt were "tremendously impressed" by her work at Gombe and entirely supportive of the research institute idea. So was Louis Leakey, who endorsed the proposal for National Geographic funds to purchase and put into place the first prefabricated semipermanent structures (the "uniports" mentioned in the letter of November 6). By the last days of December, the foundation area for the largest prefabricated building had been leveled, and the stones and sand for making concrete had been hauled up.

More immediately compelling during that year were the chimpanzee mothers and their newborns. The appearance of Flo's infant, Flint, as we have seen, was exciting enough to divert Jane and Hugo's intended honeymoon in March. Flint provided them with their first great opportunity to observe chimpanzee infant development from the earliest weeks. And then Gombe was blessed by the arrival of another newborn on September 7: Melissa gave birth to an infant tentatively named Jane — until "she" turned out to be "he" and was then rechristened as Goblin (by October 26). By early November, yet a third newborn appeared: Mandy's Jane.

In sum, the year 1964 was a productive, prolific, and momentous one indeed.

*　　*　　*　　*

[Around April 21, 1964]

Darling Family,

This must again be rather short, as I have to get several most urgent things off by the replacement of the Owens* who is flying to Dar. The urgency is because the railway is now almost entirely out of action. For two weeks there have been no passenger trains because a driver went too fast and ripped away 100 yards of line just outside Kigoma. Kris was stranded in Kigoma because of this. And still the lake is rising. Two days ago the first passenger train crawled into the station over 20″ of water! It contained one 1st class, two 2nd and 3 3rd class carriages only! People in Kigoma anticipated a funny time on its return journey because there were 50 bookings on it for 1st class and one school teacher alone had 300 pupils supposed to be travelling 3rd! They apparently reckon they can cope with water up to 24″ over the rails, after that they give up. They have had to remove the generators which live under each carriage — as if they get wet the train stops. So everything is in darkness!

---

* Perhaps Mr. and Mrs. John Owen; he was soon to become director of national parks in Tanzania.

How I know all this is because of our film show. The Owens arranged for us to go in and show the film to all the people who mattered. When Edna arrived she brought with her a message to say would we go in on Wednesday. So on Wednesday, at 4.0, the whole group of chimps had just left, and we thought we would leave in 30 mins, because of engine trouble. Well, Hassan had been working on the engine all day, and he was still working on it at 5.0. At 5.30 we were able to start out — what a slow boat. Well, bit by bit the coast line slid away, and we reckoned on arriving at 8.30, the show being at 9. We felt that <u>perhaps</u> the Owens might come to look for us in their fast boat. Then, just at the valley beyond Gombe, where is the little whitewashed hut, the last valley of the Reserve, and one third of the way to Kigoma, the engine stopped. Hassan tried everything. So then Dominic began rowing us to shore. We landed. Dominic immediately took charge of arrangements, and in next to no time he had mustered 3 of the 5 inhabitants, chosen the fastest canoe, ordered Hassan into it, then off they paddled, to the next village just round the corner, to bargain for a boat — if one was there. So Hugo, Edna and I were left with our broken boat, the film, and a suit-case of cloths to be left in the dry of the Owens' house. So. After 30 mins we opened our provisions and had some coffee. The two remaining inhabitants were watching, so I poured some for them — they didn't want it so I felt silly. One hour and 15 mins later we had made ourselves at home. Edna had tried to set light to some damp straw. One of the little boys turned up trumps and kept rushing up with pieces of dry twig and palm frond, so soon a cosy little fire was burning. Edna and I had put jeans on under our pretty dresses!! "Pwitty dwesses" read. Then a boat was heard, heading for the reserve. A tiny light far out on the lake. Thinking of the dismal prospect of rowing back to the camp, Hugo asked for a light to wave. They produced their sole illumination — a candle! Hugo held it up and it went out. So it was relit and went out again! So the boy brought a long bundle of dry straw, we thrust it into our fire, and Hugo waved the flaming torch aloft. After three of these the boat headed for us and eventually arrived. Full of Africans. To cut a very long story short we persuaded them first to go and look for Hassan, and then to take us home. So Hugo went with them, and we packed up and waited patiently by our dying fire. 10 mins later, having given the little boy a slice of bread — he licked off all the butter and then offered half to his friend! — we heard a boat. It was going straight by! Horrors! And a second boat, right behind it, was arriving towing Hassan's canoe. This doesn't sound ghastly — in fact we knew that the first one was the one with Hugo in it! However, all was well, and Hugo was with Hassan in a boat which, after one and a half hours of bargaining had agreed to take us into Kigoma and bring us back for Shs. 140. Well, by that time it was 9.15! It seemed rather pointless to go back to Kigoma and arrive at 10.30 p.m. for a 9.0 film show! So a lot more bargaining and they agreed to transport us and boat for 70/-. Sheer robbery! Still, we got back.

Well, the following day the sordid White Father stopped by. The one who always whizzes past in the fast boat without stopping. He was so foul and rude that we were not very nice to him. "Well," he greeted me "I have been passing this place for two years now, and never bothered to call in and stop, but Krus* told me a lot about the chimps, and everyone is talking about them, so I thought I'd spare half an hour". No asking if we wanted him to do anything, or anything. He even said that we should have spent a whole day in Kigoma for the film as one could never be sure of the weather on the lake.

However, Hugo and I decided that it would be a squish on all the foul Kigoma-ites if he went in by taxi, organized a new engine for us, and, at the same time, showed the film. So he went off the next day and said Owen was so rude he almost caught the next boat back. There are lots of stories to tell about how horrible are the Kigoma-ites. Owen even insinuated, apparently when everyone was waiting for us to turn up that night, that we probably just "hadn't bothered" to turn up. We were livid. Anyway, it is done now, and over. None of the important Africans came to the film — either the proper night or the night Hugo finally showed it.

Well, I started this letter at 6.30 this morning, and got to the top

---

* This may refer to Kris, with Jane imitating the White Father's distinctive accent.

of this page. Then came Huxley, J.B., Pooch, Goliath, David and Flo and family. The Owens arrived while they were still here — or anyway, Carlos* and his "take over" and the take over's wife. The two latter, though I only said hello to once, were the most soppy people. I hope they won't open this letter — they are taking it to Dar, chartering a plane, and posting it there. Edna has answered all 30 of my publishers' letters, so those will go off as well. These silly people we planned would take the mail today but, as usual, nothing was ready.

It is now early the next morning. I have lost the other part of this letter, temporarily, so I had better start on a new subject.

Flint is the name of the new baby, and he is simply adorable. He is now begining to look around with interest, watch things, make little pout greeting faces, and he scratched himself yesterday. FF† loves to play with his hands, and the other day was allowed to groom one little arm, but Flo usually gently pushes FF away from him. We saw an exciting thing the other day — what one would have expected, true, but nice to see. Flo picking leaves to wipe off dung — we couldn't see if it was off the baby or herself. The other adults disappointingly ignore the infant. But David, two days running, played most sweetly with FF — and as for FF herself — she is quite fantastic now, so tame is she.

We are started on work up the valley. It was all so difficult, trying to visualize the organization, safely, of another camp that we are ended up much nearer to this camp than the original plan. But we reckoned that, once the chimps know there are no bananas here, they won't bother to come anyway, especially if there are other tasty things for them there — blankets, shirts, etc! We should be grateful for any old clothes — used and unwashed. This is a serious request. Perhaps some could be sent by sea mail? Though that might be foolish in view of present postal conditions! Anyway, cardboard does the trick usually — even David, having had no bananas at all, was fobbed off with cardboard yesterday!

---

* Apparently a bureaucrat from Kigoma.
† Fifi, Flo's next-youngest offspring.

Saw the most funny thing. There is a strange kind of termite that circles round and round like a swarm of bees, round a tree. We cannot understand why they do this, but they do. And have now twice seen chimps trying to catch them. It is just about the funniest sight you ever saw — a chimp, standing right as far out along a branch as it can, holding on with one hand sometimes, and reaching out with a waving — or beckoning — gesture trying to sweep a termite into its mouth. I watched a stranger doing this yesterday, through my telescope. He made the most fantastic face as he was making these antics — mouth wide wide open, all upper gums and teeth showing, lower lip slightly pushed forward. It was so funny to watch. And sometimes, if they are on a secure branch, they sweep out with both hands, and sweep them to their mouths one after the other! The little chap I watched yesterday performed in this way for 2 whole hours, rushing from side to side of the tree after the swarm. He must have been quite exhausted.

Anyway, to return to the new camp. We have a superb spot, just beyond the little ridge, and all yesterday Hassan, the scouts, and our other trusty helpers made the banana/clothes store. For this Hugo bought large sheets of corrugated iron in Kigoma. We are having a hut built here, so that two boys can always sleep there, and be there in the day — and they can change around for this, taking turn and turn about. We have, finally, two tents there, and the original one will stay here. We eat and bath here in the evening — for the rest we live and work at the other camp. There is a lovely view of Sleeping Buffalo and although the scope is not as great as if we had gone further up the valley, I think it should work out fine.

At the moment only Ben is here. He is very nervy.* He has been several times, but never had any bananas till today, as he came with groups. Today we saw him in a tree over the stream, put out a pile, and he came over. He is in the tree behind the tent.

That was actually written as page 3, a part of the first part which I said was lost on the previous page! Because at the moment Edna is typing my Journal from tape, Hugo is removing his burrs,† and

---

* Nervous.
† Shaving.

sends his love, and the chimps have just gone. We went to inspect work up the valley just a moment ago, and it's coming on fine. The store nearly done, and the main structure of the boys' hut nearly ready.

Chimps here all day. And darling Olly. I don't think I told you. She came once before, goitre larger than ever. Worzle and Leakey were here. She was very nervy, and when we sneaked her three bananas she was attacked by both the horrid males and Worzle bit her in the arm. So it was very sad and pathetic. Kris told us she had only been twice since we left, but we feel sure that she came, in silent Olly fashion, peered down, and there was no one to love her and see that she was sneaked bananas. Anyway, today, although we had Goliath, David, Leakey, Huxley, Gregs, Charlie, Worzle, Flo and family, and Evered, we managed to sneak Olly 14 bananas, and no one attacked her. Hugo filmed FF holding Flint's little hand, and moving a tiny piece of food which had dropped onto his head from Flo's mouth. He is getting more of a handful for poor Flo every passing day!

Edna — Miss Peru — is turning out just fine. She is not "tough" yet, and I'm not sure if she ever will be really tough. But she is keen, interested, observant, intelligent, and great fun. So, all in all, we feel she is a great success. She adores the chimps, and we certainly feel that she will be able to cope at the end of the year. If she agrees to stay on, that is. We asked her, point blank, if she felt she wanted to go on with this sort of work, and she said yes. I hope she does. It is nice having chimps here absolutely all day long.

I'm sure there is so much to relate, but I really feel I must write some more wedding letters! Oh — a most important thing, which I forgot last time. We could not find that unbreakable china in Nairobi. Not anywhere!! What a bore — but it isn't here. So what do you suggest? Could you find out the price of the various things and then we could send a cheque for it. Do we have to have a special cheque book for our joint account? Or what? Mum.

The rain is fantastic. The stream really gets uncrossable for ages — a nuisance with the choo on the other side! Poor lone Palm is miles and miles out in the water now, and I can't imagine how it can still be standing. Hugo, now smooth, says please will I send his love to everyone. I hope Nick is well, give him our love, And tons and tons to all of you — we have had no mail yet from anyone except one from Catherine Hitchen!!!* She addressed that to the Boma!

Tons of love,
Jane

P.S. The "H" has just come off the typewriter!!

"Chimpland"
[Late April 1964]

Darling Family,

Well — we have moved our camp! At least, Hugo and I and half of the chimps have. Edna is left sort of floating between the old and the new, often trailing chimps along here with her, by luring them with bananas or pieces of cardboard!!

But let me start from the beginning. We searched around, Hugo and I, and found the most delightful shady place, palm trees overhead, and a lovely open space opposite where, we thought, when the long grass was trampled or cut down, Hugo would be able to film the chimps admirably. Accordingly we instructed Hassan to gather his forces and start off by building a banana store, of corrugated iron, and a small hut for two Africans to live in, at a spot not too far from our camp site. This took some time, but eventually was finished. And then, before moving all our things up the valley, we thought we should try and get at least some of the chimps accustomed to the new place.

So we filled the store with bananas, and I came here at crack of dawn ready to seduce early chimps which might pass with delicious bananas. No chimps passed. Our walkie talkies are still working, and we had arranged to contact at 9.0. We did so, and Hugo told me that all sorts of chimps were with them — including David himself, Goliath, J.B. — who is more horrible and beastly every day,

---

* An old friend of Vanne's.

McGregor,* and Flo and her family. Hugo asked if I thought he should try to lead some of them here. So I said yes, but neither of us thought anything would come of it. So he picked up an empty box — one they sometimes have bananas in, walked past them — they ignored him — and then held the box up and sort of waved it at David. Good old David, immediately hoodwinked, gave screams of delight and anticipation. To cut a long story short, I, in the new place, suddenly heard a frenzied voice yelling "They're coming". I flung bananas all over the place as the excited screams and calls approached — and they came — a long string of black creatures all rushing after a panting and disheveled Hugo who was still brandishing the empty box. With yells of pleasure they fell on the new banana supply. Since then we have managed to lure dear Olly and Gilka to our new place — they come every day now. Olly's goitre is bigger than ever.

Well, to return to the camping place. Having established it with the chimps, it was time to establish it for ourselves. The first thing was to flatten some of the very tall grass. So we instructed Hassan to hire an army of eager fishermen, and up the valley we trailed. Half of them cut the grass with pangas, the other half hit it with sticks and trampled it. The trampling method was much quicker — Hugo and I turned it into a sort of dance — we held hands and tramped it down sideways in a sort of St. Bernard's waltz! By nightfall all was ready. What we had not reckoned on was the fact that all the area which has been cut is now bristling with hard sharp stubble — the chimps simply hate it! They tiptoe over the hurtful area if they have to, to reach a banana — but all Hugo's dreams of the superb charges out in the open sunlight are shattered! Instead the chimps happily sit and lie in the shade of our palms, sitting around the tent, and do wonderful things where it is far too dark for filming!

To continue. The following evening we hired a longer string of fishermen porters, got the tent down, piled all the equipment into separate loads, and led our "foot safari" off along the steep little

---

* Jane often spelled this balding older male's name with a double "g"; he was named after McGregor, the old gardener in Beatrix Potter's *The Tale of Peter Rabbit*.

path and down into the valley. It was quite sort of romantic, looking back and seeing them in their rags and tatters in single file behind us, trailing through the long grass with their loads on their heads. We then set them to on making a level place for the tent. This was hard work, as everywhere here is so sloping. They had to dig about a foot down at the back of the tent and push the earth to the front. Then we had a fairly level floor, though we still find only our heads and shoulders in the bed in the morning, our feet and legs having slid off the end! This leveling had to be finished by the light of two pressure lamps as it took much longer than we had anticipated. Then we got the tent up, piled the equipment inside, and went back to the other camp.

Edna — Miss Peru — was to be left in charge there until the new tent arrives — more of that later. We had supper and then Hugo and I set off with our torch back to our new little home. It is really most super — we have our cosy supper and coffee round the fire — did I tell you we have bought a really elegant coffee percolator — one of those glass ones that push the coffee up and then let it down again? It is really most handy for out here because all you have to do is light a small flame, and remember to time it. And it makes good coffee. Then we come back to our cosy tent here. Luckily Anyango loves the trip down the valley in the evenings to make our bed and wash up the odd cups and spoons and things we have used during the day.

Next we had some drama. We suddenly noticed that there was a tall dead palm tree right behind the tent — which could have smashed everything and everyone right out of existence. After hearing from Kris about the dead palm that fell exactly where Hugo had been sleeping that night, we were taking no further chances. (We have even had our fire moved, in the old camp, from under the palm tree in case dead fronds should suddenly crash down). So we got Hassan to look at it the next evening. He at once employed a few more fishermen, one of whom had a long strong rope. The tree itself was so rotten that no one would climb up it, but luckily a good palm grew very close. So an expert palm tree climber was sent up this tree with the rope, which, by some magical manoevering, he managed to tie firmly near the top of the dead palm. Hassan and various fishermen then took the other end of the rope. The next problem was the cutting. Palm wood is really very hard indeed, so they wanted to take advantage of the big hollow quarter the way up the trunk. This made cutting difficult — they had to cling round the trunk like — well, like chimps! while they cut. They took it in turns, and by the end, though they didn't have to cut much, the sweat was pouring off them.

Hugo suddenly had horrors that the tree might, after all, fall the wrong way, and so decided to take everything out of the tent and lay it flat on the ground. This was duly done.

At last they decided they had cut through enough of the tree. The cutters scuttled off to a safe distance, and the pullers took over. We didn't think it would work, but, of course, they had judged it to perfection. There was a creaking, and splintering, and the whole tree seemed to bend as though it was made of rubber before the trunk broke at the wounded place and the tree fell gently amongst the fronds of a neighbouring palm, and there came to rest.

Yesterday Edna suddenly found a palm tree, even closer to the tent, which is quite alive but, in the middle, all the inside has gone. The whole top half is supported by three little thin pillars of hard bark! They are about 9 inches high! We are either going to put wire cable round the tree and peg it, so that if it falls it falls away from us, or else cut it down.

Gradually we are getting our belongings "chimp proofed". High time too. We have lost one sweater (and another to the rats!) a pillow and pillow case, a blanket, a sheet and various small items. In addition we occasionally may have files or notebooks literally snatched out of our hands by such cheeky individuals as Pooch, Figan or Hugo — chimp Hugo! We now have polythene hanging over shelves with books (or we are just about to!) or else they are enclosed in firmly locked wooden boxes and crates. First job in the morning is to dismantle the bed and lock up the bedclothes! I dread the day when they suddenly realize that the clothes we are actually wearing are as good to chew as the ones they steal from broken into boxes and stores!!

Whether or not you ever receive this letter is in the lap of the Gods. Kigoma is completely cut off by road and by rail. There is no mail link at all, and the only way we can get mail out is by having it sent on some small plane which has been locally chartered. The Owens have promised to send anything we let them have at the first possible opportunity. 130 mail bags are stuck somewhere on the way to Kigoma — this includes masses of equipment from the Geographic and — we hope — various letters from our families. Edna's new tent is among the delayed goods. In addition to lack of mail, Kigoma has now completely run out of butter, margarine, sugar, and various other not so important things. We have had no butter for weeks.

We had one day, last week, when it rained as I never imagined it could rain. Our little stream was transformed into a raging hurtling river, with enormous boulders being dashed along in the [remainder missing]

"Chimpland".
1st June [1964].

Darling Family,

It seems so long since I last wrote that I can't remember what I've told you of all our news. So forgive me if I repeat myself from time to time. . . .

Edna has now moved up the valley to the new camp to sleep. This is rather sad — better really, from work points of view, but not so nice and cosy for us in the evenings when we had our own special little tent. Never mind. This, of course, means that our new tent has arrived — it came through, together with the new engine, on the first mail train that was able to creep through the flood waters into Kigoma. It is the most heavenly tent imaginable, and Hugo and I plan to get one for ourselves for the future. It is more or less square — that is, it has tent poles in the middle and also at the sides of the tent, so you can stand upright everywhere inside. It has yellow mosquito netting windows all round — lots and lots of them, so that it is always beautifully cool. At the back is a little oblong which is intended for a bathroom, but which is now Edna's bedroom, so that the whole of the rest is a work tent. In the bedroom just fits the bed and a lovely wooden stand made by Hassan for Edna's trunk and other personal things. The bedroom has windows too. The yellow netting gives the tent such a nice warm light all the time. We have had white small stones carried up from the lake shore for the veranda, and from this dear little veranda one has the most lovely view over the mountains across a great open space leading to the stream, where we give the chimps their bananas. It is a simply wonderful tent. The only reason that Hugo and I did not immediately move in, is that in our own tent we now have lovely lots of room, having moved all papers etc, into the new tent. This means that as soon as chimps arrive the tent is zipped up and all the contents completely safe. Which is wonderful after having to immediately hide all papers, files, etc., as soon as we heard chimps anywhere near. The tent also has a plastic washable groundsheet, completely leakproof, and nylon guy ropes. A palace. You should have seen the faces of the Africans when they saw it standing upright in its full glory. None of them had ever seen such a tent in their lives before!

When we get back to the base camp in the evening we usually settle down wearily to a tomato juice in front of the fire, only to be at once brought to our feet by a string of patients.* One poor old man almost cut his toe off. Funny thing is that one of the chimps, Ben, has a cut in exactly the same place — just slightly worse than the old man. But what I was really going to say was that every third evening or so an extra large mob arrives, all madly inventing ailments, and then ask if Edna will play her guitar! The two who have guitars of their own are the ringleaders, and the idea is that after Edna has played for a while she hands the instrument over to one of them, and then they sit there, surrounded by an admiring circle, and play their own African tunes until supper is ready, and Dominic shoos them all away. How they love it. As a result we are getting lots of presents of eggs. We manage to eat some of the eggs, but it gets more

---

* Vanne had started an informal "clinic" in 1960, offering medicines and simple treatments to anyone who showed up, including African staff, fishermen, and people from villages just outside the reserve.

and more difficult. McGreggor has developed an absolute passion for eggs. If we even half open a container with eggs in it, when he is anywhere around, he simply rushes up, taking the shortest possible route even when this is straight through the tent and over someone's legs, scattering wadges and cardboard in his wake, and grabs the egg. The first time we noticed how strong his passion was was when we handed two to Dominic, down in the old camp, so that he could boil them for breakfast. Greggor, who was miles away calmly eating a pile of bananas, suddenly leapt to his feet, rushed, upright to Dominic (whom he is normally scared of) and snatched away the eggs — albeit with rather a trembling hand at his own audacity! Little Gilka will steal eggs too, but she is funny. The eggs are too big to fit into her little mouth, and when she cracks them she loses the entire contents, and then just chews and spits out the shell! Then there are other egg fans — Pooch will dare much for an egg. Fifi manages to get one very frequently. And, in fact, nearly all of them apart from David and Figan, will occasionally pounce on an egg they see lying around.

Our most exciting piece of chimp news concerns Madam Butterfly and her little daughter. They came to camp about 4 times last year, very nervy. Earlier this month — last month I mean — Madam B. became most attractive to gentlemen who all pursued her madly all over the reserve. This went on for two weeks, at the end of which a very exhausted and jaded party trailed wearily to camp exhibiting large bare patches where hair had been pulled out by jealous lovers, and all manner of cuts and bumps. In fact, they all came except for David. He was faithful to her even when her charms were on the decline. Then, two days later, he brought her with him. All calm and peaceful. She got lots of bananas. And then came the exciting discovery — that her little daughter, whom we have now called Little Bee — b for short! — has a club foot. Whether or not club feet are known in captive chimps I don't know. But even if they are, the fact that this little thing has survived in the wild is quite fantastic. She is now about 2 years old. She obviously can't grip properly — if at all — with the deformed foot. She walks with the foot upright on the backs of the bent toes. And it obviously isn't all that easy for her because she is constantly rushing to climb onto her mother — while Gilka, the same age, is now seldom seen on Olly's back. Even more fascinating, she is the most cheeky and impudent infant we have yet seen. She doesn't just go up to a big male and beg — she goes and grabs hold of whatever it is she wants, and pulls! She continues thus until either she gets it, or else she is firmly pushed right away — which causes her to scream in temper, rush to her mother, stare round sulkily — and then, in the next instant, she is back and trying again! No wonder she survived.

Flo's baby Flint is three months old now. He still doesn't crawl, nor has he got any teeth yet. But he takes such an interest in life, and greets any newcomer with little baby pants and hoots. Fifi is fascinated with him and spends hours and hours playing with his hands and feet — when Flo allows these liberties that is. But Flo allows it more and more often.

Hi! I'm sure there was lots more news — but no time to write it. Absolutely not. Chimps from dawn until dusk absolutely. Wack o! Thank goodness for Edna. She is now in the work tent typing the first of 6 sides of tape — 2 days! We have bananas hidden in millions of different containers — most of which are discovered by David, Figan, Melissa or Charlie. This afternoon we had a most charming party in the tent. Goliath sat on our stone on the veranda (Hugo & my tent) with one hand on the tent pole — sort of 'tent owner' style. Inside sat Flo — leaning on the tent pole with Flint cooing & gurgling on her lap; Fifi — draping the last shreds of the mosquito netting door over her head like a veil; & Figan — rocking because he knew Edna & I were 'banana pregnant' (i.e., b's under our shirts) & yawning. Flo & Flint both wee'd & then they went out. It was then super — Fifi wanted to play with Flint. Flo doesn't like that. Flo also wanted to play with Flint herself. So she play-bit Flint's face — making him give baby-choking gurgles of laughter — meanwhile sparring with Fifi — parrying her grabs at Flint. Then Fifi tickled Flo, making the old girl chuckle. And Figan sprawled in front of his family then played with Fifi, making her chuckle and giggle like mad! It was so gorgeous.

Hugo has just come in & we are going to hear these various

laughs — which we recorded — they were super! Especially Flint's. We brought our coffee here in a thermos tonight, so as to be quicker over supper. But we weren't quicker because Edna had been doing her garden & had not had her bath — & it takes her 30 mins! She is growing veg! Hugo is composing your cable, Olly! You will have had it by now! The "wispy-burr" in case you wondered, is true. You & your scissors much needed, Mummy Pineapple!

Lots more news next letter — v. soon as sordid Owens coming in 2 days — ugh.

Tons of love,
Jane

P.S. 'Nature' has not arrived. Please <u>AIR MAIL</u> reprint <u>if</u> they have.*
P.S. In next letter comes mailing list for Nature reprints.

c/o Box 8,
Kigoma.
9 July, 1964.

Dear Dr. Payne,

Please accept my most sincere apologies for the long lapse of time since last I wrote to you, and for the fact that the promised interim report has never been sent. In fact, I have been kept so busy here that I still have not found time to write an official report.

First I must thank you for your last letter — which, owing to Joanne having to return to Kigoma early with the horrible ulcer on her leg, arrived after she had left.

Certainly I understand that it is necessary to build up a story around "Jane Goodall", and we have cooperated with Joanne as much as we possibly could. However, I know she was hoping to return to Washington with all the additional footage "in the can", and this, unfortunately, was not possible. This was because Joanne's visit coincided with a period when the chimpanzees came to camp in large groups, stayed for long periods of time, and were unusually

---

* Jane's article "Tool-using and Aimed Throwing" had appeared in the March 28 issue of *Nature*.

excitable. Because of this we did not feel that it was really safe to leave my new assistant, Miss Koning, alone in the camp for long periods of time. As you know we have moved our camp, and the artificial feeding area, further up the valley and away from the lake shore. . . . In fact the whole situation has come about because the steel banana boxes, to be opened by remote control, have not yet arrived from Nairobi. These boxes were invented and ordered by Hugo in February, before he left Africa. He stood over the maker until the first of the order had been completed and tested, and then left urgent instructions that the others be finished and despatched with the utmost speed. And still not one has arrived, despite wires and messages.

However, with the help of Hassan we have constructed temporary boxes out of cement and already the situation is vastly improved, and we are able to cope relatively easily with the largest of groups.

During Joanne's stay Hugo got about three quarters of the necessary additional footage completed. We plan to finish the remainder as soon as possible. The scenes of me we have had to hold up at present because of another outbreak of my old skin trouble on my face — now nearly healed up. The scenes on the beach are held up until the fishermen get a good catch of dagaa. And the night scenes have been held up until now because the sun gun was not properly charged.

I also hope to tape a draft commentary for the TV film and despatch it very soon. I gather, from talking to Joanne, that a great deal of last year's film material may be changed for better material shot this year and so, in view of this, we are not trying to make an exactly timed commentary, but I think that all the information required is included and that this will form the basis for a second commentary to be written when the film is finalized.

I now feel that I must summarize the highlights of this year's research. I hope you will be able to see some of the film — that will tell you, better than any words of mine, how wonderful is Flo's baby, Flint. Flo is now so tame that we have been able to observe every small development of the infant since our arrival. And as you say, we are most excited about the pregnancy of Melissa since this will give us a chance to fill in the details of the missing six weeks.

As I may, or may not, have mentioned, I had to prepare a paper to be read at a conference in Nairobi. I have not yet discovered whether or not it was read (by Dr. Leakey!) but I enclose a copy as this will serve to show you how the research is progressing and how, gradually, the pattern is becoming clear. This paper, which was prepared as an oral talk only and not with a view to publication, concerns the development of the young chimpanzee from infancy until it becomes mature at the end of the adolescent period. It was completed when Flint was about 12 weeks old. Since then he has appeared twice on Flo's back. In addition his interactions with other members of the chimpanzee community have increased. Fifi now takes him more and more often, and is allowed to keep him for longer and longer periods. As she sometimes runs off with him and carries him up tall trees, with poor Flo puffing in pursuit, we can't help feeling that this might be one of the reasons for the suspected high rate of infant mortality! Best of all, Flint has taken his first few tottering steps — so far not more than two before collapsing. However, he progresses, because, at first, he cried as soon as he collapsed so that Flo gathered him to her breast immediately. Now he keeps quiet, gets up, and tries again.

Flo and her family are certainly great assets to this research. We actually saw Figan losing one of his milk teeth — one of the lower canines. So this is one way of checking up on whether the approximate ages we had fixed on for each of the youngsters are more or less correct. And it seems likely that they are more or less right.

We have also come to the conclusion that one of the adolescent males, some two or three years older than Figan, is also a son of Flo. This, of course, is not absolutely certain, but so many facts point to such a relationship that we have renamed Ben "Faben"! One important point is that Faben is the only adolescent male, with the exception of Figan, who is allowed to touch, and even play, with Flint. He is continually moving about with Flo, plays frequently with both Fifi and Figan and, believe it or not, with old Flo! The other day he was tickling her in the ribs until the old girl shrieked with laughter. And only yesterday we saw a never to be forgotten sight: Flo, Faben, Figan and Fifi (not to mention little Flint clinging on for dear life under his Ma) all chased each other round and round and round a palm tree, grabbing at each other's ankles as they went. We all agree that we have never seen anything funnier. . . .

Before leaving things appertaining to Flo entirely, I must mention that this same lady has shattered yet another generalization (it really is true that you can't generalize about chimps). I had come to believe that female chimpanzees never display in the fashion of the males — that is a charge, dragging at branches or vegetation and ending up with slapping on the ground or on a tree. But the other day Flo charged!! She even commenced with a male-type bipedal swagger, she dragged (or tried to drag) a huge log, she stamped the ground, and she swayed a sapling. She even put her skimpy hair out whilst doing all these masculine acts! And the following day she leapt at a tree and drummed on it!

There is one exciting thing which I am not sure whether we have mentioned to you or not. And that is that one of the small infants (about the age of Gilka) has what appears to be a club foot. Although I had frequently seen the mother and infant in the reserve before, and although they came to camp several times last year, not until this season, when the mother, Madam Butterfly, started coming here regularly, did we notice the club foot. Unfortunately the pair has now temporarily disappeared, but I feel sure they will reappear soon. It is amazing that a chimpanzee in the wild can survive with such a deformity — she cannot use the foot at all, and walks on the top of her bent in toes, the foot held upright in the same position as a club foot on a human.

We have now seen the chimpanzees react twice to large snakes. One was actually chased by Fifi, who moved along behind it shaking branches at it and hitting towards it. The other snake was a much larger one which moved slowly into a small chimpanzee group. On this occasion the chimps were definitely apprehensive, but showed none of the terror which is characteristic of all captive chimpanzees when they see snakes of any size. Most of the chimps made a few small worried sounds, Flo walked unhurriedly up the slope away from it, Melissa went towards it which made it streak away, and as it went Worzle gave a threat bark and hit in its direction.

We are fortunate in having a very fine drumming tree right near this camp, and I have been able to observe drumming almost daily. Previously I had seen chimpanzees stamp, in passing, on tree trunks, but never seen the actual drumming which can carry for at least a mile. A drumming tree must have large flat buttresses on which the chimpanzees stamp with their feet, either once or several times in succession. If we try stamping on the same tree we are able to produce merely a dull thud!

With regard to feeding behaviour various new insect foods have been discovered. Firstly we have seen them eating weaver ants in large quantities — and feel that they may have made quite a discovery here! They have a most exotic flavour, and we are planning ways of marketing them as tropical delicacies!! We have also seen them eating caterpillars for hours each day. Somehow this seems a strange diet for chimpanzees, but they apparently relish them. In addition we have seen them standing in the tops of trees and reaching out with one or both hands to try and catch a type of termite which swarms — rather like swarms of bees they look. The chimps look very strange when they feed in this way — rather as though they are signalling! The baboons and monkeys also reach out in this way.

Also with reference to dietary matters, we have devised a "dung swirling" technique whereby the contents can be washed easily and examined carefully. Lists of all these contents are being kept carefully.

In addition to the above I am learning a whole wealth of exciting new material concerning social behaviour — particularly with reference to one of the most fascinating of all aspects — communication. As yet all this is un-analyzed, but at last the pattern is becoming clear — the means by which one individual obtains the support of others (or at least tries to).

The new Nagra tape recorder is superb, and I should like to thank the Committee very much indeed for sending us this piece of equipment. At last we are building up a collection of calls which will be of inestimable value for analysis at a later date.

This then, is a summary of some of the fascinating data already revealed during the first three months of this year's research. If the future produces similar results — as it is bound to do — our work this year will be worth while indeed.

Before I close this letter I should like to ask your views about a proposal which I should like to put before the Research Committee requesting an additional assistant. Miss Koning is proving very valuable in helping me to keep up the scientific record — in making detailed notes of things which it is impossible to record when one is observing the behaviour of a group as a whole (such as scratching, details of individual charges, etc.) in checking the dung samples, and in keeping notes when I follow a group away from camp.

Now, however, the overall work has increased so tremendously that we are all three going flat out from about 6.30 a.m. until nearly midnight each day simply in order to keep everything up to date. I should be very happy to take over all Miss Koning's expenses if the Society would agree to completely finance another assistant who would be employed more or less entirely for secretarial purposes. At present Miss Koning spends the greater part of her time typing out part of the day's notes — usually about ten pages like this one. If we could have someone to take over this part of the work it would mean that she would be free to help me, at night, in the sorting out of at least part of these notes for analysis for my scientific reports. It is wonderful to be acquiring so much information — but horrifying when one thinks of analysing it!

This brings me to one final point. In view of this vast amount of work, and to the exciting results which we are obtaining, do you not think that it might be mutually advantageous if the writing of an article for the magazine could be postponed until the end of the year? This would certainly be a very great relief, and I feel certain that I could make a better job of the article if I was able to write it in slightly more peaceful circumstances!*

---

* The article, titled "New Discoveries," was published by *National Geographic* in December 1965.

I'm afraid this has been rather a long letter, but the contents were long overdue. Please give my regards to your wife, and to other members of the Society.

With warm regards,
Jane

Note from Hugo. He asks me to tell you that he is most happy to devote the greater part of this year to filming the chimpanzees, and that he is most grateful to the Society for thus prolonging his honeymoon! He will do his best to ensure that the Society is not disappointed with the results!
P.S. (from me) I would be very grateful, and there is no hurry at all, if you could have a few copies made of the enclosed paper, as this is the only one I have until I get back the one I sent to Dr. Leakey.

"The Hut"
Chimpland.
10 August 1964

Darling family,

It becomes more and more impossible to find any time to write decent letters to one's friends and relations! Somehow, although we daily get more organized here, the amount of work to be done increases and increases, and the more we do, the more there seems to be left to be done. All this is just to excuse the sort of letter this will be by the time it gets posted. Because I have resolved to type little bits, here and there, as a nice way of relaxing in between other things. This will be quite a short little piece as it is almost too dark to see already! The lamp is lit in the tent, but I am sitting in our new little hut so as to be at hand for Edna — who is checking over her daily "dung swirling" results. Once more we have found the chimps with meat — it was old Flo this time. I went after the group up the valley (Flo was not among them when they left camp). I found them all sitting in a cosy little huddle, gathered around Flo. As there was a new mother amongst them (new for us I mean, though hardly "new" in any other sense as she is old as the hills), I was unable to go very close, and they were almost obscured by leaves. Then Flo emerged to greet Mike, and, in her hand, was a large gory piece of red meat! I can only presume that she had stuffed herself to capacity, for she was not even eating it. The others must have been eating meat too, as they showed little interest, merely sniffing at the bloody hand from time to time. After some time, and still clutching her booty, Flo got up and set off in the direction of camp. I quickly rushed ahead to warn Hugo that Flo was bringing red, red meat to camp, not just an old dry bone or an old piece of skin. And, believe it or not, the old bag arrived without it! I don't know what can have happened — I quickly went back, going by one route and returning by another so as to cover all ways she might have come, but I couldn't see a trace. I think old Huxley must have stolen it as she got near the tree where he was eating dry leaves!

Today it has been really hot and humid. Twice I set off to follow the chimps when they left camp, but they must have felt the heat too. They just flopped down — so I flopped with them!

I am rather lost now, with what you all know and don't know. There is nothing really startling, but a number of very nice things, to tell you. First of all, our three new females. Marina, whose name you have heard, has a most adorable family. Her eldest son, we have discovered, is Peter Pan,* one of the two chimps here which beat their chests. Then there is the daughter Miff, about 6, and the most adorable little boy, Merlin. Merlin is the epitome of a mischievous and wicked little boy. His face is "little boy" all over. The way he moves — running all sideways and gangling so that he looks all the time as though he might overbalance and tumble down in a heap of long arms and legs. And he's super at walking upright. The other day he sat on the path, a tiny, self sufficient little fellow (he's only about 2), and gathered up a number of dried, black, banana skins. These he tried to shove into his "trouser pocket" (i.e. between his thigh and tummy), but there were so many that, every time he put the last one in, one of the others tumbled out. It was so funny. Then, finally, he gathered them all up in one hand, except for one, and tod-

---

* Subsequently renamed Pepe.

dled off down the path, very upright and with a completely straight back, and the one odd skin he held first over his shoulder and then over his head, so that it hung down behind — just like the tail of a little boy's red indian headdress! He looked so quaint. You have probably heard what terrible thieves are Marina and her children. She is the worst. Creeping into the tent and stealing a pair of shoes, two days running. She completely chewed up the uppers of 4 shoes! Miff took away my haversack one day. Hugo's binoculars the next because she likes the flavour of the strap! And Peter Pan, hoping to find hidden bananas, went off with two thermoses and one torch which he proceeded to bang against rocks until they smashed open! The latest craze is to lick Hugo's tripods — the whole family gathers round, pink tongues licking into all nooks and crannies, Merlin often reaching out from his Ma's back! It really is a very funny sight.

Then there is the "new" mother. Her family is most exciting to have. The daughter is about the age of Olly's Evered, and the son about the age of Gilka. The latter is the funniest little thing, though we don't know anything of his character yet as Sophie is most retiring, and has only been three times. She comes because the males insist — she being, at present, particularly interesting to them. Poor woman — if she wants to go off for a quiet drink, she has a long escort of gentlemen — if she wants to sneak off by herself for a while, one of them notices, hurries after her, hair out, and shakes branches at her until she meekly turns and follows him back to the group. There even seems to be some sort of competition for her, because all the less dominant males, including the adolescents, are in the most ghastly tempers, attacking smaller ones for no reason whatsoever.

Before I explain about this delightful new typewriter,* let me just tell you the last of Sophie and family. Her daughter, about 8, is called Sally, and she, at last, will fill in one of the big gaps in the knowledge (still not quite sure where dashes, etc, live on this typewriter!) — adolescent females. Then there is the little boy — the funniest little fellow imaginable — bold and cheeky too. His second day he came right up onto the veranda and even peeped into the tent

---

* A sudden change of typeface begins here, at the start of the letter's third page.

where we were all huddled. To remind us of Bobbie he is called Sniff!*

Yet another interruption — I have to go and try and eat I am told. So the story of the typewriter will have to wait yet a little longer. Now, back again. Well, Hugo had a cable to say he had to do all of the Kigoma shots again. You can imagine how gloomy we all were about this. There had been a piece of fluff stuck in the lens, or the camera, or something, so it all had to be done again. Anyway, he set off bright and early yesterday, with Hassan (who has to do the bargaining in the market) and Anyango who was to do the shopping while those two filmed, and Dominic. Dominic is another story which I will relate in a moment. He got all his filming done, had a nice day (for a Kigoma day that is) and came home laden with spoils of the trip. It was a nice home coming. He brought the most super watch for me, — a darling little one that doesn't need winding, and is water proof and shock proof. I simply love it. He also brought me a Parker fountain pen as mine has been lost for months, and anyway, didn't write any more. This is also automatic — you just dip it in the ink and it fills itself in a magical sort of way. It is blue and most elegant. He brought all sorts of other nice things that we wanted from Bimji, including a bottle of liqueur. And he asked for Cointreau. Bimje said that he found it impossible to get rid of a crate, and he couldn't buy in smaller quantities. "Oh, fine", says Hugo — and so he and Bimje are ordering a crate between them — 6 for us and 6 for Bimje***!!!! (How nice, I now know this machine has a *!) AND he brought this typewriter. It is a superb little machine — looks almost identical to the Diplomats that we have, is a Triumph — and we do so love this neat little type. It was cheap too, so far as typewriters go — and for once Bimje doesn't seem to have doubled the price.

Now, the Dominic story. Dominic got up yesterday — no, the day before — feeling fine. At 11 a.m. there was a whistle from the whistle tree. We went to see what was happening, thinking gloomily that perhaps we had visitors. It was Rashidi, to say that Dominic

---

* This refers to an obscure family joke concerning Hugo's sister-in-law.

was ill. He made expressive gestures with his hands, and said he'd been throwing water all over Dominic. Hugo had to go to the old camp anyway, for his battery, and to shoot some film on the boys. So he went at once to see what the matter was. Well, we still don't know the cause, but what happened was that Dominic, at 10, felt very sick. He went to the stream to get water, fainted, and fell headfirst into the water. By enormous good luck Rashidi just happened to be passing — else we should have had a corpse — he was out, and with his face in the water!! Since that he continued to feel sick, and blood was coming out from both ends, so to speak. So we thought he'd better go into hospital with Hugo — I mean in the boat when Hugo went! We still don't know the answer!

The messy ending of the previous page was due to the fact that our precious new machine went wrong! On its third page. Hugo wrestled with it valiantly, and finally, by courageously slicing bits off a plastic roller with a razor blade, got it to work. Else it would have been disastrous. So it is now some time since last I wrote, and in addition it is terribly late, as I have been writing pages and pages to an American judge* (most influential in wild life matters) all about our plans for the research station. This has hung heavily over me since our visit to Washington in February!!!

So I will not write much more now. Hassan is going in again tomorrow as we have some scientific visitors. We hope that they will be genuine and are not coming to steal all our hard-won facts. If they are nice they may do a great deal of good for us as they come from the same establishment as Konrad Lorenz.

Let me quickly tell you that we have found an ideal — THE ideal site for the future research building. It is some way up the valley, up a little slope, and there you are, right in the forest, above the level of the trees, and with the most magnificent view stretching right across the valley and over the distant mountain slopes. When I first went there I fell in love with it — I was contacting Hugo on the walkie talkie and told him I'd found the site! So he came in the evening, and we ecstacised over it together. We have all plans formulated now —

---

* Russell Train of the World Wildlife Fund.

the plans for the building, drawn by Hugo, the materials it must be made of, how it should be transported, where the people will eat, how the stuff will be carried up the valley (and at night so as not to disturb the chimps) — then Hugo and I return as the building reaches completion to see that nothing has been overlooked and to help get the chimps accustomed to their new haven. That first time I was there one of the lovely little hornbills, black and white with a red beak, came swooping down across the valley, calling his strange cry, and landed on a dead tree stump just a few yards from me. He sat there, shining in the sun and with the wind blowing his feathers gently, and peered at me, his head first on one side and then the other. Then he seemed to accept that I was all right and he pecked into the dead wood in search of insects. That seemed somehow to be an omen that all would be well with our plans.

We havn't told you yet about our bath. We go to the old camp so seldom nowadays, and we got sick of washing bits and pieces of ourselves each night in the old green plastic bowl. So we started going down to the stream. But we got a bit sick of trying to dry whilst perching and wobbling on sharp stones. And then, one night, we found a perfect bathing place. This was thanks to the pig. Do you all know about the pig? I just cannot remember. One of the scouts found a pig, freshly killed, floating in the lake. So it was carried straight here and we laid it out, hoping the chimps might eat it. The chimps didn't, but their reaction was interesting — nearly all of them were nervous, peered intently at the corpse, wouldn't go near it, but sniffed at leaves, twigs and the ground nearby. We feel sure that they suspected a leopard and were trying to detect traces of the killer. Anyway, how does this tie up with our nightly bath! Quite simple really. We dragged the carcass out into the open grass, hoping that perhaps a leopard might be attracted by the smell during the night. The following day we were all nearly sick all day long. The smell was absolutely ghastly. . . .

So we went upwind to look for a place for our baths. And came across the most charming little place, which might be made for a picture post card advertising the charm of some holiday resort. A tiny white beach from which you step down to the rushing little stream. A view to the opposite mountain. A little waterfall. So Hugo and I paddled about for ages, made a sort of dam, a lovely deep pool with white sand at the bottom, and the white white sand to stand and dry oneself on. It is particularly attractive in the moonlight.

Did Hugo tell you that he filmed a baboon eating the remains of a baby bushbuck. Poor little thing, we got the skin back afterwards — quite perfect, the legs all inside out, and the head, but no flesh left at all. Such a pretty skin. Then another baboon stole the skin away and rushed up the slope with it.

I think I must stop. It is after 11, and we still have to do the last banana work — hiding them in trees, and seeing that there are enough containers in all the big boxes so that we can nip them out really quickly and pop them under our shirts ready to smuggle to deserving chimps. Thank goodness, at long long last, the boxes Hugo ordered in Nairobi, before coming to England, have arrived. So, within the next week or so, we should have 13 chimp proof boxes — then we can stop this silly game of hiding bananas in all sorts of places where bananas shouldn't be hidden — such as under the ground sheet!

I will promise that one of us will write another letter very soon. . . .

Tons of love,
Jane and Hugo

Chimpland.
Early one morning
Approx. 21 August [1964]

Darling Families and Lyn,

This will be short, but I must write something now to tell you about the events of the past few days. I can't recollect whether or not I even mentioned, in earlier letters, the impending visit of two scientists from Konrad Lorenz's institution — viz. Dr. Eibl-Eibesfeldt and Hans Hass. The underwater Hans Hass himself. Well, we were dubious about their visit, wondering if Eibl. was the sort of person to steal facts (he is working on human greeting ceremonies which is why he wanted to come here) although we felt that, if to do with Lorenz, he couldn't be too nasty! We also wondered whether, in fact, they would ever get here when they found how far they had to come. (Sorry about the ends of all the lines.* More typewriter repair work for Hugo!). Well, they duly arrived. Rashidi blew his whistle from the whistle tree about 3 in the afternoon, when we had a whole large group here, including the new female Circe. So, we despatched Edna downstairs (old camp is always thus referred to!) to give our guests some tea, and inform them they were not allowed to arrive until Circe had departed. Duly they arrived. There were still some old hands here — David and Goliath and Charlie, so far as I remember. They were most impressed.

Well, the long and short of it was that they are both tremendously impressed with everything here — the work, the chimps, and the future plans. Eibl., which is almost better than anything, has completely undertaken to send future Ph.D. students of his here to do certain specialized studies — and this is the sort of thing which will give life to the research station, give it standing, and keep it going. Even better, they were both enthusiastically plotting means of ensuring that Lorenz himself, together with Tinbergen, should somehow get here in the autumn.† The trouble is that Lorenz is doing his trip with Tinbergen who has difficulty in getting sufficient time off from Oxford. However, it will be really wonderful if they do manage to get here. It will do us such a lot of good. They have promised to spread the news abroad — that the chimpanzee research station at the Gombe Stream reserve is a "must". In addition, which is very nice news indeed, he is assistant editor to one of the best journals on animal behaviour — German, but publishing in all the main European languages. And he has undertaken to publish any papers I may write (with lots of photographs) within 6 months. That is really wonderful. He has told us all about the most wonderful behaviour film library. You edit single "units" (i.e. feeding; tool using; locomo-

---

* The characters were jamming together at the right margins.
† Nikolaas Tinbergen was, with Konrad Lorenz and Karl von Frisch, a founder of ethology, the scientific study of animal behavior. These three great pioneers shared a Nobel Prize in 1973. Although Lorenz became a friend of Jane's and an admirer of her work, neither he nor Tinbergen ever made it to Gombe.

tion; etc). They have a negative of this, give you a print, and have a print in their library for scientific use. They sell prints to universities, etc, who are interested, and loan them for lectures on comparative behaviour etc. With the film goes a paper, which is not only circulated with the film, but which serves as a publication, and appears — I think in the same periodical as Eibl helps to edit. But one of the good ones. Best of all, this place PAYS the costs of preparing the internegative, which is quite costly. So there is one way of saving the chimp material for ever, and for it to be put to the right purposes.

In addition to all this Hans Hass has promised to give Hugo millions of contacts in all the right television places. He strengthened our opinion that, even if the Geographic do sell their T.V. film to the European market, this will not in the least interfere with the sort of film we want to make. They are both sending us copies of their new books — they showed us these. Hans Hass's has the most superb underwater pictures. And Eibl's is about the Galapagos Islands, and also has beautiful pictures. He was funny though. There is an English edition, but he said he wouldn't send us that one because he thinks the quality is inferior!! So we have to have it in German!

We took them up the valley to show them the proposed site — most enthusiastic. What amused us about both of them was that they never listened to anything we said. It was really funny sometimes. They asked us, right at the start, what animals constituted a danger to the chimps. We explained carefully that, so far as we could see, no animals did. We explained why we felt that leopards were not dangerous predators apparently — because chimps walk around in the forest without really being alert at all, and would often bump into me, when I was quite visible, and only see me when they got to about 10 yards away, or less. Well, the following day Hugo came to me in amazement to say that Eibl. had asked him all about which animals predated on the chimps here. And my amazement (sorry, had to take the paper out as the wind had blown it into queer shapes) anyway, my amazement was even greater than his, on hearing that, because Hans Hass had just asked me the same thing!!!

I think there were two things that really impressed them. One was the fact that the chimps, after eating their bananas, don't immediately rush off back to the forests, or even into the dense bushes, but sit around and do nice things — such as "social preen". It sounded so sweet, instead of social groom, and I kept thinking of David and Goliath as two strange large very black and ungainly birds! Then Eibl. went up to Figan and held his hand out, as we do, and Figan responded by patting on it in play. Not very enthusiastically, true, but a response. Eibl was delighted. Then, this being evening of their second and last day, Hugo took Eibl up the valley to take some pictures of the proposed site. And Hans Hass stayed here with David. Now David has developed a new habit. When he wants more bananas, he knows that it is quite useless to pull on boxes. He knows it's a waste of his energy. (Which, having so little of, he needs desperately to conserve in order to impress his lady of the hour.) So he comes up to whoever is nearest to the nearest full box and, very gently, pushes with the backs of his knuckles. Well, on this particular day he had tried pushing me, had pushed me all round the veranda, but I had not responded. He sat for some time, looking determined. He then approached Hass, in his deliberate way, and proceeded to push him, gently, twice. Hass was quite overcome with amazement and delight. He now feels "part of it all". It was a most thoughtful gesture on David's part, bearing in mind how useful such people may well be to his descendents.

We had a very successful evening, for their last. We so seldom go down to the old camp, and when we do some of the fishermen are quick to come for medicine. The little boy, Petro, who always wants to play Edna's guitar, had asked, the night before, if Edna would bring it down so that he could play. Which she did. Eibl and Hass both wanted to purchase an African instrument each — those small wooden ones with the metal strips that you flick with your fingers. So two of those had arrived to be sold. And, best of all, the African who is so very, very good at playing the guitar also came. So, whilst we sat around a splendid camp fire, this African played, accompanied by the two small wooden instruments (lent back to their original owners) and Hans Hass was able to get out his tape recorder and tape some of the music. They both really enjoyed the evening. So, all in all, a most successful visit.

Since they left we have seen hardly any chimps. The big group has vanished, and are nowhere to be found. I went up to the Peak the day before yesterday, but only saw Flo and Olly on their way from camp! Today we have despatched Edna off to Mitumba valley, at the end of the reserve, so as to give her some practise in observing by herself, and because the valley is full of figs. I can hardly bear to do this — memories of the valley are so vivid, and these days it is all work work work with little time to roam through my mountains. I wouldn't wish it otherwise though. Being able to observe the sort of behaviour that we see these days, and beginning to understand so much about the social pattern, is worth everything.

Sophie was most disappointing. I met her up the opposite mountain two days after her brief visits to camp. Since then she has not been seen. I have a horrible feeling she may not visit us any more. Which will be so sad.

Apart from various sundry things, of little interest — such as the fact that the terrible Dominic is now out of the hospital three days and <u>still</u> not back (we plan to reduce his salary to what it was last year), that Hassan is continually complaining about his back and we don't know what to do, and that Anyango is so often in a bad mood and grumpy in the evening — probably because he has to do all Dominic's work as well. These are not interesting, and apart from them there is no more news. We have had our tent, our poor chimp invaded tent, thoroughly spring-cleaned. Luckily our dear little toad was "out" at the time when Anyango flung dettol and soap and water all over the floor! We hardly know it now. The chimps so seldom go in now, that we thought it was safe to give it a real good clean. And so, the very first day, Hugo's namesake, having been busy with females over the hills and far away for nearly a week, returned, and for old time's sake, and to christen the unpleas- ant smelling clean tent, sat on the floor, grunted happily, — and did a wee!!! (Excuse the sentence rather running away with me). It is suddenly excessively hot here. The bare trees with their huge red flowers are in full bloom. We couldn't have chosen a more lovely camp site. Our "field" has six of these trees, and half are now a blaze of red against the green palm trees and the yellow grass of the opposite mountain. The chimps, luckily, don't fancy these blooms, but the baboons simply love them. Our cheeky Stephanie, who still persists in visiting us despite being shone at with mirrors, narrowly missed by Hugo's stones, and chased up the slope by me, is always being caught with a prize blossom disappearing into her mouth. She is a funny baboon. We are thinking of starting Edna off on these baboons later on in the year — if I can get another secretary.

I will now end the letter. Still two days before Hassan goes in to collect Malcolm MacDonald. I wonder if he really will make it this time. Anyway, if anything startling happens I will continue later.

Lots of love from us both.

"Chimpland"
8 September, 1964

My dear FFF,

We have had your last letters, the long ones, about the buildings here, and the films, etc. First, thank you a million times for all your hard work and thought re. the buildings. We have a long letter to you which should go off by the next post — we are waiting to find out the prices of the various materials.

First, though, and urgently, and this, please, keep as a secret from Ma because it has to be a surprise for her when she arrives here, Melissa has had her baby. Yesterday! It is the most adorable little thing, sex not yet known, but Jane if it is a girl. I was able to see her [the infant] when she [Melissa] first met up with some of the chimps today — they stared and stared, and their behaviour towards her has changed considerably. She really hit out and grabbed the hand of one childless female who tried to touch it. She is not scared of us at all. Didn't see the birth — we have been expecting it so long, and it came as such a surprise.

However, the point is this. If I stay on here until March, as you suggested — well, until April I suppose, do you think a) the Geographic would agree to Hugo staying on to cover the baby, and b), and more important, will you mind if, in the end, and if the Geographic agree for Hugo to stay here, if he doesn't film any of your next lecture film? We must know about this first, before asking the Geographic, or making any other arrangements at all. The value would be firstly that we could cover Flint's development until he is one year old, and second, cover the new baby over the time when it has got to the stage at which Flint is now — just seeking social contact with individuals other than the mother. It might be most fascinating because Flint is a fourth child, and the new one is a first (or anyway, a first to survive).

If we did this we could still come out here to see the final stages of the building in the summer. Hugo's long letter to you explains everything about the building, and about its supervision, etc, so don't get confused by my saying we will see to the last stages. All will be explained.

Must tell you a fascinating thing. These chimps, anyway sometimes, don't break off, bite off, or eat, the placenta. Melissa had hers dangling for probably two days. It was off this afternoon. Flo, apparently, was seen by Dominic to drape the cord around Flint's neck so as to get it out of the way!

One final point. We have got a baboon person. Edna is now really keen, and she is shaping well. We are giving her a trial period on the baboons and, when this is written up, and with some film on them, we feel absolutely convinced that money will be forthcoming. Particularly as there is a most exciting development at the moment — one adult male — a really big dominant one, is going around with a stage 1 baby (black coat) on his back all the time. It is fascinating, and we are desperately trying to get a few facts and pictures of it — via Edna, as I have no moment to spare just now!

Forgive me ending now, but it's terribly late, and supper is getting cold. PLEASE don't tell Ma about the baby being here — you can, of course, mention we want to stay till March.

Much love,

F.C.

Jane

"Chimpland"

24 September 1964

Dear Dr. Payne,

Many thanks for your last letter and for relieving my mind about the article and next season's lecture. With reference to the Franklin

Burr prize money, I much fear that the letter I wrote to you about it must have been one of the many that went astray in the floods. At that time I asked if you could put that money together with the rest of the money which the Society is keeping for me. Hugo and I have now discussed the matter fully and have come to the conclusion that it would be best if you could send the money, in Hugo's name, to his account in Switzerland. We shall then transfer it to an account of my own there, once the formalities have been completed.

We are still continuing to get exciting results here with the chimps. As you so rightly said in your letter, there seems no end to the surprises the chimps have in store for us. Once more this letter will take the form of an interim report.

To start with, as you may already have heard, Melissa has come up to expectations and we have a new member of the chimpanzee community. We did not actually see the birth, but saw the infant when it was certainly not more than 48 hours of age, and probably only one day old. The mother seemed completely dazed as though she couldn't understand at all what had happened. She walked only a few yards at a time, supporting the infant carefully with one hand and also with her thighs — she walked all the time with very bent legs. The entire placenta was dangling from the umbilical cord — on one occasion this became entangled in the vegetation and Melissa had to stop and unwind it. I was able to watch her making her nest that night — it was made very quickly, with one hand only and with none of the customary crude interweaving of branches. She was originally seen in the company of a mature male, but she left him and made the nest completely on her own.

The following morning I was able to see what were almost certainly the first reactions of some of the other chimps to the baby. The 4 year old Fifi was particularly interested, and kept approaching closely, peering, and sniffing at the placenta. This last worried Melissa who quickly gathered the cord up. (And it was interesting to find out, from Dominic, that when Flo first appeared with her infant the placenta was likewise dangling, but Flo, old and experienced in child-birth, carefully wrapped the cord around Flint's neck!) David was also interested in the baby, went very close, and peered and peered. As did Flo. Another childless female, Circe, tried to touch the baby, at which Melissa immediately grabbed her hand, and rushed to Goliath for reassurance. Her first encounter with Flo's eldest son, Faben, we are lucky enough to have on film. Faben was tremendously curious and his continual peering worried Melissa who kept reaching out her hand to him, presenting and generally trying to appease him yet keep her distance.

Luckily for us Melissa did not at all mind our close scrutiny of her offspring for the first few days — in fact she was far less wary of us than of the other chimps. So we were able to observe and photograph the infant closely. Despite this we have been unable to discover its sex — it is provisionally named "Jane"! She is the ugliest little creature you can imagine and, from Dominic's and Kristopher's descriptions, completely different from Flint when he was a baby. Flint, apparently, had a very pale and pretty face, and was very sparsely covered in hair on his head and back, and more or less naked below. This infant has a strangely marked face, dark around her eyes except for pale eyebrow streaks, and pale around her mouth. In addition she has thick hair on her head, back, and outsides of legs and arms. We have not been able to see the underside yet.

Unfortunately Melissa is now going through a spell (which I hope will be of short duration) when she is a bit shy of our too close observation and is uneasy if I follow her. She likes to keep very close to one of the dominant males, but finds it difficult to keep up with them as she is continually pausing to sit for half a minute or so and so usually gets left behind and ends up alone.

With regard to our other small infant, Flint is now beginning to walk with more determination and more success. He is still extremely unstable and collapses after every four steps or so unless he manages to keep on his feet by going so fast he simply has not time to fall over! He now regularly rides on Flo's back, or else dangles from her side reaching back at vegetation with his free hand in a most annoying way (for Flo that is). He actively seeks social interaction with all other chimps, who, for the most part, ignore him (mainly because of fear of Flo I suspect). Figan now occasionally carries him ventrally for a few steps, as does Gilka (now 2 1/2 years old). Fifi, on the contrary, although she is continually playing with him, almost to the exclusion of all other chimps, carries him around seldom — mainly, I think, because she finds him a bit much to cope with now he has such a mind of his own. She still picks him up and cuddles him when he is asleep.

Flint went through a short period when he would whimper whenever a chimp, who had been sitting or standing near him, walked away. With his little lips pushed forward he cried pathetically as he staggered and slithered after the retreating individual — it was as though he wanted to be the center of all attention. The younger chimps all responded to his crying by returning to him.

He is getting very expert in climbing, which he does much more skillfully than walking. He is also beginning to respond to Flo's "moving away signals", and to cling or clamber onto her when she reaches out to him or pauses with bent knees near the twig he is climbing on.

It is proving extremely interesting to compare the behaviour of a male infant, Merlin, with that of the female Gilka. Merlin really is "little boy" through and through. His playing, whether alone or with others, is far more "rough and tumble" than Gilka's ever was (he is about a year younger). He literally "flings" himself into games, onto other chimps, and, in fact, into everything he does, including begging food from his mother. In this latter he is invariably successful which is a measure of his persistence since Marina is extremely fond and possessive of her food!

Gilka herself is going through a most difficult period. Until the birth of Flint she was very frequently seen playing with Fifi, but now Fifi has time for no one but Flint. As Olly seldom goes around with mothers other than Flo, this leaves Gilka more and more to her own devices. Her brother, Evered, is not, at present, moving about very often with Olly and Gilka so she is also deprived of his companionship. In addition to all this, Olly is apparently trying to wean the child. I have never before observed any weaning behaviour in wild chimpanzees, and it may be that this is an exceptional case. Certainly no weaning behaviour was observed between Flo and Fifi, and Fifi was about a year older than Gilka when Flo's milk finally dried up. This weaning has a very marked effect on Gilka. When the breast is denied to her she whimpers, and she usually approaches Olly, when she wants to suckle, stands in front of her, and whimpers. If Olly does not want her to suckle she stands up and either gently bites her wrist, or "play bites" and nuzzles at the child until she stops whimpering to laugh. If the whimpering continues (and this I saw for the first time two days ago) Olly takes Gilka ventrally, carries her a few steps, sets her down, and again tickles her until she laughs. Several times that worked, but twice Gilka continued to cry. This seemed to affect Olly considerably — she returned to the child, gathered her up in an embrace and sat holding her on her lap. Then, when Gilka tried to suckle and the breast was again denied, Gilka moved away crying. But she had only gone a few steps when Olly reached out, drew Gilka back by one arm, embraced her, and allowed her to suckle very briefly. I am hoping to get more details on this fascinating behaviour within the next few days.

Three times, in the last month, we have seen Gilka playing, just as she might with a chimpanzee agemate, with a young baboon (almost certainly the same individual). It is fascinating to speculate as to whether this "friendship" has perhaps arisen from the difficult social situation described above. Young baboons and young chimps often play together, but this play is normally rather one-sided as the baboons when small are usually rather afraid of the young chimps. But Gilka and "Goblin"* play extremely gently, and on one occasion we saw most exciting interactions between the two. Firstly the baboon presented to Gilka, tail up, and she carefully inspected his little bottom. She then presented to him and he actually mounted her and gave a few thrusts, as small baboons will do in play. Next he went round and they nuzzled each other in the neck, play biting, and he then embraced her from behind and tickled her in the ribs, she throwing back her head and laughing. She tickled him in a similar way. The last time I saw the two playing was when Olly and Gilka were up the valley. Gilka left her mother feeding when she

---

* The young baboon had tentatively been named Goblin; when Melissa's infant, Jane, was discovered to be male, he was renamed Goblin. Presumably the young baboon was then rechristened.

saw the baboons approaching, crossing the valley, ran up to the small baboon that I am sure was "Goblin" and the two played gently together until the baboons had passed and Goblin scampered off after them. I hope that we shall soon be able to make a positive identification of the baboon. If, in fact, it is the same individual, this will represent a most amazing "friendship" between young wild animals of different species.

In addition to the facts relating to infant behaviour above, we have been able to make several more observations of infants pushing away males mating with females in oestrus. And this includes pushing away males from females other than the infants' mothers.

In this latter respect the little male infant, Merlin, was particularly amusing. He found the large pink bottom of Circe tremendously fascinating, and was continually running up to embrace it, and even tried to mount her by half climbing up her legs! And when one of the big males approached, Merlin appeared like magic to rush up and push the bounder off "his girl".

Before leaving the subject of infants completely, I should add that one more female, Mandy, seems to be pregnant, but we do not expect the event until next April or May.

Just recently we have seen three superb examples of masculine tyranny over females. The first two were perfectly understandable as the females were in oestrus, but it was interesting to observe how the two males concerned just _forced_ the females to follow wherever they went. By shaking branches at them or hitting at the grass and then, if the females still refused to follow, or if they tried to escape, charging at them flat out and beating them up. The third example occurred when J.B. arrived closely followed by an old female with an infant on her back. This female was in oestrus some two months ago, but when seen with J.B. had not the very slightest suggestion of a swelling. Yet J.B.'s behaviour was exactly as though she was at the height of her sexual attraction. The measure of her fear of him was well illustrated, since she is not "tame" having only visited the camp once before — when she was in oestrus and accompanied by a large number of males. Yet, although very nervous of approaching the camp he went on "branching" and charging at her until she finally followed him right up to the tent. To give him his due, he did share a very large bucket of bananas with her! And when she finally and whimperingly refused to come right onto the veranda (with us all huddled inside the tent with the flaps down) and despite the fact that he had already attacked her and pounded on her because of her unwillingness, he finally gave in and led her and her infant away.

The dung swirling technique continues to give excellent results — the latest find was the remains of bees and wax. During the first year of my study I came upon a group of chimps in thick undergrowth which I felt sure was raiding a bees' nest. I was unable to examine the place closely afterwards because of the bees swarming angrily around, and the chimps were not tame enough then for me to approach closely enough to see. In addition there are reports of chimpanzees eating honey in other areas. We now have nice proof that they do, in fact, raid nests, but the method is still unknown. Bees' nests are far from common in the Reserve.

Also, in connection with feeding behaviour, I have twice more observed meat eating. Once was almost certainly a baby bushpig. The previous day when I was following a group, they plunged into almost impenetrable undergrowth from which, after a few moments, emerged the most ghastly sounds of tumult. I was quite unable to find out for sure, but guessed that they had either stumbled across a bad tempered pig, which was "roaring" and charging heavily through the undergrowth, causing chimps to scream and race up trees. (And I did see several males displaying up in the trees and then leaping back into the undergrowth.) Or, and I thought more likely, they had been trying to catch a baby pig. Then, the following day, I heard similar sounds, but of short duration. Again I was unable to see what was going on, but some time later I found a group gathered around a male who was eating some sort of small animal (and a baby pig is very tiny).

On the other occasion the prey was a young bushbuck. It is interesting, in this connection, that Hugo was able to film a male baboon, closely attended by another, feeding on a young bushbuck. They had almost certainly caught the animal. It may well be the first time that baboons have been filmed actually eating meat (un-

less Professor Washburn shows this in his film which I cannot remember).

Also in relation to the hunting techniques of the chimps, we have
come to the conclusion that monkeys are mainly caught during the
breeding season. This might well tend to make them an easier prey.
This theory is strengthened by the fact that remains of a very tiny
baby (either just born, or, more probably, unborn) redtail monkey
were found, together with bones and skin of the mother, in one
day's dung swirling. It is possible that the mother, just before birth,
may be slightly separated from the main troop. Certainly the one
kill I have observed occurred when the colobus actually caught was
one of a group of four. Last week a group of chimpanzees approached a large resting group of red colobus. Not only did the
colobus seem unconcerned at the approach of the chimps, but several males could be observed leaping from their branches and
bounding down towards the chimps. What followed took place out
of sight, but produced loud screams from young chimps. And then,
shortly after a prolonged outburst of angry and frightened chimp
sounds, an old male chimp, Mr. McGregor (our greatest meat eater)
was observed literally running down the mountain with a mature
male red colobus in hot pursuit! I have seen young chimps running
from colobus before, but should never have believed that a mature
chimpanzee would do the same!

We had an excellent opportunity to test the reaction of the
chimps to a freshly killed bushpig. The Game Scout found a young
pig, which seemed to have been speared, floating in the lake early
one morning. It had obviously only just died as the blood was still
running from its wounds. We accordingly laid it out and awaited
the chimps' arrival.

We had, of course, hoped (though not expected) that they might
eat the meat, since it was so fresh. Instead a most unexpected and
interesting reaction was obtained, and from nearly all the chimpanzees. They were afraid of the carcass. They were interested in it.
They gave small worried sounds, and climbed trees at varying distances (according to each one's degree of boldness), and they then
proceeded to <u>smell</u> at everything all around, without actually ap-

proaching the carcass. They sniffed at leaves, twigs, trunks and branches of nearby trees. And not only once or twice, but many times and in many places.

The only conclusion we could come to as to the meaning of this strange behaviour was that they suspected that the pig might represent the kill of a leopard and were smelling everywhere for leopard smell. Even if this was not the case, they were certainly trying to get some sort of clue as to how the pig got there or who put it there. Olly and her family, together with two other males, actually saw us handling the carcass, and they did not go around smelling for clues. But apart from those, all chimps sniffed around with the exception of one.

The above facts are among the most interesting observed since I last wrote to you. Many others, of course, have been seen and recorded — in particular we are now getting a much fuller picture of female behaviour. For instance, I have now seen two other females, besides Flo, perform masculine type displays, charging and dragging on vegetation. And as for Flo — about three weeks before Melissa's baby was born, and for no apparent reason, Flo went under a tree into which Melissa had just climbed, Fifi took Flint, and Flo had all her hair out. Melissa climbed a little way down the tree, under which Fifi and the baby were sitting. All at once Flo moved closer. Melissa whimpered and held her hand towards Flo. No response, and so Melissa climbed higher. Then Flo all at once shot up the tree, shaking the branches, and Melissa leapt out into a next door tree, down to the ground and away. And Flo was after her, flat out, for about 100 yards. Then she stopped. And just sat, her lip drooping and all her hair out, and a rather mad glaze to her eyes. After about half a minute she seemed to recollect her poor baby, and returned to where Fifi had taken refuge up a tree. Poor little Flint looked quite dazed, and pushed his lips forward in a little whimper and reached out to his mother. Her hair gradually lay flat again as she climbed up and took him back. The reason for this was never known — the next day they were as they always had been.

I think that covers the main points of interest. But I should add that the boxes from Nairobi have arrived, and we have also fixed up additional cement ones. All work superbly, and we have no problems at all now with our feeding. Everything goes smoothly, and we havn't had one crisis since all were ready. We have one or two boxes more to come, and these should cope with our ever increasing number of visitors.

Dr. Leakey wrote to us to ask whether he should himself put forward a grant request for observations to be continued here during 1965. We decided it would be as well if he continued to do this, and sent him a draft estimate for Edna with the assistance of Sonia Ivey (see attached sheet) to carry on next year. I am sure that you appreciate the urgency of maintaining sustained and uninterrupted observations on the chimps here. We have been very lucky in finding Edna to assist in the work here and I am quite sure that, if the Society continues to sponsor the research here, she will do a very good job in continuing the observations on our behalf during 1965.

I think this letter is long enough now, and so will close.

With kindest regards to you and your wife.

Yours sincerely,
Jane

"Chimpland".
26 October, 1964

Dear Dr. Payne,

I am sorry that we seem to be burying you in an avalanche of letters all at once. This one concerns the possibility of my remaining here for the first three months of 1965.

The main reason for this is to enable us to make a fuller comparative study of our two infants, Flo's and Melissa's. The latter has be rechristened, by the way. I tentatively guessed it was a girl after a good look from the rear. However, a close up view from the front left no room for further doubt. "Goblin" is a little boy! In actual fact this, in itself, makes the comparison between the two infants even more interesting. To what extent, for instance, is Flint's social development influenced by the constant attention he received from sibling Fifi? Flint started to become really interesting when he was three months old as, from that time, his social contacts began to extend beyond those with his immediate family. It will be most important to follow Goblin's progress during these same months.

In other ways it is already interesting to compare the two babies. When we first saw Flint he was six weeks old, and even then Flo was continually having to support him as he had great trouble in gripping with his feet. Goblin, however, was able to cling on unsupported for quite long periods even during the first week of his life. In addition, he is far more active and seems to take more interest in his surroundings than did Flint at a similar age.

As you know, I have to keep two further terms' residence at Cambridge next year. I now feel that, from all points of view, it would be most profitable if I remained here until April and then worked flat out on my analysis for the rest of the year, with as few interruptions as possible.

We do hope that the Research Committee will approve of this plan which has been included in Dr. Leakey's grant request for this research for next year. You may have already received this. I should like to stress, at this point, how much Hugo and I appreciate the Society's generous support so far. The facts which are coming to light as a result of this support are, as you remark yourself, truly amazing.

Please give our best regards to Mrs. Payne.

Yours sincerely,
Jane

P.S. I quite forgot to thank you for your last letter with its entertaining enclosure. It was so kind of you to make such appreciative comments about my reports — which I always feel are far too brief.

Chimpland.
6 November [1964].

My dear FFF,

What super news about the grant, uniports, and everything going through so quickly and without question. I felt it would all be O.K. Many thanks for your help over it.

First — the question of what to do with the money. The amount for the Uniports . . . should certainly go to the fund which you operate so that you can pay all the expenses for them. For which, again, thank you a thousand times.

We suggest that, for the present, you keep the second sum in Nairobi but without, as yet, making any definite arrangements for it. We don't need any money here just at present, and Hugo is going to work it all out and then let you know. I feel so lucky having him to cope with all the horrid financial side of things — which I simply loathe as you may remember.

Things here are splendid — as usual. Mandy has had her baby — the most gorgeous little girl — which is splendid after the two little boys. I should be able to get really first class comparative material now. The social development of the fourth infant of one female (Flint) as compared with that of two first infants of young mothers, one male, one female. Both the latter, Goblin and Jane, are doing fine. We are rather worried about Flint — it seems he may either have something wrong with one leg or, less likely, something wrong with his sense of balance. He has been on his feet now for over 4 months, and he still wobbles and collapses all the time. Apart from that he is quite enchanting.

It would be nice if Tinbergen could come here — I rather feel he won't be able to. But I daresay we shall know by the time you get this. It was Lorenz we really wanted to see here.

Must stop — it is dark and the Africans are using the light to put in some pipes — dear J.B. found out how to break the wire of the boxes* and no Hassan to splice them for us! Hope he is O.K. Do let us know what was wrong with the poor man.

With love from us both, and many, many thanks.

Love
F.C.
Jane

---

* The latches on the steel banana boxes were controlled by wires running through buried pipes.

"Chimpland"
14 December 1964

My dear FFF,

Thank you so much for your last letter — it was so nice to have. It is such a wonderful idea of yours but, as you probably know by now, Hugo has not been granted permission to go to England with me next year — they want him to get on with the animal stills, etc. It is so sad, but do let's hope that at least they agree to one of the plans Hugo has told you about. I'm sure they must.

I wish I could see the genets — they must be lovely little things — Hugo had one that he adored, as you may remember. But we have an adorable pet too — a little mouse bird brought in when it was so tiny I never thought it could live. But it did, mainly thanks to Edna who spent a lot of time on it. I never would have thought that a tiny bird could have so much character. Did you know that mouse birds held their food with one foot when eating a large object, just like a parrot? . . .

Our new baby, Jane (species <u>Pan!</u>) is adorable. So we now have — Hugo, Leakey, Miff (Mummy's nickname in case you didn't know), Olly, Jane, and Rix (Eric's nickname)! Quite a good collection. No Jiff as yet — though we do have a Sniff. And, of course, there is a Sally. Oh yes, and a brand new mother, completely tame from the day she arrived, who is "Bessie". I'm sure Danny was jealous not to have a chimp called after her. And you know there's a MacD?

Anyway, I was going to say that Mandy is such a good mother as compared to Melissa. But I may have already told you that? Mandy is so concerned for the well being of her infant that, when eating and therefore having two hands in use (or, rather, if she is eating and happens to need both hands for the job!) she holds Jane pressed closely to her by means of her foot — which she may hold in the most uncomfortable looking position for ages. Melissa never goes out of her way to make things easy for the baby.

It will be fascinating to see whether Mandy's solicitude has the effect of retarding the baby's development, or the opposite. Certainly Goblin, who at first seemed much more lively than Flint, is apparently less advanced than Flint — and I am sure that this is because Goblin has no brother or sister to help him onto his feet.

I do hope there will be good news of Hassan. We are getting rid of the new boat boy at the end of the month, and Hugo's Anyango is going to take over the boat. Hassan did actually admit, on the day he left, that perhaps, after all, his stand in was not such a good bet.!

We are much wondering whether Payne and co. will venture this far. I do hope so. Perhaps, by then, all will be well.

I must stop now. Hugo and I both wish you a very happy Christmas, and please wish Mary and the rest of your family a happy Christmas from us too.

With love,
FC.
Jane

[December 31, 1964]

Darling Family,

Well, we are nearly at the end of the last day of 1964. What an impossible thought. What a day it has been too. Dear darling David displaying through the tent, using me as a pole first to swing round and then to drum on! His finger is hurting him a lot poor thing. Goliath back. He returned on Boxing Day which was so nice of him. Also on boxing day came dear Sophie and Sniff. Sniff now so tame that we can walk around and towards him and he doesn't bat an eyelid. And, talking of eyelids, Mum — you know Leakey's wart — we always called it a wart, on his left eye, lower lid, where the lid was torn? Well, I was gazing at his eye, and suddenly discovered that instead of being a wart sprouting black hairs, it is the skin that was torn from the lid, and the black bristle of hairs — I mean the bristle of black hairs is none other than — the eyelashes! There are no more on that lid — something must have torn it and pulled the skin to one side, and there it all healed up. The tent really stinks, as Mike and J.B. both weed into it.

Enough of chimps. How are all of you. Happy New Year. How did the tape go — we are dying to hear. No letter yet from you

Mum, though I guess one will be in the post. Bimje's niece and nephew, together with 2 friends, and Senter, came to visit us yesterday. NO MAIL!!!!!! How can they be so sordid.

Special thank you to you Danny for the calendar. How nice. It is hanging in the sitting room with the other cards. They are all absolutely super, the cards. I adore the tiger. Hugo's card from you, Olly, is an absolute hoot!

There is quite a lot to say, and I don't quite know where to begin. With "John" perhaps. Well, we sent Sonia off to meet him. That evening she did not return. We were peeved because, not knowing when they would return we had to put off our Staff party until Christmas Day. John and Sonia were scheduled to arrive on the 23rd, the party should have been on the 24th. However. On the 24th, during the afternoon, they arrived. What had happened was that poor John had omitted to report to the immigration in Kigoma. He had been told at the border that there was no more he need do. They nearly didn't let him come here. So their 23rd was spent in John taking a policeman to show him where he had slept, in the car, for the night (luckily he remembered there was orange peel there!) and Sonia weeping in the police station. Finally word came through from Dar that he could proceed, and so they arrived, with all the Christmas list we had ordered.

Hugo and I spent most of Christmas Day wrapping up presents and blowing up balloons and typing sweets into little coloured paper bags. — I mean, tying! John and Hugo went down to the beach in the morning for John to look at the engine. . . . John mended the engine, as he knew at once what was wrong with it. Being a very engine minded young man. They selected a shrub for Rashidi to put in a debe.* And that was our Christmas tree. A rather sadly drooping one by the evening when Hugo and I went down to decorate it. We had about 30 balloons, all of which we tied in a lovely bunch from a guy rope. The tree was just in the veranda there, in case of rain. And, by the way, it rained, non stop, all day until 4.30. Very worrying. We gave the presents to our boys — they were very delighted —

---

* A large tin.

thanks for thinking of the blankets Mum — and they loved the shirts. The little girls (and there were 3 so we had had to get one more of everything!) adored their tops and carried away the cases without unwrapping them. So we still don't know if they liked them! But obviously they did. They were all three very much little madams. We had bought a knife in Nairobi for a present for some-one, and never given it, so we gave that to Petro. He was quite over-come. We then finished off the tree. We even had silver balls for it — real ones from Bimje!

Then Hugo and I came back here for a quick sip of wine to start off the evening, and wait until the work up here was finished. Then down we went. Mbrisho was already there.* The two scouts came with their wives. Our own boys. (Hamisi excepted as he was getting married!) And two of the hired boys who are carrying kerais† of sand and stones for the cement bases for the uniports. Of those more anon. Then, altogether, there were 8 little children, and Petro. It got off rather badly, as partys so often do — no decent music on the wireless. Rashidi and co an extra long time doing bananas. Everyone sitting round. We amused them with balloons — they loved making the air come out so that it squeaked. And then, as it got later and later, we began stripping the tree. First they each got a water pistol — the children. Then everyone got one of the little sweet packets. And then the ceremonious meal. Hugo and I were on the ground. Sonia and John on chairs, together with the scouts, Mbrisho — yes, the scouts and Mbrisho. Hugo and I were using our hands — like you and I did Jiff. So we were brought water to dip our hands into before the fray. The food arrived on enor-mous sort of tray like dishes, and there was a great to do sorting it out — the women in one circle, children in a group where they had to wait until their elders had finished — Sonia and John cere-moniously served onto their plates. Then the dishes brought down

---

* Petro was a regular visitor to the research station from a neighboring village. Mbrisho was a distinguished older man, formerly a fisherman, living in the village of Bubango outside the eastern boundary of the reserve. He was a long-time friend and a regular visitor.
† Baskets.

for Hugo and I — I assure you we came off better than they did! Nice music started, and Chiko's cooking was simply super. A really first class super duper chicken curry. After it came the cutting of Dominic's nice but rather blackened looking cake. First he made a little speech thanking us for the food.

Then we stripped the tree. A biro each for the scouts, D and A. For each of the adults apart from the scouts, who got 10/- each, a packet of tea and a tin of corned beef. More sweets. Smarties for all the children. Lollipops. And then the toy trumpet things. Sonia got more from Bimje, but instead of 8 he only had 7 — I mean however many more it needed to get to 7 over what you got, Mum. So we handed them round. I gave the last one to Petro and suddenly noticed that there was the most darling little boy, who was standing all the time by Richard (his father) and was about 2 probably — perhaps three. He was gazing wide eyed at everything. And no blower left for him. All the others blew theirs. His eyes got wider. They never grouse, these African children. If it had been European children of that age they would all have been shouting, and some crying, because many of them didn't get one toy or another. There weren't enough to go round. But after a while Hugo and I couldn't bear this dear little boy any longer. So Hugo took Petro's trumpet — he had his knife, and anyway, he plays real life instruments. And it made that little boy's day. For the rest of the evening he chirped like a tree frog, on and on and on. He had a super time.

And so the evening drew to its close just as things were warming up. We toasted you all at only 2 mins after the right time. Mbrisho made a long speech about the usual things. The balloons were distributed and, mostly, popped. And amidst laughing, music, and the peep poop peep of the trumpets, punctuated by the popping of balloons, we left them. And returned to coffee, quantro and, as Hugo suggested, more toasts to our families!

So that was Christmas Day. Apart from the party, it was not unlike the tape, so far as chimps went. They came and went and hung around. We were awaked, and how, by Mike. He and J.B. slept with us on Christmas Eve. Gregor got his Christmas egg. So did Flo and so did Fifi.

Since then I have been working hard on the article — which, I am happy to relate, is three quarters done, first draft that is. But it is coming on. Otherwise I would have written more. . . . There only remains to tell you about the new site. We found the perfect place — near where we went that night, Mum. Just the right distance up. They have now piled, on the ridge, sufficient stones and sad. — sand. And this is the 4th and last night of the leveling of the site for the large uniport. That is the main work. We have employed 4 people, and so, with Rashidi, Ramadthani and those we have 6 people at work. Sadiki and Hamisi do the bs. This is the first evening I have not been up to the site. Hugo is up there now. . . . I must close. I must find the bird — Dodo, and put him to bed as it is dark. I will close in pen.

It is very late. Hugo is smoking a cigar that is twice as big as he is — one of the Winston type! Must end. Happy New Year to you all.

Love, Wisp

With love — Cigar Burr, Hugo

10

❧ ❧ ❧

COMING OF AGE
1965–1966

When I first set foot on the sandy beach of the Gombe Stream
Chimpanzee Reserve I never imagined that I was taking the first
step toward the establishment of the Gombe Stream Research
Centre: that, nine years later, there would be ten or more students
not only studying different aspects of chimpanzee behavior but
also observing baboons and red colobus monkeys.

— *In the Shadow of Man*

B Y THE START of 1965, Jane Goodall had already accomplished much. Thirty-one years old, she was well respected in
the scientific community and — primarily by virtue of the
first *National Geographic* article, published in the summer of 1963
— was beginning to acquire her mature fame among the larger
American public. She had already made the first discoveries —
chimpanzee meat-eating and tool-using — that would forever un-
derpin her public and professional reputation. And she had managed to habituate to an astonishing degree almost an entire social
community of wild apes. She was then, as Dr. Leonard Carmichael
(chairman of the National Geographic Society's Committee for Research and Exploration) declared in a committee meeting of early
1966, "probably the best qualified person in the world today to
speak on the subject of chimpanzee behavior in the wild." Profes-
sionally she had come of age.

Carmichael's opinion was particularly important because Jane
had by then developed a vision of her future as a chimpanzee con-
servationist and researcher. She wanted to establish a series of chimpanzee reserves in West Africa, and she emphatically intended to

continue the research at Gombe on a long-term basis. National Geographic, with its wealth, influence, and abiding interest in pursuits geographical and anthropological, seemed precisely the organization to help.

National Geographic *was* helping, of course, but nevertheless, the January 1965 visit to Gombe by three alpha males from that institution — Dr. Carmichael, along with Dr. Melvin M. Payne (executive vice president of the Society) and Dr. T. Dale Stewart (member of the Committee for Research and Exploration and director of the Smithsonian's Museum of Natural History) — obviously was an occasion of paramount importance. As Jane wrote home (in the first letter in this sequence), "What paraphernalia went into their visit, what preparations, what work, what worry." Even the chimpanzees themselves, she noted in a casual flight of fancy, appeared to recognize the visit's significance: "It was as though they all knew that, perhaps, their future depended on the impression they made." It is thus noteworthy and even, I think, surprising that a quite young woman still without formal scientific credentials had the nerve and poise and self-confidence — the maturity — to stand up to all three proud and powerful senior men. She argued heatedly and earnestly with Payne, who at one point "nearly exploded with rage" at her apparent insolence; Carmichael she cut short; and Stewart she forthrightly disagreed with. In the end the visit was a great success. At least two of the men seem to have appreciated her assertiveness, and Dr. Carmichael made the reassuring pronouncement that "this place MUST be put on a permanent footing."

While 1965 marks the beginning of Jane Goodall's professional maturation, it also marks the start of her withdrawal from an intensely intimate, day-to-day association with life at Gombe. That withdrawal she regretted. "Yet there were times," she recalled a quarter of a century later, "when I thought back to my early days at Gombe with real nostalgia. . . . But change had been inevitable: there was no way in the world that one person, no matter how dedicated, could have made a really comprehensive study of the Gombe chimpanzees. Hence the research centre."*

---

* *Through a Window* (1990), p. 26.

By March of 1965 the first buildings of the center were complete — including two prefabricated aluminum units (floored with concrete and, for insulation and aesthetics, covered with palm-frond thatch and bamboo siding) and a smaller hut to store bananas. The two buildings were, by 1966, furnished, painted, fully in use, and even given names. The larger, which included a main workroom and two smaller rooms for sleeping quarters, was called Pan Palace (a punning link between aluminum pan and *Pan troglodytes,* the scientific name for chimpanzees). The smaller, consisting of a single room to be used as Jane and Hugo's sleeping quarters, was named Lawick Lodge. By May of 1966 a third semipermanent building was begun down toward the beach, constructed partly from pieces that had originally been a veranda for Pan Palace; this building, a dining hall for the research staff, was finished by June and named Troglodytes Taverne (mentioned in the letter of June 23, 1966).

The research staff during 1965 and 1966 consisted of two or three persons who did not have scientific credentials. Edna Koning, who had arrived at the start of 1964 and remained until the winter of 1965, began the baboon studies. Sonia Ivey, who stayed, along with Edna, for about a year, from late 1964 to the winter of 1965, labored mostly on secretarial duties, of which there were plenty. Edna and Sonia were replaced by Caroline Coleman, an American Ph.D. candidate in psychology, who took over as a researcher at the start of 1966, and, in March, by a woman who came to work as secretary, Mrs. Sally Avery. A few other people arrived for short stays at Gombe during this time, including a woman named Milly or Millie (referred to in the letters of October 2, 1965 and May 1966), who helped with the secretarial work for about four months, and John MacKinnon, who came for a time to study insects.*

Jane and Hugo, meanwhile, had been forced to leave Gombe Stream for more than a year — from March 1965 to early May 1966 — and in separate directions. Hugo followed his camera. National Geographic was funding him to photograph animals else-

---

* John MacKinnon, grandson of British Prime Minister James Ramsay MacDonald and nephew of Malcolm MacDonald, came to Gombe officially as an entomologist, but he was clearly interested in the chimpanzees. He studied zoology at Oxford and went on to conduct an extended, pioneering field study of orangutans in Borneo.

where in East Africa. Jane returned to Cambridge, living once again at Cross Farm in Comberton and working, as she expressed it in a letter of November 5, "flat out on the final stages" of her doctoral dissertation. At the same time, the many enticements and demands of her astonishing professional success were starting to pour in. She finished a draft of her second *National Geographic* article (letter of February 3, 1965); turned in the typescript of her first popular, nonscientific book (late July 1966); continued a correspondence with Paul Brooks at Houghton Mifflin, the American publisher that hoped to publish her second popular book; delivered a lecture for the prestigious Wenner Gren conference in Vienna, held within the walls of the castle Burg Wartenstein; and, after a "delightful month on the Serengetti" that included a very brief visit to Gombe, she returned to "horrible oral exams, lectures, lectures, and more lectures." The lectures were given during a whirlwind tour in the United States, where her visibility was rapidly expanding, thanks to a cover appearance for the second *National Geographic* article and a CBS television special, "Miss Goodall and the Wild Chimpanzees," both in December 1965. The tour began with three sold-out lectures in National Geographic Society's Constitution Hall in late February. After a quick return to England for, among other things, a March 9 lecture in Bournemouth, the tour ended in California with Jane ceremonially cutting and consuming the first of 30,144 pieces of a 320-foot-long birthday cake celebrating San Diego Zoo's fiftieth birthday (letter of April 23, 1966). At the end of April she received formal notification from Cambridge that henceforth she was qualified to be known as Dr. Jane Goodall. Finally, back in Africa, she and Hugo showed their latest chimpanzee film to Julius Nyerere, the distinguished first president of Tanzania.

There is little doubt that Jane — and Hugo as well — enjoyed the attention brought by this new-found fame, but she took greater pleasure in returning to Africa to be with the chimpanzees. Certainly the letters written from Gombe, filled with daily news and views from that small paradise, include the most fully detailed and emotionally engaged writing of this chapter. The business and professional letters mailed from Cambridge and elsewhere pale in comparison. The Gombe correspondence continues the story of hope and excitement, including the births of two new infants (Circe's Cindy and Little Bee's Tiny Bee) at the start of 1965, and of despair, such as the horrible death of Mandy's baby, Jane, in early February 1965.

Among the notable chimpanzee events of 1966 was Jane's first observation of an entire meat-eating sequence, as reported in the final letter from May: "MEAT-EATING. Saw Hugo (chimp) hitting a baboon (young, not baby) in camp!! He had it by leg and was bashing its head up & down on the ground. Saw the whole meat-eating sequence." The event, both dramatic and gory, was fully reported and even illustrated in the book Jane was just then finishing for National Geographic — except that chimpanzee Hugo was renamed Rodolf to avoid confusion with husband Hugo. One other compelling, if depressing, set of observations from the same period has to do with the decline of "poor little Merlin." After his mother, Marina, died in 1965, Merlin fell into a deep depression, losing weight, obsessively grooming himself, and neurotically plucking out his hair, until he seemed merely "a skeleton with a pot belly" (May 7, 1966). His sister, Miff, allowed him to "climb in and snuggle up" into her sleeping nest at night, but Merlin died before the year ended.

Some long-term management problems developed and continued during this period at Gombe. In the early years Jane had spontaneously touched — in grooming and play — a few of the chimpanzees, but as research assistants began to take over the running of the center, she and Hugo recognized the importance of keeping human observers from making physical contact with the ape subjects. For one thing, there was a reasonable concern about spreading disease. And, there was the issue of physical safety. Chimpanzees are vastly stronger than humans, and it seemed like a good idea to keep them from discovering that fact. Thus Jane and Hugo made it a rule that "no student should purposefully make contact with any of the chimpanzees."* And thus we note the alarm and concern in Jane's very first letter home after her return to Gombe in May 1966: "The

---

* *In the Shadow of Man* (1971), p. 139.

chimps are fine — except that, so far as we can see, even Caroline has been touching them."

A second persistent problem had to do with the banana feeding. Upon their return in 1966, Jane and Hugo were, as she recollected in her book *In the Shadow of Man,* "shocked by the change we saw in the chimps' behavior. Not only was there a great deal more fighting than ever before, but many of the chimps were hanging around camp for hours and hours every day."[*] The ultimate solution was to limit much more strictly and carefully the dispersal of bananas. In the meantime, the banana boxes were found to be not very functional. The original steel boxes were operated remotely, with levers pulling underground cables that drew open latches. But over time Fifi, Figan, and Evered figured out how to remove the locking pins from the lever mechanism. Hassan replaced the pins with threaded screws — which the chimps soon learned to remove. Then the threaded screws were held in place with tightened nuts, but those didn't last long either. By the summer of 1966 Hugo had decided to go hi-tech, ordering from Nairobi a number of steel boxes that could be locked and unlocked electronically via battery-operated radio control (as mentioned optimistically in the last letter, of late July 1966). At last, Jane enthused, those new boxes ought to "really fox cunning little devils like Fifi!" With the boxes just about ready, a wealth of "grand" safari equipment, including their "Folkswaggen" modified to serve as a traveling office, and "the fact that for the first time in 6 years I do not have a weighty work hanging over my head," Dr. Jane Goodall was ready to go: leaving with Hugo for a photographic assignment in the Serengeti and the "icy fastness" of Ngorongoro Crater and entering at last the mature phase of her brilliant career.

* * * *

[Late January 1965]

Darling Family,

What ages since I wrote. But you must forgive me — I havn't had any seconds to do anything until now — now that the dear trio

---

[*] *In the Shadow of Man,* p. 141.

from the States have left us. What paraphernalia went into their visit, what preparations, what work, what worry. And how are we left as a result. In many ways their visit couldn't possibly have gone off better. There were lots of chimps, doing nice things. We have made the hut joined to the work tent by a great fence, with roll down mats across an opening where the path goes. So that the great men could walk from their tents to the hut, to their choo, etc. We had gone to enormous trouble with this fence, to buy and dye yards of mosquito netting so that no chimps took fright and ran away. We moved the salt block from its place on the path to the trees outside the work tent so that there was some incentive to keep the chimps, at least for a little while, in their sight. We had cut down vegetation so that by dint of peering they could see chimps by our tent from the work tent and the hut. We decided that, one by one, they could be allowed to our tent to see the chimps from close, unmosquitoed quarters. So. They arrived, with Hugo, when Sonia and I had had such a busy day that things were not really ready. We had been in hiding for over 2 hours because a very pink Sally had been in camp all afternoon. The hoot of Hugo rang through the air. Sonia and I like two frantic bees rushed to the sitting room and the work room tents and emerged laden with all the bits and pieces that we had instructions to tidy away during the day. All were dumped in Hugo and my tent and the flaps closed! Then the party was whistled on. No sooner had they been escorted by the back door into the hut than the next group came. Super arrival display by Mike and Hugo. Lots of other chimps. A very heavily preg. Circe strolled around. A few chimps peered at the four vaguely visible objects in the hut, all madly clicking.* But none of them bothered. And, the next day, one by one our resolutions were overcome as, one by one, all the chimps accepted our VIP's with a nonchalant stare and a turned back. It was quite unbelievable. It was as though they all knew that, perhaps, their future depended on the impression they made. Olly couldn't have cared less. Figan straight away brushed past Payne, nearly pushing him off his chair. Mac D, timid little Mac D, gave

---

* The visitors were taking photos.

them a noncommittal stare and continued to scrounge in the tent for bananas. Circe didn't mind. And even little Jomeo, our new latest little male who was christened Romeo until I found he was none other than Jo — even he, for whom we still hide in tents, came bouncing along the path whilst we were all standing out in the field! So. Our gentlemen from the States enjoyed two complete days of complete freedom. They were very good. Did what they were told. Didn't complain about cups without handles, cold breakfasts (because chimps always came in the middle and they wanted to take pictures and watch and we couldn't keep it all hot) and were quite happy to drink stream water in its pristine unboiled state. Carmichael, that great giant of a man, when I asked him if he would like hot water to wash with, or a bath, said I please wasn't to worry because he made his thermos top of shaving water go a long way — in fact he had almost bathed in it. Thinking of the little bird in the glass I had a hard job not to laugh out loud. Anyway, to speak of other things. Payne, dear Payne . . . nearly exploded with rage when I told him I wasn't happy about the lecture film being shown to scientific audiences. I was livid too. We let it be. And then, later that evening when we were all together, Carmichael mentioned to me that he had had the honour of showing it, and how successful it had been. I said nothing. Payne turned to me and asked if that didn't completely set my mind at rest. My opportunity, and all unasked for. So I regaled Carmichael and Stewart with the examples of unscientific things which had crept into the film. Stewart was on my side in a flash. Carmichael looked into the fire for a long time, and could only say that anyway it served to interest people in the chimps and in conservation. . . .

However, let me turn to the bright aspect of the visit. And it was very bright. For one thing we won over Carmichael, hook line and sinker. And are dying to hear, Mum, any report you may hear from Louis as to their comments when they left. When he arrived Carmichael was so pompous and so ready to pounce on every word I said — how did I know — why did I say so — was this justified — etc, etc, etc. We got almost hysterical — and this is not just Hugo and I — Payne and Stewart were usually on our side too — that we couldn't keep our faces straight. He was, in fact, being silly!! For instance, when I asked if he could remember at what age a laboratory chimp walked first, he spent 5 minutes giving a discourse on the origin of walking, and how infants new born walked by movements of their limbs through space, and walking originated by the C and then the S shape of swimming organisms — and it went on and on. And in point of fact he didn't obviously know the answer to the question, but he would never admit it! However, we had one long discussion about the meaning of a movement of Flint's, or Figan's or something. And he kept saying that when I was writing a scientific paper or my thesis I should say this or this, and not that or that. Until, in exasperation I said that I wasn't writing a thesis, but talking to him. And do you know, from that moment onwards, he was a changed man. He stopped being terrified that every opinion he gave would appear in reference to his name in some or other of my papers. He became human. He talked about chimps like we do. He commented on a satisfied expression on Gregor's face. He began extasising about Flint (only I'm sure he spelt it differently!) And we had fun. I think he rather likes it that I stood up for our views, and wouldn't be talked down, and even ventured to disagree with him on more than one topic! Stewart, the Director of the American Museum of Natural History, was also won over. He started off in a very critical vein. But changed quicker than Carmichael. In fact his turning point was when I ventured to disagree with his theory that man became man simply because an erect posture freed the vocal organs of some pressure which was the consequence of a quadrupedal gait and enabled man to talk. Anyway, the next morning he happened to mention that he had been thinking and thinking about the vocal organs and — this, that and the other. And next Carmichael appeared and said he'd been thinking during the night of something or other we'd been talking about. So both learned gents had had food for thought. And began to enjoy themselves, and relaxed, and told jokes, and we grew to really like Carmichael. And what a brilliant man he is to be sure.

Two things happened. The day before they came Faben came to camp with a whole, complete, and certainly baboon, skull. Of course, Hugo was meeting them so no record is made except in my notes and a few very poor stills — because Ben was so nervy and so certain that I wanted to steal his skull, that I couldn't get anywhere near him. The other thing is even more exciting. CIRCE HAS HER BABY! We don't know the sex. If it's a boy we are undecided as to whether we should call it Leonard, in honour of the great man's visit. Or Winston in honour of the even greater man's sad death.* How sad, but he was so old that it had to come soon I suppose. But we thought a little chimp Winston would be rather nice, and one little tribute we could give. It was Sonia who thought of it, and we thought it was a good idea. However, from the very brief glimpse of the relevant portion of its anatomy, both Hugo and I suspect a girl!

I forgot to tell you the research news. Carmichael is so impressed that he feels this place MUST be put onto a permanant footing. He feels he might get us some of the money that is available to primate research from the U.S.A. government. Countless millions of dollars. He feels sure he can find qualified people to come here and take over, because he feels as we do that there must be a continuity of observations, and the records must be kept. He was, in fact, wildly enthusiastic. He thought the Smithsonian might well finance an expedition to Liberia, such as we used to talk about. As it is an American — well, something, I've forgotten what — it sounds good. He is great friends with the President. Who is very keen on animals. . . .

So, our plans for next year are sadly changed, and Hugo will just be in England for about a month in July or August. Then he must be back for the birth session of the plains animals — and I hope that I shall be able to join him for a short time between Christmas and the Geographic Lecture which we have fixed for 10 Feb. What a relief it will be to know that I shall not need shingles for the lecture — that even though it will not be <u>our</u> film, the film of films, it will be a scientifically accurate film.† Please can someone find out when, if I do get a PhD, I would be expected to receive it, or be awarded with

---

* Winston Churchill died on January 24, 1965.

† She realized that she wouldn't break out in shingles from worry because, unlike an earlier film presented at a Geographic lecture, the current film was scientifically correct.

it, or whatever does happen? <u>URGENT</u> Also, Mum, <u>please</u> can you get Jiff, next time she is home, to look out one of her pictures of Priscilla termiting, which shows her <u>face.</u> This is URGENT — as we want to put it side by side with a strange new female who has now been twice, and who looks rather but not quite like the Priscilla of old.

Next thing, Mum. This is no urgent request — it is just something which I'd be most grateful if you could keep your eyes open for, or your ears. While I am at Cambridge I shall need someone to help me with charts, tables, etc. The work Edna should be doing if she was here now, but isn't. Otherwise I don't think I can get all the work done. If it was someone good at maths so much the better! Someone who had left school and had some odd time to fill in and wanted some pocket money — that sort of thing. You see, it COULD be someone in London, that I could meet every other weekend, or something. I shall also ask Lyn to keep her ears open in Cambridge, because, of course, that would be far more satisfactory. I could, also, take someone to Cambridge with me — could easily find them somewhere in Comberton, I should think, that would not be too expensive — that would be really ideal. Maybe you could ask Uplands [School] or something. Anyhow, just in case you do hear of such a thing.

Help — end of page. I will write again soon, now all panics over.

Tons & tons of love to all,

Jane

Hugo sends his love to all.

c/o Box 8,
Kigoma,
Tanzania.
3 February 1965

Dear Mr. Vosburgh,

Here at last is the promised manuscript! I have been trying to get it finished, in the few spare moments available, for several months, but couldn't manage it any earlier than this.

I do want to impress upon you that this is a <u>DRAFT.</u> There are several passages that I want to rewrite, particularly towards the beginning. However, I am sending it to you in this form because I feel sure you will find it too long and I should appreciate your advice on which parts to shorten. If you could write back, at some time, and let me know what you feel might be omitted or reduced I should very much like to do as much of this as possible myself.

I don't know if you were one of the members of the Research Committee to visit East Africa — if so I do hope that you enjoyed your 'safari'. I am sure you will have heard by now how well the chimps behaved for our Geographic visitors here.

Hugo joins me in sending our best regards,

Yours sincerely,
Jane van Lawick

P.O. Box 8
Kigoma, Tanganyika,
E. Africa
[Received February 8, 1965]

Miss Mary Griswold
National Geographic Society
Washington 6, D. C.
United States of America
Dear Mary:

I have received a letter from Professor Pronko of Wichita State University asking for permission to publish some photographs in a book of readings in general psychology he is compiling.

I have spoken to Dr. Payne concerning this and he agrees that we can let Professor Pronko have some photographs. He is, of course, particularly interested in tool using, and as I do not have contact sheets of termiting stills with me I should be most grateful if you could choose some for him. If you still have the list of the ones which were used in the Stanford book I would suggest the same would do for Pronko. In addition, from 1964 contact sheets — sheet No. 14A — No. 6, Sheet 19A, No. 2. (i.e. playing and grooming). The former is a female juvenile playing with nearly mature male, approx 10–11 years. The latter — mixed group social grooming.

Have you heard our latest news — that Circe has a baby? Still don't know the sex because after her first visit she has not been. But you have not heard our even more astounding news. Madam B. arrived here 1 hour ago, after an absence of 5 months, with a tiny, new born infant! We had been talking about her and saying we felt she must be dead only minutes before she arrived, because I dreamed about her last night!! Little Bee was still well, but Mama was very nervous. The new infant is "Tiny Bee". It really is most exciting — the 5th baby this season — the 2nd this year!

I do hope all goes well — we haven't heard from you for AGES.

With regards,
Jane

"Chimpland"
13 February 1965

Dear Dr. Payne,

What a wonderful surprise we had to receive your present — you can't imagine what a difference it has made to our meals out here — or perhaps you can! It was so kind of you to think of it, and you couldn't possibly have sent us anything we should appreciate more. Many many thanks from all of us.

You timed your visit here just right. If you had come two weeks later you would have been in Chimpland for the most horrible tragedy. Mandy came down the slope with a big group, and when she was way up we heard agonized screaming. And then we saw it — little Jane, her 3 month old infant you remember — had one arm dangling loose, all the inside of the lower arm torn off from the elbow and dangling down over the little hand. And every time Mandy moved she screamed in agony. She turned to the comfort of the nipple and suckled, but could find no relief. Mandy, of course, didn't understand at all, and when Jane screamed she pressed her close, adding to the infant's pain. It was about the most ghastly thing I've seen in a long while. It must have happened only a very short time before Mandy arrived, for blood was still dripping, and Mandy's own ear was torn and still bleeding.

Mercifully death came far quicker than we had dared to hope. She didn't, thank goodness, come here again with the baby. But two days afterwards we saw her opposite, carrying the body, hitting away the flies that seethed all over it. She didn't bring the body here, which we hoped she would, horrible though it would have been. It would have been interesting to see the reactions of the others. And then, two days after that, she arrived here, alone again. Her breasts very tight and swollen, but otherwise showing no ill effects. But sometimes she sits and stares and stares at one or other of the other infants.

The buildings are, to all intents and purposes, finished. Hugo has asked me to tell you that he will send the cost of the cement bases and the labour in the next mail. By then we shall know this down to the last cent. We are now busy getting banana boxes put there, and then we shall be able to leave the girls with a happy heart. The bamboo on the outside looks wonderful, and one is being thatched tonight. And with the linings inside they really are going to be nice looking buildings.

Poor Edna is still stuck — she is now in Dar es Salaam! But she is due back, definitely, on Tuesday next, just in time to help us start to organize the move to the new camp.

I do hope that the rest of your safari in Africa was successful and enjoyable, and that you had a good trip back to Africa. — sorry — America! Thank you again so much for your present, from all of us.

Yours sincerely,

Jane

c/o Box 8
Kigoma, Tanzania
20 February 1965

Mr. Paul Brooks,
Jpigjtpm ?off;om !!
Houghton Mifflin Company,
2 Park Street, Boston 7.
United States of America.
Dear Mr. Brooks,

It was nice to get your Christmas card and message. I do apologize for not writing — but for one thing we are so hectic here that it is hard to find even a moment to compose oneself sufficiently to write letters. For another thing, there is nothing I can say except that I still can't commit myself to a publisher. The Geographic is being a bit awkward as they want to publish a book themselves, and there is some question of their not liking another book on the market. I think this will resolve itself, but have heard nothing from them since I wrote about it.

Things here are going superbly. We have got two semi permanent buildings set up on the most magnificent site. They are just about ready now, and although Hugo and I have to leave in a month (me back to England and he, lucky fellow, filming in the game parks) we have two girls to leave here who will look after things while I finish my PhD. After that I hope to do another year here myself, and then perhaps our scheme will be working — that students should come here to make specialized studies. We have received enthusiastic promises of help from all sorts of sources — the Smithsonian, Professor Lorenz and Julian Huxley amongst them. I think we shall manage to find the finance somewhere.

Hugo and I also have a plan to establish a string of chimpanzee reserves throughout their range, so that, eventually, behaviour studies in the different areas may reveal cultural differences. The project has been taken up by the World Wild Life Fund, so that seems promising too.

Forgive hasty note, but I hope it's better than nothing.

Yours sincerely,
Jane van Lawick

July 25, 1965

Dear ~~Mr. Brown,~~ Andrew!

Excuse haste, but I want to answer your questions — or Dr. Car-michael's — before the post goes.

1. By all means qualify the statement that Faben is Flo's son, in the way you suggest. It is quite certain, but if people might object, we may as well qualify it.

2. No absolute proof, in positive form, that chimps KILL ba-boons. But, as I have said, we have seen them hunt baboons. I have seen one eating meat from a baboon skull. And I have no hesita-tion in asserting, dogmatically and with assurance, that <u>chimps will not, under any circumstances, eat something that has already been killed.</u>* We have tested them out in this respect, on several occa-sions, and the result was always negative, even though we had seen them kill and eat the same animals or birds.

3. No one from the Geographic had a hand in getting Edna to us. She read the article and wrote direct to me, and Hugo and I decided that, since she was so keen and was willing to get out to Africa un-der her own steam we would give her a try.

4. I do not consider the last paragraphs too anthropomorphic. I am not trying to attribute human motives to David. What he did was what he would do to another chimp. What I hoped I had con-veyed, and what I want to convey, is the impression, purely subjec-tively, that this action had upon me. I think, on suddenly thinking about it, that the one wrong part is right at the beginning where I say that "he not only tried to communicate with me, but actually succeeded" — or words to that effect. In fact it would be better to omit the "tried". Something like — On this occasion my old friend, D.G. actually established communication with me, by using a chimpanzee gesture (or the chimp gesture before the actually es-tablished).

Do forgive haste — and I see I've torn the paper!!

Yours sincerely,
Jane Goodall

---

* The behavior has since been observed on a very few occasions.

Austria.

14 September [1965]

My dear FFF,

Well, here we are, on holiday at last. I think you would already be surprised if you saw me as I look about 80% better — even to myself!

We have just got to our chalet having stayed on to the bitter end of the Wenner Gren conference. It really went off fantastically well and we had a wonderful time. . . . I think the conference has done a lot of good all round. The film went down excellently and the principle of 'reassurance' was accepted without protest from anyone. They all immediately realized they had seen it in their own animals. We planned to stay 3 days and stayed 7! Isn't it a fantastic place for a conference. We had music in the chapel garden (no one talked, but we did all freeze). Liberal wine flowed and thousands of concepts were evolved round the dinner table. In the middle of the Conference part of the Board of Directors arrived and they came in to a session. Apparently the first time they have attended any meeting in session. Primates would get in first! Lorenz didn't come, which was a pity, but a lot of other interesting people were there — Mason, Marler, and Hamburg especially.*

On the last evening DeVore & Sherry sang a song about chimps to me which, I gather, was instigated by remarks made by you some years ago but which you had not heard! It was strictly censored!

With reference to the request for money for the drawings from film. These are not only for my thesis, not by any manner of means. But we got them all out — or Hugo did — while he was going through the film, & they may just as well be all done together. Certainly I will pay if the Geographic refuse, but I see no harm in asking. Especially in view of the very large return they will get from the television film.

We got the M.G. for our holiday. Grossly extravagant but as we are going to sell it we shouldn't lose any more than if we had got any

---

* The "interesting people," all of whom were distinctly promising or already distinguished academics with a direct interest in primate studies, included William Mason, Peter Marler, David Hamburg, Irven DeVore, and Sherwood ("Sherry") Washburn.

other car, & the open air is just wonderful. Sorry about change of pen but we can't find anything else at hand!

Well, I will end for now. I bet you are relieved that Sonia has gone back, all signed and all! It is raining hard here!

Will write again soon.

With love,
FC.
Jane

Don Quixote
Kitzbuhel
October 2, 1965

My dear FFF,

Well, just a few words. We are nearing the end of our holiday. We have had superb weather, and I feel 100% fitter than when you last saw me. It will be sad to leave Austria and the cows and deer and nearly black squirrels.

We went to see Lorenz last week, and showed him the film. He was delighted with it all. Poor man is not at all well — has something or other wrong with his insides and is about to give up paper work for a spell and calmly watch his geese. He made a superb remark about Pooch when she was investigating the dead rat* — "Ah — there is the first Zoologist"!!!

There are a list of questions I must ask you, and to clarify matters I will give each one a number.

1. Have you still got Edna's signed agreement? If so, can you send it back to me. Edna is unhappy about it and only signed it thinking it concerned chimps.

2. Did you get, direct from Caroline, her passport number? Is anything working out for her? Is there anything we should be doing from here to see that she can get through quickly?

3. We hear from Edna that she is to — or was to — pay Milly's salary from the Kigoma fund. The only source from which this was possible was the "emergency fund" which she was not supposed to

---

* A scene in a film made by Hugo.

touch unless in trouble. This money was the accumulation of several months of my stipend. If she paid 4 months of Milly's salary from it it will not cover emergencies, which is why we want to know. If so, then we can arrange something else for that fund. Edna also said that you said that the Nairobi fund was depleted. What is the financial situation for the end of the year? I suppose that Edna's salary is still all right, because she will be going on holiday early next year, and will presumably want it.

4. Has the new grant request gone off yet? If so, we'd be most grateful for a copy of it as it finally stood.

5. Hugo tried for insurance (medical) for the girls from England but was unable to succeed. He therefore can do no more about it until he sees you again in Nairobi. Also none of the African staff are insured yet either.

6. A final message from Hugo. Would it be all right if he camped at Olduvai for a couple of months when he gets back — quite self contained of course. If so, could he hire your truck for getting petrol there, for 2 days — I mean hire the truck for 2 days.

There — that is all the points I think. And I am keeping the letter brief because I am now working on "reassurance and touch, etc" and must get on with my lists. I hope you got my brief scrawl after the Wenner Gren which went off superly.

Hugo sends his regards,

With love,
F.C.
Jane

1, York Mansions,
Earl's Court Road,
London, S.W.5.
5 November 1965.

Dear Dr. Wolff,

I apologize for the delay in answering your letter of 23 September, but I have been away and only recently returned.

As I am working flat out on the final stages of my PhD thesis, and shall be kept busy until my arrival in Washington in February, I feel that I shall be unable to prepare a lecture for you with the first lecture film. However, if you could persuade the National Geographic Society to allow me to lecture with the new lecture film, after the lectures to the Society, I shall be very happy to accept your invitation to speak for the Maryland Academy of Sciences.

As an alternative, perhaps the Geographic Society might be more willing to allow me to show simply a half of the new lecture film — for the other half of the programme I should be happy to introduce the work being done at the Gombe Stream Reserve and show a number of colour slides.

If you or the Geographic agree to either of the above the best date for me would be February 22nd.

Yours sincerely,
Jane van Lawick-Goodall

Ngorongoro Crater Lodge, Ltd.
P.O. Box 751
Arusha, Tanzania
1 February 1966

Mr. Paul Brooks
Houghton Mifflin Company,
2 Park Street,
Boston 7.
United States America.
Dear Paul Brooks,

Just a short note, on our way back from a delightful month on the Serengetti to horrible oral exams, lectures, lectures, and more lectures, to say thank you for the book — which we got yesterday, together with your letter.

We havn't, of course, read the book yet, but it looks fascinating, and we look forward to doing so — perhaps on our flight to the States in two weeks time!

I think we are coming to Boston to show the film there. If so it will be during the week starting 7th March. Any chance of meeting you there? It would be fun, and I'm sure there is a lot we could talk about.

If you want to know our plans, contact Miss Joanne Hess of the National Geographic Society — but she will not know the Boston dates yet, since we do not know ourselves! Roy Little has invited us — I'm sure you know him. We met him in Seronera, and he is very interested in the chimpanzee work, and our plans to make Reserves, or Parks, in West Africa — for the chimps I mean.

Hoping to see you,
Jane van Lawick

Ainsworth
Nairobi.
23 April, 1966

Darling Family,

How are you all. We had a jolly good flight back — plane almost empty, and it didn't stop after 10.30 p.m. until we got to Entebbe in the morning. We were able to sprawl out on a seat each — in fact, almost everyone could, so few seats were filled. It was a B.O.A.C. plane — the service was fantastically good — nice polite people, super food, gorgeous huge blankets — really looking up. Much better than on any of the Pan Am flights, or TWA in America.

Poor old Hassan trailed along here yesterday. Come to see Louis about what he is supposed to do in Victoria. Another of his children died. He asked Mrs. Crisp for a bit of money, and Mary, since he had none at all. They both lost their tempers with him, and sent him off to Mike Richmond.* Of course Mike didn't know what to do — it was lucky we were here. His [Hassan's] back is bad again — we are taking him to the doctor who was so good with Hugo, this morning. Mrs. Crisp is vile. In a most flying into tempery mood (notice that this typewriter too is beginning to overtype, Mum!!!!!). In

---

* Mrs. Crisp was Louis Leakey's secretary. Mike Richmond, a businessman with East African Film Services in Nairobi, came to serve, with a small retainer fee, as their factotum and general contact in Nairobi.

fact, so many things are disturbing. Caroline is making things very difficult for herself. She wrote to us to say she was sorry her last letter sounded cross — but she had been cross with us for several reasons. (1) Mrs. Avery had arrived, and been horrified at the set up, and said that she had not been at all prepared for what she found. For weeks had been terrified of the chimps but was beginning to settle down now, and was most efficient. (2) Much worse. She said she had been most cross not to hear that Mrs. Avery was arriving until she got a wire from her from Dar. Then we found two letters, written by Caroline, written about 3 weeks before Mrs. Avery got to Africa, saying she had heard a Miss Avery was arriving, and could she please take to the Reserve a long list of items!!!! What muddles we do get into. . . .

We have ordered our travelling office — Carmichael calls it a "portable" office!* He is a hoot. It is a super thing — the only one they had in stock. We have also ordered the radio telephones. Mike Richmond is the agent for them, and apparently the mountains won't affect them at all. Never recommend anyone to buy an Alder typewriter! The bus is a pale grey, and absolutely super inside. We can't get an air conditioning to work except by running on the battery, but we can apparently have a fan fitted — this would probably be sufficient to keep the temperature bearable.

There are two things which it would be wonderful if Anthea or Shirley could bring. I should forget the little white case — I really don't need the things from it. (1) the case of cups you gave us, Mum (which are in the little white case). (2) the telescope. It's not heavy, and is in the flat, with its tripod, in our cupboard in the studio. We are happy to pay the overweight which this might involve, if either of them could bear to. Also one pot of Boots Moisturising cream — No. 7 I think it is.

I had better stop now, but will write again soon — either whilst we are at Manyara, or when we get back.

Tons and tons of love to you all,
Jane

---

* A Volkswagen bus.

c/o P.O. Box 2818,
Nairobi, Kenya.
23rd April, 1966

Dear Dr. Carmichael,

Thank you very much indeed for your letter of 24 March. We were, of course, delighted to hear that our grant request had been approved, and are extremely grateful to the Society for its continued generous support of the chimpanzee research.

I understand that the Chimpanzee Research Account at Kigoma has already received $3560 for the maintenance of staff etc. until the end of April. We should be grateful if an additional $3204 could be sent to this account as soon as possible — this should be sufficient for a further four months. Could this be sent to the National Bank, Kigoma, to A/C no.10640 Caroline Coleman Chimpanzee Research A/C. We shall be in Kigoma ourselves in two weeks time.

We should also be grateful if the $3976 for the metal buildings, their transport, etc, and the $7056 for the Volkswagen portable office etc. could be sent to the Chimpanzee Research Account, in my name, in Nairobi — General Bank of the Netherlands. We should appreciate it if this could also be sent off as soon as possible. . . .

Hugo and I had a fantastic time when we returned to San Diego for their Zoo's silver jubilee celebrations. It happened, by coincidence, that the Zoo's birthday was on the same day as mine! They had made, for the occasion, a 100 yards long birthday cake, laid out along a great row of end to end tables in the zoo. The cake was for 30,000 children — and anyone else who came along! I had to cut the first piece! It was quite a performance, and the children loved it — as did all the great apes who were all given pieces as well!

We had to do heaps of television interviews while we were there and you would have been delighted if you had seen the number of times that the December issue of the National Geographic Magazine was held up before T.V. viewers, and the pages slowly turned!! We also aroused a lot of interest, and quite a bit of support, for our chimpanzee reserves plan. We have been in touch with Professor Bourliere about this, and I will write further when we have followed up his suggestions.

It is wonderful to be back in Africa — and it will be good to see all the chimps again. I'll write from the Reserve to say how things are going.

Hugo joins me in sending best wishes to you and your wife.

Yours sincerely,
Jane

[Around May 7, 1966]

Darling Family,

A hasty hasty note — we are just off, flying with Mike Richmond 'cos the road is out. So we'll be with the chimps this evening. I meant to write heaps of times — but we have been <u>frantic</u> — I have just got the paper off to Phyllis — who hasn't received from England — (Peter's) photos. I hope you got the list Mum? If not, please CABLE — & I will send you the list. Been struggling with Geographic book outline, rushing to show film to Nyerere & Tanzania Society in Dar — lots of love from Caroline Sassoon* — showing it twice in Nairobi — drama with Owen (re Park status of Reserve) — great time in Manyara with elephants <u>when</u> I went out. It was mean — we were there for 6 days — I went out only 2 afternoons!! Rest of time battling with the Wenner Gren.†

Havn't had <u>any</u> letters from you, so presume they're in chimpland?! Has Judy sent the copy of Mrs. Avery's agreement? It is rather urgent, but is really too late now to be useful as we wanted to consult a solicitor here in Nairobi.

Apparently poor little Merlin is dying — steadily and irreversibly he gets thinner & weaker, and goes blue with cold. A skeleton with a pot belly. Sad & horrible. Caroline told us that when they had a scheme in West Africa to <u>stop</u> the Mum's breast feeding for 3 years there was a drastic increase in infant mortality. This they put down to the fact that the mothers were too ignorant to know what the children should eat. Why we have to be so interfering I don't know.

---

* Caroline and Hamo Sassoon were friends living in Dar es Salaam.
† That is, with the paper she gave at the Wenner Gren conference, which she was preparing for publication.

URGENT. Hugo left some keys in his <u>brown</u> suitcase — the large one that opens in half. <u>Please</u> could these be given to Anthea — or Shirley — for us. They are for the safe & the filing cabinet. Can be left at the office or with Louis. We are <u>dying</u> to hear about the trial of Nigel. How is the book getting on?

Love,
Jane.

[May 1966]

Darling Family,

This will be a rather queer letter — I am in a crouvched position on our matress, on the floor of Lawick Lodge, with the typewriter on the matress in front of me. And, guess wha t — it is my very original dear little typewriter. It has gone through 4 years of tropical humidity, typed several papers and 2 Geographic articles — not to mention the Stanford chap ter. It ha s endured being typed on by me, you Mum, Edna, Sonia, Millie, and "Sally" Avery — and it is still quite super to typ e with. It's faults, as you see, are jjumping and a crooked margin. But neither of these effect the speed of one's typ ing, nor make it impossible to read as overtyping does. Good old Diploma t. And the new one, so generously given to us for whatever it was, is simply hopeless. So hopeless that I ahve left it in Nairobi, and we shall try to sellit and get another when we get back. Most of the mis takes, incidentally, are due to the strrange position in which I am typing — but we don't even have a proper table in here yet. The girls are in luxury, but we have our matress and a pile of old boxes in the corner — and our luggage in another. It was even worse yesterday, since all our belongings were strewn absolutely all over the floor — but dear Benjamin arrived from his holiday — you know, the one Hugo and I had on the Serengitti. He, unasked by us, at once tidyed up the whole place.

Well, I will start with first things first. The chimps. A nd the wset up. the chimps are fine — except that, so far as we can see, even Caroline ha s been touching them. It really is hopeless. Anyway, David is absolutely impossible — when he comes he takes one by the hand and leads his victim to a box. He is too dim to realize that the person should be taken to the handle — so you sit with him at the box held in his iron grip, and he gets progressively more livid because you don't open the box. So, a fter he has had h is box he is left outside and everyone ha s to remain in the buildings until he has gone! Talk about being in a cage!!!!!! But the others are fine. Flint is a n absolute little dear mischevous wicked imp. Never still for more than a few moments at a time, and a lways up to some mischieve. And Fifi is worse than ever. Really wicked. She has developed a pashion for throwing, with very bad aim (I know I spelt that wrong!) But she doesn't just throw one stone. She collects stones until her hands are full and then goes stamping off towards the poor female she is about to attack, scattering her stones all round her. Merline is a most pathetic and sad little cha p. He is actually sma ller than Flint, except that his limbs are longer. But, even worse than his skeletal form, is his ap athy. We watched Master Flint trying to play with him this afternoon — it was quite horrid. Flint jumping all over him, and Merlin just crouching down, taking it all — ra ther like a mother being attacked by a male. He does all sorts of peculiar things — for instance, when he grooms himself which he does all the time, he pulls his hairs out by the roots, with his teeth. H e is like an old neurotic little ma n.

Next — the staff. Ca roline seems to be doing excellently. She is a very conscientious and neat person, just as we thought. Very thorough, and everything is kept quite up to date and ship shap e. Sheis rat her extravagant in her tastes, but we don't think she is spending more money than she should. And she certainly likes the chimps. She is a bit tired at the moment as they have been having a terrible two months — chimps here the entire day through with scarcely a moment to even have a cup oftea or visit the choo! And Sally — we find it so hard to get used to "Sally". She seemw to be w orking out fine after all our worries. She is sweet a ctually, and also loves the chimps. Very quick typist, does shorthand so Caroline dictates the notes which saves the tapes. She seems to love trailing into Kigoma for a day to do theshopping, and since Caroline doesn't mind being on her own with a n A frican for a day, and since Sally is simply sup erb a t getting everything that can be got in Kigoma, we think that, after all, it is proba bly a pretty good idea. She is ra ther upset a t the moment because her Mother has just died — not that she shows it, but she mentioned that she couldn't sleep, and told me a bout it when I asked her why she couldn't sleep. But she trots off swimming in the lake every night, and we are having supper on the ridge as planned. . . .

Well, our flight was tremendous fun. Hair raising on 3 occasions because we were much too overloaded: Taking off, cross the Ngorongoro mountains (the ones near the crater) in thick cloud when we could not climb as high as we should because of the load. We nea rly turned round and went back a t tha t point! But made it. And, a bit, landing — beca use we went down much faster than we should have, again because of the weight. But we did a superb landing. And actually managed to get out of Kigoma quite fast. We did not get ba ck in the boat — we had told the girls we should be a rriving a dsy later, but got permission to go early when it was toolate to let them know. Anyway, apart from having to wait for ages and ages at the immigration nothing held us up.

The radio telephone is fantastic. xxxxxx Nairobi. a parantly, as clear as a bell. The aerial is a fantastic t hing, all held up withx guy ropes and 40 feet high. It is not with the chimp s, for obvious reasons, but near the ridge. Hardly visible from nywhere, really. Beautiful thing. A lso, when we were in Dar, we got a nice typewriter — were all most excited to try it out. But, believe it or not, despite its packing it had had a jolt. And one of the tab stops had got pushed up out of place so that the carriage wouldn't move past the middle. Well, Hugo managed after much difficulty to get the carriage off — then got the naughty tab stop out of the way — then the carriage wouldn't come off. — I mean, of course, it wouldn't go back on, but it is getting rather late at night! Also I am getting stiff from my wierd postion, and it is dark since the shadow of me is over the page. So I will just say, now, that the new typewriter now workds superly, and will then finish tomorrow. Page 3

Well — it's now morning. A very very windy moirning indeed. I have turned myself around for work today — instead of facing the opposite mountain where I kept thinking I saw Madam Bee, I can just see bits of blue lake through the trees. Outside are Flo, Flint, Fifi and Melissa with Goblin. I should be doing the book, but am not in the mood. The pa per is blowing all over the place in the most irritating ma nner. Hugo is getting his equipment ready and drinking coffee — and it is superb to have a typewriter that I can type fast on without it sticking. Last night Hugo and I followed Miff and Merlin. S aw Miff making a nest, and Merlin, after eating caterpillars for 30 mins, climb in and snuggle up beside her for the night. Caroline Sassoon — we stayed with them in Dar as I'm sure I already said, told us an interesting thing. That when, in West Africa, they had a scheme for stopping mother's breast feeding their infants after one year, the infant mortality rate simply shot up. Jolly interesting. But Merlin has simply GOT to live. It would be too awful if he died.

Well — as I huirriedly told you in my blue, we rushed off to Dar and showed the film to Nyerere and then to the Tanzania Society — where Hugo met an old army friend of his. As I told you, Nyerere loved the film, but it wasn' to successful a show as last time because no one else was xxxxx invited, and it is never so good when you see a film with a small audience as with a large one. The Tanzania Soc. showing was a great success — the Museum hall was packed — approximately 40% of the audience were standing or sitting on t he floor!!!!! We sa w poor Hassan in Nairobi — his back is awful — he ha s osteo-arthritis in the lumbar spine. If it is very bad for him to work you should write and tell Louis — who will otherwise put him to any sort of work he fancies. He is not very compassionate where his staff are concerned, simply because he is not for himself. But when you are doing your own work it is different. . . . Caroline and Hamo Sassoon send their love to you — Caroline was most intrigued by the story of Nigel mum. Oh — have I thanked you for your letter, telling us at last about the trial. Well — it was waiting for us when we got here, and a blue. Someone else who wanted very much to be remembered to you, Mum, was Philip Tobias. He too was intrigued by the tale. We took him out to dinner. We had fondue and the poor man burnt his lips most terribly by clsoing them on a red hot fork. Huge white blisters leapt up, and you could hear his lip sizzle. Ugh. We also took Louis and Mary and Philip out to dinner!!!! Mary is wierd — she is always so charming to our faces!! Philip is now quite O.K. so far as she is concerned — she also told C. Sassoon she planned to meet him with a horse whip. I think I must end now — I may add to this, but it is cool, and no chimps, and peaceful, and I must tackle this sordid book. So xxxxx au revoir for the present. . . .

Tons of love from us both,
Jane

Chimpland
[May 1966]

Darling Family,

Just a note to let you know that all is well — very very well re. chimps. Not so well re. book since I havn't yet had much time to write it yet! <u>Chimps.</u> MEAT-EATING. Saw Hugo (chimp) hitting a baboon (young, not baby) in camp!! He had it by leg and was bashing its head up & down on the ground. Saw the <u>whole</u> meat-eating sequence. Hugo being selfish. Mike chasing all others away from him — & getting the liver — JB begging from Mike & crying when he couldn't get any. Hugo carrying the carcass over his shoulder to drink. Lying asleep with it. Suddenly getting up & leaving it on the ground. The others, his faithful persistent followers, staring in disbelief & then all with one accord <u>pouncing</u> on it. Mike, Goliath, JB & Huxley & David. They <u>all</u> grabbed it & pulled. Mike attacked them all & finally got it. Rushed off, flailing it. But the others rushed after him and grabbed it again. Guess who got the best bit? — David!! Up a tree with rump & one leg. Then JB — one arm. Then Huxley. Other arm. Then Goliath — small bit of bone. Then Mike — head and bit of shoulder. All were allowed to share with Mike when they'd eaten their little bits (Hx, Gol & JB). But David turned his back on people. He gave Gol a <u>tiny</u> splinter. And, right at the end, let Mandy have 3 tiny bits of cartilage, & Flo a nearly bare bone! But the best is to come. When Mike's was nearly finished he stopped letting JB share. JB gave up & reclined above Mk, further along the branch. Suddenly he rushed past Mike, shot down the tree, & was gone. I peered, wondering what he had seen. Mike was staring after him with 1/2 open mouth. Then I saw. Mike's share was gone! The prettyest bit of snatch & run robbery I ever saw! He took it up a tall tree & no one bothered him! One horrid part was when Mike lay on his back, held the head above him with one foot, &, with one hand, groomed the head!!

Another thing. Sniff had been coming alone for 2 months. We thought maybe Sophie was dead. But she came, 4 days ago. And, as luck would have it, we saw the re-union. Sniff rushed up & they groomed fanatically. Sophie, Mandy, Pallas & Athaena are all pregnant!

We like Sally — still too talkative though! The new "dining room" on the ridge will be superb — it has been begun. We are painting the inside of Pan Palace — hardly know the place — cream & sky blue.

Will write proper letter anon.

> Love from us both to all,
> Jane

[Postmarked June 23, 1966]

Darling Mum — dear drunken Pineapple,

Have just read your letter — or at least the start of it — to all. Hoots of mirth, but secret commiseration that I have an old soak as a mother. Love from all, before I forget. Hugo is looking at Playboy — full of nude women. I didn't see a joke he showed me, so he said I was taking after you in my old age. What a reputation. He keeps interrupting with Olly-type jokes. Well — Olly. No — surely by now you have heard how Hugo and I went off to Mtumba, hoping to see Olly. No chimps at all. My old original tree where I saw the first chimps with Rashidi and Adolf and Mikidadi — it was full of fruit but not yet ripe. So we got back — who came that afternoon. Mandy with a new baby. And — Olly. Wasn't it fantastic. It is now three times that Olly has come back, as a regular person, soon after Hugo and I got back. Once when Kris was looking after the camp — and she didn't come for three months. Once when we got back in Jan. And now now. Can't see the page — it is in pitch darkness. So we have dear Olly with us — and a heavily-pregnant Olly. Hugo is going in a week — going to Sambura park, towards the Northern Frontier area. Where I have always wanted to go. But we felt that if I stayed here I could a) finish the book, and b) see Olly's baby. Sophie also any minute now. And a new mother, Spray — we think the original daughter of Mrs. Maggs — with a dear little girl, aged 2 — Sparrow. Another new mother — Jessica — with a little tiny baby, and a daughter of about 6 called Lita — after Lita Os.* We havn't told her yet as we are waiting to get a picture.

Pan Palace is now quite fantastic. All painted. Carpenters here for 2 days, shelves, bookcases, fantastic deck for Sally to type at. It really is super. Poor Sally fell over the other day, caught her hand probably on a tin, and cut huge flap of skin on her finger. This won't heal and is hurting, and so she is going to Kigoma tomorrow to have it looked at again. She has managed to make up 4 long, long back days of tapes with [illegible] in pictures of Flint, Fifi and Figan — for their files. They really do look super now. In fact, I suddenly thought, as I stuck in some hair of Figan's that was pulled out by Mike on 8 July 1964, that our research is the most super in the world. Oh — do you know the latest on the John Owen thing.† I suppose I did write to say that he had proposed Tinbergen for my <u>supervisor</u> if the research here came under the Serengeti Research Institute? Well, we were planning all sorts of drastic measures — he has now decided to ask Robert to act as advisory scientist to the Board of Trustees of Tanz. Nat. Parks. If Robert accepts all should, I hope, be well. We have had 2 Americans staying here all week — actually for 10 days. We thought it was going to be two boys — we met one in San Diego and he asked if he could come for a couple of days when he was travelling round — just to look. So we said yes. Well — he came for 10 days — and with him was a girl — she spells her name — Chryssee. Honestly! They slept all cosy in Trog-

---

* Lita Osmundsen of the Wenner Gren Foundation.
† There seem to have been several points of tension between Jane, as director of Gombe Stream Research Centre, and John Owen, then director of Tanzania's National Parks.

lodytes Taverne! The beds got a bit closer together every time we had supper we thought! That's when we noticed it I mean!!

We shall keep our fingers crossed for Jiff as well — hope that you will let us know when a decision is reached. I can't get over the sermon.* Am dying to hear all about it. Did Danny know in advance! Or do you mean it wasn't really about me, but an allegory. Am rather mystified. Can see down to Hugo's sordid magazine. Page filled with over ripe bosoms and buttocks. Not at all in Hugo's style really, but still. Better than James Bond which has been with us sev. nights and many days during past few weeks!!! Merlin doesn't seem to be getting any livelier or more normal. Sad though it is, it really is quite fantastically interesting — and important. I should think many psychologists will be more interested in him than in almost anything else. Flint is just superb. A real wicked naughty little boy. His whole face is one wicked little impish mask. And Fifi is more wicked too. She doesn't just throw stones when she's angry — she unobtrusively collects up handfulls and throws the whole lot together. Only female known to throw in aggressive context. Would be Fifi. She has taken on Flo's job as chief baboon chaser. Flo is really a bit too old. 2 new tools!! One a stick used to investigate — poked in and then end sniffed. Once my pocket to see if b. in it. Once stick when wasp grubs in hollows inside. Other tool — Flint and a — nose pick!!!! Mandy's baby, by the way, clings like a limpet. So her behaviour with Jane really was because of a weakness in the baby. Do hope Old Men are going well.†

Tons,
me

---

* In a sermon preached at Bournemouth's Richmond Hill church, Reverend Trevor Davies mentioned Jane's life story as an exemplary case.
† Vanne had been working with Louis on a coauthored book exploring "ten decades of thought about human evolution." Entitled *Unveiling Man's Origins* (but privately referred to as "The Old Men"), the book was published in the United States in 1969.

Chimpland
[Early July 1966]

Darling Danny,

I do hope that this letter will arri[ve] for your birthday — if it doesn't, you will [know] it was meant to, but that Tanzanian posts decid[ed] otherwise. If it does — well, very happy birth[day.]

It is early in the morning. I had meant to do more book, but I think I must have been too late at it last night — I don't seem to be able to [do] any now, anyway. It's as bad as the thesis all over again. Even to the extent of grass-widowing me all over again!

Two days ago Mike Richmond flew down, in his little plane, to collect Hugo and Michael.* We had decided that if I went too, what with messing about in Nairobi with no fixed address, driving all over the place, camping — well, I should never get the book ready for when the old Geographic wants it. So I am staying here.

There are compensations of course. Olly is pregnant, we are pretty sure, and it will be wonderful if the baby comes before I go. To see whether Gilka behaves like Fifi did with Flint, always trying to steal the baby. Also Pallas and Sophie are both pregnant too.

You would love to see the babies playing together. There are so many now, all little furry bundles — the smaller ones so gentle and sweet — the elder ones, like Flint and Goblin, little wicked and mischievous imps. Flint is really terrible — Goblin is super. In fact we have added onto his name — he is now Goblin Grub. Because he always, always has a dirty face. Hugo filmed him the other day eating a large banana. It was too much for him. He pushed the whole lot into his mouth and it was so much it fell into his hands again. So then the little grub slapped his hands onto his face, again and again — covering his face with sticky banana! It was just like a small human child let loose with ice-cream!

I followed Flo and Melissa the other day, and they both climbed a tree to feed — with their two infants, Goblin and Flint. Then they climbed down, leaving the children playing. Then Flint climbed down, and went to Flo to suckle. Goblin, half a year younger than

---

* Hugo's brother.

Flint, was left all alone. He stared down, and began to cry, very softly. His cold Mama stared, and decided he was old enough to fight his own battles. But little Flint stopped his suckling and hurried back to the tree. Up he went, flung his arms round little Goblin, and then climbed oh so slowly down, looking up at Goblin and every so often reaching up to touch the little one with one hand, as though encouraging him. Finally they got to the ground, and Flint more or less waved Goblin past him, and the two returned to the adults, Flint in the rear with one hand on Goblin's rump! It was so charming!

Our buildings really are smart now — well, Pan Palace is, but Lawick Lodge has not really been touched. It is furnished now, though, with the left overs from the newly furnished and fitted Pan Palace! Pan Palace has long bookshelves down one wall, over which is a huge framed colour print of the picture in the last article of Flo, Fifi and Flint, Fifi kissing Flint. It has two new tables, one a really good and super desk for Sally to type at. And, as you probably don't know, we already had a four drawer filing cabinet. Then the kitchen has been fitted with new table and shelves all down one wall and above the table. The store has super shelves at one end, and down the side (kitchen and store are only tiny weeny little rooms). The girls each have shelves, and proper beds. Just imagine it all — I still find it hard to believe. They, of course, take it all for granted!

We now have the most beautiful table for the supper house, Troglodytes Taverns. It is dark polished wood with two cutlery drawers, and very heavy. We were absolutely staggered when we saw it — we had never meant such an elaborate thing to be made! But it is super, in the evenings, to sit at it with candles. And for the girls, who, after all, are not here doing their life's work, I think it is an excellent thing that they should have some feeling of civilization! I, personally, preferred the early days when Mum and I, and then I, were "roughing it" — but things have changed so since then, and it's difficult to live in a tent with 50 tame chimps around!

Oh — the chimps killed another baboon. We heard the sudden excitement way down the valley, the chimps in camp simply ran, and Hugo and I hurried after. When we got there Mike had the baboon — it was very different from the time when Hugo had it. Mike shared much more liberally. And then, near the end, Hugo arrived — chimp Hugo we are talking about! He took hold of a piece of the skin of the bab, wanting to pull it off. Mike didn't mind. But Hugo couldn't tear the skin, so he just held onto it! Mike got frenzied, pulling and twisting and turning — Hugo just sat, quite motionless — even with Mike's hardest pulling Hugo's hand scarcely moved. It was the most wonderful demonstration of his enormous strength I have ever seen, and was most impressive. Finally he got a bit off. Then David came up to beg, and, just as a mother tickles her child to distract it from some naughty plan, so Mike began to tickle David. In the middle, when the two old men were rolling over and over and roaring with laughter, Hugo returned having eaten his piece. And he held on again and sat, motionless until the game had ended — just holding on! I do wish Hugo could have filmed it, but it was dense undergrowth. The final episode was Mike with the skull. He poked his index finger into the hole where the top vertebrae goes in order to pick out the brains!

I wonder if you are having a "flaming July" for your birthday. Probably cold and wet, as usual. Am dying to get your letter about the sermon!

Well — the day wears on. They have just called me over to eat a boiled egg, and then, whether I feel like it or not, I must get on with the old book. Only one more month to get it finished. Tell Mum that the first installment for you ALL to severely criticize, particularly from American public's point of view, will be in the mail after this letter. Also that the reprints and her last letter with letter from Nature, etc, arrived safely, and many thinks.

Once again, happy birthday, and I shall be thinking of you.

Tons and tons of love to all,

Your Jane

Please tell Mum — Olly v. pregnant and Gilka most independent — slept a good 50 yards away from Olly — in a different tree! P.S. Did the San Diego 8mm films ever arrive? If so, please, what were they like?

Nairobi
[Late July 1966]

Darling Family,

Just seen Shirley,* who looks terribly happy to be back here in Nairobi. She had the things you gave her to bring — what super, duper little slippers. I adore the sorts of striped ones — not stripes, but I can't think of the word for those things. The others are gorgeous too. Thank you very much whoever sent them.

We are just ready to set off to Ngorongoro for three weeks. We then return here to collect Phyllis Jay and take her down to the chimps to install the 40 electric boxes.† The four that arrived down with Hugo are not ready yet, but he fixed them up inside the building for us — you should have seen the boys' faces when we showed them! They are super — you just have a car battery — which we can charge ourselves by a generator that Hugo and I got — and this works all 40 boxes. We are having 4 panels of 10 switches each, and the boxes can be up to 100 feet away. They open towards the building, so that you can see the number of the box from the window, and press the corresponding number on the pannel. It all seems most weird, — but should really fox cunning little devils like Fifi!!

We were having a birthday party, combined for both girls, just when Hugo and the two Mikes were there. It was quite spoilt and made sad because we got this cable, when in Nairobi, to say that Caroline's brother had been killed. Her only brother, whom she adored. She took it very well — but it hadn't really sunk in at all. I am glad we were able to leave her with an older sensible person like Sally. Poor Sally met J.B. head on — the moment his head left her leg, her leg swelled up — rather like Rod's. I've got a feeling I've told you this before.

The enclosed cheque is to help me celebrate the fact that for the first time in 6 years I do not have a weighty work hanging over my

---

* Shirley Coryndon.
† Phyllis Jay, an anthropologist from the University of California at Berkeley, had organized the 1965 Wenner Gren conference on primate studies.

head. Please will you buy something for all of you that the Birches needs — or something small for each of you that each of you wants — or just anything you like.

Our safari equipment is so grand now that we shan't recognize our own camp when we see it. The new Folkswaggen is absolutely super. Our first little house. We are taking pictures, and will send to you. We have no money left in the bank, but decided that it was more fun to have nice things now and enjoy ourselves, whilst we are still able to be in Africa, than to wait until it was too late. We have taken on another African — supposed to be a driver for our second vehicle, but he's not good enough, so Hugo will give him lessons, meanwhile I shall drive it. Also he is going to help Benjamin with everything on safari — which will be necessary when we have Phyllis. After the chimps, we take Phyllis to Murcheson — where there are chimps and patas monkeys, then to another park, then to see some colobus, then we take Michael to Mombasa to catch a boat, because Hugo has to photograph Sable antelope down near the coast. Then Phyllis leaves East Africa, and Hugo settles down on the Serengeti with me. I start analysing in earnest, and he films lions with George, and hyaenas with Hans Kruuk.*

I mustn't write long now. We have to dash a last minute dash into Nairobi for last minute things. Collect various things, and buy some things, and Michael have his hair cut. We have to have lunch with Judge Russell Train — the world wild life man from America. And then depart to get to Namanga to show them the chimp film this evening. Oh — I never said about our flight back from Kigoma. Smoke, smoke, smoke all the way. Poor Mike Richmond had sore eyes — and it made it very bumpy. He didn't dare take his eyes off his panels at all, or one wing went up or down. He is an excellent pilot. You will see the plane at Kigoma airport on next 8mm films. HAVE YOU SEEN THE AMERICAN ONES YET? ALSO, did the Sunday Times thing ever materialize?

Must stop, as Hugo is fussing around and although he's not say-

---

* George was George Schaller. Hans Kruuk was a Dutch scientist studying hyenas in the Serengeti.

ing anything I know he's rar'in to go — or should it be rarin' to go? Anyway, he's anxious to be off!!!!!!!

Will write again from the icy fastness of Ngoro — will be really freezing there. It will be best if you write to 2818 Nairobi and Mike forwards, rather than to Ngorogoro. For one thing, we can contact him about changes by means of the radio telephone.! What a thought.

Tons and tons of love to all — hear the proofs are done Mum — jolly good show. Dying to read your book.

Jane

Hugo sends his love too. How is your knee Olly? Thanks tons for your letter — will write to you soon. How is Dido? And Figgy?

ILLUSTRATION CREDITS

Illustrations not otherwise credited were provided by the Goodall family.

The manor house in Kent: Dale Peterson
May Day at Oxford: Jane Goodall
Jane dancing with Brian Herne: Brian Herne
Jane Goodall at twenty-three: Brian Herne
Annabelle gets a ride: Jane Goodall
Flo and Flint: Jane Goodall and Hugo van Lawick
Cartoon by Jane Goodall: Jane Goodall
Jane Goodall and Hugo van Lawick: Jane Goodall
Flint reaches out: National Geographic Society
David Greybeard: National Geographic Society

INDEX

In the Shadow of Man

"One of history's most impressive field studies."—Time

IN THIS GROUNDBREAKING BESTSELLER, Goodall recounts the remarkable discoveries she made in her first ten years of studying chimpanzees at Gombe Stream Reserve. With an introduction by Stephen Jay Gould and a postscript by Goodall. ISBN 978-0-618-056767

Through a Window: My Thirty Years with the Chimpanzees of Gombe

"A humbling and exalting book."—Washington Post

PERHAPS THE BEST BOOK EVER WRITTEN about animal behavior, *Through a Window* is the dramatic account of three decades in the life of a community, of birth and death, sex and love, power and war. ISBN 978-0-618-05677-4

Africa in My Blood: An Autobiography in Letters, The Early Years

"A fitting tribute to the woman who first made science friendly."—Biography

THIS EXTRAORDINARY SELF-PORTRAIT in letters and commentary, edited by Dale Peterson, tells the story of how a girl who loved animals became one of the greatest scientists of the twentieth century. ISBN 978-0-618-12735-1

Beyond Innocence: An Autobiography in Letters, The Later Years

"[Goodall] has become one of the most famous people on earth."—USA Today

THE SECOND VOLUME of Goodall's autobiography in letters tells of some of her greatest triumphs, her deepest tragedies, and the events that changed her from a rather private observer to a public crusader. Edited by Dale Peterson. ISBN 978-0-618-25734-8

Jane Goodall: The Woman Who Redefined Man

A NEW YORK TIMES NOTABLE BOOK

IN THIS ACCLAIMED BIOGRAPHY, Dale Peterson shows how truly remarkable Jane Goodall's accomplishments have been. Candid and illuminating, this magisterial work will be a revelation even to readers who are familiar with the public Dr. Goodall as presented in her own writing. *Houghton Mifflin hardcover* ISBN 978-0-395-85405-1

Visit our Web site: www.marinerbooks.com.